D0722875

3/10/00

A Social Ontology

A Social Ontology

David Weissman

Yale University Press

New Haven and London

Chapter Six, "Free Speech," was adapted from an article that appeared in *Metaphilosophy,* volume 27, no. 4, October, 1996.

Set in Adobe Garamond with Stone Sans display type by The Composing Room of Michigan, Inc.
Printed in the United States of America.

Library of Congress Cataloging-in-Publication Data

Weissman, David, 1936–
    A social ontology / David Weissman.
        p.   cm.
    Includes bibliographical references.
    ISBN 0-300-07903-6 (alk. paper)
    1. Social systems.   2. Ontology.   I. Title.
HM701.W45   2000
301—dc21   99-26249
                                   CIP

A catalogue record for this book is available from the British Library.

The paper in this book meets the guidelines for permanence and durability of the Committee on Production Guidelines for Book Longevity of the Council on Library Resources.

10 9 8 7 6 5 4 3 2 1

In memory of Justus Buchler

Contents

Preface

Ontology is the science or study of being. It identifies the generic features that every thing must have in order to exist. The thesis of this book is *social* in two ways: first, in the respect that every existent is alleged to be either a system or the constituent of a system; second, in the respect that the book applies its claims to human societies.

Three theories are considered—individualism, communitarianism, and holism. Individualist—atomist—theories emphasize the self-sufficiency and moral autonomy of persons. They speak of freedoms, rights, and exemptions; rarely or never of reciprocities, duties, and connections. Individualism dominates our self-perception. It encourages us to deny the ligaments and nerves of our social lives. Perceiving every society as an aggregate, it assaults or diminishes the systems—including families, schools, businesses, and states—where personal identity, security, and satisfaction are achieved. Every such system is, in atomist eyes, no less an aggregate than the passengers in a bus.

No one who participates in a family or friendship fails to distinguish aggregates from systems. It is unwelcome news that our dominant social theory cannot do as much. Individualists paw the ground, saying that systems are distinguished by the mutual sympathies or habits of the members or by laws that bind them. But surely, these thinkers ignore something obvious and important: namely, causal relations. This book proposes that causal relations are the root of the difference: systems have them; aggregates do not.

The first chapter is abstractly metaphysical. It argues—in opposition to the views of David Hume, endorsed by individualists—that causal relations are the efficacious relations of interacting people or things, not the spatial, temporal relations of things that are merely contiguous. It says that systems are established by reciprocal—mutually modulating—causal relations. The later chapters apply this claim to concrete issues, including personhood, sociality, and value, free speech, conflict, and ecology. These later chapters confirm that the ontology proposed here is applicable to the details of our personal, moral, and political lives.

Why should we care about metaphysical theories, or the evidence for or against them? Because metaphysics is important information. Not knowing our character or place in the world leaves us puzzled and incomplete. People lost in the woods are grateful for a compass or map. Our rabid individualism is equally disorienting. We need a better theory. This book supplies one.

Acknowledgments

I am grateful to Elaine Sternberg for her critical comments and for helping to prepare the manuscript for publication; to Jean van Altena for editing that required me to rethink every word; and to my wife, Kathy, for her care. Most of all, I am grateful to Jonathan Brent, editorial director of the Yale University Press. I could not have written as I have without his support.

Introduction

Imagine that people surge out the doors of a commuter train, dispersing through a station already crowded with riders. They move in waves through the exits onto the street. Some walk together, but most go alone, strained or composed, full of purpose, complete. Social atomism could tell most of its story by describing these commuters. Separate bodies and trajectories distinguish and explain us, though we are sometimes joined under rules or laws that limit the terms of our mutual duties. Everyone does, or can, arrive at the destination of his or her choice. Crowding delays but never captures us. Togetherness is ephemeral.

One aim of this book is the formulation of a substitute ontology. I shall be saying that reality is social in this dynamic sense: many things, including galaxies, friendships, crystals, and elementary particles (but not aggregates), are *systems*. They derive their coherence or integrity from the reciprocal causal relations of their parts. Sometimes the reciprocities creating a system are elementary and inflexible, as when neither person falls because each leans on the other. Other times the mutual modulation of a system's parts promotes their excitation or inhibition, hence negative feedback and self-control. Atomism, whether physical or social, has no comparable notion of system, because Hume reduced relations to resemblance and spatial or temporal contiguity. The atomist analysis of relations barely suffices to describe dispersing commuters. It ignores the vital features of friendships, work crews, families, and communities.

Atomism is entrenched in our thinking because Hume's notion of cause abets these other, mutually supporting ideas: Democritean atomism and Aristotle's doctrine of primary substance affirmed the separability and self-sufficiency of material things; Jewish and Stoic thinkers, then Luther and Calvin, emphasized the moral autonomy and responsibility of individual thinker-actors; Descartes affirmed that I exist each time I think or pronounce it, though possibly nothing else exists. Together, these claims entail that reality is composed—materially, morally, and mentally—of self-sufficient entities, each one having an existence and character that are independent of other things.[1]

One may defend an atomist ontology without considering its social implications, or favor atomist social policies without invoking an atomist ontology: Descartes did the one; most social theorists do the other. Yet both practices are objectionable, because they are incomplete. Atomist ontology has plain implications for social policy, while specific policies may have little or no justification additional to their sponsoring ontology. We see the link between atomist theory and social policy in the phrase *separable if distinguishable*. It implies that human agents are distinguishable and separable, hence really or ideally self-sufficient, and that human organizations—businesses, for example—are described enough when we specify their defining tasks, without regard for their reciprocal relations (and responsibilities) to other social formation.[2] I contest social policies that have atomist ontology as their principal justification.[3]

My second concern—a backdrop to the first—is the character of metaphysical inquiry. How should we proceed? One approach requires that a position be formulated, criticized, then revised to make it invulnerable to dialectical objections. Evidence to the contrary, especially empirical evidence, is ignored. The thesis is then repeated, as if repetition and the consensus of believers were a test of truth. The social atomism I criticize deploys a version of this strategy: neglect the evidence; repeat the principles. A different strategy settles irresolution by appealing to the higher authority of rational intuition or innate ideas supported by a divine guarantee. These are traditionally the courts of last resort for disputed matters of fact. I don't invoke these powers, because we have neither one.

I suppose that metaphysical claims are hypotheses about the character of the world and our place within it. Taking our bearings, measuring our hypotheses against the evidence, we declare that this is the way the world seems to be. This test is sometimes hard to apply, either because the same perceptual data support two or more hypotheses—physicalism and phenomenalism appeal to the same data—or because there is no empirical difference consequent on an alleged factual difference. God's infinitude is an example: it could have no empirical expression because perceptual data are finite. We may explain the absence of empirical evidence—the dog who doesn't bark—and we may justify our preference for a claim that is unsupported empirically: it leaves less that is unexplained. But these are extrapolations from a base of empirically confirmed hypotheses. Indeed, skepticism about the possibility of decisive empirical tests seems overblown. We are sometimes misled by our hypotheses, but we go back and forth using one assumption as a control on others. This is a commonplace to someone confused by the dirty lenses of his eyeglasses: he takes them off and squints to see better; he asks someone else how things look; or he cleans the lenses. Quine's animadversions about empirical testability[4] never stop us for long, because factual differences, categorial ones included, typically make empirical differences. Having lamplike data, we infer lamps. Seeing smoke, we infer fire. Or we see fire and smoke, and infer cause and effect. Each of these inferences is a hypothesis—what Peirce called an *abduction.*[5] Hypotheses are testable if their truth would make some empirical difference. Empirical testability is problematic for every hypothesis whose claim exceeds the data used to confirm it. But it is not so problematic as to deter us from making many judgments—about one another, governments, restaurants, the weather—that exceed the evidence for their truth. Equally, it is no bar to testing metaphysical hypotheses. Finding evidence in data or theory for a categorial difference, we infer its character and role. Is reality constituted of aggregated individuals, or of systems constituted by the reciprocal causal relations of their parts? We weigh the alternatives, choosing the hypothesis that best accounts for the data while cohering with other claims for which there is evidence. The surviving hypothesis is the one affirmed: here, we say, is our best surmise about the matter at issue.[6] I shall be applying my hypothesis about systems to a trove of examples from our experience of ourselves and one another. More than a test of this ontology, these psychological and social phenomena are a standpoint from which to compare it with social atomism: which is the better description of us and our circumstances?

A metaphysician's hypotheses resemble any other in the respect that they are applicable if there are instances of the things they specify. Metaphysics is distinctive because it also requires that its theories be adequate because complete, meaning that they specify all the categorial features of either being or one of its domains—literature, for example. The ontology proposed here is applicable but not complete: some categorial features (for example, motion and spacetime[7]) are exploited but not explicated. Some others are only mentioned.

My emphasis on the testability of metaphysical hypotheses seems odd if one assumes, as positivists do, that all the cachet of metaphysical claims depends on their untestability. Some metaphysicians have hoped to defend unverifiable beliefs about God or the One. Yet most claims about the categorial features of things do have empirical, hence testable, implications. Reality includes the perceivable, while exceeding it, so that every waking moment overflows with evidence of the things about us. No one could responsibly ignore this evidence when adjudicating hypotheses about matters of fact. The differences between atomism and the notion of systems proposed here are a test case for this trial by evidence. Atomism is not devoid of supporting evidence. But even those data are better explained by the claim that reality is an extended network of systems, each one independent of some but reciprocally related, overlapping, or nested within others.

One conception of metaphysical theory does seem to make empirical data extraneous. Theories of this type speculate about the generic character of possible worlds by reflecting on certain logical principles. Contingencies have no place in such theories, for there are no counterexamples to the principles of noncontradiction, identity, and excluded middle: nothing violates them, because nothing could. Yet even these universal truths need instantiation if there are to be particular, actual worlds. We live in such a world, so that states of affairs obtaining here should supply empirical evidence of universal logical truths. They should, and do, confirm the identity of things with themselves, the absence of contradictions in nature, and the forced choice between contraries. Nevertheless, some metaphysicians are more concerned to formulate universal principles than to show their realization in our world. Kant argued that every infusion of space or time—hence every thinkable experience—must have quality (for example, a color or sound), magnitude (for example, size or intensity), and relative position in space or time. He gave less thought to the distinguishing expressions of these categorial properties in our world. (Though one might argue, conversely, that Kant assumed the specific—Euclidean—character of space in our world, before supposing that any possible world must also be Euclidean.)

One rationale for the philosophical dedication to universal principles is a belief that successful inquiries are specialized: let everyone do what he or she does best. Common sense analyzes experiences that are practical and local. Science identifies the regional or pervasive features of our world. Metaphysics does its part by describing principles that are common to every possible or thinkable world. This division of responsibilities, apparently so judicious, hides a failure of nerve. Metaphysicians are encouraged to restrict themselves to speculations about the logical form of any possible world: meaning worlds where nothing contradictory is possible or thinkable. They are absolved from having to make specific, testable claims about our world. Refusing to make such empirical claims has two benefits for metaphysicians: it enables us to avoid empirical error, and it excuses us from having to compete or cooperate with scientists regarding the categorial features of our world.

This division of labor—some to practical experience, some to science, some to metaphysics—is also faulty for another reason: it obscures the fact that a principal aspect of the world is neglected. There are, for example, an infinity of possible, mutually contrary spaces. Our world instantiates one of them, thereby barring the others. Is our space Euclidean? This is a factual question, one to be answered by hypotheses tested by empirical evidence. The correct hypothesis is part of a theory about the *categorial form* of our world. It specifies the distinctive expression of factors common to many worlds—space and time, for example—as they are instantiated in our world. Such a theory distinguishes the contingency of our world's form from the parochial necessity—*parochial* to distinguish it from universal, logical necessity—that everything in our world satisfy its form: everything in the space obtaining here—be it Euclidean, Riemannian, or some other—satisfies its intrinsic topology and metric. Science doesn't usually make itself responsible for a synoptic view of our world's categorial form, or for remarking the differences between the categorial forms of this and other possible worlds. These tasks fall naturally to metaphysical inquiries that couple theory formation and analysis with observation. What, for example, is the character of the lawful regularities in our world: are they static or evolutionary? What are this world's things? Are they atoms—self-sufficient individuals—and aggregates, or systems? Metaphysics should not restrict itself to truths that obtain in all possible worlds, because we want to know the distinctive application of these universal truths in our world. These are questions of fact. A priori answers are not credible. Having no power to intuit them, and no innate ideas about them, we can only hypothesize about this world's categorial form, using empirical data to test our hypotheses.

Aristotle is the exemplary metaphysician of categorial form; but he would not have described this world's form as I propose: namely, as the contingency that our world instantiates one of the possible contrary forms for properties such as matter, space, and time. Ignoring the backdrop of possible worlds makes it harder to conceptualize the contingency of our world's form. Aristotle's meta-physics is, nevertheless, dominated by his concern for the categorial features of this world, including their relations to one another and the necessity that things occurring here observe the constraints imposed by its form.[8] He agreed that claims about the world's general features require the support of empirical data, and he adduced reams of evidence to support his hypotheses that things were as he said they were. Much of everyday life confirms his view that such things as acorns, statues, and we humans are stable and discrete, and that we and they engage other things with specific, predictable effects. Left to ourselves, we and they retain our identity until some external force destroys us, or until we are disabled by an internal flaw. Ordinary experience, morality, and the greater part of science still make these assumptions.

Suppose, however, that we choose a different paradigm for reality. Think of weather and its evolving formations of cyclonic air. Their integrity—their apparent stability and separateness—is ephemeral rather than sustained, as air masses form and dissolve. Nor are these systems mutually independent. Every formation has crystallized within a flux where its relations to other emerging, stable, or dissolving systems, no less than its internal order, are conditions for its character and stability. Which is the better hypothesis about our world's categorial form: one that founds its metaphysical claims on examples of this sort, or one, like Aristotle's, that starts from discrete, self-sufficient particulars? This is an empirical question, one requiring that we elaborate the alternate hypotheses, while showing how (or if) each analyzes or explains the examples used as paradigms by the other.

This book assumes, without further argument, that metaphysics should not restrict itself to the a priori demonstration of truths having application within all possible worlds; it formulates a (partial) metaphysics of nature appropriate to our world; and it shows the applicability of its hypothesis to a domain of empirical examples. I shall be saying that the separability observed in earthbound things, and prized in our moral lives, is real but fragile. Self-perception is distorted when we treat such things—principally ourselves—as models for reality, making separability and independence, not reciprocity, our moral ideal. Weather is the better paradigm for inquiries regarding the categorial features of things, because weather is systemic. Every system evolving within the atmosphere has a merely temporary integrity, and a character determined as much by its conditions as by its internal states. Each thing is formed from others, and each one sustains itself by drawing substance and energy from them before it is dissolved and reincorporated, piecemeal, into its successors. We are not inclined to forget—as typically we do with earthbound things—that every eddy and storm is generated within a system differentiated hierarchically into systems that are local at one extreme and global at the other. There is some independence. The internal states of a local system are constitutive of it. But every system overlaps some others, and every system is nested within hierarchies of overarching systems. If there is no single, comprehensive, highest-order system, there are several or many highest-order, overlapping systems. Nothing is, or is what it is for reasons wholly intrinsic to itself: the existence and character of every thing are conditioned by its relations to some or many others.

This is a sketch of the metaphysical theory proposed in these chapters. I intend it as an answer to this succession of charges: Metaphysics has nothing to say of particular worlds, but only of truths applying to all possible worlds. Or, metaphysical claims are untestable empirically. Or, metaphysics has produced no set of naturalistic categories applicable and adequate to all of nature since Aristotle and Hobbes: the one as he established the applicability of his physics, psychology, and ethics;[9] the other as he proposed a psychology, morals, and politics.[10] These are grave charges, but only the third is true. The absence of a naturalistic alternative adequate to the science of our time diminishes metaphysics and disables our sociology and morality. We ignore the cost to metaphysics because science (revered as "philosophy enough") replaces it with hypotheses that extend from local phenomena to particular features of categorial form (theories about spacetime, matter, and energy, for example). We wait patiently for the time when scientists will formulate a rich, comprehensive account of nature's categorial form, one that may direct us as we locate ourselves within the world, making such accommodations as are appropriate to it and ourselves. But there is no serious commentary that integrates and interprets science for the rest of us, focusing and orienting our moral and psychological reflections. Moralists defer to the versions of categorial form that are available and comprehensible—principally those of Aristotle and Hobbes—but these accounts are outdated because their supporting ontologies are mistaken. Using them distorts our perception of the world and ourselves. I shall be saying that we have a more subtle psychology and more cogent social policies when we have a more accurate ontology: one whose categories enable us to describe, explain, and predict human behavior and social relations, while they imply some prescriptions for moral and political behavior.

One may resist my ontology of systems for either of several reasons. It may evoke images of life in a sea of treacle, where everything is engulfed by other things or soldered to them. Isn't it better for everyone's freedom and integrity that things divide into self-sufficient particulars? Or readers may agree that relations are critical for the times when things are made or used, but affirm that a thing's identity is founded only in itself (granting that it may embody a network of relations). Isn't the evidence of these separate identities prominent everywhere? Don't we profit from it, as when spark plugs not whole cars are replaced? Justice, too, requires separability: we reward or punish individuals, not whole families or cities. Examples like these support our intuitions about the separability of things; but they claim too much. We replace spark plugs; we don't expect them to work without a starter or that engines will work without them. We want to believe that the criminality of the wrongdoer lies altogether in him (as the good in us is unconditionally our own). But we know better, partly because criminals are made, rarely or never born; partly because many crimes result from petty miscalculations; partly because punishing individuals is, very often, a ritual contrived in circumstances where punishing some larger group of collaborators is not feasible.

There is a solution to this puzzle—separability or interdependence—in the difference between separability and self-sufficiency: things that are separable under certain conditions are not thereby self-sufficient. Separable structures may be mutually conditioning, so that the character of each structure's behavior (and even certain aspects of the structure itself) is determined by the behavior of the other. The separability of structures is consistent, this implies, with mutually conditioning relations. Aristotle's description of functional interdependencies within living things (the relations of a flower's petals, pistil, and stem, for example) speaks for the social character of thinghood. It invites extrapolation to things of larger scale and complexity, to families, friendships, businesses, schools, governments, and nations. Those who speak for the self-sufficiency of primary substances[11] reject this inference. Things affiliate, they say, without creating societies that mimic the integrity of individuals. For autonomy is never compromised; what a thing does or can do is determined by its structure, as knives cut because they have sharp edges. We are to infer that structures are separable, hence self-sufficient. We may sing together, but each of us has vocal cords such that each can sing alone.

Do such examples confirm that having structure guarantees the physical autonomy of individuals? Consider the integrity of a spark plug. It is separable from the engine in which it operates; but is it separable, without loss of its autonomy, from every other circumstance, including the external conditions that tolerate or support it? Grant that a thing's structure is not separable from its constituents or some of its circumstances, and we get this result: *structure is the ef-*

fect of its internal and external conditions. A knife does not cut unless its internal conditions and external circumstances tolerate or sustain the internal order of its parts (whether proper pats—blade and handle—or molecular parts).

Things may seem to be self-sufficient, because they are separable; but we err by taking this appearance as the elementary truth about them. Astonished readers will say that things are moved or changed, one independently of others. The claim justified by such observations is nevertheless different from the Aristotelian claim that separability is evidence of self-sufficient structures. Consider, for example, the integrity of things that suffer no apparent change of shape or size when moved. Suppose, more strongly (but falsely), that the appearance is accurate: things are not changed by motion. Does this establish that a primary substance is self-sufficient, because its structure and function have internal determinants (matter and form), but no external ones? No, it proves only that whatever conditions support or establish a thing's character and apparent singularity (conditions, such as acceleration, which we assume to be little changed or unchanged) tolerate this change of relative position. This point is easily tested: rather than move a thing slowly, we move it, with nearly instant acceleration, at half the speed of light. Now it doesn't remain the same (it vaporizes), thereby confirming that the separability of structures is sustained only as variables such as velocity and pressure are little changed. Alter these conditions dramatically, and the integrity of structures (and their capacity for specific behaviors) is compromised: they collapse or explode. A structure's integrity is, therefore, derivative: its integrity—its separability—is a function of the structure's relations to the pervading conditions that operate within and upon the materials that compose it. Self-sufficiency is an idealization that applies to nothing but the universe itself (ignoring the possibility that our universe may be one bud among others in a matrix of an unknown sort). Individualism (Aristotle's and our own) avoids this inference by suppressing the generative, sustaining, internal and external conditions of things. We don't know these conditions, or they are ignored, because—being roughly constant—they have a constant effect: namely, structural integrity. Observing the separability of things, we seek an absolute grounding for their self-sufficiency. Aquinas is paradigmatic. He supposed that each thing is distinguished by its signate matter and by a separate act of being.[12] For it isn't enough that things look and act distinctly. Aquinas hoped to validate the appearances with a metaphysical writ of integrity: substantial particulars are separable in themselves, once and forever, because they are (in the order of finite things) self-sufficient. God could annihilate them, but even he could not eliminate their (ideal) differences. Later thinkers, including Descartes, Luther, Leibniz, and Kant, extended this act of authenticating self-sufficiency to thinkers, immortal souls, and moral agents. Beings of these sorts are said to confirm their separability in two ways: first, as we discover ourselves; second, as we are reinforced by the metaphysical theses and arguments that found our separability in an unassailable ground. I discover that I am, before learning that my existence derives from an idea in God's mind and an act of God's will. God may withdraw the act of being, but not a difference that he—a being whose acts are perfect, hence error-free—once acknowledged or created.

This belief in our singularity has some useful moral implications: that duties cannot be alienated, that we are responsible for things we do, and that punishments and rewards are rightly ours. There are also elaborations that go another way: toward rights rather than duties. For singularity is reasonably construed as a power to act on one's own. As moral autonomy, this is the idea that each of us moves voluntarily, that each can resist intrusions or demands made by others, and that each is a locus of rights, including the right to be left alone and the right to do whatever satisfies us, up to the point of harming other moral beings. Our separability and self-sufficiency—with respect to consciousness, thought, will, feeling, action, and responsibility—promote the individualist, atomist doctrine that society is an aggregate of autonomous agents. We assume that every man, woman and child is, or wants to be, a center of entitlements, including freedom from the demands of others and freedom to do such things as he or she is competent to do. Systems are ignored, or acknowledged only at the margins of experience: we marry (for a time) or take a job, but every such coupling is perceived as an aggregate, one whose reality reduces to the individuals that compose it. "Distinguishable and separable" expresses our atomist self-perception. It nicely suits the competitive spirit of the market economy and the conviction that each is master of himself as he (or she) reflects on his domain and perquisites. The audacity of our narcissism, the ferocity of our entitlement: these are distortions of the perception that certainly I exist, though possibly nothing else does.

This persuasion has ancient roots. Aristotle argued that primary substances—self-sufficient material particulars—are the elementary things of the world. Hobbes described us as self-driven, human animals. Their heirs have eradicated the persuasion, common to Plato,[13] Augustine,[14] and Hegel,[15] that reality is a network of systems, each one independent of some, but overlapping, nested within, or reciprocally related to others. Reality, say these heirs, is dispersed and flat. Luther's souls[16] and Descartes' thinkers[17] spiritualize this claim. Kant's kingdom of ends[18] and Mill's liberalism[19] give it moral dignity. Yet all these atomist formulations are mistaken if the things claimed as particulars are systems. For then the existence and character of such things are conditioned by the internal causal relations that establish and sustain them and by their causal relations to other things. Everything, says this systemic view, is conditioned and conditioning, effect and cause. Efficacy is local and selective, but pervasive. Most important, because, contrary to the impression garnered by thinking of nature in terms of notions such as those of statistical mechanics, relations are not merely additive or aggregative, as molecules interact or slip past one another. Instead, *reciprocal* causal relations create systems having a sustained integrity, one that limits the freedom of a system's proper parts, as marriage limits the freedom of husbands and wives. Reality is a network of systems, some of them mutually independent and related casually or not at all (gravitation apart), others that are reciprocally related, overlapping, or nested.

Causal reciprocity (hence mutual determination and limitation), networks, and hierarchies—all the paraphernalia of systems—are offensive to liberals, free-marketeers, and some metaphysicians, because systems are alternative centers of power. Governments often refuse to tolerate this competition, so that evidence of "factions" intermediate between individuals and the state was and is the occasion for ardent purification. The state controls these intermediate systems, denies them social, political, or metaphysical recognition, or eliminates them. Only individuals or their aggregates are to be acknowledged as real. Aggregates may be accidental, like passengers in a bus; they may also be contractual, as in citizenship or marriage, so that their occurrence implicates the only adjuncts to this spare ontology: namely, laws, government, and the state in whose name it rules. Laws establish our rights as individuals and our obligations as contractors within associations we have entered voluntarily. But laws are stipulations, so they, like the government organized to make and enforce them, reduce to the acts of individuals organized to govern themselves.

This atomist story distorts the self-understanding of people living in democratic, industrial societies. Our participation in systems is, we suppose, voluntary and conditional: we could, perhaps, refuse to participate in every one. Enjoying the freedom to choose our obligations, we can scarcely imagine the self-perception of ancestors who believed that their responsibilities to other members of critical systems—family or church, for example—were inalienable, natural duties. This persuasion changed when the rule of law, free markets, and secularized values superseded the family, village, and church as guarantors or providers of justice, commercial life, and values. We passed from systems having multiple functions—the family that raised children, worked together, and dispensed justice—to systems that multiplied when their functions were differentiated: we leave home to go to work; justice is dispensed by courts, not by a council of family elders.[20] Social atomists misconstrue our history when they interpret this change as passage from life within systems to freedoms that exempt us from them. Expecting that systems will be discrete, material, and local, as families are, they look for comparable structures to perform these newly differentiated tasks. Not finding systems of the old, familiar sort, atomists infer that no systems have inherited responsibility for these functions. The justice once dispensed by family or village elders is now presumed to be extra-systemic and transcendental because conferred by natural law. Or it is merely conventional: we create aggregates, such as states, to make laws that bind us. Neither inference is warranted, because relationships are no less systemic or effective for being intellectual, ramified, national, or global, or for being established and sustained by signs and intentions, such as those expressed in courts, legislatures, or commerce.

Atomists say correctly that many human relations require no system to supply their context: people meet, do their business, and separate. But is this the whole story? Are states or markets mere aggregates established by the contractual relations of the members? Or are they systems? The answer depends on the character of the relations that bind the members. No system is formed if reciprocal causal relations do not join the contractors. Jostling for space on a crowded sidewalk, we move around, rather than through, one another: physical bulk, not reciprocity, limits our interaction. There is reciprocity, hence a system, only if the interaction between us is mutually modulating and sustained, as when each responds to the other in a negative feedback loop: one of us is slow, so we interact and adapt as the other draws back to make way. This loop stabilizes and sustains the relationship. Let marriages and friendships be our example. They acquire flexibility and strength when the reciprocity of the partners overlays their merely contractual relations. Formal rights and duties become the mutual obligations of people who are dedicated to the system that joins and alters them, hence to one another. Systems such as these are local and palpable. Others—states and markets—are more abstract. It may take a while to learn the practice of citizenship, or the rhythms of commerce, in buying, supplying, or banking. Still, roles are learned, and systems established. Let bond traders be our example. They establish reciprocal relationships, hence systems, though competition among them is sometimes fierce. Some of these arrangements are barred, because they monopolize or otherwise manipulate the market. Others are tolerated or encouraged. They overlay the rules that prescribe standards for participation in the market. Systems, this confirms, are sometimes created by the

reciprocities of individuals who are otherwise aggregated. Indeed, mere participation in a rule-governed activity typically requires the mutual accommodation of the participants. Such accommodations—implying causal reciprocity—
create systems. So traffic in some places is aggregative and chaotic; but other
places, where discipline and reciprocity override impulse, it is a system.

Systems of this more abstract kind are sometimes puzzling, because they encourage initiative while tolerating indifference. Fifty percent of the American
electorate fails to vote, yet the democratic system persists. Where is the system
if it constrains us so little? Some people rationalize their failure to vote as a rebuke to the candidates, though most suppose that the system will go on whatever they do. Yet the system is fragile. It depends on the participation of its members and will surely disintegrate or be transformed if their indifference is coupled
with structural changes that empower some of the system's members at cost to
its democratic procedures. These considerations remind us that rights and freedoms are perquisites of a political system, not entitlements of the state of nature. People who enjoy the rights without fulfilling the responsibilities sabotage
the system and themselves.

Atomists rightly believe that the duties acquired by virtue of our roles in systems limit freedom, understood as self-sufficiency and exemption from the will
of others—freedom *from*—and as the power to choose—freedom *to*. How is
duty to be reconciled with these two kinds of freedom? We have the intimation
of an answer in the experience of freedom expressed as choice. There was less
choice in small isolated villages where members relied on the village's norms and
resources for justice, material well-being, and values. Every person would likely
feel the tribal loyalty that Socrates expressed by refusing exile: he relied too much
on his neighbors to believe that he would be better off if relieved of his duties to
them. Obligations were sometimes reduced because conquerors imposed different rules and practices, because the social or cultural disparities induced by
conquest or revolution invited comparison, cynicism, and choice, or merely because one escaped one's duties by traveling to another place. But then new rules
were learned and enforced, so that all of life's social functions fell again within a
few overlapping systems. Duties were clear; choice was limited. The experience
of freedom was intensified when the modern differentiation of functions—of
family and school, for example—required people to move among the systems
that engage them, sometimes following routes or schedules of their choice.
Goods and services were now sold to anyone who chose to pay for them, rather
than given to the patron in whose entourage one lived. The rule of law defends
us wherever we are within such systems, though we may test its application—

intensifying the experience of liberty—by moving from system to system, the better to confirm that it protects us everywhere.

These experiences illustrate three aspects in our experience of freedom: the discovery that we participate in systems that guarantee our rights irrespective of family, caste, or class; the realization that we can choose some, at least, of the systems that engage us; and the power to rank our commitments, thereby choosing a path among these systems. This complex experience is more than an impression. It expresses our discovery that we live within systems created to fulfill the tasks of government and commerce. The experience is deceiving if we construe it as evidence that duties are annulled by our freedom. We err in this way if we forget, for example, that the rule of law is a practice, one sustained by the reciprocity of mutual respect. Its constitutive features—including majority rule, minority rights, legislative authority, judicial review—are abstract; but they underwrite the roles available within states that embody these practices. Citizenship implies the obligation to assume these roles.

Suppose we acknowledge the reality of systems and the contingency of rights acquired because we participate in them. Notice this incipient tension. Participation in a democratic society endows us with the right to enter or leave particular systems, whether families, businesses, or schools; responsibilities, nevertheless, fall to us because of our roles within such systems. We sometimes take our duties lightly—we may enter or leave systems at little or no cost to ourselves—though the systems we join or establish rely on us for certain reciprocities. How shall we temper freedom with duty? How do old duties limit new initiatives? This is the conflict of socialization with unencumbered individualism. It pits the views inherited from Luther and Descartes—I exist, though maybe nothing else does—against the evidence that who and what I am are conditioned by the systems in which I participate.

Dewey had a two-part solution. Provide for individual freedom and initiative by acknowledging that a democratic society is an open playing field, where associations are created when individuals unite for common advantage. Then take care that people satisfy the obligations acquired when they ally themselves. This solution acknowledges, but limits, our freedom by obliging us to fulfill chosen duties. It adds that individuality is qualified when so many of our features and powers—including language, ideas, morals, practices, feelings, and aims—are socialized, and that every activity implicates antecedents or contemporaries who prepared the way. The associations engaging us are merged into a network where many of them are mutually independent; but all are reciprocally related to, overlapped by, or nested within some others. This is not an undifferentiated continuum—each system has a boundary, hence a distinguishing character and privacy—but there are causal links between and among systems, so that the existence and character of each are affected by the existence and character of some others.

This solution recognizes the efficacy of systems, while it struggles to defend the individualist emphasis on autonomy. Dewey acknowledged Mill's three regions of liberty: consciousness and conscience, tastes and pursuits, and the freedom to unite with other people to satisfy shared or complementary interests. Still, Dewey believed that autonomy is an acquired power, the effect of good care and the teaching that emphasizes initiative, not an ontological condition. It is learned, rather than inherited—perhaps as a special endowment from God. It is circumscribed by duties that befall us because of our roles in systems. This is conspicuously true of people who participate in many systems, but also of people who distance themselves from every local system (including families, businesses, and religious sects). For there are few of us living in democratic states who alienate ourselves from the protections and sanctions of the law. But states too are systems; and they too obligate their members. Accordingly, every human system has these two effects: it enables members to do some or many things, while limiting the autonomy Dewey defends. No one chooses his affiliations from a position that is unencumbered by duties to other systems.

Has Dewey preserved the core of the story told by Descartes and Mill? They supposed that we, who discover ourselves as thinkers, learn to decide what is true and good, and that we join with others to secure and satisfy ourselves. Privacy is never compromised, because each of us has cleared an inviolable space within consciousness.[21] This space is a fortress. It confounds the holist persuasion that every position in psychological and social space penetrates and limits every other. Dewey wanted to satisfy both interests—the liberal regard for autonomy and the ontology that locates us within systems. His success is tempered by the ambiguous status of systems, his *associations.* Do they exist as we create and intend their perpetuation? Or is their existence independent of conscious aims? Atomism, with its strong voluntarist emphasis, implies that systems should dissolve when their members are inattentive, or their objectives are achieved. But some systems survive our neglect or the satisfaction of our aims, either because we continue to need them or because rules, laws, or habits keep us from eliminating them. Their survival guarantees that our participation in newly created systems is encumbered by our roles within systems that exist already. Atomist freedom and self-sufficiency are, hereby, compromised: the autonomy for which Dewey argues—we are free to create new systems—is limited by the associations in which we already participate, hence by our duties to them and their other members.

Public rhetoric in America is equivocal: incessant appeals to "family values" are coupled to policies and practices that encourage the dissolution of every association that frustrates the perception of one's liberty (families included). The spaces cleared within consciousness or in the regions we inhabit are presumed empty but for the articulations that each receives from the efforts of its individual thinker-actor. Freedom *from* is subsidiary, this implies, because it is the condition for our freedom *to* make something of ourselves. Mill provides our formula: each of us claims to be free to do as he or she likes, up to the point of damaging others. But damage, even contact, is unlikely if the domain of our behavior is large and nearly empty, as America once seemed to be. Now, when American cities are more a plenum than a void, this libertarian model needs rethinking. We should encourage the intellectual and moral development of individuals and their freedom to choose. But we need not, and should not, disguise the systems that engage us from infancy to death. Their effects upon us are a matter of fact, not speculation. Prescriptions for effective behavior, whether practical, moral, or political, are less cogent—they may be irrelevant—if we ignore these systems and our roles within them. This is not the death of freedom, because the freedom to choose is learned within systems—families especially—that make us competent and bold, and because we express our freedom by participating in other systems.

Readers will object that America is not a plenum. Dense networks of systems are alien to people who don't live in or near cities and towns. Many such people are oblivious or hostile to systems that capture the rest of us, hence to roles that compromise our self-sufficiency. Still, their fantasy of a simpler life, independent of systems, distorts everyone's self-perception. The more accurate rendering of our circumstances requires that we acknowledge several things: frontiersmen and explorers adapt their habits to their circumstances (systems remembered are likely to be the ones installed); an apparent void is not so empty that there are no systems and constraints, whether physical or social, within it; a plenum is never so full that there is no space for reciprocities that establish a new system. People living in Idaho or the Australian outback participate in fewer social systems than those in New York or Shanghai. But now the implications are confounding. Does having fewer systems entail more autonomy because there is less constraint? Or is there less autonomy if there are few systems, because there is less opportunity to acquire the skills required to participate in absent systems? This option—plenum or void—is overdrawn. The American frontier is mostly closed. Settlements in space are more anticipated than real; their technological complexity will make interdependence—and duty—incumbent. The vast majority of humans live in richly articulated communities, where systems are overlapped or nested like a paisley print. Autonomy in them—freedom to and freedom from—is constrained. What is more, most of us do not want the unconditional freedom that atomists idealize. Character forms in us as we fill roles in systems, in families, schools, teams, work, or the army. We are frustrated or despairing if there are no available places in the systems to which we aspire.

These implications for freedom are one likely basis for objections to the ontology proposed here. The ontology itself is a more conspicuous target, one that is focused by this example. Suppose that three line segments are joined to create a right triangle. This entity, several new properties, and a law emerge. The properties include angularity and closed-sideness. The new law is the Pythagorean theorem: the sum of the areas of the squares on the sides equals the area of the square on the hypoteneuse. We sometimes dismiss such theorems as stipulations of formal systems, despite counterexamples like this one: it specifies a law that obtains in flat, Euclidean space, hence in any world instantiating such space.

I shall be saying that new properties often or always emerge when systems form. *Emergence* signifies that new properties are generated when relationships are established by a system's proper parts. Their generation may be static or dynamic: geometrical configurations are the one, chemical bonding, metabolism, and conversation are the other. This explanation implies that the conditions for emergent properties are always relational. All secondary properties—perceived color and sound, for example—are properties of this sort: they occur when animal nervous systems are affected by the light or sound emitted or reflected by other things. Intelligence, feeling, and cooperation are also emergent, for they occur when a system's proper parts are joined. I suppose that none of these properties is reducible to its lower-order constituents or conditions: angularity is not reducible to separated line segments; human intelligence is not the property of single neurons. This proposal defies the almost universal conviction that all complexities are aggregates of simpler things, as statistical mechanics establishes that heat is the effect of aggregated molecular motion. But what argument (*argument,* not program) convinces us that a friendship centered on the reciprocities of the friends is explained *exhaustively* by describing the aggregated molecules or the separate behaviors of the friends? Something is missing in explanations that cite no relations but the additive ones of statistical mechanics, as impacts are additive.[22] Triangles supply useful examples of emergent properties and relations, but they are static. The more important relation for the dynamic emergence of properties is causal reciprocity. Here, each of two causes is affected and stabilized by the other: people conversing are affected and stabilized. This is the relation that establishes systems and thereby the properties that emerge when systems form. The emergence of laws is more suspect, for reasons considered in Chapter One.

My ontological hypothesis may seem retrograde, because it divides reality into partitioned, layered domains of emergent entities and properties. I see the result differently: my proposal legitimizes the medieval persuasion that reality resembles the small plots of tenant farmers seen from a neighboring hill, each one distinct from the others because of its crop and shape. The ontology I favor embeds this claim within a more ample physicalism. Green eyes are not evidence of demonic possession, but only the effect of uncommon genes. The genes are molecular; the eyes are molecular; the effect in us who see them is neural, hence molecular. The wholesale reduction of complex phenomena and behavior is not a promise or a threat, but the daily practice of science and technology. Nevertheless, this program is oversold. It does not, and cannot, do all that is claimed for it, if one or more distinguishing properties emerge with each system's creation (as the gestalt of a face emerges with the configuration of its parts), and if the inception of stable systems marks the occurrence of relations that are causal and reciprocal, not merely additive. Let physics go as far as it can. Let it prove the applicability of fundamental physical laws to every event and behavior. Let it also acknowledge what reductionists have heretofore ignored: that reciprocal causal relations construct successive orders of emergent systems and properties, always in ways that satisfy the laws of motion. Contesting the reductionist promise that merely additive—aggregative—relations will eventually explain everything, I espouse this Aristotelian heresy: nature is rife with pockets and layered domains. Its systems emerge and stabilize, because causal reciprocities bind their proper parts. This formulation may be less off-putting if we think of it as ecologism. For nature is a network of systems, one that locates and engages each of them. Relations to other systems reduce each system's autonomy: human freedom is limited by our roles within systems and by other systems that supply a context for those in which we participate.

These chapters are an ontological propaedeutic to theories of human social relations. Some such theories are descriptive, hence true or false. Other theories are recommendations. Telling us what to do and when to do it, they require that human behavior be construed and appraised in the light of values. We who describe such directives as *theories* thoughtlessly assume that the truth claimed for descriptive theories also applies to theories that prescribe. This is problematic. Truth entails that things are as we describe them, though moralists use *truth* honorifically to commend their values. We see this equivocation in the conflict of moral claims, all of them described by their sponsors as true. Descriptive theories are more or less accurate; but there are no contradictions in nature, hence no irresolvable inconsistencies that are generated within or among theories that are true of nature. Compare the internal inconsistency or mutual inconsistency of moral theories: they demand regard for ourselves and others in circumstances where no one can give both at the same time; or one theory celebrates the poor, another disdains them. There may be no moral theory so supple that it makes no inconsistent demands, and no way to expunge the inconsistencies of competing theories.

This failure is somewhat obscured by a familiar strategy: we warrant a moral or political theory by mooring it to a material ground. We then suppose that our theory's directives are entailed by or appropriate to this ground, and that inconsistencies consequent on applying the theory result merely from irresolution in our statement of it. They can be purged when the theory is elaborated. Let equality be our example. We agree to treat people equally with respect to a set of benefits or rights, because all humans are created in the image of God; because all have immortal, moral souls; because each affirms his or her existence, though everything else is doubtful; because each proves his or her rationality by willing maxims that are universalizable because noncontradictory; because each is sensitive to pleasure and pain; or because each can have a life that is satisfying in itself and useful to others. Our egalitarian theory is assumed to be "essentially" true, because true of a ground such as one of these.

Such claims to truth are rhetorical only: their "justifying" material grounds do not eliminate inconsistency in theories that express or acknowledge as few as two distinct values. No matter that such values are complementary on most occasions: there seem to be no values that are not mutually confounding on some occasions. Nothing is gained by shifting the material ground, affirming, for example, that every moral or political theory may cite either of several grounds to justify its norms. The delicately calibrated tissue of recommendations that moralists proposed will sometimes generate inconsistent prescriptions whatever the material ground, so long as they are driven by two or more values. Accordingly, moral and political theories are sometimes motivated, but never confirmed by the material grounds that moralists cite. Inconsistency is the probably ineliminable effect of diverse, sometimes irreconcilable values. We wait for someone to produce a moral theory so subtle that it averts every conflict among the values it assumes.

These remarks justify a different way of construing our moral and political theories: we acknowledge that such theories are programs for remaking people and their societies in the ways prescribed by ideals. This is the familiar point that differences in morals or politics sometimes express differences of value, not disagreements about matters of fact. Information about our circumstances is, nevertheless, critical: directives prescribed by our values should be appropriate to them. Coupling these circumstances with other values would justify different recommendations and practices. The ontology proposed here does nothing to avert the inconsistencies that result when two or more values cannot be satisfied concurrently. It does supply pertinent information about the circumstances wherein moral and political ideals are formulated and applied. Facts are pertinent to values; accurate descriptions of our social relations and their products somewhat limit differences of value, hence aims, recommendations, and practices. People who value themselves may also value the conditions of their identity and well-being, including the families, intermediate systems, and states that engage them.

This assumption explains another of my contestable assumptions. I shall sometimes infer from role to duty, thereby supposing that *is* limits the possible *oughts*. I do this because of assuming that our condition is a baseline for recommendations about our conduct: no Earth-bound human is asked to run the mile in ninety seconds. The constraints upon us are determinable: many different sorts of conduct are possible within them. Still, the conduct required or commended must come from the range of behaviors that creatures of our abilities can perform in these circumstances. *Ought* is always restricted by *is* or *can*. Conversely, our place within a system often determines what we ought to do, as when our moral task is that of filling a role as best we can, whatever the cost to our autonomy. There is, to be sure, an important presumption here; that we have expressed our autonomy by seizing an appropriate role and its duties, so that choosing a situation, we inherit its duties. None of this compromises the familiar limits to the *oughts* entailed by *is*, as coercion is no basis for duty. Is this "propaedeutic" a way of insinuating my own communitarian political views? The verse is true; this ontology mitigates my preference for initiative over community.

These points converge on a single objective: I intend to establish an ontological theory that is applicable to things of every kind and scale, and thereby an ontological basis for psychological and social theories more accurate than the atomist notions that dominate moral argument and popular perception. Never doubting that we humans have a distinguishing character and privacy, I challenge the psychological and moral self-sufficiency ascribed to individual persons. The individuating conditions for persons—our separate bodies—are not in doubt. The conditions for our psychological, moral, and cultural identity are a different matter. Their development is a process of engagement and dependence, not one of monadic self-articulation. If John Rawls is correct about our responsibility for one another,[23] he is wrong to postulate a domain of creatures that live within Mill's three regions of liberty, where the formation of intellectual, moral agents—each pursuing its self-interest—precedes our ad hoc and limited relations to one another.[24] I shall be saying that nature—social life included—is a dense network of systems and relations. Each of us consolidates a self within this network, a self that is qualified to participate in disparate roles, though it is not reducible to them. Once infants, we have assumed successive roles in systems that stretch from families through schools and friendships into jobs, adult friendships, and families of our own. We have rarely or never lived outside of systems, and now, as adults, we are primed for responsibilities to the other members of the systems that engage us. Our bodies are separate; yet, our psychic postures are distinguishable, not separable, from the postures of others: every child's attitudes bear the traces of his or her caretakers.

Atomists tell a more fantastic story, one that hungers for confirmations like the one of today (5 July 1996), when a seventy-year-old, single-handed British yachtsman sailed into his Hampshire port, six months after his last landfall in New Zealand, four months after he was presumed dead at sea. Wasn't it reckless of him to make this vogage, given his age and the fact that he does these things (his third trip around the world) on a shoestring? "I have been married twice," said this man, "but I have no children or heirs. If I want to kill myself, that's my business." Robinson Crusoe stories excite us. We romanticize single-handed yachtsmen. But few of them build the boats they sail. The reciprocities that engage them are attenuated, but not extinguished.

Chapter One characterizes the things of our world. It describes complex systems—I call them *stabilities*—from the complementary standpoints of nature naturing and nature natured. Chapters Two, Three, and Four apply the claims of the previous chapter to us humans, our societies, and values. I argue that the ontology of our world has regulative force on selfhood, sociality, culture, and morality. These are aspects or functions of community. We rightly describe it as "an association of people who share some values and a history, participate in certain common activities, and have a strong bond of solidarity to each other."[25] Chapters Two, Three, and Four embellish these ideas, given Chapter One's claims about systems. Chapters Five, Six, Seven, and Eight apply the ontological claims of the previous chapters to particular issues: deliberation, free speech, conflict, and ecology. All seven of these chapters test my claim that the metaphysical notions elaborated in Chapter One have application in our world, even to the grit and detail of disputed, practical questions. Chapter One is abstract. Most of the points made there are applied in the subsequent chapters. A reader could skip the first chapter and discern these points in the context of their elaboration. Chapter Three, section XI, is a more accessible restatement of Chapter One's ontology.

I shall say very little about realism and idealism. Idealists will suppose that my ontological claims are merely ways of speaking, the world being nothing in itself or the product of whatever notions we use to think it.[26] I construe these claims about systems as testable hypotheses intended to represent things whose existence and character are independent of the ways we talk about them. The empirical confirmations are described throughout Chapters Two to Eight. My reasons for discounting idealist persuasions are expressed in four previous books.[27] They argue for the existence of an extra-mental world, one that we have not made but know by way of empirically testable hypotheses.[28] Here my concern is the formulation of a naturalistic metaphysics, one that applies to the structure and detail of everyday experience.

Readers may perceive the strong affinity of this book to Justus Buchler's *Metaphysics of Natural Complexes*[29] and to Mario Bunge's *A World of Systems*.[30] We express many of the same ideas in different ways. The convergence of my philosophical ideas with those of biologists and some others is especially gratifying.[31] Why shouldn't philosophers elaborate on ideas we share with the sciences, in ways that are responsive to philosophy's traditional concerns? This is sure to happen as philosophy recovers its interest in nature.

Chapter 1 Systems

Thing is typically an all-purpose word used to signify any topic of thought or conversation. The things that concern me are material particulars, including cats, cultures, and cyclones. I shall say that such things are systems, and that they are established and sustained within tolerant environments when causal relations bind their parts. Any material particular that is not a system is an aggregate of systems, as people are systems and crowds are aggregates.

Section I describes the inception and character of systems. Section II appraises the various arguments that purport to eliminate relationships in favor of their terms. Section III considers the views of metaphysicians—Aristotle, the atomists, and Whitehead—who ignore or disparage relations, thereby implying that systems are aggregates. I affirm, as they deny, that the mutually determining relations of systems (their reciprocal causal relations) create wholes that are distinct from the sum of their parts.

I. SYSTEMS: THEIR INCEPTION
AND CHARACTER

Stabilities (systems) have parts which are themselves systems. First are the elementary particles from which complex systems are constructed; second are the higher-order systems having these parts, as quarks may be elementary, while atoms are stable systems composed of them. Stabilities are complex, because each one embodies several properties or parts (themselves comprising properties and relations) in a network of relations that is spatial, temporal, and causal. A complex is stabilized within a tolerant environment when the energetic bonds within it have established an equilibrium of its parts, one that sustains this thing's integrity until some greater energy destroys it, or until the energy sustaining the bonds has dissipated. Think of Plato's ideal republic, or an orchestra. Both are complexes having properties appropriate to them, as justice in the one and sonority in the other are corporate, systemic properties. Change the balance of the parts, and the system fails; or it reforms to some different effect. Or systems evolve without losing their integrity. Parts are altered or replaced, or relations change so that the corporate character of the system is changed. Cadavers dissolve; caterpillars are transformed.

My emphasis may seem familiarly Aristotelian, because it favors things over the actions or processes that create or change them. This impression is unintended: every stability is the expression of actions within and outside it: entities themselves are structured, enduring events. We recall Spinoza's distinction between nature naturing and nature natured:[1] the one is nature as a dynamic, self-differentiating, self-organizing process; the other is nature as the array of created, more or less ephemeral things. This difference is sometimes translated as the one of being and becoming. Being—in this context—is the condition of systems that are sustained by their internal order and by their relations to the other things in their environment. Becoming is the process whereby these systems are created and sustained, then disassembled. This is a difference of emphasis only. Things are never static—there is action in the reciprocities that sustain them—because they are inseparable from the processes whereby systems are created or sustained, as a storm blows up and passes away. This doesn't preclude their temporary stability and relative autonomy: we ponder an organization's current design without also considering its history or likely evolution.

The analysis that follows may seem less obscure if my principal assumptions and conclusions are apparent. I suppose that things are constituted of their properties, that property values—including position, velocity, or particular shades of color—are effects fixed by the relations of properties; that these relations among properties are expressed as the relations of efficient and formal causes; and that systems are generated and sustained by the reciprocal determination of property values. Systems are networks of reciprocal determination. Systems may also couple with one another in ways that are mutually determining or constraining, so that systems may be mutually independent, or reciprocally related, overlapping, or nested. Nothing is exempt from the reciprocities of every system, because gravity, at least, guarantees that each thing is conditioned by everything in its light cone. Higher-order modes of determination—conversations, for example—have effects that are more restricted.

1. The Constitution of Things
by Their Properties

Why does it happen that reality's elements are systems, not autonomous simples? One reason is speculative but critical. Suppose that every thing is constituted of its properties (a claim defended below); then consider the determinability of properties. A boat at sea is a useful example: it goes in some direction at some speed. These two—direction and speed—are determinables. Their specific values are fixed by determining conditions: a certain wind velocity determines the direction and speed the boat will go by filling and driving the sail.

Every such example exhibits these three factors: a determinable property, a determining condition, and a determinate expression (a specific value) for the determinable. This threefold distinction may seem to be a misrepresentation of actual states of affairs, where values are always determinate: everything has a specific speed or direction, a specific color or size. This is accurate but misleading. For every property is determinable within a range of values, though it has a specific value at any moment: one who is walking at a certain speed in a particular direction could go in any of several directions or speeds. The determinability of properties is disguised, but not eliminated, by the specific values of instantiated properties.[2]

This threefold distinction—determinable, determining condition, and determinate value—has two features that are characteristic of systems: irreducible complexity, hence a minimal diversity of properties, and the functional (causal) relation of a determinable to its determining condition (or conditions). Consider the boat. Not being self-moving (in an ordinary sense, not Newton's), it needs a cause if its determinables are to achieve specific expression. Determinables always achieve determinacy in the actual world: every property has at every moment a determinate value, thereby supplying evidence of pervasive causality. (The justification for saying that causality is pervasive is detailed in section 1b.) Are these two factors—complexity and causality—sufficient to account for the establishment of systems? No: systems are created and sustained by the *reciprocal* causal relations of their parts,[3] as friendship or a conversation requires mutual determination. There is causal interaction, but no reciprocity, in the relation of the wind and boat: wind determines the boat's speed and direction, but the boat can be discounted as a cause of the wind's velocity. Still, this example does have two of the features that are critical for systems: namely, irreducible diversity in a system's properties and ineliminable causality (including the mediated causality described in sections 2b and 2c) in the relations of all or some of its properties.

(A) EVERYTHING IS CONSTITUTED OF ITS PROPERTIES

This section and the next locate the basis for the relationship of a determinable, its determining condition, and determinate value in the character of properties. The explanation I propose may seem arcane and needlessly speculative. Anyone who loses patience with it can safely revert to the case of the boat. This and examples like it already confirm that complexity and causality are the conditions for fixing property values.

We begin by restating the principle affirmed above: everything is constituted, exclusively, of its properties.[4] This jars our intuitions, because Aristotle distinguished form, meaning the properties with which a quantity of matter is organized or festooned, from the matter which grounds it.[5] Matter has bulk, inertia, position, and separability. Properties that qualify discrete matters sometimes make a difference to the efficacy of things, as pointed projectiles have effects different from round ones. Still, thinghood derives from the bulk and separability of bits of matters, not from their qualifications.

This Aristotelian doctrine—a plausible gloss of information derived from perception and practice—is unsatisfactory, because of an ambiguity in its notion of matter. Is this prime matter—something having no properties of its own, but able to accept any set of properties introduced into it—or is it matter of a particular kind (for example, wood or marble), matter that is constituted of, and distinguished by, its properties? Aristotle said both things;[6] his scholastic successors emphasized the former.[7] Neither he nor they could defend prime matter effectively, because it lacks the minimum condition required for any being whatever: namely, the constitutive properties that would give it determinate character. Having no properties of its own, it cannot support the constitutive, distinguishing properties of things. Prime matter is salvaged if we define it functionally, as that which is qualified by form. There is nothing in this functional definition to imply that matter has no properties of its own, or that it is not constituted only of its properties. Indeed, it is only matter's properties that supply its character and justify the inference that particular kinds of matter behave as they do because of them: marble chips because of the crystalline structure of its molecules. Accordingly, we refine Aristotle's account of matter by saying that the properties of form qualify the properties of matter, as clay is shaped. We have this result: things are composed of their properties.

Suppose that an elementary particle is nothing but the assembly of, say, mass, spin, and charge. We add that mass is primary, so that charge and spin are its qualifications. This is not an adequate analysis of particles that have no mass, because there is charge in them but nothing in which the charge inheres, unless we say that a small region of spacetime is electrified (under conditions we may ignore). Mass is, nevertheless, a primary qualifier of spacetime regions. Every such primary qualifier may be qualified by secondary or higher-order qualifiers, as mass is more or less dense, and each patch of spacetime has a qualifying shape or topology. Accordingly, each thing is constructed from a few primary qualifiers, then by successive layers of secondary and higher-order qualifiers. We also credit things with properties that are effects of their relations to other things (the red ascribed to apples, for example, is an effect in us who perceive it). We correct this mistake by distinguishing a thing's constitutive properties (whether they are primary, secondary, or tertiary qualifiers) from the relational properties for which it qualifies because of its constitutive qualifiers, as apples look red. The order of priority among a thing's properties is, therefore, opposite to the order in which they are known: we discount the glitter of fool's gold.

The properties constituting a thing include both determinables and the determinate properties that are their specific expressions: shape, triangularity, and right triangularity are determinables; right triangularity of specific dimensions is determinate. A determinate property gives manifest expression to a hierarchy of determinables; all the determinable, higher-order properties of its hierarchy are present—immanent—wherever the determinate property is a constituent. A red, crested whistler is a cardinal, a bird, and an animal.

(B) FIXING PROPERTY VALUES

Things are constituted of their properties, including determinables (i.e., generic properties) and their lower-order, determinate values. *Causality* and the systems that eventuate from it are implicit in this claim, because the determinability of properties prefigures the relations that fix their more determinate values. Property-fixing relationships have three terms: a determinable property, a determining condition (that is, a cause), and a more determinate expression for the property. These relationships are our focus, but their significance is obscured by some foundational questions. We start by considering them.

Properties, in themselves, are often thought to be disembodied, so that things composed of their properties may seem insubstantial. We avert this inference by supposing that mass is both a property and a primary qualifier of spacetime regions. Still, the feared impalpability of properties is justified, if they exist in the first instance as eternal (logical) possibilities.[8] This aspect of properties is contentious, because Aristotelian naturalism deplores the idea that properties may exist *ante rem*. It denies that the structure of properties existing as possibles may be consequential for actual states of affairs, hence for the character of systems. I shall, nevertheless, assume that properties do exist originally as possibles, because doing this enables me to exploit the discovery that properties are structured in sets of three.

Suppose that properties exist in the first instance as possibilities, as being five-sided is a possibility whether or not any actual thing has five sides. This claim, entailing the *ante rem* existence of possibles, is sanctioned by the principle that anything not a contradiction is a possibility: properties that embody no contradiction exist as possibles, whether or not they are instantiated—whether or not there are instances of them in spacetime. I suppose that possibility is itself a mode of being. Actuality, its counterpart mode, is distinguished by the quantitative and qualitative determinateness of things.[9] These are some conclusions. Here are some reasons that make them credible.

Every thing in spacetime is constituted of its properties. Each property has a specific value: shape and size, for example, have specific values, rather than being determinable. Properties existing as possibles are determinable with respect to some or all of three marks—quality, quantity, and relation—that are common to every property.[10] Quality is distinctive character. Most properties existing as possibles are qualitatively determinable, meaning that generic properties set limits on their lower-order, more determinate expressions, without deciding what those expressions shall be. So color and red are generic properties such that color limits red, and red limits scarlet. Not every property existing as a possible is qualitatively determinable. Some—the lowest-order determinate expressions of determinables—are qualitatively determinate (a specific shade of scarlet, for example). Every property existing as a possible is, however, determinable numerically, because each may be instantiated an indefinite number of times: many, one, or none.[11] Relations too are mostly determinable, though one—self-identity—is always determinate.

What factor decides the lower-order expression that a determinable shall have within the order of possibles? What fixes a property's lower-order, more determinate expression? For the matter is decided: determinable possibles do have lower-order expressions, as happens when triangularity achieves determination as right, isosceles, or scalene. The determinable itself cannot make this determination, for either or both of two reasons: it is neutral with regard to its lower-order expressions, because nothing in it prefigures them; or they are prefigured within the generic property, but no lower-order determination can issue from it because the lower-order expressions are contraries, hence mutually defeating: red, yellow, and blue are the contrary, lower-order expressions of the determinable, color. What is left to determine that a determinable shall have a specific, lower-order expression? Higher-order determinables within this hierarchy are excluded, for the same reasons that the determinable at issue is excluded: they are neutral or confounded by the contrariety of their lower-order determinations. The hierarchy's lower-order determinations are excluded, because they presuppose determination of its higher-order determinables: they are not self-selecting. Suppose that neither a determinable nor its lower-order contraries can determine what lower-order expression this possible shall have. What other property or properties can fix its lower-order expression? There is an infinity of candidates for the role of determining condition: namely, all the possibles that are not related hierarchically to the one whose determinability is to be resolved. Any possible that is not related vertically to the determinable—any that does not fall within its hierarchy—can play this role, barring contradiction. Accordingly, properties, associable with a determinable and resulting in its lower-order determination, are christened *determining conditions*. Properties, this implies, have three principal kinds of relations: they are self-identical; they are related within hierarchies; and they serve as determining conditions for determinable properties in hierarchies other than their own. We say that possibilities within a hierarchy are *vertically* related, whereas determining conditions are *laterally* related to the determinables whose lower-order expressions they fix. In addition, we say that no determinable receives lower-order determination in the absence of a laterally related, determining condition.

We are reluctant to acknowledge the efficacy of properties, because we think of them as uninstantiated. Grant their instantiation, and properties are as palpable and efficacious as anything is or can be: one hits one's thumb with a hammer, whose principle property is its mass. The contrary persuasion—that properties have no efficacy—is enforced by the subject–predicate forms of our language. Saying that things—not their properties—are the agents, we turn a grammatical point into Aristotle's metaphysical doctrine of primary substances. We speak as he did, so that any implication to the contrary must be an error: it is things that act, though they have one or another effect because of having some property. This is misleading dogma if things are composed of their primary and subsequent qualifiers. A moving billiard ball transfers motion on impact because of its mass, not because of the number painted on its side; but mass too is a property.

The efficacy of actual things is prefigured in the relations of properties existing as possibles. To see this, consider the vertical relation of a determinable to its lower-order, more determinate expression, and the lateral relation of a determinable to the determining condition that fixes the value of its lower-order, more determinate expression. This formal relation among possibles translates into actuality—the domain of instantiated possibles—as the relation of an efficient or formal cause to its effect. Wind fixes the speed and direction of a boat; the shape of a torus determines that the straight lines inscribed on it are circles or arcs.

(c) OBJECTIONS AND CLARIFICATIONS

This is my argument for complexity in the relations of properties: determinable properties must be made determinate if they are to be instantiated; they achieve more specific, lower-order expression because of determining conditions. The argument will be dismissed, because it invokes properties that exist in the first instance as possibles, and because the qualitatively determinate properties that require determining conditions are generic properties such as color. It is hard to know which is more despised, possibilities or generic properties—one an "invention," the other an "abstraction." We need a substitute argument, one that supports my conclusion—that determinables require determining conditions—while dispensing with reference to possibles and generic properties. The wind-driven boat described at the beginning of this discussion is a place-marker for this point. Here is its justification.

No determinable property is self-determining: no property determines its own specific value. The point of saying this is easily lost if we generalize to networks of properties, as when the complexity of things composed of their properties makes them self-determining: one chooses to learn a second language. We narrow the point to eliminate this implication: it is individual properties, and sometimes complexes of properties, that do not determine their own values. Consider a barber and his clients. He cuts hair that does not cut itself. Hair is longer or shorter. Each change in length has a cause other than the hair's specific length at the moment. This is the barber's role: he is a determining—altering—condition. What length shall the hair be? There is the range of possible lengths between the current one and a shaved scalp. The barber—perhaps on advice—makes a determination by cutting the hair. A different example—one that includes a determinable, its lower-order expression, and a determining condition—is Newton's second law, $F = ma$. Each of the variables is a determinable; the values of any two variables are determining conditions for the third. Conversely, any value for one of the terms is a function of the values of the other two.

We have, therefore, the same result as before: a property achieves a specific value because of a determining condition. We say this without having to introduce properties existing as possibles. This stripped-down way of stating these functional relations—of determinables to their determining conditions—is complicating, however, in this other way. The relation of possibles, like the functional relation of force, mass, and acceleration, is an instance of formal cause. The relation of the barber to his clients is one of efficient cause. How shall we provide for both formal and efficient cause when we invoke the relation of determinables to their determining conditions? I suggest, with more detail below, that determining relations (relations of form) among possibles are expressed among actuals as the relations of *either* efficient *or* formal causes to their effects. It is one, the other, or both, depending on the properties and relations at issue, as the traditional division of dynamical relations from their background condition, spacetime, encourages us to believe that determining physical relations are instances of efficient cause, while the determining relations of geometricals are expressions of formal cause. (The acausal form of Newton's law is, by implication, the result of abstracting from the actual circumstances in which there is covariation among mass, force and acceleration. For there, their mutual determining relations are efficient, formal, or efficient and formal, as a change of mass or force causes a change in acceleration.)

Now, having confirmed that we can derive a conclusion that is similar (though not identical) to the one above (but without its offensive assumptions), I revert to those assumptions. Our point of reference continues to be the one of relations among properties that exist in the first instance as possibles. We also assume that the possibles of our examples are instantiated, and that determining conditions among possibles translate into actuality as causes. Why continue to speak of possibles when actuals are the primary concern? Because we can revert to the more schematic character of properties existing as possibles when ambiguities occur in our thinking about the relations of properties.

There is, for example, the difficulty of providing for determining conditions in contexts where determining and determined properties are not primary qualifiers: cars handle well, and well-handled cars brake and turn, but fine handling does not brake or turn: How is this determining condition—fine handling—translated into an efficient cause? It is never more than shorthand when we credit such properties with a direct efficacy of their own. There is no ambiguity if both properties—the one whose value is determined and its determining condition—are primary qualifiers: one thing is crushed by the mass of another. Precision is required when action is explained by reference to some property that is not a primary qualifier. For then, the simple formula—laterally related properties determine the specific values of other properties—needs details of these two sorts. First, the properties are instantiated, so agency is ascribed to these instances, not to properties (universals) existing as possibles. Second, citing secondary or tertiary qualifiers seems to detach them from primary qualifiers, hence from the first-order conditions for action. We cover this misconception by agreeing that it is things that act, though we understand that things are assembled from the instances of primary, secondary, and subsequent orders of properties. Saying that one of a thing's secondary or higher-order properties has determined the value of a laterally related property in that thing itself or in another thing is shorthand for a more complicated story about these properties and the primary qualifiers presupposed by this determination. Pressing the valves—not only the remembered notes—determines what phrase a trumpet plays; the color a stoplight—not instances of red or green alone—determines that cars stop or go. Accordingly, the notion that some properties determine the value of other properties is not the error of ascribing agency to things of the wrong category, to properties rather than things. Describing properties as determining conditions is an innocuous abstraction, not a solecism, if we suppose that things are assembled from their properties, so that every higher-order qualifier presupposes such first-order qualifiers as mass. I am assuming that efficacy requires motion, and that things do not move (with exceptions) if they have no mass.

Also pertinent is an ambiguity concerning the two senses of *part* when properties are the parts of things constituted of their properties. First are the several properties instantiated in the spacetime region the thing occupies: its parts are these properties, whether they are primary, secondary, or tertiary qualifiers of the spacetime. This is the distributive sense of *part*. Second is a focused sense: parts of this sort are composed of a primary qualifier, mass especially, and the one or more secondary or tertiary properties that qualify it. Talk of parts in either sense may ignore the manner of a property's integration with the other properties constitutive of a thing; it must not describe the property in a way that would imply its independence from all of them. For every property is integrated with some others, including its higher-order determinable and determining condition.[12]

(D) SIMPLE SYSTEMS

What is the structure of the simplest system? It has two determinables, each with a lower-order expression. Assume that color and shape are the determinables, and that red and square are, respectively, their lower-order expressions. Add that shape is the condition determining that color shall have red as its lower-order expression, while color is the condition determining that shape shall have square as its lower-order expression. Here (formally) is the mutual determination that occurs as reciprocal causality in the relations of actual properties: each of two determinables has more determinate expression because each is a determining condition for the other. Accordingly, our red square is a system that embodies two complexes, each having three terms: a determinable, its determining condition, and determinate expression. Each complex shares a term with the other, and each is a pistol pointed at the other, as happens if each of two thinkers supplies the others with content on which to reflect. (Which is first to fire? We hide the paradox implicit in the example by supposing that each determinable is concurrently a determining condition for the other.)

(E) TWO KINDS OF SYSTEM

Two kinds of system concern us. First are systems created when two or more three-termed complexes are assembled. Suppose, for example, that positive and negative ions are scatted and mixed randomly, with the effect that many or all bind to ions having the opposite charge. The products of these couplings are systems that are stabilized internally by their causal reciprocities: each side complements the other. Second, and less common, though familiar in human affairs, are systems having negative feedback.[13] Imagine that the entities distributed are obsessive talkers, and that each captures and binds to another. These couplings are stabilized by the shared interests of the partners. Yet every speaker has limited interests, so each informs the other when the other has strayed from his or her concerns. There may be a lengthy period of mutual adjustment, as either learns the domain and limits of the other's tolerance. We get this result: a partner's interests or tolerances are learned and honored, or the system dissolves.

Systems of both kinds may be more or less tightly integrated: meaning that each of a system's parts may be directly related to only a few others and mediately related to the rest, or directly related to all. Either sort of organization may be efficient. Modularity (discussed below in section 9e) somewhat isolates subsystems from one another, as parallel processing effectively distributes tasks. Yet orchestras and restaurant kitchens work best under a single integrated command. Too much mediation makes negative feedback systems inefficient: the sensing circuit garbles the information, the control circuit is ineffectual or slow, the train passes before the crossing gates are lowered.

2. Elementary Particles

The simplest freestanding array of properties is an elementary particle. The composites that result when particles are joined may be aggregates or systems. Aggregates are joined by contiguity or in a mechanical way that does not require the mutual, dynamic engagement of the things joined (but for the exception of gravity, considered below). Do elementary particles qualify as systems? Are they autonomous—freestanding—hence separable from one another?

(A) A LOWEST ORDER OF THINGS

Why believe that there is a lowest order of things? Because the construction of complexes from least particles is conceptually coherent, because we can explain the generation of elementary things—they may be precipitates of the superheated plasma from which our universe evolved after the Big Bang—and because there is empirical evidence for a lowest order of things. The alternative view—that every candidate for a lowest order is discovered to be the complex of more elementary things—has its principal justification in the false analogy to infinitely divisible line segments: line segments are virtually, not actually, divisible into an infinity of points. The analogy is plausible only because of the brief history of inquiries that discover more elementary parts of particles that were thought to be lowest-order.

The issue seems unresolved, because of this history and because of an anomaly: the alleged least order of elementary particles is set against the infinite divisibility of space, time, or spacetime. We justify this disparity by remarking that atomizing spacetime has intolerable consequences: it entails either that motion is discontinuous, stopping at every break, thereby limiting the mutual accessibility of interacting causes; or that motion is propagated across the gaps in spacetime. Can the gaps be measured, and if so, what do we measure, given, *ex hypothesi*, that these are not spans of space or time? Perhaps, we needn't infer that an atomized spacetime implies breaks between atoms: the discreteness of its regions may entail only that spacetime has some equivalent to the fracture lines in glass. These lines might resemble color lines, implying no break in spacetime, but only a local geometry peculiar to each bordered region. This interpretation implies that the moments or regions of a fractured space, time, or spacetime would be exactly contiguous, without overlap. The situation thereby represented is all but indistinguishable from an unbroken continuum, so that we avert the prospect of breaks in spacetime, hence limits on the propagation of motion (of light, for example). The principal qualification is the difference between a uniform continuum and the prospect that the "atoms" of spacetime are geometrically idiosyncratic local regions having a distinctive shape, geometry, or topology. either way, we are saved from questions about the unifying ground for a fractured spacetime, and from the puzzling implications of motion in a spacetime laced with gaps.

No comparable dialectic inclines us to deny that matter is composed of elementary particles. The evidence of atoms, electrons, photons, and quarks, together with our comfort with the principle that things are constructed from bricks or Tinkertoys, molecules or cells, encourages the surmise that there are such things. Supplying a mechanical model for them is more problematic: particles may not be discrete, as raisins in a pudding. Physicists (responsive to questions about the criteria of separability and identity through time) are the only ones competent to supply such models. I assume, temporarily, that there are elementary, autonomous particles. What are the relations, internal or external, that establish and sustain them.

(B) AUTONOMY, ALTERABILITY,

AND SIMPLICITY

Three questions direct inquiry: Are particles autonomous? Can they be altered? Are they simple? These are traditionally philosophers' questions: there were thought to be a priori demonstrations that resolve them. Now we concede that each of these claims is a fallible hypothesis. Hypotheses require dialectical elaboration and an empirical test.[14] What follows is an elaboration of my surmise that elementary particles are alterable, but not autonomous or simple.

Consider the idea that elementary particles are *autonomous*. Autonomy implies that particles are complete and self-sufficient. Higher-order systems are assumed to be constructed of them, though the existence and character of the particles are independent of the configurations in which they participate. Think of a pomegranate as though it were composed only of its seeds, so that dissolution of the whole leaves these parts. Or autonomy is qualified, because a particle's property achieves a specific value because of its relations to other particles or systems: the polarity of a particle's magnetic charge is the effect of its relation to something external.

The question of *alterability* is decided if the autonomy of particles is limited in the way just described: a change in the circumstances that fix the value for a particle's property alters the particle by altering this value: change the magnetic field in which a particle lies, and its polarity changes. An autonomous particle might have a fixed character, or it might evolve in predictable ways: changes within it could be cyclical. Chaotic changes are also possible, but they assure its dissolution.

Now *simplicity:* are particles simple—meaning qualitatively simple, hence homogeneous—or complex? Two sorts of complexity are universal and innocuous. Every actual property is the lowest-order, qualitatively determinate property of the hierarchy of generic properties to which it gives manifest expression: a triangle of specific shape also instantiates triangularity, closed-sidedness, and shape. Also conceded, but ignored, is the fact that every property has the three marks cited above: namely, quality, quantity, and relation—if red, it has a certain intensity and is self-identical. I ignore these considerations, because each of them precludes simplicity. Equally, we discount the prospect of particles having secondary qualifiers—agility, for example—since these presuppose primary qualifiers, hence complexity. This leaves the substantive question unanswered: is anything simple, because of having a primary qualifier—mass or a patch of spacetime—but no other property?

A particle would be simple if it had only a single property, and if that property's determining condition were external to the property (imagine, for example, that a sailboat is simple, and that the wind determining its speed and direction is external to it). The particle must be complex if the determining condition for one of its properties is another of its properties. Suppose that an elementary particle is complex because of having two or more properties. Suppose, too, that the value for each of the properties is a function of its relation to one (or more) of the particle's other properties: it has color and shape, where the specific value for each of these determinables is a function of the value of the other. Such a particle is a system, and autonomous. It is also unalterable, because there is nothing within the particle to change the values of its constitutive properties once they are fixed. How the values are fixed is so far a mystery. We may stipulate that each is the complementary function of the other, by analogy with the mutual determination of squares on the sides and hypotenuse of a right triangle.

Notice that autonomy and simplicity are suspect wherever property values are fixed. For they cannot be fixed without the three-part relationship having a determinable, determining condition, and determined value as its terms. Hence this question: Are all three terms present in each particle whose property value is determined, or is one of the parts—the determining condition—located elsewhere? Consider the alternatives: (i) In the simplest possible world, a particle has one, lowest-order determination for a hierarchy of determinables (Peirce's example, the smell of rotten cabbage). Its determining condition would be some feature of space, time, or spacetime, there being nothing else to decide values for the cascade of generic properties that terminates in this lowest-order, qualitatively determinate expression. (ii) In a world that is more complex, the elementary particle has two properties, each one's value fixed by the other. Or we suppose that specific values for each of the particle's two properties are determined by the other property's value in conjunction with the determining effects of spacetime. (iii) Finally, we postulate a world having two elementary particles, each of which has one or more properties whose value is wholly the effect of a determining condition in the other particle, with or without a contributing determination from spacetime. This last possibility implies that neither of a particle's properties (supposing it to have more than one) is a determining condition for the value of its other property.

All three worlds, the simplest included, embody the relational form of a determinable, its lower-order expression, and their determining condition. This relationship compromises the autonomy of anything having a determining condition distinct from itself. It compromises the simplicity of anything having a determined and determining condition within it. Now distinguish complexity from system and consider this other question: Which of these hypothetical particles embodies the structure of mutually determining properties: meaning that there are two or more three-termed relationships, each supplying a determining condition for the other?

The first and third alternatives do not credit particles with complexity sufficient to qualify them as systems. This is so because the first alternative postulates a particle having only one property—a determinable but no determining condition—within the particle, and because the third option makes neither of a particle's properties the determining condition for the determinate value of the other. Both versions of the second alternative do qualify particles as systems: in them, each of a particle's two properties fixes or contributes to fixing a specific value for the other. An amended version of the third alternative also qualifies its particles as systems: each of a particle's properties is the determining condition for the value of properties in other particles, thereby qualifing these properties to act as determining conditions for other properties of the original particle. We suppose that properties A and B in particle X are determining conditions for, respectively, property C in particle Y and property D in particle Z, while C in Y is the determining condition for B in X, and D in Z is the determining condition for A in X. These are systems in which the mutual determination of the constituent properties of parts is mediated by a system's relations to other things.

The next question is factual and empirical: Which of these alternatives obtains in our world? The alternative version of the second alternative is plausible, given the character of higher-order things such as protons and the hypothesis that particles were formed in the explosion of a singularity: it supposes that constituent properties plus spacetime are determining conditions. The amended, third scenario—mediated determination—is also likely to obtain, given the mutual effects that particles have on one another. Together these alternatives affirm that a particle's property values are fixed by some feature of spacetime and by either the accommodation of its properties to one another or their mediated, mutual determination. Particles that satisfy this description are systems: the values of their constituent properties are mutually determining, whether directly or mediately.

The question of fixed or variable property values—what considerations decide that a property's value is variable or not—is still to be resolved. The answer depends on factors in the possible worlds considered above. I describe them again, with an altered emphasis. (i) In the simple world of an elementary particle having one property, that property's value is invariant, because its single determining condition derives from the spacetime in which the property is embedded: π is the invariant function of the ratio of a circle's circumference to its diameter. The question of variability shifts to the determining property: is it variable? If not, the value of the particle's property is fixed. If the determining condition is variable, as the value of π shifts if space is flexed, so is the value of the particle's single property variable. (ii) We suppose, alternately, that the one elementary particle has two or more properties each of which fixes the value of the other. If each of these properties has only the other as its determining condition, then the value of each is invariant. So values for the magnitudes of the angles and the relative proportions of the sides are mutually fixed in isosceles triangles. This invariability depends on the contingency that the embedding space of such triangles is uniform, as when flat. Distortions in its space would liberate each of the mutually determining values from the rigid determination of the other: there are warped spaces in which the angles are equal but the sides are not. (iii) We also consider the possible world in which each of two elementary particles having one or more properties supplies determining conditions for the other. Where each of the two particles supplies an invariant determining condition for the other, there are fixed values of the property whose value is determined. Variation in a determining condition, or rotation in the properties serving as determinants may cause variation in the value of the determined property. (This qualification—"may cause"—expresses the possibility that different causes may have the same effect.)

Again, the next question is factual and empirical: Which of these possibilities for fixity or variation is realized in our world? There seem to be no particles having only a single property: even quarks are credited with spin and polarity, or perhaps polarity because of spin. This complexity entails the second alternative: namely, elementary particles having two or more properties that are mutually determining (with or without the added determination of spacetime or properties in other particles). This possibility is realized by some invariants in our world, protons for example; and perhaps by elementary particles, too. In them, as in the right triangle, the mutual determination of properties produces a fixed form. Compare scenarios of the third sort: determining conditions for properties in each of two (or more) particles are supplied by companion particles. This formula also has many expressions in higher-order systems, as each of two friends determines the other's beliefs or feelings. This too has rigid effects if neither friend has an alternative source of information. But typically, friends talk to several or many others, and this feeds back into property values—effects—determined by their friendship. Accordingly, the condition for variability in a property's values is variation in its determining condition or conditions.

This result confounds the traditional claim that elementary particles must be invariant, as Democritus, Leibniz, and Wittgenstein supposed that atoms, monads, and objects respectively are unalterable. It implies that the identity of such particles is protean: each has a generic feature that achieves determinate expression somewhere (perhaps anywhere) within the range of its possible values. One thinks (perhaps too figuratively) of the hundreds of apparent particles reduced to twelve by Gell-Mann's quark hypothesis. The accepted model supposes that one gets the many by variously configuring the twelve. Could it be true instead that some of the inflated many are variations that occur when a small number of generic properties achieve one or another specific value because of changes in determining conditions that are internal or external to the particles having these properties? (String theorists speculate that fermions and bosons are different determinate expressions for the determinable properties of strings.) Elementary particles subject to a range of variations are chameleons. They compare to determinables that have only two values: properties that are, so to speak, turned left or right, on or off, by their determining conditions.

Consider again the questions asked above: Do particles qualify as systems for the reason that the property-fixing relationship of a determinable, its determining condition, and determinate expression is doubled and reciprocal within them, whether directly or via mediation supplied by external particles or spacetime? Notice that the condition for being a system does not require that determining conditions within a particle are sufficient to fix the values of its determinables, merely that internal factors are contributing determinants of a determinable's value. There are plainly some *nearly* elementary things that are systems: we infer from the stability of protons that their properties are mutually determining (formally or efficiently), with or without an additional determining condition (or conditions) supplied by their embedding spacetime.

Suppose that quarks are the elementary particles we are seeking. Are quarks systems, given that each has several properties? They are systems if each property's value is determined (partially or wholly) by one or more of the other properties comprising it. Quarks are autonomous, complex, and unalterable systems if all property determinations are decided by the relations of these constituting properties (as the property determinations of a right triangle inscribed in a flat space are unalterable). Quarks are complex and alterable, but not autonomous, if one or more of their determining conditions is external to them, in other particles or spacetime. It is likely, given the stability of some quark states, that determining conditions for them derive principally from the quarks themselves and from spacetime. (I assume that the best guarantee of stability in property values is the stability of their determining conditions, as the structure of spacetime is presumed stable.) Determining conditions for other quark states may be supplied by things whose own properties are variable, thereby explaining changes that occur in quarks.

(C) THE FORMATION OF PARTICLES

We know from experience that personal autonomy is never absolute. This is partly the effect of complexity in our lives: independence in one or several respects is consistent with dependence in one or many others. Elementary particles exhibit minimal complexity. They have one or few determinable properties. Each of them implicates one or more determining conditions, hence a specific value for each of the determinables. With them, the question of autonomy is not easily fudged: they are autonomous or not. Still, we avoid a categorical answer by rephrasing the question: What is the degree of a particle's autonomy or dependence? We say that dependence is maximal if all the determining conditions of a particle's properties are external to it. The particle is autonomous if no determining condition is external to it. It is likely that no things (hence no particles) are fully autonomous, despite the contrary evidence of protons. For their autonomy is the contingent outcome of a history of dependence. They were probably created in the early moments after disequilibrium in a dense singularity caused its abrupt expansion. We infer that such particles had, at the moment of their creation, determining conditions—heat and compression perhaps—that were prior and external to them. And we infer that the continued existence of these particles, as separate, autonomous entities, presupposes the hospitable condition—the cooling—of the environment where they are sustained.[15]

This speculative history further qualifies the autonomy of elementary particles. They are basic in one sense, but not another: particles are the things from which more complex systems are constructed, but they are not elementary in the respect that *all* change is explained by citing their reconfiguration or interaction. That cannot be so, because particles are themselves derivative. Their existence and character, including the form of determining relations within them, were generated and are now sustained by their circumstances: circumstances that formed them are now altered to the point of tolerating them. This is not a state of indifference: the particles are stabilized in circumstances that favor their perpetuation. I infer that elementary particles, too, are effects of both the dynamic environment in which they were created and the hospitable one in which they survive. Their autonomy and stability would dissolve were the current universe to collapse into the compressed state of a future singularity. Therefore, determining conditions include both historical conditions which do not currently obtain and such contingencies as are relevant to the sustained character of a thing: it is contingent and relevant to the autonomy of protons and quarks that the universe has cooled. This is an additional reason for saying that elementary particles in our world are not autonomous: one determining condition external to them is the environment, now altered, that once generated and now sustains them.

(D) SUMMARY

Elementary particles are complex in three ways. First, and incidentally, each of a particle's properties has quality, quantity, and relation as its marks; and each embodies a hierarchy of ascendingly generic properties. Second, particles are complex because they embody all or part of the relational form composed of determinables, their lower-order determinations, and determining conditions. This relationship fixes specific values for a particle's properties. Third, particles are complex because they embody and conform to the geometry of spacetime. All three complexities obtain, whether the particles are considered as possibles or as actuals (that is, as possibles instantiated). All three obtain, whether or not elementary particles are systems: meaning that their properties' values are fixed by mutual determination, with or without mediation. What does this imply for our atomistic prejudices? It implies that no particle in our world is simple. Where particles derive some determining conditions for their property values from other particles or spacetime, we infer that no particle is unqualifiedly autonomous. Where determining conditions are variable, we infer that particles, too, have variable property values.

Consider now that the autonomy of elementary particles is not so vital an issue as atomists would have us believe. Indeed, the autonomy of particles—the condition of having all of a particle's determining conditions within it—is unnecessary if there is access to determining conditions in other particles or in spacetime. Equally, it is unimportant to the claims I shall be making that elementary particles are or are not systems. Much more important is the complexity that catches particles in its net. For each property in a particle is fixed by a determining condition (that is, an efficient or formal cause). It is less critical that particles be systems—hence self-suppliers of mutually determining conditions—if particles can obtain determining conditions by coupling themselves to one another. Systems do emerge—there is mutual determination of property values within them—at successively higher orders of organization, as in molecules, cells, and bodies. It is unimportant to us (because unimportant to the human systems that concern us in later chapters) if systems that are relatively autonomous do not emerge short of domains where entities are more complex than elementary particles. Is it mistaken to identify thinghood with systems if elementary particles do not qualify as systems? No: it implies that so-called *particles* may be abstracted free radicals that are not identifiable apart from the systems in which they participate.

3. The Mutual Accessibility of Things in Spacetime

Spacetime is important to the determination of values for the properties of particles and higher-order systems, for two reasons: because particles are embedded within it, so satisfy its geometrical and topological constraints; and because spacetime supplies access to a particle's determinables by its determining conditions, whether they are within the particle or system or external to it.

The first of these considerations—that spacetime is everywhere the basis for the linkages between and among particles and systems—is founded in the character of possible worlds. Each of them is an array of properties (some related, some not) within a possible spacetime. Actuality instantiates a possible world, with the effect that its spacetime is the mediator of relations that obtain among the actuals, determining relations included. Particles, higher-order systems, and all their relations are embedded within it. This step from possibility to instantiation, hence actuality, is contingent. Most possible worlds—perhaps all such worlds but our own—are, presumably, uninstantiated. It might have happened that no possible world is instantiated. There is, this implies, an ambiguity (or error) in the question, why is there something rather than nothing? For there would be an infinite array of possibles, if nothing were actual. The question is better phrased in either of these two other ways: Why is any possible world instantiated? Why is this particular world—with a spacetime having its distinctive topology, geometry, and metric—instantiated? There seem to be no answers for these questions. We can only consider and describe the *fait accompli:* namely, the instantiated properties of our world in its spacetime.

Spacetime individuates the properties it instantiates, giving them dates and addresses, while supplying the relations that make them causally accessible. More, these properties are inscribed in spacetime, not merely present there. For this is no waiting room or featureless container. Spacetime is the medium that shapes, however subtly, everything embroidered within it. Let me show that this point is consequential, not merely allusive.

Two claims are made above. The relation of a determinable and its determining condition within a possible spacetime is an instance of formal cause: the value of the one is a function of the value of the other. Equally, the formal, static relations of possibles—the relations of determinables and their determining conditions—are expressed in actuality as efficient causation. Now consider: how does spacetime affect the determining force of one property as it fixes the identity of another, whether in possibility or actuality? Does it merely supply the medium in which agents are mutually accessible? Does its immanent geometry constrain their interactions, as a riverbed directs the flow of water? Does it alter the character of the interaction, because of being, itself, one of the causes?

Here are two metaphors that suggest the force of spacetime's determining role. Imagine an active telephone system, one so advanced that there are neither wires nor handsets. Callers have access to one another because of occupying any place in the system where calls are made or received. Things in spacetime are also mutually accessible: motion in any region has access to every other, but for the limitation imposed by the speed of light, hence of signals. Reciprocity among mutually accessible particles or higher-order systems is, therefore, inescapable. Everything is affected to some degree by everything in its light cone: that is to say, by everything whose energies can reach and affect it. Accordingly, a system's properties and the steady state established within it are to some extent a measure of the effects imposed by its environment. Whatever it would be in isolation, it is different because of them. Nor are other things exempt from its effects. For the many particles or complex systems establish a web of interacting centers.

This has the significant corollary that everything is the effect of many causes, not only the effect of whatever causes interest historians. What considerations limit the causes that fix a determinable's specific value? Whitehead answers that everything "prehends" (is caused by) all the antecedents having access to it. It grades them, from effects that are inconsequential—"negative prehensions"[16] —to those that are significant or critical. Less metaphorically, a thing in spacetime is affected gravitationally, but not in every other way, by things in its light cone. The mechanism of selection—oblivion, inhibition, or intractability in the presence of an irrelevant or unassimilable input—is the modularity and hierarchical organization of systems (discussed below in sections 9e and 9h). Advice tendered in Japanese cannot determine specific values for my plans or attitudes because I don't understand the words.[17]

These first considerations imply the spatiotemporal connectedness of things, but not that the manner of their connectedness is itself a determinant—a cause—of the things connected. Is spacetime the neutral arena in which motion occurs, or is it both the medium for interacting causes and a formal cause of the result? This depends on the character of the spacetime. We are unaware of its constraints, because our spacetime—or the scale of our place within it—

approximates a Euclidean space: motion seems unconstrained in every direction, because of its symmetries. Constraints would be apparent (and unnerving) if our space were, for example, a torus.[18]

We annul the impression of spacetime's neutrality by supposing that it resembles a grid of rubber bands under tension. The stretched rubber bands somewhat resemble a trampoline. Each place is dynamically connected to every other, with the further condition that these dynamic relations conform to the topology, geometry, and metric intrinsic to the spacetime. Put anything anywhere, and there is a shift of tension throughout the system. The narrow localization of mutually determining relations, as happens in the autonomy of protons and the privacy of conversations, occurs within the framework of this pervasive, dynamic weave. Does this universal connectivity preclude autonomy? No: the modularity discussed below offsets the mutual accessibility of things in spacetime.

Talk of a spacetime under dynamic tension is ambiguous in this respect: is the character of spacetime one of the determining conditions that fix property values? This is the implication of saying that the quantity of mass is altered, or that mass is transformed into energy (and the reverse), as it moves within the geometric constraints immanent in spacetime. Think of cotton candy generated in a swirl of motion, or of a roller-coaster transformed into butter by its speed and trajectory. The familiar distinction between spacetime, the container, and the things contained therein is naive, though we still have to determine whether spacetime is an efficient as well as a formal cause. (This point is also discussed below, in section 4, where complementarities are the issue.)

A different, less empowering notion of spatial relations supposes that they are configurational only, making no difference to the character of the things organized. I ignore this alternative, because it is empirically false: a rutted spacetime or one having mutually inaccessible regions would limit causal interactions, hence the alterations they effect. Our spacetime does not seem to be restricted in such ways (though how can we be sure that this is so?). Seeming to move freely within it, we infer that it is infinitely continuous in all directions, and that it has no efficacy with regard to things or relations located within it. Hume and Wittgenstein took these appearances at face value. The internally formless space they described does nothing to energize, constrain, or alter the things configured within it.[19]

The mutual accessibility of things and the relatively greater efficacy of things operating at short range remind us of the motive for thinking that elementary particles may be systems: that they may have some or all of the determining conditions for all their determinables within them. What considerations favor this state of affairs? Other factors being equal (determining conditions could be supplied internally or externally), the critical conditions are access and efficacy, hence constant—unimpeded—determination of a property or properties, whether unilateral or mutual. Spacetime attenuates efficacy: our sun is potent enough to sustain the whole solar system, but distant stars of the same size cannot affect us with the same intensity, given the inverse square law of gravitation. The same considerations operate at the smallest scale. One imagines a possible world in which determining conditions operate telephonically over long lines; but this world is less likely, because determining relations between or among agents remote from one another are subject to interruption and break down. The mutually determining relations of properties within small things may be secure to the degree that protons are all but indissoluble. These are building blocks that don't come apart. Autonomy in them is the formula for stability, even at the ineliminable cost of complexity. The proximity of determining conditions and determinables may be one condition for this result.[20]

4. Reciprocity

Higher-order systems are formed when reciprocal causal relations are established between lower-order systems (starting with elementary particles). *Causal reciprocity* is the relation of agents whose characters or behaviors are mutually determining, hence mutually controlling, over a cycle of back-and-forth interactions. Reciprocity may prevent either term from changing; or, like extemporizing jazz musicians, each may progress as it does because of its response to the other.

Reciprocal relations may be formal only, efficient only, or formal and efficient.

Formal reciprocities are *complementarities*. Mathematical identity is paradigmatic: a change on either side of an equation requires a change on the other, if equality is to be maintained. Geometry, too, is a principal source of complementarities: the relation of the radius and the circumference of a circle is an example. Others are everywhere apparent in nature, practice, and aesthetic life. They include mountains and valleys and the symmetries of etiquette and sonata form. Complementarities differ in one significant way from the causal reciprocities that concern us. Each of two or more values is a function of the other, but there is no mutual engagement—no interaction—in matters that are complementary. They occupy prefigured places in a unifying form or function. Imagine a painting whose weight is balanced by figures at the vertices of a long scalene triangle, its base at the painting's top left corner, its point at the lower right. The figures offset one another—without their causal interaction—because of exhibiting this form. Such material examples suggest that complementarities may not be merely formal and analytic, hence irrelevant to nature. There is, for example, a geometrical match—like lock and key—between neural receptors and the molecules that affect them. There are also the gravitational effects of spacetime's curvature: they are complementary and pervasive. We reasonably suppose that the geometrical complementarities of spacetime itself (not only those of material agents) constrain and direct the interactions of things embedded in it.

There are also complementarities of form in domains such as language and music. Each of them intimates something about the distinct character of its domain, while establishing the systemic relations which create it. Rules of grammar are an example. Subjects require predicates; the grammatical role of a word may depend on its place in a sentence. Rhythm, too, is an example. Though formal only, its relations are powerfully constraining. We discern the variable but virtual structure of its medium by way of the relations embedded there: shifting rhythms expose the virtual structure of time.

Reciprocities having efficacy—*causal* reciprocities—add motion and energy exchange (or its interruption) to the relations of a system's parts. Efficient causation is energy transfer that alters or sustains the property values of the interacting causes. Every cause is affected by its interaction with others; but causal reciprocity is distinctive among interactions, because each of the agents captures the other by controlling its property values. Such properties may be positional or constitutive: spatial or temporal relations are the one; quantity of mass, charge, or shape are the other. Reciprocity is established when one cause sustains its determination of one or more property values of another, because (assuming just two causes) the other sustains this one's property values. This is the relation that constructs systems from their parts.[21] Results vary, as reciprocity promotes or inhibits activity.[22]

5. The Kinds of Systems Constructed

Systems form when reciprocal causal relations establish and sustain a balance of forces between or among their parts. There are many such systems, including standing archs, molecules with positive and negative ions, and films of soap stretched across wire rings and sustained because of equal pressure on both their sides. A balance of forces may express itself in either of three ways that are significant for later chapters: (i) Some systems are static. The relative motion of the parts is routinized, not stopped, as in atoms and the solar system; or their relative motion is (nearly) stopped, as in the bricks or stones of an arch. (ii) Other systems are created by positive feedback. This happens in the case of fires when the burning caused by an initial source of heat sustains or raises the temperature so that other things burn in a cycle that continues until the fire is extinguished (because it exhausts the supply of combustibles or because some other factor denies it fuel or lowers its temperature). Growth and war are also examples. Growth occurs when cells divide repeatedly under the stimulus of nutrients. They promote division. Division promotes the search for more food, until growth is arrested by the absence of food or an internal inhibitor. War is mutual incitement that terminates, sometimes, in mutual exhaustion.

(iii) Negative feedback complicates reciprocity when each cause responds to the other by provoking or inhibiting the other. These effects may be more or less calculated, as people monitor their effects on others. Quarreling friends are careful not to violate the other's self-esteem. Negotiators talk back and forth, each side modifying its position, given the other's responses. How many cycles of negative feedback are required to establish a system? Suppose that a cycle is completed when each of two interacting agents responds to the other by inhibiting or promoting its action: *B* responds to *A* by affecting *A*, while *A* responds to *B* by affecting *B*?[23] Is this enough reciprocity to establish a system, irrespective of its later evolution? One cycle is not sufficient for any of three reasons: because one agent (or both) is affected by the other in a way that defeats the other's control; because an apparently cogent response is tentative and needs consolidation; or because an apparently cogent response is accidental. Confounding, tentative, or accidental responses by one or both agents (supposing there to be only two) are ineffectual. They preclude or abort the nascent system. Accordingly, one's response to the other requires confirmation (consolidation) by a second cycle of reciprocal effects. Having heard one another, each of us believes that he understands the other. But now we speak again, only to discover that nothing passed between us. Or we consolidate our mutual understanding, so that we have a conversation and a system. Like partners in a dance, we move in response to one another. This, the negative feedback of systems that regulate themselves, is especially critical for human social systems.

Each of these three forms of reciprocity—whether static or negative or positive feedback—is an expression of control: each of the causes engaged falls within the control of another. (One thinks of the two sides of an arch and of oppositely charged ions: each controls the other.) Control is nuanced in the case of negative feedback: each cause modulates its control of the other by altering its response to an input from the other: a thermostat shuts down an overheating boiler when the temperature of its thermometer rises to a cutoff point.

All three kinds of system-creating reciprocities are promoted by principles whose applications are pervasive. They include gravitational and electromagnetic forces, the constraining effects of a least energy principle, the peculiar topology and geometry of spacetime (this is one basis for the requirement that a system be organized to minimize its use of energy); and the dynamics of scale: increases in scale require disproportionate increases in mass.[24] Notice that systems of all three kinds are subject to each of these constraints, and that any particular system may illustrate one or more of the three types. Crystals exemplify the first two: their growth requires positive feedback; the finished crystal is static. Living things embody the features of all three.

6. Responsibilities For and To

The parties to a dynamic reciprocity are responsible in ways that couple mutual control with mutual demand. Each is responsible *for* the other, as each fixes a value or values for one or more of the other's properties. Each is responsible *to* the system (hence derivatively to its other members) for acting in ways that sustain the other's character and efficacy, hence the system that engages them. These complementary responsibilities—*for* and *to*—distinguish systems from the ephemeral encounters of agents that affect then escape one another, like clapping hands. Reciprocities are more than ephemeral, because the causes capture one another, each gaining some degree of control over the other. This control is not fail-safe: subsystems often fail to satisfy their responsibilities to the system or to one another, because of more powerful forces acting upon them or because of an internal failure. Higher-order systems disintegrate when this happens, or they reform: stability is reestablished by resetting the reciprocal relations of the parts.

Responsibility *to* others may seem obscure; but illustrations are close at hand. (i) Think of partners: each one's behavior is sustained because the other's posture incites and demands it. Each accedes to the other's demands, because each prizes the relationship and grants it a regulative power in his choices and actions: being responsible to the system, one acts on its behalf. (ii) The corporate effect of a vocal quartet requires the harmony of the several voices, so that each is responsible to the whole and to each of the other three for the vocal clues that support his or her line. Each one's responsibility to the quartet and its other members may be expressed as a conditional: if the system and its effects are to be sustained, then each member is responsible to it and the other members for certain actions. (iii) Imagine a play in which one character provokes fury in another. We redescribe their relationship, saying that one actor is responsible to the other for his cue. Or suppose that real anger flares between men who are members of warring clans. Each has supporters murmuring in his ears or resonating in memory, so that he acts as much for these others as for himself. Their battle has a ritual quality: the antagonists deliver open-handed slaps to one another's shoulders, each taking care to land a blow that damages the other's pride more than his body. Even pride is respected, as both men step back after moments of chest-to-chest bravura, each snarling while half-bowing to the other. Chance encounters of enemies sometimes end explosively; but this meeting is never out of control. For these are behaviors occurring within an established practice. Its signature is the set of relations that constrain and direct these interactions. Each man fulfills his responsibilities to the other, given the expectations that shape their stylized combat.

One may object that responsibility *to*—with its emphasis on expectation and intention—presupposes a system whose proper parts are conscious agents. This inference is appropriate to the examples above, but not to the point they make: responsibility *to* is characteristic of every causal reciprocity, whether or not its parts are agents with conscious expectations or duties. Responsibility *for* is efficacy: changes are suffered by interacting causes. We use the word *responsible* in this way without ascribing duty or purpose to the cause. We can also purge these implications from the idea that causes are reciprocally responsible to their system and to one another. For responsibility *to* is the demand that each of a system's proper parts perform in ways that sustain it.

Is there, nevertheless, the ineliminable taint of final cause in the notion that a thing is responsible to the other components of the systems that engage it? We answer by distinguishing two aspects of final cause: one is the principal target when this idea is scouted; the other is less apparent, with the result that we uncritically renounce the second because of objections to the first. More prominent is the notion that each thing's motions are impelled by an aim, though planets rotating around the Sun, even squirrels hiding nuts, do not have aims. Less prominent is the normativity of reciprocal causal relations. Normativity has the two aspects specified above: the subsystems comprising a stability lay down constraints on each other's behavior, and each part stabilizes the system by satisfying those constraints. This second consideration is elided with the first when we suppose that the normativity of reciprocal relations has no foundation but the intentions (whether conscious or not) that motivate human behavior. Commercial pilots are responsible to their passengers for their safety; but such examples of intentional behavior mislead us, if we generalize from them to every case where proper parts are responsible to a system and its other parts for sustaining it.

Consider the solar system: massive bodies turn around a larger body in precisely determined orbits. Their uniformity is evidence of an equilibrium founded in the reciprocity of their gravitational relations, as each planet's orbit is the function of its relations to the Sun and other planets. Each planet is responsible to the planetary system and to its other parts in this complex respect: the system of bodies, less any one of them, lays down gravitational constraints on that one's orbit; it is responsible to the system and to them (the system is just the array of reciprocally related parts) for behavior that falls within the limits they have determined. There is no intimation here of obligation. Rather, this planet helps to sustain a system that will not survive in its present form if the planet does not continue to act within the limits laid down by the other, reciprocally related members.

Causal reciprocity has these complementary features: the causes are responsible for effects that create the system and responsible to the system and its other members for behaviors that would sustain it. We may believe that responsibility *to,* with its hint of obligation, is appropriate to human systems only; but the reverse is true. Human agents have to be reminded of their obligations because they are easily distracted. Other things are reactive, with little freedom to vary their responses to the actions that provoke them. If the Sun and other planets establish a set of limits for the orbit of one of them, it behaves as they prescribe: their normative demand is satisfied mechanically and almost without qualification (ignoring the possibly chaotic, long-term outcome of apparently steady-state systems). Nothing in this formulation implies that the part or member having responsibility to others is aware of their demands or that it wants to satisfy them.

This moral demand—to fulfill our responsibility to a system and its other members—is, less contentiously, a distinguishing feature of human systems. Our responsibilities to them—to families, work teams, and states—may have either of two outcomes: they add conscious resolution to the mechanical stimuli that provoke us to sustain systems we prize; or we reject our duties to abhorrent systems because we acknowledge that further participation would implicate us in their effects. This second alternative reminds us that responsibility *to* is not always a positive duty. Indeed, responsibility *to* is amoral, given that members may find themselves responsible to odious systems. Sometimes these duties are consciously fulfilled or rejected. More often—even among human societies—they are honored, unconsciously, because of the reciprocal causal relations that mechanically bind a system's parts. Careless or distracted members fail to override reciprocities they should abjure. Responsibilities *to* are critical to the chapters that follow.

There is also this historical note. The reciprocity of determining conditions distinguishes systems from adventitious causes and effects—people brushing past one another on the street—and from accidental but sustained conjunctions—neighbors, for example. Hume could not acknowledge this difference, because he reduced causality to spatial, temporal conjunction, while declaring that such relations make no difference to the character of the terms related. Precluded from describing the efficacious reciprocal relations of a system's parts or even the productive relations of adventitious causes, he could not describe the generation, life, or death of systems. Humeans should test their notion of causality against such systems: explain the reciprocities that sustain them or agree that constant conjunction is an incompetent notion of cause.

7. Accessible Energy

The parts of stable systems—cells of bodies—or the parts of their constituent subsystems—molecules, then atoms—are moved or braked by a balance of forces. There is no reciprocal action and no steady state—no routinized motion—if there is no energy. Whence comes this stabilizing energy? There are three sources: the system itself, the spacetime in which it is embedded, and the energy or material supplied by the system's relations to other things. The steady state established within a system—its stability—is a product of the interplay among these three. Systems sustain some particular internal form, because the energy required to stabilize them is greater than the energy available to disrupt them. Some things are rarely dissolved. Others endure for fractions of a second before being transformed: external determining conditions overwhelm whatever energies they have for sustaining themselves. The trick for stabilizing a system (absent collapse of its parts or external disruptions) is organizing it to make maximal use of its energy supplies. I assume that the energy transferred within and among systems observes a patter of constraints. This pattern is the network of causal relations among value-determining and value-determined properties. These relations embody the geometry of the region occupied. For spacetime is more than the passive arena in which particles and systems are dispersed or interact: this is the plastic medium where energy is transferred along paths that satisfy its intrinsic geometry.

What is the status of energy within an ontology that acknowledges possibility and actuality as the two, complementary modes of being? Energy in actual worlds is a function of motion, mass, and relative position: this includes the potential energy stored in mountain snow and glucose. Energy, too, exists originally in the possible worlds that prefigure dynamic, actual worlds. In them, it is a function of possible trajectories or structures. Energy is not characterizable, this implies, apart from possible or actual paths or structures. The inability to distinguish energy from paths and structures—to specify energy in itself—reminds us of the distinction between nature naturing and nature natured: the character of change as a process shows itself in the things created and changed, hence moving or energized.

8. Functions Contrasted with Structures

My characterization of reciprocally related, overlapping, and nested systems assumes that successive orders emerge when physically distinct entities—starting with elementary particles—are organized into systems that include individual persons, families, clans, and nations; or atoms, molecules, cells, and bodies. This formulation is too simple. Relevant stabilities are sometimes identified more effectively by citing their roles in higher-order systems: firemen may be described in terms of their work, without regard for the style of their uniforms or the color of their trucks. Indeed, too much emphasis on typifying structures may blind us to different ways of accomplishing an objective. Thinking that children belong to families, and that the standard family is composed of them and their parents, we neglect some other ways of nurturing children, including aunts, schools, and street gangs. This belies our ingenuity, for we are adept at finding new ways to do the same thing, and adept at distinguishing functions performed concurrently by individual systems (proselytizing and teaching, for example). Emphasizing roles is also useful when the complexity of a system's parts and relations obscures its function. As with a Rube Goldberg machine, we can't tell what it does. Or we remark that functions integrate systems that are anomalous in most respects, as happens when an individual engages a nation-state by passing through its custom's post. Such relations are structurally obscure: two people meet, one a "visitor," the other an "officer." We avert confusion by specifying the functions or roles of the system's relevant parts—in this case the two people.

The convenience of emphasizing functions is, nevertheless, subversive in this other way. We find ourselves saying that functions have an abstract integrity of their own; each could be realized in different ways. We then talk as if functions are distinguishable from their realizations, so that the character and complexity of supporting structures is incidental to the work done. Nothing is accomplished, we concede, if there are no physical systems—no hardware—to do it. Still, the material character of these realizations is a contingency: we can use vacuum tubes or transistors to make radios. Where reality includes physical systems and their functions—agents and their effects—we say that functions are the salient part. This understanding of nature should make science easier: we need only model a function, perhaps mathematically, leaving it to the drudgery of smaller minds to discover the physical mechanism that realizes the plan. Let architectural practice be our guide: the architect designs, then leaves construction and the choice of materials to a competent assembler.

This abstracting persuasion is more rhetoric than reality: there is no spinning without the wheel that turns. Some people ignore this truism, because of wanting to liberate functions from their physical realizations. Separable if distinguishable is their assumption, though the roles or functions separated have integrity for thought but no efficacy. We right the balance by emphasizing their material realizations: they are performed by systems or their parts. We replace mathematical descriptions by physical models; or we study actual systems and the contexts wherein they stabilize, reform, or dissolve.

9. Higher-Order Systems

Elementary particles and the systems formed of them enter into reciprocal relations, thereby creating higher-order systems. There are eleven points to consider.

(A) ESTABLISHING HIGHER-ORDER SYSTEMS

Reciprocity couples two or more of the relationships having determinables, determining conditions, and determinate values as their terms. Imagine two things, each of which supplies a determining condition for a determinable property of the other. We (who are systems) talk to one another, thereby determining our respective ideas and attitudes. Our conversation occurs just once or sporadically, or it is almost continuous: either way, we establish a higher-order system. Various couplings are possible: A talks to B, who talks to C, who talks to A; or A, B, and C talk concurrently to one another, so that A and B are jointly determining conditions for C's beliefs. Members of the system may be differentially and mediately connected, each connected to some, thereby to all; or each may be connected directly to all.

(B) PROPER PARTS

The members of any system are its proper parts: meaning the first, lower order of reciprocally related parts from the standpoint of the system, as individual persons, not their organs or cells, are a family's proper parts. Proper parts may be differentiated structurally or functionally. The human body's proper parts are, structurally, its skeleton and organs; functionally, they are systems that include its digestive and immune systems. Only the skeletal system meshes (nearly) with skeletal structure. The proper parts of functional systems are themselves functions. Particular functions may be performed by any of various systems, so that the character of a function precludes simple inferences to the number and kinds of structures engaged to achieve it: there are vehicles powered by gasoline, electricity, or magnetic attraction. Conversely, the proper parts of structural systems are mechanisms or their parts; though here too there is uncertainty, because identifying a system's constituent structures may tell us nothing about their functions, as thumbs are used in many ways. Accordingly, systems are described incompletely if we do not specify their proper parts in this complex way: we tell what structures they have and the work they do.

(C) PROPERTY VALUES FIXED WITHIN A
SYSTEM OR BY DETERMINANTS OUTSIDE IT

How much autonomy do systems have in determining values for the properties of their proper parts: do all the properties of an animal body's proper parts have particular values because of causal relations within the body, or because of causal relations connecting it to other things? This question was asked of particles. Three alternatives were considered (though not in the order that follows): values for all such properties have determining conditions that are native to the system; some determining conditions are native to the system, while others are not; or all determining conditions for all the properties of a system's proper parts are external to the system.

These are alternative survival strategies. The first alternative—autonomy, as in protons—is an effective defense against environmental changes. Total reliance on external determinants—the third alternative—eliminates internal reciprocities, hence system, though it may sustain a system's parts: think of actors who desert their play in order to take their cues from the audience. Strategies of complete autonomy or dependence—having all determining conditions within or without the system—are, nevertheless, risky: there is no provision for alternative support when primary causes fail. Complex systems are more viable, though less autonomous, if they participate in nested and overlapping systems, where external determinants supply energy, information, or materials. It also helps if a determinable accepts determination from any of a range of determining conditions, for then dependent systems are less vulnerable to the loss of particular sustaining causes.

The balance of autonomy and engagement is also critical for the many tasks that isolated systems cannot perform. The power of speech is an example. This is a complex property introduced with the evolution of brains. The capacity for speech is nevertheless undetermined—it remains determinable—until the person having it participates in a society where the language in everyday use decides the language that he or she learns to speak. The effects of environment are not always so benign: latent aggression may not achieve a determinate value until civil society has disintegrated into a mob.

It is the second option above that dominates in our world: the determinables of this world's systems typically have internal and external determinants. One's heartbeat is the function of internal causes, but altitude is also a constant cause, and fright a sporadic one. There may be nothing else so autonomous as a neutrino or a proton.

(d) AGGREGATES

Systems of every sort are different from aggregates: causal reciprocity binds the parts of systems, whereas aggregates are established by the contiguity of their parts. This distinction lapses when gravitation is the factor at issue. For aggregated grains of sand are a gravitational system: each grain helps to determine the weight of the others.

Aggregation due to gravity is the most primitive and pervasive system of reciprocal relations. Higher-order properties and relations are generated within gravitational systems when successive orders of complexity are created and sustained by motion and the intrinsic geometry of the spacetime in which mass, then its secondary and subsequent qualifications emerge. (Thinking again of swirled cotton candy, abstract the sugar added to the hot, quickly turning bowl. All the properties and things of our world are contrived, perhaps, from equally rudimentary stuff.)

The difference between aggregates and systems is muddied if aggregates are gravitational systems, for then every collection of things is a system. How shall we distinguish aggregates from systems? There is this two-step procedure. Identify the proper parts of the thing at issue; then determine the character of the relations that bind them. If properties of the parts other than gravitational properties—weight, for example—are determined reciprocally, then this thing is a system, however few the properties or their relations. If no properties other than gravitational properties are mutually determined—the parts are otherwise merely contiguous—the thing is an aggregate. Equally, we could say that gravitationally bound aggregates are the most impoverished systems.

(E) MODULARITY

Every stability has the integrity of a module, one that stands apart from its environment because of the integrating relations of its parts. A module's organization works in two ways. Within a system, organization is enabling; it facilitates the system's use of the energy, material, or information it has appropriated. Outside the system, organization is a barrier that filters inputs. It reads signals, for example, finding some intelligible, others not.

We emphasize this difference by saying that every system has an *inside* and an *outside*. Inside is the relationship of the parts. Energy or information is cycled through these bonds, so that every dynamic relation to things outside a system is mediated by its properties and their relations, or by that representation of the outside created by this agent's interpretation of the available information. Its every response expresses, however obscurely, something of these systemic properties or products. Extracting energy or information from the things outside itself, the system metabolizes them in its own terms. This is its distinguishing privacy and integrity.[25]

A module's inside is usually organized within a space enclosed by a more or less permeable surface. But this is not always so. Imagine that speakers of diverse languages are evenly mingled, so that *inside* signifies the relations among speakers who are widely dispersed with gaps—filled by speakers of other languages— between them. Inside, for these purposes, is a place within the network of reciprocal relations. Things that are outside this network are not thereby denied efficacy within it; but such things have a significantly weaker effect on things within, as uncles and strangers are usually less influential on children than their parents. The network of reciprocal relations that comprises a system is also, therefore, a filter or barrier. Diffuse barriers are evidence that a system has a merely tentative integrity: it barely hangs together. Its closure is incomplete; stability is precarious. Its constituents are easily dispersed; or they await some missing item so that they may reassemble. We are reminded that systems come to be, dissipate, and sometimes reform in a flux wherein the integrity of every system is compromised by its reliance on determining conditions located in other systems.

Modularity also explains this anomaly: a stable system affects everything in whose light cone it falls; yet many of them responds differently to it. This is no paradox when we remark that a system's pervasive and uniform gravitational effects compare to the differentiated effects it has when it acts as a system having a particular character. The transfer of information is an example. Considered as physical energy, it has the gravitational effect just cited. Considered as information, it is pertinent only to those stable systems able to interpret and use it because of the character of their parts and relations. It makes no difference to this example that the information is propagated by a radio transmitter, by whispering in someone's ear, or as a virus read by a body's autoimmune system. Whichever, it is the particular parts and organization—the modularity—of a system that qualify it, or not, for interpreting the information supplied. Whitehead was somewhat too literal when he proposed that each of his "actual entities" grades all the inputs it prehends:[26] systems cannot read (construe, interpret, understand) most of the effects that other things have upon them. Such effects are not so much graded and rejected ("negative prehensions") as ignored.

(F) DISSOLUTION

What is it, more specifically, that averts a system's dissolution? Two things are critical: an energy supply (whether internal or external to the system) and reciprocal causal relations which sustain the system's parts while using the energy efficiently. Unsustainable arrangements are common enough when the effect of causal relations is an uncontrolled reaction, one that continues until the system is destroyed or until the energy or material fueling it is exhausted: there is no internal brake within a fire. Compare self-limiting processes, with their self-regulating causal loops. Systems of this sort are organized so that interaction turns one or more of the interacting parts on or off when a critical value is achieved. The thermostats that activate furnaces are familiar examples. Elections have a similar role in democratic states. Systems that are organized for this self-regulating effect promote actions that serve their purposes, but stop or divert those which impair them. They resist dissolution.

(G) STEADY STATES

Equilibrium, as it concerns us, is a steady state in the sustaining distribution of a system's tasks and energy. (Thermodynamics says that systems in this condition are far from equilibrium, meaning far from a state of minimum free energy.) Three conditions promote this steady state: (i) quantities of energy, material, or information sufficient to sustain it are supplied to a system; (ii) each part does work whose character is determined by its qualifications; (iii) the timing of each part's work is determined by the manner of its interaction with one or more of the system's other parts.

A system's steady state has either of three effects: (i) it sustains a system's parts and organization and the interaction of the parts; (ii) it sustains a succession of replicated parts, their organization, and interactions; or (iii) it sustains parts, organization, and interactions when each has evolved from some antecedently stabilized condition. A working engine is an example of the first alternative. A body and its cells, a team and its players, and a species and its members are instances of the second. The successive development of pupae, caterpillars, and butterflies is an instance of the third. The apparent stasis in some of these examples is, more precisely, the effect of routinized motion.

Every system relates to other systems in one or more of four ways: they are mutually independent, reciprocally related, nested, or overlapping.

Independence: A system is not affected gravitationally by systems that do not fall within its light cone. Moreover, each system is a module stabilized by its internal, reciprocal relations. Having an inside and an outside, it is exempt to some degree from the influence of the systems in which it is embedded: its property values are fixed principally by causes internal to the system.

Reciprocity: Systems sometimes engage one another reciprocally, thereby creating higher-order systems. How much stabilizing reciprocity is required before we justly say that the products of these encounters are systems? (We want a criterion that distinguishes system-founding reciprocities from interactions that do not capture the participating causes.) Is it sufficient that there be a single round of mutual effects? Adventitious causal relations are, almost tautologically, those that fail to create systems. Still, one pass—one causal interaction—may succeed, as when gravitational bodies capture one another. Systems established by the negative feedback of their parts are more demanding: they require two or more cycles of interaction. Suppose that each of two causes is reoriented or fortified by the first effect it suffers, and that it responds by prompting (signaling) the other cause to act again as before or to alter its behavior in some respect. This second round of effects confirms the mutual control of the system's constituent parts. (See section 5 above.) Systems having positive feedback also require two or more cycles of reciprocity, though confirming that control loops are established is irrelevant here because there are no control loops in them. Positive feedback systems require two or more cycles of reciprocity, because they are not established if not sustained: there is no fire if striking a match does not create a blaze hot enough to burn the match or other things.

Nesting: Systems may be nested, each having an integrity peculiar to itself, while each is constrained by the succession of ascending orders: the Borough of Manhattan, in the City of New York, in the State of New York, in the United States, is an example. It may seem odd that lower-order stabilities are constrained by a higher-order one, when the higher-order system has no existence separate from them, its parts. Yet, this makes sense, because the supervening system controls them by way of the organizing, reciprocal relations which are the only basis for its existence. Such constraints may be more or less subtle. The United Nations makes few demands upon the citizens of member countries. The European Union is more demanding. Particular states may be coercive indeed.

Overlap: Systems overlap (a kind of nesting) when a part of one is also a part of one or more others. Is there also determination in the reverse direction—from the bottom up? There usually or always is, because the character of the parts determines the character of the reciprocities that may engage them, hence the character of the higher-order system. So any orchestra has supervening powers on its musicians, though its authority is responsive to the difference between violas and oboes. Many systems overlap, as the society of father and child overlaps the one of mother and child. Disparate claims made by overlapping systems on the part they share are often the cause of tensions between them. Ethnic or religious groups compete for control of a school; or a court is asked to declare that New York and New Jersey share jurisdiction over Liberty Island. We invent effective compromises; or the overlapping systems waste their energies fighting one another.

Human social relations (and tensions) may illustrate one or more of these four styles of relation. Mutually independent people or systems compete for space; reciprocally related systems disagree about the best use of a resource they jointly need and control; a higher-order system competes with a lower-order part for a resource (as state and city governments compete for tax money); or systems compete for the loyalty of their shared part. Each side sets prescriptions for the part they share. These demands may be compatible or contrary, as happens when dialects overlap. Speakers in the region of overlap are intensely aware that each version of the language prescribes its distinguishing norm, where either may preclude the other. Other times, one or both competitors tolerate choice in the shared part, because freedom survives in the spaces left determinable when causes fix values incompletely. Amalgamation—a common patois, for example—is the likely result.

We may resent the constraints imposed by systems, but then our situation is awkward, for we have these unsatisfactory choices: repudiate one or the other of the systems that compete for our participation; repudiate both of them in favor of a third; or repudiate each of the competitors in order to live in a void, exempt from the demands of the systems abandoned. Having left a big city, I am careful not to live in another. Any city would constrain me in ways I find intolerable, so I live in a much smaller town or in a cave. These substitutes also constrain me, but differently. My new freedom is of two sorts. I can do here some things I could not do there; and I don't have to choose among alternatives that were forced upon me there: I am not called on to speak to anyone. Still, my freedom is costly in a different way: I am unformed in ways that could not escape determination in the other place. Everyone there insisted that I have an opinion on every point of controversy: here no one asks what I think, so that I think less.

The spaces that tolerate self-determination are critical in the chapters that follow, because they justify the insistent impression that we humans are both determined and free. We participate in stabilities, where reciprocal relations constrain us. Yet, there are often degrees of freedom in the application of these reciprocities, as when speakers tolerate idiosyncrasies in one another's accents, choice of words, or grammar. There may be scope for liberty and individualism, even for anarchy, within stable systems: laws barring nudity don't prescribe the clothes to be worn. None of this implies that we may remove ourselves (death apart) from all the conflicts cited above. Indeed, much of the creativity and excitement of human social life is an accommodation to these tensions, as standard English is enriched by its dialects.

There are also strategies for exploiting the spaces for variability and choice that are left open to us in circumstances where we are, otherwise, constrained by reciprocity, nesting, overlap, or the competition of systems independent of us. Sometimes, for example, there is no determination from any side regarding the matter at issue: I may wear any hat or none. Or there is freedom to choose among competing determinations within an order, given that I must choose one or another. Or freedom at a lower level is forced by a determination originating at a higher one: the choice of desirable suitors is presented in the context of an arranged marriage.

There is, finally, the advantage of living within a network of systems where each supplies a different, but complementary, support. Think of the talented child whose parents buy him a piano because he wants to play it, inciting a teacher to offer lessons, so that this well-trained musician impresses the sponsor who arranges recitals that make his reputation and fortune. It all seemed so easy, says the pianist at the end of his career. We are usually oblivious to constraints and obligations that confine our choices.

(I) A CRITERION FOR ASCERTAINING
ORDERS OF SCALE

Sometimes the subsystems of a higher-order system are systems of the same order, as a family is higher-order, and its members are things of the same order.
Often, however, there are differences of complexity and scale among the parts
of higher-order systems: a foreign national goes into business with a sovereign
state; a city is established by the reciprocal relations of citizens, corporations,
buildings, and a transportation system. We want a criterion for determining
whether systems belong to the same or different orders of complexity. How
should this scale be established? We may propose to number the orders: counting elementary particles as zero, we move through the number series as systems-
become-parts are successively joined by way of reciprocal relations to create
higher-order systems. This project quickly fails, because we find ourselves having to make arbitrary choices. We decide, a little tentatively, that the number of
a system's subaltern parts is irrelevant to certain functions (so that Luxembourg
and China are stabilities of the same order); but then we have more difficult
cases. How many stable structural systems does a living animal embody? Do tissues count as intermediate systems, or should we only count cells and distinct
organs? Having given one too many uncertain answers, we abandon the project;
or we accept a pragmatic substitute. We say that various orders may be compared
and judgments made about their relative position within a ranking, as molecules
are lower-order than cells. We agree that systems located at different orders of
complexity on the scale of structures—elephants and amoebas—are to be classified as same-order for the purpose of some task: both survive and reproduce.
We acknowledge that our choices are somewhat arbitrary, with no principle that
would reduce the patchwork of stipulations to an objective order. This is not a
surrender to relativism. We assume, as before, that higher-order systems comprise successive orders, from elementary particles through intermediate orders
to higher-order structures. We merely concede that the mere counting of structural orders, from simplest to most complex, is problematic; and that analogies
of function often concern us more than equality or disparity in the order of structural complexity.

(J) PRINCIPLES FOR GENERATING SYSTEMS
OF SUCCESSIVELY HIGHER ORDERS

The creation of successively higher-order systems suggests a question: do these
successive assemblies result from the recursive application of the same generat-

ing principle or principles? There may be such principles, though I don't know
what they are. Is there evidence from which they may be inferred? There are
some common features of stable orders: they include the proximity in spacetime
of the systems assembled (though one imagines pen pals communicating over
great distances at the speed of light); similarity or complementarity of composition or organization; similarity or complementarity of scale (no systems but
gravitational ones created by coupling ants to comets); similarity or complementarity of internal rhythm (as of work, growth, or reproduction); and community or complementarity of intention or practice. Relationships that do not
satisfy conditions such as these are likely to be unstable, hence ephemeral. But
this list is less than a specification of the principles sought.

A negative principle—one having apparently universal application in our
world—is easier to state: no higher-order system is sustainable if the energy required to create and sustain it is drawn from the energies sustaining the constituent systems. There can be no higher-order system if the price of establishing it is the dissolution of its subassemblies.

(K) LIMITS ON THE ASCENDING
ORDERS OF SYSTEMS

There are physical, but no logical, reasons for limiting the ascending orders of
systems. There may, for example, be insufficient energy to sustain a network of
reciprocal relations among a system's parts; there is no way to deliver the energy
required, or the cost of the energy is unsustainably high. These are warning lights
for systems of overreaching complexity: they risk outrunning the stock of energy or the means for delivering it.

What is the highest-order system achieved? Is nature a unitary system of systems, one such that the mutual accessibility, interaction, nesting, and overlap of
material stabilities are reinforced by the unity of their embedding spacetime?
Holism is entailed if every system is located in spacetime in such a way that each
makes a dynamic difference to every other system in whose light cone it falls, or
if systems that do not fall in the light cone of another are connected to it by an
intermediate system or systems: one falls in the light cone of another, which falls
in the light cone of a third. This is, to be sure, a very qualified holism. For many
systems have no reciprocal relations but gravitational ones between them.

Modularity is also relevant to this holist dream: it limits the connecting effects of spacetime, because a module's subsystems are reciprocally related to one
another, but not to most things outside it (gravity apart). Spacetime may con-

strain a module's subsystems, even to the point of determining some of their properties. Still, it does not overwhelm the modularity of the myriad systems inscribed within it by making the value of each module's every property a function of all the systems connected to it in spacetime. Accordingly, modularity averts the full-court press—the thesis of comprehensive and universal internal relations—that holism promises. We are saved from having to say that everything affects and is affected by everything else in every respect.

Holism is sometimes less ambitious, as when it dispenses with comprehensive internal relations, requiring only that things be located within a suitable container. Spacetime and God's mind are the principal candidates. But there is no evidence that a conscious being thinks the world as one. Indeed, there is no evidence of a highest (because universally inclusive) order of any sort save for the ones of spacetime and universal gravitation. (The second may be the intrinsic kinematics of the first.)

There is, therefore, an upper bound to the complexity of nested systems: complexity is limited by the availability of the energies required to organize large systems and by the mechanics of transmitting these energies over vast distances. There are, for want of these energies, clusters of nested systems, but no single system—other than spacetime (hence gravity)—that supervenes on all of them.

10. Disparate Kinds of Higher-order Systems

The class of higher-order systems includes things—such as animal bodies, families and markets, athletic matches, and species—that are very different from one another. The first of these examples passes Aristotelian muster. Atomists bristle at the second, calling them aggregates. They ignore the third: events, on their telling, are not *things*. They are mystified by the fourth. But all of these are systems, as we confirm by rehearsing their features.

A system has properties whose values are determined by the causal interaction of its parts, or by the interaction of its parts with things external to the system. By itself, this description is appropriate to every causal interaction: actions of any sort have effects. Systems take causality one step further: mutual activation and inhibition—causal reciprocities—stabilize interactions that have created a system. Something you say provokes me to respond in a way that incites you to further words. Each holds the other in place as we talk. Our conversation may be utilitarian and short; but what we discover in one another impels us to carry on, now and many times again.

Reciprocity is sometimes easy or obligatory because of circumstances. Heart and lungs have no choice but to coordinate their action. Orchestra and family members are equally constrained, the one by employment, the other by marriage or birth: violinists who want to keep their jobs cannot refuse to play with cellists. Athletes are constrained by the character of the games they play, as football teams are reciprocally engaged for just the hour of playing time. Within this period, their pitched battle is a stability (with considerable internal variability), each team playing as it does because of its talents and organization and because of the other team's style. But then the game ends, and players disperse.

The reciprocities of breeding populations have some distinctive constraints. (A species is an array of disparate breeding populations, all or most of whose members can breed with some at least of the species' other members.) They include each member's genes, the features of this population's ecological niche, and those regularizing forms which operate within or upon various orders of complexity. Genes determine the character of successive generations of the population's members: first, by making other kinds of things sexually uninteresting or invisible (this is an instance of figure and ground: one sees things of one's own kind against the backdrop of the rest), then by supplying the template that activates proteins from which individuals are constructed when breeding has occurred. The ecological niche supplies nutrients and opportunities for encounter: one to nourish bodies, the other to facilitate cooperation and reproduction, as bats, not geese, find partners in caves. Regularizing forms of order operate in domains where order emerges from disorder. Apparently random behaviors become regularized: a disorganized school of feeding minnows suddenly organizes itself into a sinuous, moving column in response to predators. The apparently autonomous and unrelated behaviors of a species' members turn orderly and social, as happens when they mate.

Still, there is this question: Where shall we look in animal or plant populations for evidence of the stabilizing interactions that create a system equivalent to molecules, conversations, or football games? Swans mate for life, though breeding is capricious and quick for most other animals. Where is the stable system—the thing—in a breeding population of swans, not a pair of mated swans?

Remember, to start, that many systems are distributed across a terrain, so that reciprocities bind one of the members or parts to a relatively small number of others. Armies are systems, but typical foot soldiers relate directly to few others, so that command structures are obliged to unify diffusely related parts. Breeding populations lack this unifying form, but they have compensating benefits. Nutrition may promote reciprocity. Mating guarantees it, however briefly. Child rearing sometimes prolongs it. Systems emerge, however casual the mating and nurturing routines, when spasmodic or sporadic mating establishes ge-

netic continuity: meaning that genes are transmitted to carriers able to reproduce them. We interpret genetic continuity distributively for sexual species by
adding that members of a gene pool—the system at issue—include a reproducer
and all those members of the complementary gender who could breed with him
or her. Accordingly, we designate the system by emphasizing the possibility of
interbreeding, hence the *virtual* reciprocity of the species' members (any male
could breed with any female), not by requiring direct or mediated reciprocity of
each member with every other.

These are some fundamental considerations that qualify breeding populations as systems. Two others are also prominent. First, each of a population's current generation occupies a niche (or many similar niches) where its typical behaviors are a part of the stable context for the behaviors of the niche's other
species: humming birds reliably pollinate the flowers that supply their food.
Both quality and quantity are relevant here, because other species are not supported and the niche collapses if there are too few individuals to perform the
niche-sustaining chore, too few birds to pollinate the flowers. Second, a breeding population is stabilized internally when the random coupling of its members creates variability in the offspring, hence the viability and survival of some
variants (and the breeding population) when circumstances are altered. Differ-
ence-in-sameness—variability—is a good strategy for surviving in a more or
less subtly changing ecosystem, because sameness is stabilizing and adaptive
in established circumstances, while difference is adaptive when circumstances
change.[27]

These conditions for stability are different from the stabilizing conditions for
other systems; but they are not so different as we typically believe. So a team is
stabilized by the relations of its members and the stability of the league in which
it plays, while a breeding population (and more remotely, its species) is stabilized by reproduction, the viability of some of the variants produced, and the
stability of its niche. Stability is the result, both times, of causal reciprocity. This
is apparent in team members who adjust their actions in ways appropriate to the
behaviors of teammates and in games where teams of equal strength stymie and
provoke one another. Reciprocity is equally apparent in the relations of a population's breeding members (sometimes in nutrition, always in mating) and in
its relations with other populations of its environment: each one's behaviors condition, and are conditioned by, the behaviors of its neighbors.

Why are we troubled by the thinghood of breeding populations and, more
remotely, of species? Perhaps this other consideration is decisive. We suppose
that human societies earn description as systems because they embody negative

feedback. Human systems, including army platoons and businesses, register their effects, then alter their behavior and effects to the advantage of the system and its parts. Compare systems that use natural selection to shape and prune their behaviors. Selection assures that members will not survive to reproduce if their inherited variations disable them from accommodating themselves to their ecosystem. Members having other variations survive to breed, so that the species enhances its viability when their genes come to dominate the gene pool. The mechanism is different: selection rather than negative feedback. The effect is the same: greater viability within an ecosystem. We say for these reasons that breeding populations are systems and in this sense things.

What does this imply about the status of asexual species? Systematicity is attenuated in the breeding populations of sexual species. It is all the less conspicuous, but not eliminated, in those that are asexual. Suppose, for example, that an asexual organism relates reciprocally to the other organisms of its ecosystem: it purifies their water; they supplies its food. The need for this activity supplies a niche for the species that satisfies it. Previous members established the space currently filled by this occupant. Its demise would leave space for a successor. But where is the system in the relations of the asexual species' members: where are the reciprocal relations that establish a system by binding its parts? The only apparent reciprocities bind the organism of our example to individuals *of other species,* not to members of its species. There is this analog to reciprocity among the successive members of the asexual species: the space occupied by any current member was established by its antecedents; the current occupant maintains this place for itself and for its successors. Hence, it does for one of its kind what another has done for it: each secures a niche for the next. The asexual species is a system in this attenuated respect: each presupposes one of its kind, while anticipating another. Critically, relations among these successive members of the species are mediated by the ecosystem that needs and engages them.[28]

I conclude that breeding populations are systems in all three of the respects considered above. There is sometimes positive feedback in their exponential growth, negative feedback in their relations to some other species of their niche, and a steady state in their relations to some of its other species and structures.

Breeding populations evolve: an evolving population is a system and a lineage. Does it follow that lineages too are systems? Imagine that one molecule deflects the path of another, which deflects a third. This too is a lineage, one encapsulated in the path of the third. Lineages of this sort are also characteristic of intellectual history, as Kant embodies Descartes who embodies Plato.[29] Still, there is no reciprocity in such cases, hence no system. How do biological lineages—whether of individual living things or breeding populations—differ from lineages such as these? Do the differences justify saying that biological lineages are systems?

They do not. Living bodies are systems: they are established and sustained by the reciprocity of their parts. Such systems evolve—they grow, mature, and die. These systems are lineages. It doesn't follow that lineages are systems. (Wolves are feral. Not everything feral is a wolf.) Living bodies are established and sustained by the reciprocity of their parts. A breeding population has no comparable network of pervading, reciprocal relations: most of its members never mate with one another. A species is all the less integrated. Breeding populations and species are, therefore, attenuated systems. Still, these systems endure and sometimes evolve, so that breeding populations and species, too, are lineages because they are systems, not because lineages themselves are everywhere and always (essentially) systems. Indeed, many lineages are histories without reciprocity—intellectual histories, for example.

The difference of lineages and systems is somewhat obscured because lineages may be continuous or discontinuous, and because this difference among lineages is also relevant to systems. So, living bodies are sustained, from conception to death, by their constitutive reciprocities. Their lineages are continuous. Compare the lineages of breeding populations and species. Their histories resemble the discontinuities of intellectual history: generations of individuals differ somewhat from their parents; and there are temporal gaps between reproductive cycles. No generation is skipped, but reproduction is spasmodic, not continuous. Accordingly, lineages may or may not be systems, though every system is and has a lineage: it endures and has antecedents.

11. Teleology

I have been supposing that a stability forms when reciprocal causal relations are established between or among its proper parts. This is too simple for many cases. Molecules may be organized as animal cells; yet the cell is not stabilizable until it is reciprocally related to the other cells of a tissue. Neither is the tissue stabilizable until it is reciprocally related to the other tissues of an organ. Nor is the organ stable until it comes to be reciprocally related to the other organs of an animal body. Similarly human bodies are something more than autonomous organisms: they have characters that are not fully formed or stable outside the systems where individuals have specific roles, hence responsibilities for certain effects and responsibilities to other members of these systems. Different again, but parallel, is the progression of stages in the development of human social systems: a prayer group is unstable until it becomes a sect; the sect is precarious until it becomes an established religion. Each of these examples illustrates the transition from precarious, lower-order systems to more stable, relatively autonomous, terminal states. Systems that fall short of terminal states disintegrate: they fall back to the next lower-order, self-stabilizing level. Progressions of systems may be represented in diagrammatic form:

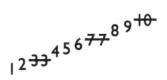

Figure 1. Progressions with terminal points at 3, 7, 10.

Notice that the same system is the end point of one progression and the starting point of another: animal bodies terminate the progression from cells through tissues and organs; they start the progression from unstable affiliations to stable systems. These progressions are disjunctive insofar as the first may obtain, though the second does not. They are conditional insofar as a later one presupposes the ones before.[30]

The first of these sample progressions is critical for foetal development, healing wounds, and the relative self-sufficiency of human bodies. The second is vital to human sociality. (The examples correspond to the second and third progressions of the figure.) We too often confuse the end states of these two progressions, claiming for one what is only legitimately claimed for the other. We ask, for example, if individual humans are self-sufficient, and we answer that typically they are. This is true if we consider only the first progression, from cells through tissues and organs to self-nourishing, self-perpetuating animal bodies. It is mistaken if the self-sufficiency ascribed to us is social. For then self-sufficiency has been misconstrued: the observation that we move and nourish ourselves does not entail our social autonomy. For this is a higher-order achievement, one that is not effectively stabilized until the last step of the second progression. We can speak, because of bodily structures. We learn to speak by listening and responding to those who speak already. Social autonomy presupposes, but is never reducible to, the bodily autonomy of the first progression.

These progressions—from provisional to autonomous stabilities—*mimic* teleology: earlier stages in a progression are sustained because they achieve a final state. Why emphasize that this is not final causation? Because lower-order stages are not sustained *in order* to achieve their terminal state. Terminal states sometimes eventuate in ways that stabilize lower-order states before they disintegrate, but this is the outcome of efficient, not final, causes: we are genetically disposed to have bodies, not merely organs. Still, the development of bodies from gametes is the effect of self-limiting, mechanical processes, without the overlay of teleological ones. It is irrelevant to progressions (hence disqualifying to all but the appearance of teleology) that earlier stages—molecules and cells, for example—have no foreknowledge of a final stage and do not intend it. Nothing in this precludes negative feedback mechanisms in the systems of a progression, as happens when people intend to fill the roles for which they prepare and stabilize themselves.

Accordingly, we distinguish two kinds of benign teleology: *attractor* states, which are the highest-order, self-stabilizing systems in progressions and purpose or intention, which drives thinkers to action on behalf of their values. Both are expressions of efficient cause, though each needs careful specification because it invites misunderstanding.

Attractor states are more accurately described as *selector* states: meaning that these states are selected. Being selected is a consequence of mechanical processes and physical contingencies only: these are least-energy states. So tissues are not selected for self-sufficiency—they are not the terminal states of progressions— for the reason that they do not control a sufficient energy supply. Compare animal bodies. Their internal processes are energy-efficient. Further, they control external energy supplies by appropriating the stored energy of things they gather or hunt. This is a story about selection, not attraction. Selected states satisfy norms of energy efficiency; but these norms do not seek or attract fulfillment.

We hanker after the contrary view because some selector states are critical for human well-being. We dearly like to believe that health or justice would capture us—like a magnetic field—if ever we could organize ourselves to approach it. Something like this does happen when we create systems of civic roles, hence of rights and duties; we satisfy these duties in order to perpetuate the state that crates our rights. Final and efficient causes seem to turn on one another in such cases, for the system created is secured by members who satisfy their obligations while enjoying their freedoms.[31] This too is selection or election—we invent the system—and not a pseudo-mechanical attraction from the side of the ideal. The mechanism promoting it is negative feedback: wanting rights, we are careful to satisfy the duties that secure them.

12. Emergent Properties, Laws, and Rules

Both properties and laws emerge with the formation of higher-order systems. We consider them separately.

(A) PROPERTIES

My claim that property values are fixed by determining conditions—causes— is incomplete. It supposes that a determinable already obtains, so that deter- mining its value is the only issue. This account does not provide for the intro- duction of new properties, as angularity emerges when line segments are joined to create a square. We infer that new properties—in geometrical systems and in the dynamic systems established by the causal reciprocity of their parts—are generated with the formation of higher-order systems. This has the corollary that a system is specified (incompletely) by citing the properties that emerge with it: atoms have properties distinct from those of quarks; cells have proper- ties distinct from those of molecules. The values for emergent properties are fixed in the way described above: by laterally related, determining conditions. The facility for language emerges with the organization of the human brain; the particular language spoken is determined by an infant's caretakers. This hypothesis—that properties emerge with the formation of higher-order sys- tems—is problematic in five ways.

First is this ambiguity: what is it that emerges, a generic property (color, for example) or a specific value for an already established determinable (as green gives determinate expression to color)? It is plainly the specific value, not the de- terminable, that emerges in the experience of someone who knows yellow and blue, but not green. Yet such examples are misleading. There is a clue to their deficiency in the fact that the visual system already qualifies us to see green as well as yellow and blue. This subtlety would be wasted on someone who has just acquired vision, someone for whom green is the first color seen. The generic property and its particular expression emerge, for him, at once. Still, this con- flation of a determinable and its lower-order expression is the accident of these circumstances: red, yellow, or blue would have done as well as an introduction to color. It is, accordingly, the emergence of generic properties—determin- ables—that signals the creation of higher-order systems, as eyes see colors of many shades, not only green.[32]

This finding introduces an epistemic difficulty into an ontological claim. How shall we identify properties that are emergent, hence evidence that a higher-order system has been established, when perception multiplies properties without informing us that its presentations are merely variants of generic properties? The plausible answer is that we should survey the apparent differences—perhaps thinking of them as different properties—before checking as best we can to learn if these are different values for a generic property. The generic property may be obvious if some of its other values are known.

This suggestion is contentious, because it challenges the judgment that Berkeley defeated Locke in their argument about generic ideas.[33] Locke supposed that we have generic ideas. Berkeley responded that what we call generic ideas are words tied to a range of different and always particular perceptions. It follows that there is no generic idea of cat, though we may believe otherwise if we separate the word *cat* from the percepts that give it specificity and reference. Empiricists infer from the alleged absence of generic ideas to the absence of generic properties, as the generic, color, is said to be an abstraction from particular colors.[34] Their argument is a non sequitur, because nothing about the character of extra-mental things is entailed by the form of our percepts, thoughts, and words. It is, for example, irrelevant to this question about properties—are there generic properties?—that there may be no generic images.

Is there evidence of such properties, evidence that survives the acknowledgement that percepts are always specific? Imagine that a piece of clay is molded continuously by turning it in one's hand, sometimes pulling, other times rolling it into a ball. The clay has, at any moment, a specific shape. Yet the shape is forever changing. How should we describe this situation? Those who agree with Berkeley suppose that particular shapes are the only reality, while shape itself is an abstraction. But isn't it more plausible that shape is the constant that receives a succession of specific values? Nominalists respond that the constant is merely the respect in which successive shapes are similar. They support this claim by supposing that time is atomized: each moment is the successor of the one before, though the moments are not continuous. This reduces the constant— generic shape—to a class of things: namely, the many moments when clay has one shape or another. Distinguishing the generic constant from its particular values is, therefore, a solecism, one that resembles running one's hand through a box of variably shaped beads in order to pull out the generic bead.

Suppose we reject the atomist conception of time, saying instead that moments are continuous, each fading into the next. Suppose, too, that shape is a plastic form suspended or embedded in spacetime, so that every particular shape is a transitory state of this determinable. It is less compelling to say in these circumstances that shape is an abstraction, and that ephemeral states—particular shapes—are the only pertinent realities. For this atomist persuasion loses the generic property amidst its expressions; it extinguishes the constraint that shape, the topological determinable, imposes on its every determinate expression.

The reality of generic properties is also supported by the hypothesis that properties are, in the first instance, eternal possibilities. Admission to this status requires that the principle of noncontradiction is satisfied: anything that is not a contradiction is a possibility, as there is nothing contradictory in the notion of generic properties. Their variability over time is exactly what one would expect of an instantiated determinable: the principle that precludes a shape from being round and square at once allows that it may be one after the other. These considerations imply that determinate properties are specific, but contingent, values for generic properties. Some determinables have only a single, determinate, constant value: the President-for-life. More often, values for generic properties are its more or less ephemeral expressions.

I claimed above that the emergence of generic properties requires the establishment of systems. But now—with color as our example—we have evidence that complicates the story. Identifying color with sensory data presupposes systems that perceive: perceived color emerges when they are established. Suppose, for comparison, that color is identified with the frequencies of light that provoke perception, so that we refer talk of color's emergence to a lower order of phenomena. We say that color's wavelengths are variations within a determinable—electromagnetic radiation—that emerges with the ordering of perturbations in spacetime, not with the establishment of perceptual systems. The system relevant to color's emergence depends, therefore, on the referent for *color:* objectively, this is the cosmological system in which electromagnetic radiation emerges; subjectively, it is the physiological system that qualifies us for color vision.

Second is Descartes' objection to emergent properties. The range of actual properties is limited, he said, to the mechanical ones of matter in motion: namely, magnitude, shape, and motion.[35] What looks emergent—including colors, tastes, and sounds—is not. Every such property is merely the complex, unanalyzed effects of mechanical forces in us.

This "nothing but" objection may seem overwhelming. For how can we refute someone who objects that properties alleged to be emergent are not (or—still harder to refute—that they may not be emergent)? Do it, I suggest, in two steps: point out that this response is a slogan until or unless it is proven that every other property is the obscure expression or overlay of the several, elementary, mechanical properties; then add that we may establish the possibility of emergent properties in a way that is consistent with the hypothesis of universal mechanism.

We do this by distinguishing two aspects of the mechanistic project: first is the claim that every phenomenon in the actual world is the state or activity of one or several physical entities; second is the claim that the only properties obtaining in our world are members of the small set that includes the properties of motion, mass, energy, and spatiotemporal relations. The separability of these two considerations—one may affirm the first but deny the second (though not the reverse)—reassures someone who concedes the reality of emergent properties, while agreeing that the actual world is exhaustively a mechanical system (a system comprising a spacetime qualified by material things in motion). Granting the hypothesis of universal mechanism, we defend emergence by means of the analogy invoked above: triangles are constructed of lines but have properties additional to those of lines. Equally, mechanism need not claim that every property generated by a relation between or among bodies reduces to one or several of a small set of physical properties.

Now this question: Are there physical properties which do not reduce to more elementary properties, whether those cited above or a simpler list such as that of Descartes? Human behaviors and institutions are a mine of such properties: one is pleased or fretful *about* something; the national budget is perpetually in deficit; the team is weak defensively; he or she is generous with friends. The mechanist thesis supposes that each of the activities exhibiting these disparate properties occurs because a small set of basic properties is engaged. But one will wait a long time before any of the properties just cited is reduced to figure, magnitude, or motion, or to entries in a richer, more contemporary list of elementary, mechanical properties. Emergent properties are not the obscure, complicated, aggregates of them.

Mechanists who believe in the reducibility of every apparently emergent property are embarrassed by the list of hard cases. Here are four others to beguile them: laughing at jokes derives from reciprocities among nerve bundles in the brain; the agility of a bird in flight is founded in the reciprocity of wings and tail; the health of endless species results from each one's reciprocal relations to species in supporting niches; exhaustive chemical and nutritional analyses miss the role of birthday cakes. Every such entity or event is only physical; but it does not follow that its only salient properties are those of elementary mechanics.

Third, two kinds of properties emerge. First are properties that emerge at one or many sites in a newly established order, as metabolic processes occur at various places within cells or tissues. Second are global or corporate properties, meaning properties of the system at large. The balance of a string quartet is an example. New properties of the first sort are not surprising or controversial; the behaviors of assembled parts are typically different from the behaviors of the parts alone. Corporate properties are less welcome, because of their political associations. But holism is not always pernicious: accurate cornering is the corporate and desirable property of a well-designed car.

Fourth, does the establishment of a new order, with its distinguishing properties, require that the properties of preceding orders be sustained? There seems to be no general rule, though there may be distinctive factors that decide the issue in particular cases. Sometimes properties established at one level survive when the assembly of systems from this or lower orders create a still higher order, as inertial properties survive into every higher order of physical phenomena. Other times, the properties of lower orders do not survive, as when the properties of village life are eradicated when villages are incorporated into towns or cities.

Fifth is a question that is harder to resolve: Do new properties emerge with every different kind of system, whether ants, beetles, or butterflies? Or is there a generic basis for their emergence, so that different systems of a particular kind give determinate expression to a determinable that emerges with this class of systems: any bug?

There is the hint of an answer in the fact that chaotic behaviors sometimes have orderly resolutions at distinct energy levels, or at specific orders of size, complexity, velocity, or temperature. Several of these factors may converge in systems that are fruitful for emergent properties. Is there a principle that foretells the emergence of such systems? Startlingly successful predictions extrapolate from physical laws and information about the spacing of particular systems on a trajectory of scales.[36] But there may be no well-founded thermodynamic hypothesis that predicts and explains all the junctures, all the energy levels, at which systems are established. Can we tell a priori that a new order of systems will introduce emergent properties, rather than specific values for determinables that are already established? We do it often, using powerful physical theories, clever fiction, newly invented games, or mathematical models.

(B) LAWS

The laws of motion—$F = ma$, for example—apply to everything within space-time, though one may not recognize these laws as they apply to special domains such as gases or springs. Reductionists who believe that all complexity is merely the aggregation of elementary things affirm that every additional physical law is only a restatement, in terms appropriate to its domain, of the laws of motion. The statements of laws applying within higher-order domains—thermodynamics or biology, for example—are, accordingly, provisional. We eventually come to understand that they are obscure expressions of those more fundamental laws that determine the relations of variables that are elementary and pervasive. We identify the molecular motions that are objective conditions for heat, then the relations of neurons, and finally those molecular motions within neurons that are the subjective experience of heat.

We may be skeptical about this outcome, because we construe the idea of emergent systems or properties to signify that they are "more" or "other" than their parts, hence not derivable from laws that constrain the values (hence, the behaviors) of the parts. This implies that emergent systems and properties entail emergent laws. But they do not. The emergent system or property is distinct from its individual parts and from a disordered set of them, but it is nothing apart from the properly ordered ensemble of its parts: a triangle comprises its three, joined, line segments. A law that sanctions the formation of an ensemble, emergent properties included, explains and predicts it, given initial conditions. Do such laws also prefigure subjective looks or feelings? Distinguishing acquaintance from description (as laws describe), I suggest that they specify all the aspects of and conditions for acquaintance without being acquaintance itself.

It is more apparent now that my paradigm for emergence is flawed. Right triangles and their properties emerge when their parts are connected. The emergence of laws—the Pythagorean theorem, for example—is more ambiguous. This theorem emerges with the formation of right triangles if we consider only the separated line segments are joined to form them. It is not emergent if we credit geometry with a rule that sanctions every possible ordering of line segments—they may be crossed, separated, or joined—that leaves them intact, because uncut. Such a rule covers circumstances where joining segments creates right triangles, hence the Pythagorean theorem. Here too we have emergent systems (better, figures) and emergent properties; but not emergent laws.

Emergentists resist this conclusion, because we can specify many laws that emerge with systems. Every such law couples a system, or the sufficient conditions for forming it, with the properties that emerge when it forms, as loyalty emerges with friendship. However, emergent laws of this sort are merely descriptive. They correlate the generation of systems and their emergent properties, and they are safely predictive: given the system, we have the property (always or to some degree of probability). Still, these laws are shallow. They describe without explaining: they cite correlations without specifying generative conditions for the phenomena described.

But is it sure that there are laws of only two kinds, not three or more? Michael Ghiselin mentions a possible third. His examples of biological laws fall into one or the other of the two types suggested here: they are biological expressions of physical laws (the second law of thermodynamics, for example), or they are descriptive laws appropriate to the domain of living things (population density, or size advantage). His descriptive laws explain a phenomenon by treating it as an instance of the correlation specified by a law, or as the property that a descriptive law ascribes to all the members of a class. With one possible exception, such laws do not explain phenomena by specifying values for their generating conditions. Ghiselin describes the possible exception:

> Darwin divided selection into three modes: artificial, natural, and sexual. These terms derive from whether differential reproduction results from the choice of the breeder, the struggle for existence, or from the organisms' efforts to attain a monopoly with respect to mates. . . . So far from being an ad hoc hypothesis that was supposedly devised to explain away facts that cannot be explained in terms of natural selection, Darwin's theory of sexual selection is a crucial element in a more general theory of selection. It accounts for three distinct classes of phenomena on the basis of differential reproduction, but specifies that they will occur under different circumstances and predicts different outcomes for each of them.[37]

The factors cited—breeders, the struggle for existence, and efforts to attain a monopoly with respect to mates—seem to be generative conditions. The laws describing such conditions are different from merely descriptive laws. Yet such laws are not the laws of motion—hence the implication that they are laws of a third type. This is a mistake we can avoid: there is no additional third type of laws.

For it is only the laws of motion, sometimes formulated in ways appropriate to a domain (springs or gases, for example) that specify he generative conditions for phenomena. We may think otherwise only because so many kinds of generation are never explained in terms that introduce either the language of fundamental physical laws or the terms of special force laws. So, Ghiselin writes of "ornamental poultry produced by the breeder." We might infer from such remarks that there are emergent laws appropriate to the generative conditions within domains established by the emergence of systems and their properties (the domain of living things). For there are, presumably, no special versions of the laws of motion—no special force laws—appropriate to sexual reproduction.

This last sentence must be mistaken if there are only two kinds of laws: fundamental physical laws that specify the generative conditions for all phenomena (as a relationship of relevant variables) and the descriptive laws that specify correlations or distinguishing properties within particular domains. For then, every domain distinguished by its emergent systems and properties has an apposite force law. Every such law applies only within a domain; or it is the more determinate expression of a law that applies within domains of a kind (for example, the force law that applies to the joining of complex molecules, as in reproduction). Either way, there are a large number of special force laws, all of them reducing to the laws of motion. We reinterpret Ghiselin's example in these terms. We say that Darwin's theory of sexual selection is explanatory in the deeper of the two senses at issue. It specifies the generative conditions for reproduction, though it fails to translate these factors into the terms of the deeper laws they instantiate.

Translating every such result into the terms of fundamental laws is the unfulfilled promise of a unified science. The reduction of thermodynamics to statistical mechanism is our paradigm for such translations, though we don't expect Freud the psychologist or Darwin the biologist to supply them. Still, the unity of science is more than a dream, if every law explaining the generation of phenomena is a force law that brings the laws of motion to bear on a specific domain.

We cover this same ground in another way by asking if the difference between descriptive and explanatory laws precludes saying that some explanatory laws have emerged. For there could be two kinds of explanatory laws. Such laws are not emergent if they explain the emergence of systems and their properties merely by receiving values for their variables, as laws of motion take on values within a restricted range as they explain sublunar motions. Emergent, explanatory laws would add constraints to the laws of motion, constraints that are not explained by the basic laws: Darwin's theory of sexual selection or the principle of least energy might be an additional constraint required to explain the formation of every higher-order system from elementary particles, as crystals form from molecules. But this isn't so: such constraints are not new and have not emerged, if—as is the case—they result merely from applying the laws of motion. These laws entail the principle of least energy, and, presumably, they are the determinables that receive determination in the domain of sexual selection. Accordingly, we break the suspected logical and ontological link between systems, properties, and laws: emergent systems and properties do not entail the emergence of explanatory laws.

We affirm that the generation of every emergent system and property is explicable by way of nature's fundamental laws (laws such as Newton's or Einstein's law of motion, or the Schrödinger equation). This is the conclusion to an argument that parallels the one concerning the generation of geometrical figures. Such figures are created by applying the rule for joining line segments: it sanctions the formation of triangles, hence right triangles and the Pythagorean theorem. Equally, we suppose that higher-order complexity and emergence in physical systems have a fundamental generating principle.

Is this conclusion faulty, because it ignores the difference between explanation and prediction? We could not have predicted many effects that are explained by fundamental laws. So current theory anticipates that water molecules will slop past one another, but not the feel of water. Shouldn't we distinguish explanation from prediction, hereby acknowledging that the distinctive character of many phenomena falls outside the circle of explanation? Don't we require perception, in addition to theory, if we are to grasp whatever is distinctive about such systems or properties?

The irresolution in these questions has an obvious source. We are not surprised when the rule for joining line segments sanctions right triangles, because we see triangles constructed. The creation of red sensations is less transparent. We concede that sensations are generated within networks of stimulated neurons, but we don't understand how such processes can have these effects: such effects are explained, after the fact, by fundamental laws and initial conditions; yet we, who don't understand the relevant processes, could not have foreseen their outcome. This conclusion expresses a failure of analysis and understanding, not a deficiency in the range or sufficiency of the laws. We would understand that the laws explain and predict every natural phenomenon, including our perceptions of distinctive phenomena, were we to understand better how fundamental laws constrain the generation of emergent systems and their properties.

This would be the end of the matter, but for this startling consideration: one kind of emergent system does introduce explanatory principles which are not reducible to the laws of motion. The systems at issue are we humans. The newly constraining explanatory principles are rules we invent to direct and control human practice. Think of marriage and tax laws: their applications satisfy the laws of motion, but their significance and normativity do not reduce to them and are not explicable by way of them. Consider poker games, or the practice of exchanging gifts on birthdays. These are emergent systems, each one distinguished by the rules its members apply.

Suppose we play a round of poker, behaving as its rules prescribe. Having dealt the cards and bid in the manner required, we rank the hands of the players so that three of a kind beats a pair. Our activity is drenched in significance: we interpret one another's behavior, we construe the rules, we appraise the results when bidding ends and hands are disclosed. All these actions are the behaviors of physical systems, our bodies and brains, so that our behaviors are explained, we suppose, by complicated applications of the laws of motion. Yet the actions performed when applying or construing rules are distinct from their meanings, so that bidding out of turn, anteing too little, winning or losing, are notions that are not derivable from the laws of motion. Here is a case where rules enjoin our behavior, though their meanings, as distinct from the behaviors they enjoin, are not explicable by way of basic physical laws.

Human practice is suffused with rules of this sort, rules that endow our actions with significance, purpose, and norms. The inception and status of these values annoy reductionists. For these are properties that cannot be explained, as consciousness and intentionality are explicable in principle, by applications of basic laws. Such values are ideal. Like justice, they exist in the first instance as eternal possibilities, though they are, or can be, the objects of human intentions or signs. We signify them, as when we contrive rules that would direct their realization—Plato's ideal state, for example—were the rules applied.

The ideals introduced by rules may be regarded as emergent determinables that limit the appropriate expressions of their sanctioning rules. In courtship rituals, the determinable is the "space" in which men and women disport themselves. In families, it is the separate duties that go with the idealized roles of parents and children. In music and speech, it establishes the domain of sequences that exhibit appropriate harmonies, rhythms, or syntax. It is, presumably, true in every case that systems and their behaviors are physical only, and that they form in accord with the laws of motion. Yet each of these contexts introduces additional, idealizing constraints—marriage vows are an example—by way of its determining rules.

The implications seem mysterious, or confused. I agree that every system and property is constructed from the small set of properties whose values and relations are constrained by the laws of motion. Yet I affirm that human behavior is often directed by possibles construed as ideals.[38] How are these ideals integrated with actual states of affairs, when every norm implies a difference between the actual and the ideal? There is no bridge from actuality into possibility, hence no need for extra-physical intuitions of the possibles.[39] We learn of the possibles by seeing them instantiated, or we use imagination to extrapolate from the actual to the possible.

Poker is still our example. Its "space" is established by players who know its rules. This space is articulated by the dealer (he or she decides what game to play), by the chance distribution of cards, and by the successive, clockwise declarations of the players. Do poker's rules reduce to the laws of motion? The movement of the cards has no other explanation. Equally, the physiology of the players—the material basis for applying poker's rules—is explicable in terms that reduce to the variables of these basic laws. The rules themselves are emergent. They constrain our behaviors in ways that are additional to the constraints imposed by the basic laws; or, more accurately, rules overlay physical events generated by applications of the basic laws with additional, normative meanings. We are reminded that human life is passed in two domains. One is the order wherein physical processes, whatever the emergent systems and properties they generate, are explained as applications of the laws of motion. The other domain is the order of practice: the one of norms, values, and significance. It expresses our habit of impressing the actual with the ideal.

Are the laws of motion sufficient to explain human practice? Yes and no. Such explanations are (or could, in principle, be) complete if our focus is the individual postures, states of mind, and behaviors of the persons engaged. However, states of mind include intentional states and the signs they construe. The objects of these signs are possibles construed as ideals, then used as directives for action. Idealized possibles cannot affect actuals except as they are actualized or represented. We often satisfy this requirement by intending the ideal, thereby overreaching ourselves and actuality too. This is a commonplace of thought and action, one that is realized in every novel, unsatisfied aim or false but consistent theory. Some ideals are fully realized, as card games are won or lost. Others— justice and beauty—are only intimated. The laws or rules appropriate to these ideal possibles are not always reducible to the laws of our world.[40]

(C) PROPERTIES AND RULES

There is a question or priority: which comes first, a determinable property or the rules that apply within the domain where the property emerges? The answer depends on the example. Rules are, typically, prior in the case of practices created by their rules, as being a pawn or a queen is an emergent property that derives from the rules of chess. But properties are sometimes prior to rules; children's play often creates properties that are only loosely constrained before their games are codified by rules.

There is a lesson in this asymmetry: there are no rules without the emergent properties whose expressions they regulate, but there are sometimes emergent properties without rules. Systems whose formation does not implicate newly introduced rules fall to the control of whatever rules or laws apply to their proper or lesser parts.

13. Determining and Facilitating Conditions

Emergence is balanced by this offsetting consideration. It too exploits systems, though now for the purpose of explaining the generation of properties whose occurrence at higher orders belies their origin in a system's parts.

Consider a child's red hair, then the two conditions—call them *determining* and *facilitating* or *enabling*—for its occurrence. Genes are determining conditions: they are proteins that activate the processes eventuating in red hair. Every condition that contributes to their expression—including bodies, behaviors, and circumstances—is facilitating or enabling. Critics who deny that genes are, or could be, the only condition for inheritance rightly emphasize both the plant or animal bodies that reproduce, and the circumstances that favor the mating of some but not all. They rightly say that natural selection works on populations, not directly on genes. Distinguishing conditions of these two sorts clarifies the motive for saying that plant and animal bodies are "mere" gene carriers. Ignore the hyperbolic use of "mere": something is neglected if we emphasize determining conditions—genes—but derogate the bodies that transmit them. Conditions of both sorts are necessary if features are to be inherited; neither is sufficient.

Disputes that turn on the difference between determining and facilitating conditions are often coded arguments about different issues: nature and nurture in race and gender are two examples. Distinguishing these two kinds of conditions does not settle this quarrel, but it does supply considerable footing to those who emphasize nurture over nature. For we need not suppose that facilitating conditions merely provide a context for the display of properties that genes determine, as if genetic information were always an unequivocal message. It is not: facilitating conditions often transform a genetically coded determinable into a specific talent, as the genetically determined power to speak a language is expressed—because of facilitating conditions—as a competence for English. it is relevant too that conditions may be disqualifying rather than facilitating: there is no gene for illiteracy.

Is red hair emergent? It is: though the gene for a trait is not the trait itself. Realization of the trait waits on the provision of facilitating conditions. They include fertilization of an egg and development of the person having the trait.

14. Change

History is the process and record of nature naturing. While most of this chapter is devoted to the products of change—stabilities—and their context, the following are remarks about change *qua* change.

Change is not separable from the things—the particles and more complex systems—that change. The consequences are perceived and understood better than change itself (as some of us prefer the things cooks make to the cooking). Notice the priority of observation over inference: seeing order established or undone, we infer that this is the effect of a process having three distinguishing aspects: alteration, energy, and disposition. Change is both the alteration effected and the altering. Either way—as effect or process—change requires energy and a direction. Energy stored as mass is released by one or another kind of motion, as when matter is heated or accelerated. Energy fuels changes that are biased by the dispositions of the agents in motion, as X and Y chromosomes are differently biased. Systems that qualify for one process or effect may not be qualified—may not be disposed—for another. All changes, whatever the biases of the agents involved, are constrained by the immanent topology and geometry of spacetime. This geometry and the dynamics of our world already prefigure—they favor—those distributions of matter that are energy-efficient. Change is only sometimes chaotic, for it often creates orders that catch and hold. Sometimes the orders created are more ephemeral than static, and pass away with any next change in the balance of forces. Other times, positive feedback creates a skein of orderly changes, or negative feedback stabilizes the agents that are mutually engaged, so that systems are stabilized. Orders created in either way may provoke a cascade of further orders, so that disorder is the cradle for the stable diversity that is everywhere apparent. And always, change is as often destructive as it is fruitful. Material disgorged by systems disperses. It may be incorporated into other systems, but eventually, when all the energy is turned to heat, there is entropy, random change, no order, and no system.

Change, as a process, implies motion. Change, as the altered state of a thing in spacetime, is the effect of motion. Relevant changes include a dented fender and the aging that makes citizens eligible to vote at twenty-one. These are the complementary aspects of this book's topic: there are processes that establish stable systems, and their effects, these systems. A formulation appropriate to both affirms that change sometimes defies entropy by stabilizing and routinizing energy exchange. The exchange occurs when mutually determining systems give to, and get something from, one another in a cycle that sustains them and their reciprocal relations. The effects of these exchanges are higher-order systems and their new properties.

The interconvertibility of mass and energy, the conservation of their total value, and the conservation of momentum partly define the economy of these stabilizing changes within a plastic, self-differentiating One. This One was diversified (we infer) when some disequilibrium in the dense plasma of our singularity produced, first, particles, then successive orders of organized particles. Where motion is perpetual, these systems come and go. Like waves in the sea, they form, endure for a while, and dissipate. Nothing is lost but the ephemeral, hierarchical order of systems established by the reciprocal relations of each system's parts. Change (as it concerns us) is the making and unmaking of these systems, always (in the history of our universe) from the same elementary particles.

Having well-ordered bodies and stable routines, living in stable buildings and states, we may think of ourselves as cocooned in layers of stability. But each of these systems is the expression of an internal dynamic, and some of them disguise by their stability the nonlinear changes that occur within them. Cells and brains, for example, embody chaotic processes which eventuate in orders that are elaborated by positive feedback, then stabilized. Disorder lies before, after, and within us.

The principal changes within a stability are those of its developmental history. Every system is generated and transformed as antecedent stabilities interact and evolve. They and their relations are successively altered, eventuating in a new complex; or established systems give up matter and energy, thereby supplying material—but little or nothing of the previously established relations—to their successors. This new complex is a system having parts and an architecture that are sustainable though plastic. Every child's developmental history is an example. He or she is a system whose parts and organization are stable but malleable through a course of changes. Better, he or she is the successively transformed product of development, not the enduring matter that abides through change or the entity that somehow underlies it. Each is generated and sustained in the nourishing broth from which it derives energy or information and substance.

Developmental history does not start or terminate, however, with the life of individual stabilities. It begins with their most remote antecedents and moves on with their successors. Our obsessive individualism blinds us to the sweep of this process. Seeing only the punctuated moments of stability, ignoring the continuities, we miss the economies and patterns that characterize generational transformations. Equally, we miss the stabilities that survive dissolution, as stability at one or several orders is consistent with dissolution at an intermediate one. Their societies and molecules survive when humans die.

It would be good to have a view of the whole from a distance such that the stabilities of our world are seen as eddies in a cosmic swirl. But no one has this perspective. These transformations are grasped, if at all, by a system that is itself in transition, as people aging judge the young. We need to be careful when making such judgments that we do not abstract either ourselves or the systems observed from the networks that engage them and us. For every system, observing or observed, is assembled, stabilized, and dissolved within the context of hierarchical systems whose strata may themselves evolve. Knowing any particular stability requires that we know its locale within a network of reciprocally related, overlapping, and nested systems.

Let an epoch or nation-state be our context. What factors, internal or external, lower- or higher-order, disrupt or stabilize it? A state's history is its transformation as a corporate entity, including the assembly and alteration of its constituent stabilities, be they persons, families, tribes, bureaucracies, or economies. The circumstances and lives of single persons are implicated, hereby, in the careers of grander things. Any narrative that ignores this complexity must distort history by ignoring the context of same-, higher-, and lower-order systems, hence the demands and tensions that shape a stability, whether collaterally, from above or below. The tempo of change may differ among systems of the same order—persons or families, for example—and from level to level. Consider this nest of anomalous systems and their circumstances: a chronic disease, the person who suffers it, his or her family in the years when children are born and reared, a period of political or religious change, and global warming. Each system has a span of its own, but each may be considered from within the span and perspective of individual lives. Every such life resonates, harmoniously or dissonantly, with the rhythms and cycles of these disparate systems. Its internal rhythms are enhanced if the rhythms of subaltern, overlapping, or nested systems are compatible or reinforcing. More often, systems are strained, their reciprocities and purposes disrupted, because their rhythms are not synchronized or harmonious with those of related systems. Historical narratives too often abstract particular systems—persons, especially—from such contexts. They highlight individuals against more or less obscure backgrounds, thereby distorting their actual lives. History is harder to write, but more accurate, if lives are perceived within the context of multiply overlapping and nested systems. Individuals who flourish when the rhythms of such systems are mutually reinforcing are destroyed when the rhythms clash. Think of people who founder when an international trade agreement strangles their factories and towns.

These complexities may seem incidental to the development of a child whose stable family has occupied one house since birth, in a stable town where reliable neighbors are a constant backdrop. The adult who reminisces about this childhood may remark that little changed through all of it, except for the recurring cycles of school years and summers, memorable blizzards, and the occasional disaster happening to people far away. There is no faulting this perspective: the life it describes was stable. But it wasn't static. Many things did happen, and this child's development was often a forced accommodation to small changes: there were new books, new teachers, new friends, a parent's anger, a new technology. The child's environment was not so much static as reliable. The many small changes were eased by rhythms that were familiar and congenial. Parents who reflect on this span of time may remember them as tumultuous. It is their poise in the face of change that explains this child's impression that nothing much ever changed.

These opposed impressions of stasis and change may also be expressed in this other way: the changes in individuals and their circumstances contrast with recurrent patterns of change. Such patterns are frequently repeated trajectories. Children mature; families go through the cycle of marriage and dependent children, then maturity for the children and senescence or death for the parents. Details vary. The cycles are generically the same in humans and families, economies, the seasons, and even the evolution and burnout of stars. Perhaps every system in nature evolves in ways that are consistent with the trajectories for things of its kind. Are trajectories that are stable in the short run (the run of human experience and memory) stable in the long run. Do they have attractors that are stable or strange?[41] We can't say. Is this also true of the universe? Think of the plasma from which our universe is alleged to derive. Could it have been the medium or ground for a system of singularities—some exploded, some not? We would want to know the relations and trajectories of loci such as these. Speculation is stymied, just now.

15. Reality As a System of Relations

Can we ignore change, saying that a system of stabilities—our universe—is identical with a shifting matrix of relations? It may seem that my hypothesis entails this claim. For I allege that the complexity of things is guaranteed by the relations of determinables to their determining conditions, then, derivatively, by complementaries in the structure of spacetime, by attractor energy levels, by the probability of orders that emerge and take hold in large populations where change is random, by positive feedback, and by the negative feedback of stable systems. The network of these relations is, I say, the crux of all that is intelligible in things. Why not express every such relation as an ordered triple—a determinable, its vertically related determination, and their laterally related determining condition? Follow by integrating these relations in a way that represents their relative rank or position within the whole. Provide for free matter—those particles not engaged within any higher-order system—by locating it within the grid of relative spacetime positions. Then describe the result as a comprehensive picture of the actual world. Actuality, this implies, is nothing but the instantiation in spacetime of a system of relations prefigured in possibility. For possibility—described extensionally—is logical space: meaning the array of possible worlds, each one a system of relations. A fragment of logical space— one possible world—supplies whatever structure and content there is within our actual world.

Is it sufficient that there be nothing to reality (whether its mode of being is possibility or actuality) but relations? Something is missing: namely, the properties related as a determinable, its determining condition, and lower-order, more determinate expression. We could ignore properties only if we presuppose them—as happens if we speak about relations while construing them as having terms. References to structure—as in the claim that reality is a structure or is constituted of structures—are ambiguous in this way. Assume that structures include the properties related, and this way of speaking is plausible, and—I believe—partly correct. (Partly only, because change—transformation— would be missing.) Ignore the properties that are terms for these relations, and we have a logician's model of the world: all syntax, no semantics.

This error is apparent if we cite the three marks described above as essential to properties: quality, quantity, and relation. The proposal now mooted is incomplete, because it reduces each property to one of its three marks: namely, its relations. Recall the purpose of relation as it was considered earlier in this chapter: properties' values are fixed by way of their relations to other properties. But then it follows that reality cannot be constituted of relations only. Emphasizing relations and systems of relations, we ignore both the property values determined and the identity of the properties that are their determining conditions.

We amend this formulation accordingly: we say that reality is constituted of relationships (not merely of relations) and also of (many) free particles, both in spacetime. This provides for everything except the difference between the two modes of being, possibility and actuality.

I propose, in summary, that the things of our world (excepting free matter and aggregates) are successive orders of forming, stabilizing, or dissolving systems. Those that achieve a steady state are stabilized by their internal organization and energy and by their currently hospitable environment. Many causal relations are adventitious; those that are concerted and reciprocal establish or sustain systems. Some causal relationships are self-stabilizing, some are not: there are clouds and thunderstorms, matches and fires.

II. REDUCING SYSTEMS TO OTHER THINGS

The hypothesis just explicated precludes the materialist reduction of every event and effect to the motion of elementary particles, whatever their character. This limitation is consistent with a qualified determinism: the organization and interaction of particles having particular properties may be sufficient to produce every effect, though there may be no way to predict their effects—systems and emergent properties especially—merely by citing the particles and their aggregative relations.

The meaning of *reduction* is ambiguous. It can signify that the character or behaviors of a complex are the aggregated characters or behaviors of its parts, or that one can predict or explain the character or behaviors of a complex by citing the character or behaviors of its parts. Call these, respectively, *metaphysical* and *epistemological* reduction. Reduction signifies (with either emphasis) that the entities, properties, or laws of a higher-order domain derive from the entities, properties, or laws of the domain of things aggregated or joined causally to create it. So psychological laws or properties are alleged to be obscure expressions of the laws or properties of the physical elements that compose the mind (and brain). Empirical research coupled with conceptual analysis should expose the one as a complex expression of the other.

This section's remarks about stable systems drastically limit the opportunities for reduction. For if it does sometimes happen that apparently higher-order phenomena—thermodynamical ones, for example—are entirely the effects of aggregation, many other phenomena, including properties and behaviors, emerge with the formation of stable systems. A triangle does not reduce to its parts (ontological reduction); nor does our understanding of it reduce to a comprehensive understanding of its parts (epistemological reduction). Both kinds of reduction are precluded, because the factor that establishes a system, distinguishing it from the collection of its parts, is the set of relations that bind the parts.

Here are three strategies for reducing systems to a prior ontological ground: cite the dispositions of their parts; or show that a law having application within a domain of systems is a version of a generic law that applies within this and other domains, or that it is replaceable by a law or laws that apply to the aggregated behaviors of things native to a lower-order domain; or establish that the basis for a complex is located in the structure of spacetime. Reducing relationships to the dispositions of their parts or to their merely aggregative relations is pernicious. The other reductions are benign.

1. Dispositional Reductions

We suppose that the formation of systems is prefigured in the dispositions of their parts, as locks open to keys of complementary shapes. Or we explain the liquidity of water by citing the dispositions of water molecules. Such analyses are useful if they explain an effect by identifying relevant properties of the causes. They are severely reductive if they purport to eliminate a relational property— liquidity, for example—in favor of the dispositions of the things related. Worse, dispositional analyses are self-defeating. Suppose we explain the picture created by assembling the pieces of a jigsaw puzzle by remarking that the irregularity of each piece's shape is complementary to irregularities in the shapes of its neighbors. Assembling the pieces creates the picture, but nothing is lost—reductionists say—by returning the separated pieces to their box, for the picture is implicit in the shapes, hence the dispositions, of the pieces. This analysis is faulty, because it loses the picture while falsely supposing that the dispositions of its parts can be identified without reference to the assembled picture.

These considerations apply equally to the ontological and epistemological questions. Ontologically, relationships of reciprocally related terms are not identical to their terms (even supposing that the relationship is prefigured in the dispositions of the terms). This conclusion is all the more obligatory on the side of epistemological reduction. For we cannot know the dispositions of a thing or kind until we observe instances of the relationship for which the thing or things are qualified. *Relationships are not reduced by replacing them with things that qualify for relatedness.*[42]

2. Generic Law and Bridge Law Reductions

Generic law reductions affirm that the law applying within a domain is an expression of a more determinable law: one narrows the range of expression for the variables of the other. Consider thinkers unfamiliar with liquids or solids who live in a gaseous world. Suppose that they know a law or laws that correctly predict the behavior of gases. Could they also predict that water liquifies at room temperature? They could anticipate this effect (though probably they couldn't tell how water would feel to touch) if their gas law were shown to be the more specific expression of a generic law that applies to molecules in all their states—gas, liquid, or solid. The generic law explains that molecules "slip around" one another in reduced-energy states. This is reduction of a sort that explains relations of a specific sort—the molecules of a liquid—in terms of relations construed generically—molecules in motion. We now vary the example to emphasize the point. Consider family dynamics. Human families give determinate expression to a determinable relation that is common to all great apes, or even to all mammals. Assuming this determinable relation, ethology describes its alternative, determinate expressions. Here, as before, we reduce a law or domain by locating it within the context of a more determinable law or domain. We explain a system's behavior and its specific covering law by citing the relevant generic law.

Generic law reductions leave the integrity of systems intact, as human families are acknowledged, not reduced, when they are identified as mammalian families. Reduction by way of bridge laws[43]—correspondence rules—is more problematic for the ontological status of systems. The classical example of reduction is the one that reduces the laws of thermodynamics to those of statistical mechanics, as heat reduces to molecular motion when the laws of thermodynamics are derived in conjunction with bridge laws from the laws of statistical mechanics. The success of this example vastly warps our attitude toward reduction: we expect that every complex phenomenon will prove reducible to the movements of its parts. But is it?

Consider the relation of entities that fall within the domains of two laws, one that applies to phenomena of a higher order, the other to phenomena of a lower order. Is this a one-to-one relation, a one-to-many relation (one in the reducing domain to two or more in the reduced domain), or a many-to-one relation (many in the reducing domain to one in the domain reduced)? One-to-one relations (this sheep is a goat and behaves as goats do), and one-to-many relations (one neurosis explains many symptoms) are not at issue.

Reductionists typically suppose that many-to-one relations are their target, as the human body is nothing but its cells or molecules or atoms. This policy is stunningly effective in statistical mechanics and quantum theory. Yet these successes make us reckless. We generalize to every high-order "thing," arguing that its relations or relationships reduce to their terms. The dispositional analysis of relationships is an instance of this many-to-one pattern of reduction: the dispositions of the parts are thought to explain the relationship for which the parts qualify. Or we confirm that the integrity of some "thing" is merely apparent, by using bridge laws to show that it, like heat, is the aggregated effect of its constituent parts. Reductions of this latter sort proceed in the following way. We use bridge laws to show that laws applying to systems are reducible to laws applying to aggregates; we then infer that entities—systems—of the domain covered by the first law are aggregates in the domain of the reducing law. The alleged causal reciprocities of the reduced domain dissolve, because their constituents in the reducing domain have the merely spatiotemporal and "additive" relations of gas molecules described by statistical mechanics: the effects of their mutual impacts are additive.

Ernest Nagel favored reductions of this sort:

> Though a system has a distinctive structure, it is not in principle impossible to specify that structure in terms of relations between its elementary constituents, and moreover in such a manner that the structure can be correctly characterized as a "sum" whose "parts" are themselves specified in terms of those elements and relations. As we shall see, many students deny, or appear to deny, this possibility in connection with certain kinds of organized systems (such as living things). The present example therefore shows that though we may not be able *as a matter of fact* to analyze certain highly complex "dynamic" (or "organic") unities in terms of some given theory concerning their ultimate constituents, such inability cannot be established as a matter of *inherent logical necessity.*[44]

And:

> If the word "sum" is used in this sense in contexts in which the word "whole" refers to a pattern or configuration formed by elements standing to each other in certain relations, it is perfectly true, though trivial, to say that the whole is more than the sum of its parts.[45]

It is not trivial that a tune (Nagel's example) is a singularly ordered sequence of notes, so that these notes in any other sequence are not this song. Nagel corrects the impression that he is cavalier about relations: there is, he says, "no inherently insuperable obstacle to analyzing such wholes into elements standing to each other in specified relations."[46]

There is, however, an issue to consider:

That issue is whether the analysis of "organic unities" necessarily involves the adoption of irreducible laws for such systems, and whether their mode of organization precludes the possibility of analyzing them from the so-called additive point of view. The main difficulty in this connection is that of ascertaining in what way an "additive" analysis differs from one that is not. The contrast seems to hinge on the claim that the parts of a functional whole do not act independently of one another, so that any laws that may hold for such parts when they are not members of a functional whole cannot be assumed to hold for them when they actually are members. An "additive" analysis therefore appears to be one that accounts for the properties of a system in terms of assumptions about its constituents, where these assumptions are not formulated with specific reference to the characteristics of the constituents as elements in the system. And a "nonadditive" analysis seems to be one which formulates the characteristics of a system in terms of relations between certain of its parts as functioning elements in the system.[47]

Nagel preferred the additive, reductivist account of "organic" wholes. But why was he alternatively sensitive to the relations that bind a complex, then indifferent to them when discussing the summing of their terms, their "constituents?" This is a difference of emphasis, not an inconsistency. The additive account does not ignore relations; it merely *seems* to do that because it assumes that pertinent relations are always the same: they are the relations of bodies in motion, relations which are generically the same though different in their specific values—velocity or distance, for example. Equally, the laws of both the reducing domain and the one reduced are not oblivious to relations. But here too the relations assumed to obtain among entities of the reducing domain—bodies in motion—are generically the same, so that one can emphasize the entities of the reducing domain rather than their relations.

Nagel avoids examples—relations of friends or husbands and wives—that are not propitious for his reductionist program. He may do this because there is little or nothing that is additive about them, or because he assumes that they are additive but too obscure just now to support his claims. He waits to see how far the stepwise reduction of intermediate levels progresses, from biological systems to their chemical constituents, though he is confident of the outcome: every apparently "holistic" phenomenon will prove to be an aggregate, one that is explained in the terms Nagel proposed. Yet friendship and marriage are selective and reciprocal. Nothing but a Spartan ideal of theory construction—the minimalism of elementary entities, motion, additive spatiotemporal relations, and, after Hume, nothing of cause—supports the hope that reciprocities such as these may be explained in the additive terms that Nagel proposed. He said noth-

ing to make us believe that mutual dependencies are reducible to additive relations.

Nagel was defiant:

> The upshot of this discussion of organic unities is that the question whether they can
> be analyzed from the additive point of view does not possess a general answer. Some
> functional wholes certainly can be analyzed in that manner, while in the case of oth-
> ers (for example, living organisms) no full satisfactory analysis of that type has yet
> been achieved. Accordingly, the mere fact that a system is a structure of dynamically
> interrelated parts does not suffice, by itself, to prove that the laws of such a system
> cannot be reduced to some theory developed initially for certain assumed constituents
> of the systems. This conclusion may be meager; but it does show that the issue under
> discussion cannot be settled, as so much of extant literature on it assumes, in a whole-
> sale and a priori fashion.[48]

Nagel claimed more than he proved. The additive, mechanical relations he
stressed—impacting molecules—are a decisive feature in nature. Reciprocal
causal relations presuppose them, because they acknowledge the spatiotemporal contiguity and impact, hence efficacy, of reciprocal causes. Still, Nagel has
not shown in any single instance that reciprocal causal relations reduce to additive relations. Do all physical—dynamic—relations reduce to the fact of motion, hence impact in spacetime? Or is something additional accomplished by
the reciprocity of causal relations? The simplest molecule is evidence that relations are more than additive and that systems are not aggregates.

3. Reductions to Spatiotemporal Structure

Consider again the leading principle stated above: don't reduce relationships
to their terms, otherwise you lose the relations. Here, in relationships founded
in embedding media, we have a style of reduction that satisfies this principle.
Space, for example, is the medium in which triangles are inscribed. But space is
not indifferent to the figures assembled within it. Having an immanent topology, metric, and geometry,[49] it tolerates some configurations, but not others
(not, for example, those represented by Escher). Indeed, space is narrowly constraining, as when triangles in a flat space have internal angles equal to 180 degrees, while those in curved spaces have angles equal to fewer or more degrees.
Reducing figures to their embedding space is, therefore, another way of reducing the determinate to the determinable. Reductions of this sort refer the actual
to the virtual.

Is there an embedding medium for all properties, so that knowing its structure would enable us (or a god) to ascertain the generic character of properties that emerge when higher-order systems are formed within it? Two questions come to mind: Is everything in nature embedded in spacetime? And are there embedding media other than spacetime? For if spacetime is the only embedding medium, we should infer that there is evidence of its constraining effects in every state of affairs. Knowing those constraints, we would know some things about any phenomenon that might come to be embedded there. This is an extrapolation from views like those of Plato's *Timaeus,* Descartes' reduction of matter to extension, and Einstein's theory of general relativity. They converge on the idea that every qualitative difference is a determination of space or spacetime. This is true if every actual world instantiates possibles that are accommodated to their individuating spacetime. Notice, however, that some possibles signifiable within a world may not be realizable there. For grant that spacetime is the medium in which Jack and Jill are embedded: is it also true that this medium constrains their semantic intensions and moral ideals? Can't we talk about and want things that are not instantiable in our world? These would be possibles that are not prefigured in the spacetime of our world.

In summary, reducing systems to the dispositions of their parts or to the merely additive relations of the parts risks losing something important: namely, the reciprocal causal relations that transform an aggregate into a system. Benign reductions proceed in either of two ways: by identifying specific formations as the determinate expressions of a determinable or by identifying the embedding medium which tolerates but constrains them.

III. ARISTOTLE, THE ATOMISTS, AND WHITEHEAD

This hypothesis about the constitution of things (aggregates apart) is clarified by comparing it to the more familiar views of Aristotle, the atomists, and Whitehead. One question directs us: Is every thing complete in itself, so that its identity is unconditioned by its relations to other things; or is each thing's character the function of its relations—topological, geometrical, and dynamic—to one or more others?

1. Aristotle

Aristotle distinguished the form of things—their mode of organization—from their matter.[50] Matters are discrete, autonomous, and determinable, with respect to quality and magnitude. Forms are universals: each may have an indefinite number of instantiations. A form—also called *essence* or *substantial form*—achieves particularity when it supplies qualification to a quantity of matter: chiseled marble is a statue, clay enlivened is a man. Things that have matter and form—*primary substances*—are freestanding. Each is self-sufficient in the two respects just cited: its character is established by its organizing, internal form; its existence and character are sustained by the stability of its matter, as wood holds the form of a chair. The limit to self-sufficiency is apparent when living things wither in the absence of nourishment. But this is a subsidiary point. The principal contrast opposes qualified, empowered individuals to their two, abstracted constituents—form and matter.

Aristotle would have us believe that a thing's relations to other things—including spatial, temporal, and causal relations—are incidental to its identity.[51] He reasoned that identity is established by form, so that relations to other things may only support, somewhat disguise, or threaten the thing. Being a parent entails relatedness, but being a man or woman—the substance's primary identity—does not. Scraping or breaking a knee impairs it, but neither alters the ideal type of which the knee is an instance.

Motion has ambiguous implications for primary substances. Motion within the human body is plainly critical for its functioning. Self-initiated motions are also vital, as in the case of searching for food. They compare to the motions of things affecting the body: they are more often threats to identity than conditions for it. Indeed, there would be no motion in an ideal, enmattered world, except for the circular orbits of the stars. Every other thing, qualified by its identity-bestowing form, would occupy its suitable place, motionless. More generously, it would be restricted to its appropriate region, whether earth, water, fire, or air, moving and changing there in ways appropriate to its nature, as a bird or a stone.

These are some considerations that distinguish Aristotle's individuals from the stable systems of my hypothesis. Stabilities are not inert: each one (not only living things) is stabilized because motion has been routed through its parts. The dynamic relatedness of the parts is plain in living bodies, but the point needs some explaining in the case of things, like chairs, that are inert. Their parts, bonded by nails or glue, seem to have little in common with the reciprocally sustaining organs of animal bodies. Yet the reciprocal relatedness of a system's parts is not an all-or-nothing affair, or one having only a single modality. There are disparate styles of reciprocity: bonding by nails is different from that by glue, as both differ from the interaction of heart and lungs. But neither style is merely static: nails bind pieces of wood because of the opposed pressures exerted by nails and wood; things are joined by glue because of molecular bonds established between it and them. These are rudimentary systems. Yet here, as in complicated ones, stability is dynamic: there is motion in the parts, in the reciprocities of parts, and within the environment where things interact, sometimes creating higher-order systems.

Aristotle's characterization of individuals is not dynamic; but this would have seemed a quibble to him. He never acknowledged that a thing's character is established by the reciprocal relations of its parts. It is, he supposed, the embodied form of man (a secondary substance)—only derivatively a beating heart or the blood it pumps—that establishes and sustains a living thing. Nor did he agree that the separability of matters is superseded by the reciprocal relations that establish higher-order systems. Such things are aggregates.[52] The result— Aristotle's ontology—satisfies his principal aims: secure instantiation for Plato's Forms, while acknowledging that stable, material particulars are the primary constituents of our world.

Readers may object that Aristotle often described the internal dynamics of things. The acorns that grow into oaks have formal, efficient, and final causes within them.[53] Animal hearts beat; but their relations to other organs were thought to be instances of ideal types, as though a man would still be a man if all the motion within him stopped. Motion was assumed to be accidental to the relations of a body's parts; we require it only because effort and motion are needed to overcome the recalcitrance of matter as it resists form. This is Aristotle's Platonism, and the reason he is inimical to the view proposed here. I suppose that reciprocal causal relations sabotage the alleged separability of things. Aristotle demurs: an orchestra must always reduce to its constituent members: it never achieves a corporate identity.

These criticisms do not obscure my debt to Aristotle. It is his notion of form, especially form in living things, that is generalized in my characterization of the reciprocal relations that establish and stabilize complex systems (both internally and externally).[54] Consider the modularity of things, as described in the previous section. Modularity is achieved when the reciprocal relations of the module's parts have routinized the flow of energy, information, or material. It is the stability of these relations which justifies describing a system as "substantial," meaning that it has a density of its own. Aristotle said as much when he described the integrity of living bodies: networks of relations supply the avenues—the circuits—for efficient causes, hence for motion. These networks of form define us, in ourselves and as they bind us reciprocally to other things. Aristotle resisted: all the integrity and substantiality of a body derives, he thought, from its finite and informed, freestanding matter.

This claim is the one I dispute. Elementary particles are the only things whose stability and character may derive principally from the reciprocity of their constituent properties. Everything else has laterally determining conditions—causal conditions—in other complex systems. Add that reciprocal relations are established between and among many things, thereby creating higher-order systems. The ontology proposed here is more ample than Aristotle's but only because it exploits his idea of form beyond the domain to which he applied it.

Why didn't Aristotle generalize his claims about formal cause in the ways proposed here? Perhaps he disliked the idea for either or both of two reasons. One is his hostility to forms that are differentiable from material particulars, as when a form organizes several substances without being their accident. Distinguishing form from particular matters—by making it the relational network whereby matters are joined—may have seemed too much like Plato's idea that forms exist *ante rem*.[55] Second is the array of tasks that Aristotle assigned to matter. It stabilizes form and instantiates universals while individuating and separating primary substances. Matter works too well, with the effect that substances are made excessively independent of one another. Relations between or among them are disparaged as accidents.

My proposal obviates this isolating effect in four ways: (i) by categorizing matter—mass—as a property (not as stuff that underlies qualification), then by acknowledging that the quantity of mass is a function of a thing's motion and relations to other things; (ii) by affirming that each of a thing's properties achieves determination, hence specific values, within a web of determining relations that are internal or external to it—values determined by cycling energy, information, or material through causal networks; (iii) by recognizing the reciprocal causal relations that establish systems, some that are mutually independent, others that are reciprocally related, nested, or overlapped; (iv) by acknowledging that the topology and geometry of spacetime are further determinants of property values, because they constrain every relationship embedded within it. *Form,* as redescribed here, is a network of causal and spatiotemporal relations. Each network's architecture is sustained, because it routinizes energy flow, thereby nourishing the causes it binds. These are some amplifications of Aristotle's ideas about form.

2. The Atomists

Atomism, from Leucippus and Democritus[56] to Wittgenstein's *Tractatus,*[57] is inimical to my claim that things are systems established by the reciprocal causal relations of their parts. Philosophical atomism infers from the observed complexity and integration of things to the simplicity, autonomy, and isolability of their lowest-order parts. It typically alleges that atoms fall into and out of configurations that make no difference to their existence or character.

I would alter this persuasion in five ways. (i) Atoms—meaning elementary particles—are internally dynamic rather than inert. (ii) They are established and sustained (at least partly) by the reciprocal relations of their constituent properties, so that they are complex rather than simple. (iii) Atoms are not autonomous, because some of the determining conditions that fix the values of their properties are external to them. (iv) Particles are not unalterable, because changes in their external determining conditions may change the specific values of determinables within them. (v) Many are not freestanding, because the reciprocal relations that bind them within complex systems (intra-atomic or molecular forces, for example) stabilize these higher-order systems, making it difficult or expensive (in energy) to separate the particles from one another.

The independence claimed for particles is better described as *modularity,* meaning that every system is exempted—more or less—from the internal economy and effects of other systems. Nothing is independent in the way required by the atomists: nothing is fully formed, with a fixed character that is unaffected by repeated reconfigurings. The stability of elementary particles is, therefore, no basis for the inference that particles are simple or inert: their stability is an (almost) autonomous steady state, or it is the orderly, internal transformation of a particle that is affected by its relations to other systems. Atomists reduce change to the reconfiguring of objects. What sustains configurations? Atomists don't tell us, though there is an answer: namely, the reciprocal causal relations of the things configured.

3. Whitehead

Whitehead challenges my hypothesis in a different way. He never supposed that the events he called "actual occasions" or "actual entities"[58] are inert, or that relations are extraneous to these prehending, self-integrating moments. There are, however, some other features of his claims, all of them objectionable from the point of view espoused here.[59]

First is Whitehead's characterization of actual occasions. They are atomic and self-contained: each one comes into being from nothing, only to be annihilated when the sensible endowment of its creation has been organized in accord with its feelings, thoughts, and aims. This material is presented by antecedent occasions, then "prehended" by a current one,[60] though there is no contact between them. There could not be, because every antecedent has expired at the moment—but before—it is prehended. Worse, each actual occasion is less than ephemeral: each is a becoming that takes no time. This would be odd but for Whitehead's debt to Leibniz. For actual occasions can be seen from either of two perspectives. Like monads, each actual occasion is a discrete, logical moment in the mind of God. More familiar to us humans, each occasion is a "drop of experience,"[61] a phrase that locates us squarely within a psycho-centric ontology. Everything is either a mind or its qualification. There are the small minds of finite actual occasions and the large mind of God. Each has its prehensions, values, and aims.[62]

Actual occasions have only two kinds of relations to one another: they are successive, each one created to replace an antecedent just annihilated; or they are contemporaries, so that neither affects or prehends the other. The order of occasions—more similar to a mathematical series than a change over time—is Whitehead's candidate for process. He proposes cogently that each individual is a lineage of becomings; there is point to saying that things having an internal dynamic evolve. But Whitehead's things—actual occasions—can only interpret their inputs and expire: having no history, they do not develop or evolve through time. Contemporaneous occasions may be related in either of two ways: both may prehend the same antecedents, and both may be prehended by the same successors. There are, however, no reciprocities, no causal relations, between them. Compare marriage, friendship, or conversation, three familiar bases for sociality. There is reciprocity in marriage or friendship when each partner's feelings anticipate and respond to those of the spouse or friend. Reciprocity in conversation implies that each party listens and responds to the other. Reciprocities of both sorts require that each of the agents outlive the effects of interaction—receipt of a signal—long enough to respond. Nothing in Whitehead's theory but God and eternal objects survives long enough to establish reciprocity with anything else. God has no companions; eternal objects are splendidly alone, each one distinguishable and separable (like the Forms in Plato's *Sophist*[63]). surely there are some other things that abide, as protons and individual persons survive long enough to establish reliable reciprocal relations. Stable systems—societies—are the result.

Equally problematic is Whitehead's belief that space and time are confused modes of intuition,[64] not the setting or organizing medium of a universe independent of minds. This deflating notion of space and time deprives us of a locale for actual occasions. This is critical, for what alternative site might they have? What locates and integrates the drops of experience, if not space and time? Whitehead's solution—after Leibniz and Hegel—is that actual occasions, like monads and finite spirits, are contemporaneous parts or moments in the mind of God.[65]

In themselves, contemporary occasions are mutually oblivious. Their separability recalls the atomicity of sensory data schematized, according to Kant, by the transcendental ego.[66] Equally, the network of occasions is the analog to a Kantian schematized manifold. So God, like Kant's transcendental ego, is said to be passive to the occasions prehended—God's primordial nature—before he uses his ideas and values to impose relations hence unity, upon these atomized, inert contents.[67] God then surveys his work—his consequent nature—apprehending a unified network of occasions. The actual occasions benefit, because each finally achieves relatedness to every other. Indeed, each is a perspective on every other, because of having a position relative to them within the ample span of God's thought. We are reminded of Leibniz's windowless monads: they have perspectives on one another because God thinks, organizes, and unifies them.[68] We get the appearance of togetherness—community—but only the co-presence of occasions in God's mind.

This is less process and less reciprocity than we require. Nothing in it implies that the existence and character of any occasion are a function of its reciprocal relations to one or more others. We need naturalistic answers to questions that Whitehead cannot answer without invoking his God: namely, how are system-creating reciprocities established, and how are these relations stabilized? Is it true (or even plausible) that effective togetherness is never achieved without a mind to order and join the things unified? There is better evidence that sociality is the effect of reciprocal, causal relations. Some things—both particles and other systems—are active and connected. What is more, they do abide. "Drops of experience" is the wrong paradigm for them.

Chapter 2 Persons

The schematic claims of Chapter One require a test: are they applicable to some domain of things? We humans are mutually independent systems, though we often join ourselves to one another to form higher-order systems that are reciprocally related, nested, or overlapping. Here, in talk about family, friendship, and work mates, we have ready evidence that networks of systems are pervasive. Yet the evidence comes too easily; the examples seem trivial. Shouldn't the idiom of metaphysical authority be abstract: shouldn't we keep our distance from the details of everyday life? This persuasion wrongly scorns the perspective and concerns that first inspire philosophic reflection. It encourages our neglect of critical evidence for the claims of Chapter One. The offsetting fault is banality. My examples are commonplace.

I. HUMAN SYSTEMS

Human bodies are stable assemblies of reciprocally related parts. Each part—hence the system that engages it—is constituted exclusively of its properties. Typical properties have values that vary within a range, values that are fixed by other properties in the same system or by properties in related systems. Compare the alternative: that human bodies are merely aggregates, without reciprocal determination of their parts. Myriad examples confirm the one and falsify the other: metabolism and the brain fix the rate of one's heartbeat; metabolism is increased or diminished as the heart works or rests.

Every stability is set apart from its circumstances—it has an inside and an outside—because of the functional membrane established by the reciprocal relations of its parts. In us, this barrier is a tissue, skin, that mediates external stimuli and the corporate response of systems within the body. This separating membrane protects the sustaining relatedness of the body's parts without blocking the effects of the external world. Step on my foot, and my pain and recoil are this system's corporate response. Other reactions are mediated and considered, as when I respond to something you tell me by interpreting the new information in the light of memories, beliefs, habits, and attitudes, all of them stored and aroused endogenously. Previously, I responded involuntarily to an assault. Now, I reply by interpreting and controlling the effect within me. Every such response expresses the relations between or among distinct systems, whether conceptual and linguistic, perceptual, attitudinal, neural, or muscular. Every such response is channeled through reciprocally related, physical structures.

These last sentences mix cognitive psychology with physiology, though joining them is problematic. The human body is a stabilized system of reciprocally related parts, but there is no equally compelling reason to say that every person is also a stability from the standpoint of his or her psychological functions, or that aspects of the psychological system map simply, one to one, onto parts of the body. The design and relations of bodily parts seem unproblematic, though they are known incompletely. The design and relations of psychological functions (including responsibility, initiative, or ego strength) are obscure, their structural expressions uncertain. The systems that concern us are somewhere in the skull, though our problem—hardly changed since Freud's *Program* of 1897—is to discover the brain's way of accomplishing these effects.[1] Techniques that use brain imaging to identify the sites of particular brain functions begin to reveal the work its structures do; but this is preliminary. For the problem of relating mental function to structure is very much as it has been: we know more of some things brains do than we know of their ways of doing them.

This is my excuse for characterizing psychological systems known functionally, but not structurally, in this way: I infer from what is done to conditioning dispositions or faculties. This is the traditional way of ascribing mental functions to the brain, without doing the empirical research that would enable us to locate these behaviors within it. The claims I shall be making are, in this respect, the IOU's of someone who has no way to pay them.

This style of generating psychological claims is also risky in another way. We infer from effects to their conditions, as if the conditions were causes—someone has acted, we say, because of guilt—though the causal model invoked derives from explanations of bodily behavior: seeing a man run, we infer that running engages his legs, heart, and lungs. Functions and powers ascribed to mind rarely get this more detailed specification: we say that the brain is the organ of guilt, without being able to tell how or where the brain generates it. Our use of causal explanations for mental activities is sometimes more show than substance, as Kant invoked the unity of experience before inferring to an agent— the transcendental unity of apperception—that grasps and unifies its inputs from outside space and time. This is the outcome when the causal model, pressed too far, founders. With Kant as our warning, we suppress transcendental inferences. What do we know of the causes of our psychological states and behaviors? Information about the causes is, principally, information about the states and behaviors that justify causal inferences. We infer from agitated behaviors to agitated mental states, though physiologists—informed by machine modeling of psychological functions—begin to know more.

Wanting additional information, we introspect: perhaps mind will perceive its own structure and powers. The result is frustrating. Self-perception supplies the evidence for many things mind does, but little or nothing of how mind does it.[2] Inferences from these behaviors is, so far, the principal evidence for the postulated faculties. There would be no other, readily available evidence for them but for the theory of mind embodied in ordinary language. We talk confidently about mind's attitudes, intentions, self-reflections, and intuitions. The story we tell is endorsed by everyone who uses language to communicate his or her states of mind. "I see what you mean," we say, implying that mind inspects or grasps the thing known. This way of speaking is as common to physiologists as to dualists. But there is this difference. Dualists often interpret ordinary language reports as accurate expressions of mind's achievements: they believe that introspection—mind's self-scrutiny—reveals mind's states and structures as they are.

This conclusion cannot stand if mind is an activity of body, especially the brain, and if self-awareness is not the auto-perception of brain's structure. Plato, Descartes, Berkeley, Husserl, and legions more have thought otherwise, because they were deceived by the apparent evidence of introspection, by ordinary usage in Greek, French, English, and German, and by the seeming contradiction of supposing that matter thinks. We avert their mistake by taking care that cognitive psychology does not justify its explanatory rubrics merely by citing the rules of our naively mentalist language. For these are early days in the translation of cognitive psychology into physiology. We admit that our characterizations of mental systems are tentative and incomplete. We infer from bodily behaviors and intrapsychic events to presumed behaviors and systems within the brain; but we cannot yet confirm that the functions and relations specified can be mapped onto specific neural systems. Because aligning cognitive psychology with physiology will likely require additions and corrections to both, we are careful not to short-circuit physiological inquiry by supposing that mind acts as no brain could do: we do not suppose that mind has unmediated perceptions of anything, or that it has a comprehensive view of itself from outside space and time.

There is also this residual problem. People often present themselves to understanding as systems of functions, not as systems of bodily parts: they are known as characters in a novel, neurotic patients, or people known only by letter or telephone. Knowing such a person's bodily parts and physiology may not tell a sensitive observer more than he knew already about these behaviors: he could discern and predict them without this additional information. Still, psychological functions are not freestanding; they do not exist without the physical system that grounds them. It is incidental to this ontological point that parents and friends may know us very well without knowing anything of our neural activity.

II. COGNITIVE-AFFECTIVE POSTURE

How do we connect functions to structure? We make abductive inferences of the sort that are familiar in science, common sense, and faculty psychology. Seeing smoke, we infer that a fire may be causing it. Seeing an over-excited boy, we infer an inability to recognize his situation and control his impulses. Or we compare this child to another, the one as social pressure reduces him to primitive, unintegrated behavior, the other as he organizes himself in ways that are appropriate and effective. We infer that information and affect are mutually supporting in the one, but not in the other. Proceeding in this way, we identify the salient functions and their relations. But critically, these inferences hardly exceed the matters to be explained: "impulse control" is not so much an explanation for behavior observed as it is a gesture in the direction of its cause, or filter. This is another instance of the problem mentioned above: we know very little about the brain, hence very little about the causal condition for mental behaviors, whether bodily or intrapsychic. Progress is piecemeal and slow. It goes faster if the inferred causes for our mental life are specified (fallibly) by a directing, cogent theory. That theory should be sensitive, I suggest, to the following issues.

We navigate between desire and fear, using what information we have to secure and satisfy us. These are the behaviors of a system that I call *cognitive-affective posture,* or *balance,* implying an accommodation—not a harmony—of parts.[3] This system's "parts" are functions, one cognitive, the other affective. Each part is itself a system having several relatively autonomous constituents. Systematized beliefs are an example. They comprise more or less autonomous networks. Each is more or less constantly adjusted as changes in one of its constituents require adjustments in others. There are also principles for smoothing relations among disparate systems of beliefs and principles for isolating systems that are mutually inimical or exclusive. The result is a higher-order system of functionally described, cognitive subsystems, some that are compact, others that are gerrymandered and loosely or badly mated with their neighbors.

The affective side is also complex. It includes hierarchically organized attitudes together with shorter-term desires. Coordinating attitudes is problematic, as when someone conflicted struggles to make his feelings cohere. We do it by exploiting relations that bind attitudes to information and belief. So we reduce the incommensurability of attitudes by using information to alter one or more of them: someone who is hostile to jockeys but likes horses learns to think better of riders who adore their mounts. This is evidence that beliefs affect and rationalize attitudes; though just as surely, mutually supporting attitudes may determine what beliefs are formulated when information is considered. Someone who prefers horses to people may always assume that casual damage to horses is the work of malign or careless people. The influence goes both ways, though the integrity of beliefs and attitudes is also notable. Having the same beliefs, we behave differently because of having different attitudes. Having the same attitudes, we act differently because of having different beliefs. Information alters some attitudes; more typically, attitudes determine what information is salient and how we construe it.

The system that incorporates cognitive and affective functions is the one I shall be emphasizing in this chapter. Cognition and affect are described as acts, feelings, attitudes, or capacities. Some of these terms signify introspectable events, but all are shorthand for missing information about the electrochemistry of the brain and body. The underlying system of bodily parts and processes is implied but otherwise ignored.

Each person's cognitive-affective balance has its idiosyncratic evolution. There is, however, this common developmental task: each of us is fragile and needy, so that each must secure and satisfy him or herself. We do this by acquiring a stable psychic posture and by filling roles within systems that satisfy and secure us. These two are co-temporal: one cannot do either without the other. We distinguish them here, starting with psychic posture, because it makes description easier.

Cognitive-affective posture forms and evolves as we test our circumstances, partly to secure or satisfy ourselves, partly to learn the mix of attitudes (perceived as feelings), information, and skills required for successful interactions. These three are cross-referenced and mutually adapted, though each is distinct, and each is a system of functions. I assume that infants are suffused with needs and obscure desires, and that attitudes are acquired when we satisfy needs by learning and applying information and skills.

Information, attitudes, and skills are plastic, ill-defined, and somewhat unaffected by one another in our early days; but more and more, each is tested against the others when circumstances engage us. Having learned that misinformation (or irrelevant information), inappropriate feelings, or useless skills get us into trouble, we seek validation for each by checking it against the others. This mix of feelings or inclinations, information, and skills—mutually reconciled and circumstantially appropriate—directs our interventions. Reciprocities—the mutually conditioning, causal relations emphasized in Chapter One—are conspicuous in the relations of this functional system. So, information is a function of my attitudes (including interests) and skills. For it is no good telling me to learn all I can about French postage during the Third Republic if philately bores me. Equally, what I like is usually a function of what I do well; and what I learn to do is a function of my information, such skills as I have already, and my persuasion that doing this will enhance or please, not damage or annoy me.

The measure of success is different for each of us. Having different bodies, we have different capacities and a different affective tone. No matter that our circumstances are identical, one of us withdraws, waiting passively for the outcome; the other bobs and weaves, looking for opportunities, often finding them. Each of us acquires an idiosyncratic mix of information, attitudes, skills, and strategies for securing and satisfying him or herself. Some of these strategies are applied frequently within several domains. Others are applied in one or a few domains only, as an imaginative cook is otherwise conventional. We explain the difference by saying that cooking is the one activity in which he or she was encouraged, initiatives in other activities having been suppressed. Most of the plasticity in our development is early. We are bent by late adolescence into the psychological form that will distinguish us until late middle age. Illness or radical changes in our circumstances may then constrict us further; or they may shake us loose from an old, cramped style: it is too late for fear, thinks someone taking the measure of himself. Why call this psychic balance a "stability"? Because it is each person's established way of securing or satisfying him or herself. It is stable as one's accent or gait. More than either of them, this posture vibrates with all the affect and style that distinguish us as we engage other people and things.

Compare the stolidity of cognitive-affective posture to the ephemerality that Nietzsche ascribed to successive versions of the self. His conclusion derives from several Kantian assumptions. First is the belief that empirical reality has no standing apart from interpretations that schematize it. This implies that the empirical self—the situationally qualified self having particular experiences, memories, and aims—is a product of interpretation: it is created by the story or stories that we or others use to construe us. Still, there must be something more to us, because interpretation is not freestanding: some agent schematizes realities by imposing character and relations on sensory data. Nietzsche met this objection by exploiting Kant's distinction between transcendental and empirical egos. The transcendental subject is prior to, and untouched by, the constraints imposed by the schematization that creates a particular empirical ego. One ego creates order from chaos (or nothing). Coupling freedom and power to law, it is at once Dionysian and Apollonian. The other has the specific character of its situation, history, and prospects. Empirical selves are ephemeral, because the transcendental ego can (and does?) alter its schematizations spontaneously. The instability of the empirical self is the price of transcendental freedom.

Will is Nietzsche's shorthand for this Kantian legacy:

> "Truth" is therefore not something there, that might be found or discovered—but something that must be created and that gives a name to a process, or rather to a will to overcome that has in itself no end—introducing truth, as a *processus in infinitum*, an active determining—not a becoming-conscious of something that is in itself firm and determined. It is a word for the "will to power."[4]

This passage appears in the context of Nietzsche's claim that we should relinquish the notions of "subject" and "object." We abjure them, because all creative power resides in an interpreting, world-making will to power; and because the person hereby formed is not separate from the schematizing act that creates and sustains it. The empirical ego resides "within" (that is, it is a contingent expression of) the reality-creating transcendental ego.

Kant and Fichte embellished these claims when they distinguished the transcendental will from effects that include the empirical ego (me, here, now, "thrown" among the contingent details of my situation):

> It should especially be noted that the practical concept of freedom is based on this *transcendental idea*, and that in the latter lies the real source of the difficulty by which the question of the possibility of freedom has always been beset. Freedom in the practical sense is the will's independence of coercion through sensuous impulses. For a will is sensuous, in so far as it is *pathologically affected*, i.e., by sensuous motives; it is *animal* (*arbitrium brutum*), if it can be pathologically *necessitated*. The human will is certainly an *arbitrium sensitivum*, not, however, *brutum* but *liberum*. For sensibility does not necessitate its action. There is in man a power of self-determination, independently of any coercion through sensuous impulses.[5]

Is the empirical self unstable, because of transcendental whim and freedom? The instability Nietzsche described is rarely observed. Nor do we expect it, if we repudiate the idealism and transcendental freedom which imply it. Selfhood resides in the information, attitudes, and skills acquired and integrated in our many roles. There is no transcendental ego that alters or obviates them merely by supplying a different interpretation of us.

We should also be suspicious of this claim:

> *One thing is needful*—To "give style" to one's character—a great and rare art! It is practiced by those who survey all the strengths and weaknesses of their nature and then fit them into an artistic plan until every one of them appears as art and reason and even weaknesses delight the eye.[6]

We survey selves, this implies, as the transcendental ego observes its empirical product. Yet, self-consciousness never justifies this transcendental aspiration. For there is no standpoint from which to observe and alter "all" our nature. Unlike the authors of novels (they create their characters by coordinating bits and pieces of description), we have a partial view of ourselves and a limited power for altering our aims and attitudes. Every person has a psychic posture because of the forced, often crude integration of their information, attitudes, and skills. We exploit the psychic posture we have (by elaborating our exposing one part while ignoring or hiding others). We don't pretend to sculpt or see all of it.

This is so, because the greater part of cognitive-affective balance, like an iceberg, is submerged. Consciousness and self-consciousness have, by comparison, a much smaller field of view, with access to selected aspects of oneself or the world. Each person's selfhood is, in this respect, either unknown to him or a thing of which he learns by seeing its effects on others. This is the truth in

Hume's claim that others may know us better than we know ourselves. For if we know the character of a singer's voice only by hearing it used, so, too, we understand a person by seeing him or her in everyday circumstances, then in situations where ordinary demands are altered. Introspection supplies only a partial view of the psychic posture that exhibits itself in these ways. For Hume was mistaken if he believed that what we see is all there is. Think of the singer: she is only as good (*qua* singer) as her singing; but singing is different from the capacity to sing, otherwise there would be no trace left by her years of lessons and practice. We may perceive something of the resolve that moves her—as she does—but not the conditioning integration of information, attitude, and skill. This partial perception of it is no justification for skepticism about it. Cognitive-affective balance is a condition for behavior; it does not reduce to the behavior itself. The posture abides, its behavioral expressions familiar, its physiology obscure.

Is cognitive-affective balance the ghost in our human machine? Ryle thought that we eliminate the embodiment of Cartesian minds by saying that mind is in behavior, all the rest being reduced to capacities of the kind signified by saying that someone can walk if he does walk.[7] Ryle's analysis is false to dispositions of every sort—as Austin showed[8]—hence false to those of cognitive-affective postures. More salient here is the empirical error that eliminates all interiority—save dispositions—in order to reduce mental activity to publicly observable bodily behavior. No one gushes about a car's performance, while denying everything to its innards but a capacity for going fast. Cognitive-affective balance has a role like that of a motor and gearbox. Better, this stabilizing system is our internal gyroscope. This, for the purposes of psychology, is what and who we are. That we are sometimes conscious (self-conscious) of this system's parts (never of the system in its entirety) is apparent. That we begin to understand the physical basis for this self-experience—in parallel processing and hierarchically organized nerve networks—is more salient.

This self-system is socially engaged, but centrally organized: the qualifications for our various roles are mutually inflected by our disparate experiences and by reflections that somewhat reduce anomalies among them. Cognitive-affective posture is, therefore, antithetic to the disengaged, "thin" selves that Rawls postulates when he describes the agents who participate in the "original position."[9] Those spectral selves are the place-holders of rights. They are the legal, political selves that emerge when democratic societies create a *public*: we organize ourselves for self-regulation, thereby endowing ourselves with certain rights and duties. (See Chapter Three, section VIII). These juridical selves have no freestanding reality. They are not achieved until and unless our material, socialized selves—our cognitive-affective postures—have come to understand the advantages of corporate self-regulation. The procedural justice achieved within a self-regulating public is, this implies, an *aim*. It would be unthinkable and unachievable by the bare, mutually disinterested, but entitled selves that Rawls postulates. For aims are the developmental engine of our crystallizing selves. Learning our roles, reflecting on them and our interests, we acquire the skills and internal order that qualify us to control (somewhat) our choice of roles. Justice is the abstract aim of mature selves, not the primordial achievement of fictive selves.[10]

III. SOCIAL SYSTEMS ESTABLISHED BY THEIR MEMBERS

Stabilities may relate to one another in either of four ways: mutually independent systems interact without reciprocity; or reciprocity is established between them, thereby creating a higher-order system; or systems are related hierarchically, one nested in another; or a system falls within two or more higher-order systems, so that they overlap. Consider the three systems-forming relations. (We ignore the interactions of independent systems that do not form higher-order systems). Here are five venues of human interaction and alliance, each one the instance of one or more of these relations: family, friendship, work, citizenship, and moral, aesthetic, or religious affinities. These systems are the backdrop for the following remarks about persons. Systems *qua* systems are the topic of Chapter Three.

We may be inclined to describe these modes of socialization as ideal types, then to consider the types by analyzing such concepts as *family, friendship,* and *work.* This a priori reflection is less than we require of a metaphysics that is more than talk about talk: we need empirical evidence that systems of particular kinds do exist, not merely that they are possible because our notions of them embody no contradictions. Apriorist reflection also errs because of its normative bias. It encourages us to believe that systems must have the character ascribed to them by our concepts, as we may suppose that ideal families comprise male and female parents and their children. I shall usually assume that families do have this structure, but only because doing so facilitates exposition. That there are other kinds of families and many kinds of friendship, work, government, and affiliation is assumed. There is only this much essentialism in my claims about systems. Each has a characteristic form (or forms) of interaction, as children and their caretakers, friends, workers, citizens, and fellow believers forge distinctive reciprocities. Could we be socialized—or recognizably human—without having a part in any of these systems? This is hard to imagine.

1. Family

Each of us bootstraps himself from raw determinability to a settled cognitive-affective system within a family. The child participates in, and helps to maintain, the stability that engages him and his caretakers before he or she has acquired more than a primitive psychic posture. For no child is a blank slate. We are born with heuristics that direct us as we gather information and with needs that shape our values: we are hungry and want feeding. It is this primitive balance that acquires content and form in the midst of relations to caretakers who are, from the child's point of view, the unalterable features of its world.

(A) DEVELOPING A PSYCHIC POSTURE

No one chooses a family until later in life. Perhaps infants are the target of Heidegger's observation that we are "thrown": each discovers him or herself, as though adventitiously, in the midst of some particular family.[11] Links with its other members are the basis for the child's psychic posture. His or her behavior expresses two points of view. From the child's perspective, other family members supply the information, values, and skills appropriate to securing him or herself among them. Caretakers see these needs through the screen of complex demands they make of the child, demands that are reflected in his or her beliefs, attitudes, and skills. Every child's emerging cognitive-affective posture is a mix of powers and constraints, skills and duties. Its determinables achieve specific values when the child interacts with the other members of its family.

Each child's posture is an accommodation to a particular state of affairs. He or she has learned to recognize and want security and satisfaction in whatever terms the family provides them. It is incidental that the circumstances are good or bad, supportive or abusive. This situation is the one that the child—and the adult he or she later becomes—tries to sustain or re-create. Why is it difficult to learn that abuse is not the required condition for well-being? Because the development of a psychological system in each of us is monadic and perspectival: this point of view is our only one. Like young geese who follow the first "parent" they see, we are forever imprinted by this first participation in social stabilities. This experience is the developmental ground of the self-stability that joins information, values, and skills. This may forever restrict the kinds of reciprocity that make us effective or happy. Other strategies for securing and satisfying us will not be learned until later, if ever.

What is changed when the child-become-adult makes his or her own family? Nothing may have changed: the adult may struggle to duplicate the family of his or her childhood. More likely, an adult has learned that his or her strategy for managing family life is not the only viable one. Someone who doesn't know this must be lucky to succeed in family life: he or she needs a mate of complementary attitudes and skills. The alternative is mutual laceration: each sorts through his or her assumptions while trying to guess the bias of a partner's information, values, and skills. Friends or counsellors prescribe "compromise," but this is useless advice if neither understands the other or himself well enough to engage the other in ways that would sustain the stability having these two as its parts. This change could occur only if each partner were to alter whichever aspect of his or her psychic posture impedes affiliation with the other: one or both needs more in formation, different values, or new skills.

Reflection and flexibility of this sort are not to be expected in children: they usually assume that their circumstances are an unalterable given. Their psychic identity is largely fixed by the manner of their engagement in circumstances their parents or caretakers supply. We also realize that our first instincts, probably the ones learned when we were children, may not be ideal for our children. Family membership is, therefore, much more problematic for a thoughtful adult than ever it was for the child he or she was: we struggle to change ourselves in order to alter the psychic economy of the higher-order system we have created.

One's power to secure a family by altering oneself should not be exaggerated. Parents in most cultures lack the information or opportunities to change their cognitive-affective postures, hence their behaviors. Think of cultures where mothers are young, poor, and unmarried. What are the chances that their children will not incorporate the information and values that shape their caretakers? This cultural inheritance is alterable in principle and often in fact; but it may not be much changed for generations. The persistence of an original formation—in the cognitive-affective postures and practices of subsequent generations—is the conservative reality of our lives. This effect is relieved somewhat by self-consciously altered practices, as when adults read experts to learn about child rearing. But usually, adults are inclined to do what was done to them; the books merely justify their inclination. America was permissive before Dr. Spock.

The intergenerational constancy of cognitive-affective postures may be explained by saying that children imitate their parents; but this cannot be a complete explanation, when the child's dominant caretakers may differ radically from one another. Which one will the child copy? The answer depends on the sex of the child and the degree of intimacy between the child and each parent. It is also a function of the balance of affect and authority within the family. Whose affective style is dominant? Who dominates when problems are solved? Is the child shielded from the effects of one because of his or her intimacy with the other? Many children acquire a mix of styles learned from their several caretakers. A few learn to be satisfied with rewards like those that satisfy one of the parents—they replicate that parent's internal form and ways of behaving. This is rare, because a child's self-perceptions are different from those of his or her parents: wanting different things, children cannot get them merely by believing, feeling, or acting as their parents do. Or the children are reactive: they refuse to believe, feel, or act as their parents do. This is sometimes imitation in the making: like a rubber band stretched against itself, we recoil to a point much closer to the other extreme.

These outcomes are functions of four variables—the four determinables—that achieve specific values as family members interact. They include the innate inclinations of the child, the postures of the caretakers, the psychic spaces that caretakers leave open to the child, and the accord or discord between parents as they encourage the child to fill one space or another. That children differ in their abilities and sensibilities seems obvious enough, however difficult it is to quantify the variations. That caretakers within a family differ from one another, and differ in the style with which each fills his or her several roles, is also apparent. The sea captain is no less imperious at home than at sea. Or he gladly surrenders authority as soon as his boat is moored: his wife has held it while he is away and keeps it when he is home. The particular personalities of a child's caretakers open some possible lines of development for the child, while closing others. Accord or discord between caretakers further distorts the options by driving the child in one direction, or by confounding him in several ways at once.

The variability of cognitive-affective formations is all the greater if we add a fifth variable: namely, the family trade. What differences are there among farmers, miners, and fishermen? One to emphasize is the organization of their families, an organization that varies with the work that breadwinners do. Each trade has a particular economy of effort and reward. Miners and fishermen work together but without their wives. Farmers work alone or with their wives. Miners and farmers are home for dinner. Deep-sea fishermen are ashore more rarely, so that they are less comfortable at home, and less familiar to their children. Families of all three sorts may be stable, but they differ in these ways, so that each style of organization supplies a distinctive context wherein cognitive-affective postures are exercised, imitated, and learned—hence inherited.

The possibility that a child may acquire a cognitive-affective posture merely by imitating one of his or her caretakers now seems remote. For there is no way for children to discern and abstract the effects of work from a caretaker's personality. The child sees a complex: someone having a particular cognitive-affective posture situated in a particular economic and social arrangement, with a particular history. The child never understands these arrangements or history, and never perceives the inner form and articulations of the complex. He may not infer until later, if ever, how particular feelings, habits, or thoughts were inflected by other things. Was a father sad in himself, sad because of his job, or sad because his wife left him no space? His children incorporate something of their father's character without knowing the answer. But this is just one of the effects they integrate. Every child internalizes something from each of his or her caretakers, so that his or her cognitive-affective posture is a unique synthesis of habits, attitudes, and strategies that are learned as the child responds to them (and to friends, teachers, and co-workers). The child who resembles only one of his parents is like someone bred by parthenogenesis: he is weakened by having too fragile a base.

(B) SOME ONTOLOGICAL IMPLICATIONS
OF PSYCHIC POSTURE

Consider the categorial points, made or implied in Chapter One, that are illustrated by these claims about child rearing. Suppose that cognitive-affective balance is the stabilizing organization of a human body under its own, intelligent, affective control, and that the family is an emergent, higher-order stability. Considered from the side of the parts, this new stability is created by their interaction and mutual accommodation. Each has captured the other or others, though coercion alone will not hold them. Relations between or among the family members must be appropriate to their several characters. Think of binary stars, each one circling the other, their gravitational masses determining their distance and relative velocity. Speaking as atomists, we say that this "system" is nothing additional to the parts related: namely, the stars. But surely this reduction ignores the dynamic that explains the stability of their orbits. The import of these relations is equally plain if we imagine the final rehearsals for a concerto. The conductor and the soloist accommodate themselves to one another: each is responsible *for* playing his part and *to* the other for playing it in a way that does not transgress the other, as happens if one plays at the wrong tempo or too loudly. This system, minus orchestra or soloist, lays down a set of expectations for the missing part. These expectations are the normative conditions for participating in the system. Play in some other way, and the system of relations goes awry; play as the expectations require, and the performance works. Or imagine that two of us greet a newcomer: you may talk to us in our language about things that concern us, but not in any language whatever and not about topics that annoy us. You enter our system on these terms, because these are the terms required to sustain it.

Atomists may respond that I have not yet made a case for the emergence of a sustained, higher-order system of relations having normative force on its interacting parts. Isn't the orchestra merely an assemblage of players, each one taking his or her cue from the score? Isn't it enough that interaction creates complexity and the mutual demands of the players, without adding that their reciprocity establishes a network of reciprocal causal relations, hence a system? We enforce this point by imagining performances contrived by an engineer: he mixes the tapes of single musicians who record their parts in a studio with none of the others present. Or each part is played by several or many musicians, each contributing a single note. No higher-order stability is exhibited in performances created by mixing the many tapes required for this experiment. Why is there a difference in principle when an orchestra's players perform together? There would be no orchestra without the players, and no music without the notes, but each of them—orchestra and music—is an ordered aggregate. Neither earns description as a higher-order system.

Remember that nominalism may be either of two things, and that we are concerned with only one of them. The nominalism that is incidental here denies the reality of kinds, saying that there are dogs but no Form of dog existing either *in rebus* or *ante rem*. Nominalism of the sort that concerns us emphasizes the terms related, but disparages or denies the reality of relations. Where Peter is taller than Paul, it says that we have Peter and Paul, each a different height, but nothing additional named by the phrase "taller than." Nominalists of the second kind (*atomists* I am calling them) are undeterred by the fact that a concerto comprises ordered notes (not merely notes), and that it is played by musicians responding to one another (not by disengaged soloists). Order, say these nominalists, is nothing additional to the things ordered.

This is plausible when claimed of things whose static relations are spatial or temporal, not causal and reciprocal: patterns in tile or music, for example. Are such patterns *more* than the sum of their parts? Yes and no: no, because a pattern is not separable from the ordered tiles or notes which are its sufficient condition; yes, because pattern is the spatial or temporal relationship of things, not merely the aggregate of things related. Remember the complementarities discussed in Chapter One. These are static relationships that exhibit a form intrinsic to the medium in which the relationship is formed. Such relationships would not be exhibited without the elements or parts configured; yet some properties of relationships are not identifiable with, or reducible to, those of their parts. So the Pythagorean theorem applies to the sides of right triangles, not to detached line segments. There is no rhythm without notes or other sounds, but rhythm is a sequence of intervals in time, irrespective of the quality of the sounds. The shape of one and the intervals of the other are forms immanent in space and time themselves, or forms to which space and time are susceptible. Drawing a triangle or beating a drum exposes one such form. Atomist nominalism makes no sense of examples such as these.

Its failure remains apparent when we pass from static forms to the higher-order systems created by the reciprocal, causal relations of their subsystems. Cells behave as molecules do not; a bag of parts is not a radio. These are wholes created by the coupling, not merely the aggregation, of their parts. Each higher-order system has a sustaining economy, one that exchanges energy, matter, or information with its neighbors. The punter, not his cells or molecules, reads the *Racing News;* the violinist, not his parts, enjoys his musical friends. Each system is distinct from the aggregate of its parts, as we prove again by thinking of a triangle: this is a figure constituted only of line segments; but they, in any other configuration, are not a triangle. This difference is explained only by the relations that create a triangle from its parts.

I proposed in Chapter One that the proper parts of systems have responsibilities of two kinds: they are responsible *for* their effects on the other same-order parts of a system (and sometimes also for effects on systems of other orders) and responsible *to* the system and its other parts for behaviors that have these effects. Responsibility *to,* at its inception, is mechanical, not moral: it implies that a system would fail if its parts did not cause a system-sustaining behavior in one another. Reductionists will find it unintelligible that a system (a nonliving one especially) should be said to make demands of its parts; or they will say that this is an anthropomorphic fantasy. *Demands* signifies a mix of requests and entitlements. Can they be made by anything other than us humans?

Suppose, by way of an answer, that systems have identity and integrity, because of the causal reciprocity of their parts. Being stable, they have *inertial iden-*

tity: they lean into the future. Doing as they have done, systems survive, though not by indifference or accident, and not necessarily because of anything that is intentional or teleological. Other, straightforwardly mechanical conditions explain it. So enduring systems are energy-efficient (or blessed with a great supply of energy). Their parts—or members—are qualified for their roles, and organized so that each one's actions control one or more of the system's other parts. These system-sustaining actions have several aspects. Each does some work, thereby provoking additional system-sustaining work from one or more of the other parts to which this one is reciprocally related. We infer from the system's survival that each of its parts, or enough of them, fulfills its responsibilities to the system and to the other parts. Most of the systems that illustrate this responsibility are subhuman. Such responsibilities do, nevertheless, obtain: the reciprocity of the parts has established the system; only their continued reciprocity sustains it. It is incidental that a system's members acknowledge the responsibility, and no matter if the system constituted by their mutual relations has value for them or anything else. Responsibility *to* is just this conditionality: the system survives if its parts (including successor parts) continue to act upon and control one another. So a hive of bees is a stability, and bees are responsible to one another for behaviors that sustain the hive. Yet this responsibility—of one to others—is mediated by the interest of the hive. Bees are responsible to one another, but only as a condition for sustaining the system. Destruction of the hive liberates member bees from this complex responsibility, at cost to the bees. They respond by establishing a successor system, though now the focus of each bee's responsibility has shifted. Before, responsibility to one another was mediated by a system's inertial identity, as expressed in the sustained reciprocity of its parts. Now, the system is reestablished because of the mutual efforts and interest of creatures that cannot survive apart from self-regulating organizations where each has a role. The status of responsibility *to* in these revised circumstances is less certain. Is it unmediated, because the bees are responsible directly *to* one another for remaking the system that will engage them? Or is their mutual interest mediated by an absent higher-order system—the prospective hive—when bees organize to reconstruct it? Responsibilities *to* have either or both vectors.

First is the consideration that the members of a system—its parts—are responsible to their system for its perpetuation, and responsible to one another for such actions as preserve it. This is not a moral point. As before, it is formulated from the standpoint of a system that survives: the sustained reciprocities of the members or parts are the condition for its survival. Nothing in this entails that surviving systems are good in themselves or good for their members. There are deplorable systems as well as good ones. Prisoners are only too happy to lose their places in political prisons; one doesn't chastise their liberators for encouraging them to ignore responsibilities to their jailers.

Second is the consideration that the members of a system dissolved or destroyed may suffer because of its demise. This situation alters the basis for their responsibility to one another. Before, such responsibilities were predicated on the inertial identity of the system: it survived as each fulfilled its responsibilities to the others. Now, when the system is defunct, these mutual responsibilities have a different basis. This other foundation is self-regard. For each member of a hive will die if it does not join another hive or help to remake the one that was lost. No bee can do all the work itself, yet each has a life-or-death interest in having it done. A thoughtful bee would want other bees to be responsible to it, as it accepts responsibilities to them. This is the implication when each bee has a responsibility for itself, one it expresses by undertaking such responsibilities to other bees as will join in remaking the hive. Bees do not think about such things, but they are social animals—meaning that they act as if each accepts its responsibility to the others.

Join these two considerations, and we have this result: the responsibility of a system's parts (or members) to the system or to other parts marks the inception of normativity and discipline within systems. This is a very qualified normativity. It presupposes the stability ascribed to systems above—*only* implying that a system survives until its energy supply dissipates or until energy sufficient to disrupt it is applied to one or more of its parts. Assuming the system's survival as the point of reference, we say that each part is responsible to the others for such behaviors as would sustain the system. The normativity having this conditional, mechanical basis is feeble: pigeons are not obliged to take care of their chicks; they merely do it because of hormonal or other triggers within them. These behaviors have a complex effect: first, pigeon families; then, the responsibilities that birds have to their families. These responsibilities are less than obligations or duties. They fall to individual pigeons because of the mechanical prejudice— the inertial identity—that favors a system's survival. Nothing more is implied by the normativity within systems; but this is all the basis required for natural obligation in members that can, do, or should perceive the value of perpetuating the systems in which they participate. Reciprocities in the molecular bonds of a snow-flake are not prized by the molecules; there is no moral failure or guilt in them if it melts. Compare us humans: we cultivate and treasure our responsibilities to systems we value. Their perpetuation becomes our interest, and the evidence of our virtue. This follows from the other foundation for responsibilities to others: we join with them when self-regard is best realized in cooperative undertakings requiring that we commit ourselves to them.

The normativity having these effects is embodied in one's cognitive-affective posture. Each of us learns, or can be taught, information, attitudes, and skills appropriate to our roles within systems. So children learn roles within families, with books, movies, and other children to model the behavior required of them. Children also undergo an apprenticeship, under parents or other caretakers, that anticipates their careers as parents. This is evidence that normativity is learned, either by doing the things we are required to do or by observing others in roles that may someday be ours. Remember now that character is cognitive-affective balance, and that learning roles adds articulation to one's psychic posture. Responsibility *to* in us humans has an intention, a locus, and a development. Its intention is the perpetuation of the system or systems in which we participate. Its locus is cognitive-affective balance. Its development requires that we learn the information, attitudes, and skills that qualify us for particular roles. We learn to be participants in systems whose continued existence depends on us.

Responsibility *to* is apparent in families, where loyalty and affection soften, without compromising, the hard edge of mutual demands founded in mutual needs. Family members may act upon the responsibilities to their family and one another without questioning or even thinking about them. Those who are feckless may also come to acknowledge and act upon them. This recognition does not create the responsibilities, for we suppose that the family is already an established, if shaky system. Act upon these responsibilities, and the system stabilizes. Ignore them, and it dissolves.

Systems of this human kind differ from others in the critical respect that responsibilities to a system and its members are redescribed among us as *duties*. There is no moral fault if a piston fails and an engine stops. We humans distinguish ourselves from the parts of other systems by imbuing our behaviors with moral depth: we consider ourselves culpable if our responsibilities to valued systems—our duties to them—are ignored.

Skeptics will say that this characterization is irrelevant to the mutually forgetful members of contemporary families. Worse, they will say that the responsibilities to systems and the normativity claimed for reciprocal relations—the idea that a system's parts are responsible to it and the other parts—are an extrapolation to all reciprocities of the mutual expectations common to relations among morally sensitive humans. For it is a fact about us, not a feature of all causes in negative feedback systems, that we conduct ourselves with the expectation that others will behave in complementary, system-preserving ways.

This objection is half right: the responsibilities of a system's parts to the system and to one another do not become a focus for morality until we humans discover and redescribe them as duties. Such responsibilities also obtain within the families of apes and the hives of bees, though apes and bees assign no moral value to them. We humans, more reflective about ourselves and our circumstances, prize our families to the point where our responsibilities to them become, for us, reciprocal expectations favoring particular behaviors. But this is a matter of emphasis, not creation: responsibilities *to* are not contrived when we interpret human action morally. Knowing that disintegration is a risk, we resist it by emphasizing our mutual duties—though always, our responsibilities to one another have antedated this reading of our circumstances, as families antedate it.

Atomism makes us defensive. We fear that anything overlaid on the terms—especially relations more binding than spatial, temporal relations—derives from the value-driven conceptual system used to organize them: we say that ideologies are disfiguring blueprints used to organize human beings. Or we reject the perspective of the system itself. Emphasizing the interests of the separate parts, we say that each acts independently of the others. Such reactions ignore the ample evidence of systems whose parts are bound by their causal reciprocities. These are relations in which each part (somewhat) *controls* the behavior of one or more others, causing it or them to behave in ways that control this agent, their cause. Some causes, principally ourselves, do this purposely, to sustain systems we value.

(c) CHARACTER AND ROLE

Consider, again, that the family is a stability, one established when a network of sustained, reciprocal relations joins the family members. Individual members are responsible for their effects upon one another and responsible to the corporate entity—the family—for such behaviors as sustain it. Members are expected to contribute to the family economy in established ways, whether materially or psychologically.

Emphasis upon a member's responsibility to his or her family is somewhat plainer if we distinguish two kinds of psychological treatment. Individual therapy—whatever its style—credits each person with a distinctive developmental history and psychic posture, one that is independent of his or her current cir-cumstances. Altering some aspect of a subject's cognitive-affective balance and behavior is this therapy's aim. The effects of his altered behavior on other peo-ple and systems are usually incidental, except as their responses deter this sub-ject from doing what he has newly learned to do. Compare family therapy. It supposes that the family is a corporate entity, a system sustained by the recipro-cal relations of its members. Each one's behavior is controlled, somewhat, by his or her relations to the others. There may be considerable variation in the fine grain of these relations (mother and son versus son and daughter, for example), but each typically acquires a characteristic form, so that each person comes to play a more or less well-defined role—guardian, clown, confidant—in relation to all or some of the others. More, the expectations of the other members make each one responsible to the family as a unit and to them individually for sus-taining his or her particular role. These demands are written into the cognitive-affective postures of the family members: each learns what the others expect of him or her, and (more or less) how to do it.[12]

There is often convergence between an individual's character and his or her role within a family: the one may seem to be formed exactly by or for the di-mensions of the other. Yet both kinds of therapy—individual and family—would have us acknowledge that character and role are distinct. For it often hap-pens that roles are declined by people who are qualified or nominated for them. Should we generalize the point, saying that roles make no difference to one's cog-nitive-affective balance? This would err on the other side: it would imply, mis-takenly, that the roles one learns make no difference to one's character. Let us cover this ground another time, differentiating character and role where we can, acknowledging, too, that character is sometimes a function of role.

We emphasize the difference between roles and candidates for them by re-marking that each of us has learned to qualify for several or many roles, so every character has more dimensions than those required for a particular role. Still, this observation should be construed carefully, lest it encourage the inference that our various capacities are unintegrated. For cognitive-affective posture is not an aggregate of skills—like a rack of costumes—appropriate to one's many roles. The information, skills, and attitudes that qualify us are integrated as a singular style. Attitudes, for example, are organized hierarchically, so that shift-ing interests or prospects are considered, then rejected, or accepted and ranked given one's short-term urgencies and longer-term commitments. Information is integrated via one's general assumptions about how the world works and one's place there. Skills may be coordinated or mutually sustaining. Information confirms our attitudes and supports our skills. Convergences such as these justify the impression that we cohere internally, each of us having his or her peculiar shape. Never mind that each person's style is a gerrymandered compromise of disparate habits and sentiments, not a harmony of parts. Knobby and uncoordinated in some ways, occasionally at war within ourselves, each of us has an established character, a shape that is distorted to some degree by every particular role. None of us reduces to his or her roles.

It is critical that we distinguish character from role, the one as a set of powers making us responsible for things do, the other as it fixes our responsibilities to the systems that engage us. As individuals having cognitive-affective postures, we are causes responsible for what we do. As creatures having roles within families or other social systems, we answer to corporate demands as they define the spaces in which we act.[13] Shall we change the character of the actor or alter his environment? This contrast is too often effaced when atomists emphasize individuals but ignore the higher-order stabilities created when sustainable reciprocities—hence roles—are established among them.

Are these two, character and role, separable or merely distinguishable? Certainly, each person's cognitive-affective balance is stamped—crippled or merely shaped—by his or her experience within a family. Each of us has a role therein, and each learns prospective roles by watching and mimicking his or her caretakers. One may spend a lifetime recreating a network of relations in which to live out the responsibilities to others first learned in a family; or we survive our families but want distance from their entanglements. Neither response—repetition or reaction—implies the conflation of character and role. For every agent's fidelity to his or her roles is mediated by this person's responsibility to him or herself: we make ourselves responsible for a set of graded self-directives. They reach from the imperative of survival through a yearning for dignity and self-satisfaction to exalted ego-ideals. Particular roles are more or less desirable as they achieve these objectives. The objectives may change: they may be remade to suit the possibilities of a comfortable role. But always, the attitudes expressing these values are the rudder and gyroscope of our being: they—more often than declarative sentences or ideas—constrain and direct us. Responsibility to oneself is a commitment to them. They endure, however much they are overlaid and obscured by roles. Some of us seem made for our roles: we are effective parents or company men. But this is the convergence of character and role, not the subsumption of one by the other.

Their difference is apparent wherever character and role are separately propulsive, though mutually reinforcing: we want to do what our roles would have us do. These goads to action also have distinct moral bases: namely, duties to the system and its fellow members and duties to oneself. Which ones are decisive? Are we goaded to action by ourselves, or by others on behalf of our obligations to them or ourselves? This ambiguity—action is overdetermined because we want for ourselves what we owe to others—disguises the gap between character and role. Their difference is more apparent when interests diverge. For it often happens that systems have interests different from those of their proper parts. Imagine a child too young to engage in systems other than his or her family. Such children are paradigms of the accommodation—the fusion—of character to role: the child does, and wants to do, what is expected of him. Suppose, however, that the child's behavior is, for this very reason, intolerable to his parents: punishing the behavior they encourage, they reject him. The child faces a double bind: his parents reprove the thing they command. Sanity requires that he learn the difference between character and role.

The theory of family therapy encourages us to believe that (some of) the principal relations binding a family's members are the specific expectations that individuals have learned as habits. You expect me to behave in certain ways; you repeatedly structure situations so that I shall do what you expect. Having interpreted your expectations as responsibilities to the family, hence to you, I do what you expect of me, even though it is agreed that these behaviors are often intolerable to you and to me. My cognitive-affective posture was shaped when experience confirmed that these behaviors secure my place within this family. This is the fusion of character and role: the child is deterred from changing his way of engaging other family members because his relations to them are regulated by their expectation that he will behave in this other way. Why does the child continue to do what they dislike? Because other members subtly reward him for it, if only by expressing distaste for behaviors that would help him to become something different. Being as he is maintains the settled economy of the family. Needing this arrangement for their own purposes, other members don't want him to change. Reforming this child is the colossal task of altering both the family system and the information, values, or skills in each member's cognitive-affective posture.

Family therapy has (ideally) two effects, one conditional on the other: family members acknowledge the conflation of character and role, at least in the case of some targeted family member, so that relations within the stability—its responsibilities *to*—are altered to allow for changes in the behavior and character (the cognitive-affective balance) of family members. The family's psychic economy otherwise reverts to its former equilibrium; the victimized member recovers his established role in the perception, feelings, and behavior of the others.

Certainly, one's character is often, or typically, shaped by one's role as an infant or child. This implies that character may be fused with role, rather than distinguishable and separable from it. Should we generalize, saying that other principal aspects of character are determined subsequently by one's roles in school, work, or friendship? This would affirm (contrary to the paragraphs above) that character is not separable or even distinguishable from one's roles, except that character shows itself differently as one fills a particular role. There are these two, plainly opposed lines of thought: we emphasize the integrity (the idiopathy) of character in order to distinguish and separate it from its roles; or we tell a more complicated story, saying that a developing character is enlarged and articulated by the succession of roles it occupies. One is different after five years in the army, and different after raising one's children. The roles are past, but their effects endure, because one's stock of information is enlarged, and because habits and values are altered. It may be said that these alterations are traces of the former role. This is right if it means that character was altered by the role. It is wrong if meant to imply that each of us is a kind of mechanical toy that sings one or another song if one of a range of buttons is pushed. Roles are not so many separate tracks or tapes stored within us, each one set to play if the stimulus is right. We learn roles, and they do change us; but we integrate the information, attitudes, and skills learned from them into our stock of other beliefs, attitudes, and skills, even before we have abandoned the role.

Why emphasize one side, then the other—character or role—as though the balance of their relation eludes us? There is an explanation and solution for this indecision. I suggested in Chapter One that the formation of sustainable systems requires the nesting of lower-order systems in a progression of systems before either the highest-order system of the sequence or its lower-order constituents can be stabilized: molecules are ordered as cells, cells as tissues, and tissues as organs; but none of these systems is stabilized until the organs are joined as a self-nourishing, animal body. Similarly, character is not stabilized short of the higher-order systems in which characters are engaged: namely, the human societies where individuals have roles. This explains the equivocal answers to questions about the separability of character from role. For, yes, character is separable from roles, as a man may be fired from his job. Yet some of the man's habits, or even the style of his character, may be his learned response to a role. Separating the man from his job is often devastating, because it decouples him from the context where his character is stabilized.

Accordingly, we acknowledge the inseparable but complementary consti-tuents of the tension within us, starting with these three marks of character. *First,* cognitive-affective balance has an integrity which does not reduce to the one or many roles in which the individual participates, because each integrates his or her several roles in distinctive ways. Differences in information and skills ex-plain the difference. Or we have the same information and skills, but we value and rationalize these roles differently: the costs and rewards of doing one thing or another are different for you and me, because your hierarchy of attitudes is different from mine. *Second,* one's distinctive character is, in part, the conse-quence of having various roles, while never satisfying them exactly. (The con-vergence of character and role during infancy disguises this elementary differ-ence.) Perceiving this imperfect fit provokes reflection: we distinguish ourselves from our roles, thereby confirming that each of us is more and other than the role at issue. There is further evidence of this integrity in persons who decline desirable roles, preferring circumstances that may seem to lack the status and advantages of significant roles. (Think of Spinoza declining a university ap-pointment.) *Third,* the difference of character and role energizes our initiatives. For there are two sources of energy: one—any role—imposes regularizing be-haviors; the other expresses each character's singularity, its desire to discover and express something that is stubbornly peculiar to itself. One is a conscientious objector during a popular war; or we decline the assigned roles in order to go as far as we need to go before joining others for an undertaking that suits us. Re-versing the emphasis, we describe character as the executive power for organiz-ing time or energy in order that the appropriate information, skills, and atti-tudes are brought to bear as one fills successive roles: one is, alternately, parent, worker, spouse, and friend. Other people perceive us as filling one role or an-other. They may glimpse the supervening character; but they see it plainly only as they follow us through several roles, remarking the pattern of our initiatives and responses. We too may lose sight of ourselves while obsessed with the du-ties, opportunities, or insults of a particular role.

Do we, nevertheless, touch or hear the part of us that is more or other than a role-player? Do we know—rather than merely exhibit—the hierarchy of atti-tudes and values that makes us distinct? Probably, no one has a comprehensive idea of the attitudes and values, information, and skills that make him or her different, despite Descartes' and Sartre's claim that everyone can have a com-prehensive perception of him or herself.[14] What would we discover if they were right? Someone who is multiply engaged, someone whose moments of personal consolidation come sporadically or cyclically after engagements—roles—that change him or her. We would never discover the fully formed, freestanding individual of atomist theory. Mill supposed that freedom to unite with others is the third region of liberty, one that comes after liberty of thought and liberty to pursue ones tastes.[15] We are, he believed, fully formed before we enter the contractual and ad hoc associations from which we disengage ourselves, unscathed, when our aims are satisfied. This is an atomist fiction if one's cognitive-affective posture is formed as one occupies a diversity of social roles, especially those of child, student, worker, and friend.

Every child's development within a family (of some kind) is a case in point. His or her character is distinguishable and sometimes separable from the systems in which he or she has roles; but character is not stabilizable apart from every role. Family is an intermediary stage in the progression that engages human bodies after they stabilize and terminate the one from molecules, cells, tissues, and organs. The families that engage us are the incubators of our character and a first domain in which to stabilize and show it; character is merely incipient in the progression that terminates in whole bodies. Cognitive-affective posture is never secure, this implies, short of the social contexts—families or other higher-order human systems—that are self-sustaining. Is this odd, or plainly mistaken, because families dissolve all around us? Neither one: it means that character is feeble rather than firm for want of the context where it is first acquired and secured.

2. Friendship

Friendship is an early and important intrusion in lives that are formed by the demands of a family. Here is the first extra-familial association, the first alternative stable system having expectations different from the now formulaic ones of a child's family. Many of the powers required to sustain this association are already present in the child's stock of information, attitudes, and skills; but there are some differences. For no matter how flexible a three- or five-year-old may be, he or she is puzzled somewhat by the responses of other children. Having to reply to them is a vital provocation to psychic growth: the child extends himself, trying different strategies as he secures the interest, affection, or loyalty of his playmates.

Doing this has several effects. *First* is the stabilization of this new engagement, with its demands and satisfactions. *Second* is the extension of a still pliable and teachable cognitive-affective posture. *Third* is a certain flexibility and space that the child acquires in relation to other family members. For the child discovers unfamiliar powers and responses within him or herself. Given these strengths and the pleasure they evoke, he is better able to distinguish himself from his role within his family. Its demands are compared for the first time with personal preferences, or with responsibilities that have a focus separate from the family. More conscious of his own nature, the child learns—probably for the first time—that family relations are contingent and local, not necessary and universal. Satisfying those demands is not, always and everywhere, the necessary and sufficient condition for being oneself. Friendship is, therefore, both liberating and a cause for anxiety.

Families sometimes resent a child's friends, even to the point of punishing the child for wanting them. Still, parents disguise their anxiety, because they understand that friendship is a first step beyond the stability of the family into the freedom where the child chooses roles for him or herself. A child unable to distinguish character from role, a child whose character is only a reflection of the demands made within the family, is disabled from participating in other stabilities that are critical for his or her further development. The family's fears are infantilizing. They express the parents' own distress, especially fears about their worth, and fears that the child will abandon them. This anxiety is dangerous for children. They are crippled if their parents prevent them from participating in other systems. They become isolated, as remote from their parents as from everyone else. Since health is, in part, the ability to achieve one's own well-being, parents need to realize that the child's autonomy is a real but fragile power to move beyond this first, higher-order system—the family—into other, hopefully complementary systems.

Cognitive-affective balance is enlarged beyond family and friendship (though often by way of family and friends) as children learn the styles of production, play, discipline, and interpretation that distinguish the people with whom they live. Baseball is a team sport; there are no teams comprising only a shortstop. Learning such practices engages us in additional systems. Their diversity is legion; still, there is a smaller set of social tasks that is fixed by our individual and corporate needs. The latter include material wants, sexual passions, outlets for aggression, intellectual curiosity, and a need for social regulation. These are constants among us humans. The systems that express them often change, as television and computer screens replace books. The needs abide. The routinized behaviors that satisfy them are social, because we are not self-sufficient, and because behaviors we enjoy often please us more when they are done with other people. We satisfy our core interests by making alliances that are diversified internally by the complementary roles of the participants. These alliances are systems of a higher order. They include teams, companies, schools, governments, and religious communities. What follows is a survey of three critical social practices: work, government, and the use of myth.

3. Work

Skilled workers organize to produce food, clothing, and shelter, to teach, to heal, or to serve the myriad interests of a complex society. A few workers—chimney sweeps and shepherds, for example—are almost self-sufficient. But most work cannot be done at all, or done effectively, unless tasks are divided among workers whose skills and outputs are coordinated within networks of reciprocal causal relations. This interdependence has several implications: that we work within systems to produce things or services that are needed or merely wanted; that work engages and alters us; that we prepare ourselves for it by learning the skills it requires; and that we are good for something beyond ourselves, including the systems in which we participate, the other people with whom we work, the products we make, and those for whom we make them.

Atomists concede the need for skill and cooperation. They know about factories, equipment, suppliers, and costs. They resist the inference that the reciprocities of work established systems that have a reality distinct from their workers. Atomist paradigms enforce this skepticism. Imagine that someone who picks apples by himself finds others picking fruit from nearby trees or from the other side of his tree. Such people may find more complex work, work that requires cooperation with others; but, says atomism, their separability is uncompromised. Each one's career and objectives are different from those of his or her fellow workers, as workers prove when they disperse but survive. Something in this atomist gloss is confused: worker's bodies are separable; but where is the evidence that tasks required to achieve complex effects are also separable? I can wash dishes without you helping me, but I cannot wash them unless you bring them to me; nor can you put clean dishes on this restaurant's tables unless you get them from me. The owner can fire either of us; he could replace me with a machine and you with a cafeteria line; but he cannot maintain the current arrangement without a reciprocity like ours. It is the coordination of workers and the conditions for these reciprocities—in developmental histories, cognitive-affective postures, and social recognition and support—that atomists neglect.

Atomist theory (together with technology and economic circumstances) inspires the advice that children should train themselves for a succession of different careers. Atomists encourage the savvy contractors, whether doctors, lawyers, accountants, or engineers, who shun permanent jobs, preferring profitable short-term contracts. Like a commando, one parachutes into a job, does the work, and leaves. Such metaphors and examples illustrate the remaking of work in ways prescribed and justified by this atomizing conception of it. Atomism concedes the need for cooperation, skill, and even complementarities of skill, as rowers and a helmsman ride in the same boat. But so does a tape of popular music seem to be a continuous whole, though engineers have created it by splicing and overlaying lines and bars from disparate performances. The message is plain: apparent reciprocity disguises an aggregate. Hearing us converse, the atomist has a simple reduction: you talk, then I talk. Reciprocity—mutually modulating, causal relations—is ignored, thereby implying that the cogency of our successive replies is a mystery.

There is also this more pernicious effect: atomism discounts vital features of the people whose interactions create reciprocities. The pianist isn't just passing time; he plays to play well, to be heard, and to earn a response. Most workers don't want to be dropped into a context, then plucked out of it, like tubes in a socket. Fungibility is cost-effective only if money is the sole, or principal, measure of worth. Other costs include the degraded skills of workers, who learn that they are required to satisfy a moderate standard only, loss of skills for working with others, and the eroded commitment and demoralization of workers who know they are replaceable. Indeed, the atomist program for work culminates when separability and substitution dictate that employees be replaced by machines that do the "same" work at less cost. Where does this leave workers? Unemployed and deprived of the activity that is their principal mode of engagement in the physical and social world. Atomist ideas about us humans are, therefore, more than mistaken. They are a dangerous program for remaking work in response to economic and technological changes that make human workers expensive and dispensable.

Consider the effect of such ideas on children. Their first work is school. We may sugarcoat the early days and years of class, telling the child that these are times for playing, singing, and lunch; but he or she quickly learns that school is an introduction to systems where responsibilities to others are more urgent and abstract than those in the family. Requiring more than the pleasure of our company, teachers judge our work by standards we barely understand. There is also the ambiguity encouraged when teachers (like the parents and friends who have also committed this socially useful mistake) conflate the demands of character with those of role. The child is taught or infers that his or her character will be improved merely by satisfying the demands of teachers and staff. Most children learn to distinguish character from role, but the ambiguity remains a part of us and prepares us for work: there, too, we are judged by what we do. The years spent in school are preparation for working together, for now as then, we are mutually committed and reliably prepared. Work, this implies, exploits the moral character, as well as the talents, of people whose years have been spent preparing for it. How much of this moral character survives when work has become ephemeral, or when sweatshops displace businesses that respected their workers?

Mill's atomism is strangely oblivious to the developmental and moral nuances of people who anticipate the fellowship, fruitfulness, and discipline of work that is shared. Could it be that his atomism expresses the disengagement of people who don't have to work because some others work so well. Isn't it true that most Americans don't worry about growing their own food, because American farmers do it for them? The people supported by a society's wealth are thought to be some of its luckiest members; but they risk being extruded from its productive life. This is not because investing capital is ineffective; rather, because investing socializes wealth, not its owner. Investors may study their opportunities carefully, using newspapers, libraries, and advisors to make their choices. All this is socializing; but all of it is distinct from the activity that investors generate. They relate to that activity as Aristotle's unmoved mover relates to the natural world: it supplies the initial impulse to changes in which it does not otherwise participate. Investors (*qua* investors) have this same marginal status relative to the projects they support. Imagine a medical school named for its donor. Students and teachers thrive; but he—an amateur cook and gardener, an avid reader, volunteer, and letter-writer—has no place among them. This generous man must learn to prize himself in the absence of an affiliation that would use his talents for the benefit and in the company of others.

We who fear hard work or value no work that is not highly paid should reconsider our priorities. Our alternatives are spare. First are tasks that are boring, dangerous, or revolting: perhaps most work falls into one of these categories. Second is leisure (often aimless) that kills retirees. Third is work that gratifies, work that is driven by passion, distinguished by the talents it exploits, and supported by the worker's reciprocal relations to the other members of a team, craft, or profession. This last alternative is plain but elusive. Few of us realize all its parts, as miners know the pleasure of reliable mates but not that of cultivating their principal talents.

Many people, perhaps most, do not like the work they do. What would change these attitudes? One, morally vigorous response makes workers responsible for their attitudes: let them come to terms with their choices. Yet there is less "good work" available in the confluence where atomism, technology, and a concern for profitability have eradicated many opportunities for joining oneself reciprocally to people with complementary talents and aims. How shall we manage an economy so that workers can form systems that provide satisfying work? Employers are puzzled by the question. Why are they responsible for inventing work that better exploits the talents of the people they employ? Having work to be done, they offer it to qualified employees. Why are they obliged to make life interesting for their workers? Workers often agree. Where employment is insecure and hard to find, they are grateful for whatever jobs they have. Matching talent to work, or militating for a society that does so, becomes the vocation of radical thinkers, including Plato and Marx. They believed that the reciprocity of roles is the best guarantee that workers shall have the fourfold satisfaction of using their talents for the benefit of those who enjoy them, with the support and companionship of other people, for benefits that support and secure them. We who confuse salary with satisfaction are almost oblivious to the benefits of reciprocity, and to the claim of Plato and Marx that this condition—like health and justice—is natural and ideal.

There isn't a simple solution to these oppositions. Most work was never gratifying, even when its reciprocities were secure. Who prefers digging subway tunnels to trading bonds? The latter is a subtle, abstract skill, one or more steps removed from the physical engagements—the factories, bridges, or schools—it supports. Work of this sort is preferred and esteemed, though its effects are ambiguous.

We prefer jobs that are less dirty, physically demanding, or dangerous, because of our intellectual and aristocratic traditions, and because nature intimidates us. We don't like being frustrated, engulfed, or defeated. We want to feel and believe that nature has been pacified and controlled, that we can safely turn our backs on it. We don't want to engage nature in the more direct way of sandhogs, firemen, farmers, miners, and fishermen. Working with things that resist us, things that are malleable to our hands and tools, they seem oddly primitive. Think of the great museums of tools—of *arts et métiers*. The work was (and is) often complicated, requiring different talents and several hands to do it. We who flee direct encounters with nature lose sight of these advantages. Better to be rich and leisured, or educated and exempt. We forget the satisfactions of productive physical labor and the work crews that are cherished as much for their fellowship as their efficacy.

Marx scorned factory work because it alienates us from nature, one another, and ourselves, while exploiting and degrading us in other ways. Salaries and work conditions are different and better now; but the repetition or ambiguity of many current forms of labor—what am I doing? why does it matter?—have the same enfeebling consequences for our beliefs, attitudes, and skills. The isolation of workers from one another is all the more extreme: think of people working at separate monitors. Pushing buttons, diverting streams of data, we relate to virtual rather than actual others. There are few supple skills here, less craft, and little participation in reciprocities enforced by loyalty, purpose, mutual reliance, friendship, and achievement. We who do these things may be more prosperous and longer-lived than fishermen or miners; but we have lost their skills and their firm social identities. Love and work, Freud said, are fundamental to our identity and well-being. This includes love for work mates and for the work we do together. But coal mining is deadly, whatever the courage and loyalty of the men who do it. It is hard to regret the machines that make these men redundant. And anyway, the coordination of workers and the elaboration of their talents are values that sometimes survive our technological victories. The crews of spaceships and submarines are not less skilled or coordinated for working in environments that are alien to our natural selves.

One imagines that the skills of such crew members are specialized to the degree that they could do no other job. Think of the apprentice who works at the side of an artisan, acquiring skills that prepare him for a specific task. Character and role should be nearly joined in him. It is not, because people are more plastic and teachable than is assumed when individuals are identified with one or the sum of their current roles. Some cooking students learn only the recipes they memorize. Other students learn the knack of cooking. They cook extraordinarily well, without books, wherever they find decent ingredients and implements. Plasticity is as much a function of attitude as of skill; having it or not is an effect of one's developmental history, not one that is learned for the purposes of any particular role. There is a similar point to be made about skills: most of the skills we learn, with the information and attitudes pertinent to them, have multiple applications. One may have them without also having or anticipating the role in which they would be deployed.

These are considerations that mark the line between character and role. Do we reduce, psychically and practically, to the roles for which we are prepared? Or is there something of us that resists this reduction? Personal experience speaks loudly to this point. Unable to conciliate character and role, I settle for goods that are mutually compromised: hating a job, I keep it because it pays the family's bills; but then I distance myself from it—saving a part of me. The elision of character and role is always mistaken. It neglects two things that are fundamental to cognitive-affective balance. First is the consideration that our several skills are not separate beads added to a string, each one making no difference to the others. There is an economy of skills, such that any new one may alter one or several already learned. A singer learns a new song in a way shaped by some other songs she knows; the startling rhythms of this one alter her way of doing some of them. Surgeons accustomed to doing a procedure in one way learn a different one, and don't repeat the other. The previous technique nevertheless shapes, somewhat, their way of performing the new one. They profit from the tendency (of psychic economy) to conserve and simplify: we acquire new information, attitudes, and skills on a base that is already articulated in all three respects. For no one is the aggregate of skills required by different jobs; though each of us is more or less skilled at marshaling what we know and value in ways that are appropriate to particular roles.

The conflation of character and role also ignores this other aspect of our psychic economy. It concerns some more than others, but each of us reflects on things we have done or ought to do. Approving or regretting our deeds or choices, imagining the alternatives, we take stock of ourselves. Looking forward or back, we reorganize and alter our information, our attitudes, and even our skills. We take the measure of ourselves, our place in the world, or our options for the future. This may be a reflection saved for leisure or one provoked by some unexpected opportunity or disaster. Either way, these reflections have the effect of distancing us from our diverse associations and roles, one or all of them. That these moments occur is plain to every child at odds with parents or school, to every spouse who has left a marriage, to every priest at odds with his church. Were role the only determinant of character, these altered perceptions of what one is and might yet be could not occur; or they could only be moments of doubt or disengagement that prepare us to swing from one role to another. But this is not so: not every one enters a new marriage at the moment of leaving an old one; most people in this perplexity spend considerable time stewing in their own juices, testifying to a power common to all of us. Do computers think? They do have representations, and they do calculate. What they lack is psychic identity, an identity conditioned by this power for reintegrating information, attitudes, and skills.

We want character to dovetail with role, without reducing to it. Both interests are satisfied if there is a good fit between a worker's cognitive-affective balance—his information, attitudes, and skills—and his work. These accommodations are never perfect, because each one's psychic posture leaves him somewhat unprepared for the work at hand. A friend's father went to sea at the age of ten—there was no food at home. This sailor didn't please the captain, who kicked him regularly with his wooden shoes. The boy was wretched and bruised when he disembarked a month later. He did better as time passed, himself becoming a successful captain. What had changed, his character or his way of fulfilling the role? Character—cognitive-affective balance—is plastic. It has developed over time, and it changes somewhat as circumstances require. But character has an inertia and vector of its own. We cannot remake ourselves for every occasion or for every job. What happens when work requires reciprocities that we cannot satisfy? We change enough to satisfy these demands; or we quit or are fired because we fail to do so. Too often, the reciprocities creating a higher-order, more complex stability are costly to the constituent subassemblies: we who need work suppress every contrary impulse in order to satisfy the demands of the job, though we are crippled—and angry. We go through the motions, convincingly, though our duties—our responsibilities *to*—violate our beliefs, inclinations, and self-esteem. We realize that the character qualifying us for participation in a system is rarely or never suited exactly for the role played there. No wonder that atomism was contrived to justify our flight from odious roles.

We sometimes believe that character and role may be perfectly reconciled, as Plato and Augustine supposed that harmony—justice—is an ideal that falls just the other side of our ability to make it actual. They were mistaken: there is no such peace, or there is little of it in the relations of us humans to the higher-order systems formed for the purposes of work. Most of us feel used by our jobs, without power to alter the rhythm of the system that employs us. We want our money or our peace, when we cannot have both. When family members misconstrue one another, there is family therapy to ameliorate the confusion of character and role. Arbitration panels having members from union and management are an analog, though few managers (or family members) concede that the roles demanded by a work routine should be appraised or modified because they violate the cognitive-affective postures of their workers. Sensitivity to these conflicts begins to affect managerial thinking, because of the increasing numbers of women at work. Routines that were required of men seem inappropriate for women, so roles are altered to suit the character of the workers who fill them. Here is a place where men—often too stolid and fearful for their livelihoods—can profit from a sympathy they would not ask for themselves.

We should expect a comparable revelation as managers discover that roles made obligatory for the purposes of work cannot suppress the diversity of roles for which workers are qualified. Why is it that workers fail to suppress other interests in order to devote every waking hour to doing or thinking about their jobs? Because there are other tasks for which our cognitive-affective postures prepare us, roles we fill in order to satisfy firmly established personal interests (including other social roles). Here, too, the concerns of women raise the issue to public attention. Women are expected to have and care for children, so that demands for maternity leave and child care alter private and public policy. There is no equivalent biological and social imperative peculiar to men, although there may be any number of deeply held interests—not only a father's concern for his children—that justify an equivalent recognition. Managers nevertheless affirm, and workers usually agree, that the corporate interest supersedes all others. Workers (both men and women) do as they are told, for the interest of the business, its suppliers, and its customers, and because of fear they will be out of work for promoting personal interests to an equivalent status. What could justify this self-denial, prudence apart? Only the willingness to conflate character with role. Some workers do have positions that use their best talents, while gratifying moral and aesthetic needs within a network of reciprocities. Think of celebrated teachers, concertmasters, athletes, and craftsmen. In luck or sagacity, these workers address the world from the perspective of work they like and a supporting team. Most of us are not so perfectly adjusted. Work is not the one satisfaction in our lives; parts of us are suffocated if work dominates us at cost to every other interest and role. Character fairly screams its priority over role.

What do these proposals tell us about workers who are set apart from other people by their vocations? Writers find burrows or barriers by which to isolate themselves from other people and duties; writers, especially, make an art of conflating character with role. Still, a writer's thinking is not a daydream. He has learned from other people. His thinking is a response to them. He finishes his manuscript and submits it for publication. He waits for objections and answers the ones he gets. The author oblivious to his predecessors and his possible public is rare. Most work within a system of relations, not all of them reciprocal, because some interlocutors are dead. Others (he hopes) aren't yet born. This too is a social act.

This mix of ideas about work comes to resolution in two questions that are common to all the environments where work is done: namely, is reciprocity good for us; and how, if it is, should we promote or preserve work that requires it? Answers to the second question are recommendations, not proofs. They are policies for ordering social life in the one way or the other: toward atomist singularity or reciprocity. Shall we encourage styles of work that isolate workers from one another, or should we create reciprocities that reward talent, purpose, discipline, and our desire for fellowship?

4. Citizenship

Citizenship is a condition—the citizen has rights and duties—predicated on a relation. This relation, like those of family, friendship, and work, locates us within a system of several or many parts. The system may be as small as a neighborhood or club, as vast as a nation-state, or as inclusive as the world community. One is a "good citizen," whatever the scale or purpose, if one does such things as make the system work. My concern is more restricted: I shall be writing of those political associations—states—that create the civil status described as *citizenship*.

States are often identified with a certain history or bordered terrain, with a culture, or with economic, military, or religious power. These are established and legitimate ways to think of states. But my point of reference is different. *States emerge,* as I shall be writing of them, *when some or all their people organize themselves for self-regulation.* They choose rules for conducting themselves and officers to oversee the tasks of self-regulation. Citizens are members and participants in states. It is their status and behaviors that concern me.

When is a citizen responsible to the state? At every moment, one may say: the good citizen's actions always satisfy the state's laws, whatever his motives, be they fear or approval. Lawful behavior is no trivial basis for appraising citizens when many of us break laws, from careless habit or because we calculate a personal advantage. Nevertheless, this emphasis is odd: stopping at red lights seems too slight a basis for proving our citizenship. We don't break laws for the reason that we were taught not to do such things, parents and lawmakers having understood that it is better (and cheaper) to use habit and conscience, rather than police and penalties, to enforce laws. But then the purpose of our behavior may be lost on us: we may suppose that good conduct is important only because it satisfies us, not because it is required of citizens. We forget that one earns a citizen's rights only as one's behavior satisfies the states's laws.

Lawful behavior is one of a citizen's principal duties to the state. Some other duties—to pay taxes, vote, serve on juries, or in the military—apply more sporadically. Indeed, citizens in democratic states may ignore or avoid these duties most of the time. No one is required to vote; service in the military may be voluntary; jury duty is easily avoided; taxes can be minimized. A state is shortsighted if it consigns these burdens to the margins of awareness—as when the draft is replaced by an army of volunteers. Extend the requirement for military or other service to men and women, and it seems a reasonable way of recruiting everyone to national service, hence to the shared experience of participation in national life. Cancel or minimize such obligations, and we eliminate civic duties and roles from the information, values, and skills required of citizens. They become indistinguishable—in respect to behavior and cognitive-affective postures—from the permanent visitors who also pay their taxes and obey the laws.

The idea and demands of citizenship are equivocal. This is sometimes the engagement of people who cooperate for common aims that include jury duty and military service. Or (within industrial democracies) citizenship is a permit to live and participate in an ample economy. Or it is principally the rite of committing oneself to public symbols. Citizenship of the first and second kinds is continuous with the practical, instrumental character of family, friendship, and work. Like them, it requires complementarity of roles: you do this, I do that, and we get a result that is satisfactory to both of us. The state, too, may be established by the complementarity of roles established in the give-and-take of everyday, productive life. But citizenship becomes the apotheosis of a different—symbolic—style of participation when these opportunities for mutual engagement—including jury duty, taxes, voting, or the army—are suppressed or ignored. We have an example of the symbolic state when we stand as the national anthem is played, thereby expressing our shared ideals, confirming our solidarity. Or we stand as a challenge to other citizens: demonstrate your loyalty as I show mine. Family, friendship, and work also rely on symbolism—whether birthdays, flowers, or gold watches—to support their reciprocities. Still, the similarity is shallow. Families use symbols of affection or respect to support or embellish relations that are reciprocal and productive. A citizenry reduced to emblems substitutes gestures for reciprocities. It sentimentalizes an affinity for which there may be little effective history. Having no experience of working together, each fearing the other's alien ways and hostility, we look for ways to neuter our differences. Mutual fears are reduced as we commit ourselves to a common ideal, or to its banners and rhetoric. These affiliations sometimes have an exalted aim, not only that of reducing our fears of one another. But devoting ourselves to the universal rights of mankind, or merely to life and liberty for our neighbors, is less common, though more stabilizing, than using flags and songs as a test of loyalty.

Societies differ as they use symbols in the one way or the other: to regulate the participants or to intensify and secure their sense of affiliation. Both uses imply that symbols are *signs*; but there is this difference. Signs of one sort are thoughts or words used to inform the members about salient states of affairs and thereby coordinate their behaviors. Signs of the other kind—symbols—have significance: they express or portend something valued. These are signs (patriotic songs, for example) that provoke the reverence first reserved for their associates (the state). Compare words used as signifiers: they are signs of something else, not emblems deserving reverence for themselves. They rarely provoke veneration or fear. (The Hebrew Tetragrammaton is an exception.)

Citizenship invokes signs of both kinds: there are the mutually informing words exchanged within a trial as lawyers and judge inform a jury and the words used to intensify affinities, beliefs, or values. We expect democracies to emphasize the use of signs as signifiers, because citizens (whether acting for themselves or the state) need information, accurately conveyed, about the rules of behavior, the plans of their fellows, and the availability of resources (as Dewey and Habermas rightly say[16]). This emphasis on informative signifiers—intensified by distrust of signs used to evoke mob feeling—prompts us to overlook the vital role of symbols and significance in societies of every sort. Yet their importance is magnified in societies that fear disintegration, a risk exaggerated by theories that reduce societies to aggregates. There are symptoms of this fear in citizens who react to their attenuated civic relations by emphasizing the symbols of their unity. Flags, sacred documents, and festivals may be gestures in a void. Compare them and their effects to the cooperative endeavors that require reciprocity among the people so engaged. We rightly worry that citizenship is being reduced to symbols, lip service, and a formality.

There are few occasions (short of elections, wars, or other disasters) when citizens prize the state in the ways that people care for their families. For the reciprocities of a small group are hard or impossible to duplicate among the members of a state. Submission to symbols becomes a substitute for the loyalties that would be created if reciprocities among citizens were to promote each one's wellbeing. Words used as symbols are an important substitute, as when citizens interpret their civic roles in ways specified by political or historical narratives. Think of stories about Lincoln or Paul Revere: these narratives explain who and where we are, and what we are responsible for doing. They confirm us in doing what we may habitually have done, though now our behavior is informed by a meaning or value that was forgotten or never heard. We also confirm one another's perception of the stories and their meanings. For I repeat to you the story I know, one that you too have heard but believe all the more firmly when someone repeats it to you. Like gossip, the narratives are told and retold, until everyone hears and believes them. This is the causal reciprocity of symbol telling and learning: each repeats to the other what he or she has learned; everyone comes to believe a story that has so many sponsors.

These meaning-bestowing narratives give substance to behaviors that would otherwise reduce to gestures. For now saluting the flag has the symbolic effect of exhibiting our shared values. We are loyal. Those who share our values bond to us as we cleave to them. Why are we so easily roused by flags and anthems? What provokes each of us to identify him or herself with the state? Every sustainable social system solves this puzzle by exploiting our need for idealizations. These ideas, suffused with reverence, are easily sparked. They are levers of political control available to the officers of nation-states.

Despotisms respond with rote learning and obligatory hero worship. Democratic societies are more demanding. They require that feelings help us concentrate on a practical aim: namely, a complex act of self-regulation, one that explains, justifies, and coordinates our affiliation. Songs and flags are its tokens, but none of its substance. Older democracies use history to focus the attention of their citizens. American students take (or took) civics classes as a way of informing themselves about the historical bases for affiliation among us. For civics, more than history, is the ideology of the American state. It supplies the strategy and rationale for our participation in a network of reciprocal obligations: responsibilities to one another and the state are to determine our style of self-regulation.

What do citizens learn in a careless democracy? To love their freedom and abhor interference, but little or nothing about conditions for the reciprocities that create mutual respect among citizens and legislation for the public good. Dewey, writing about the eclipse of the public, worried that factionalism and mutual ignorance would destroy the conditions for freedom among us. There would be songs and flags, rhetoric and social intimidation, but no public of self- and mutually regulating citizens. Each one's cognitive-affective balance would lack the information, habits, and attitudes that would enable him or her to participate in a system that organizes itself for making and administering a code of public behavior.[17]

How should democratic states engage their citizens in the acts of self-regulation—in government, the army, or courts—that are the life of the state? How should they defend themselves from the inattentiveness of their people? States having stable, homogeneous populations, a longer history, and a smaller terrain are more effective than vast, pluralistic democracies at encouraging the active participation of their citizens. Constitutional monarchies have the additional advantage of a king or queen who personifies the state. An accessible monarch, one who gladly participates in the ceremonial occasions that relate citizens to the crown, becomes the paradigmatic public person. Add pomp and privilege to the monarch's role, and every citizen enjoys, vicariously, the special treatment received by a person who is—almost—like himself.

What can a popular democracy do to recommend itself when there is no monarch to evoke awe or affection and no despot to provoke fear? It should uniformly impose those kinds of service which enable every citizen to identify him or herself as a, sometime, officer of the state. It should promote reflection on the advantages of citizenship, and its conditions. Newspapers and political parties should regard political reflection—what are our priorities and circumstances, what requires fixing, and how might we fix it?—as a principal task. Every child's parents should have been educated by a political process that encourages discussion and participation in the practice of government. Do these things, and citizenship would no longer be a nearly free ride in a system that wins our loyalty merely because it feeds us well. Despotic governments never hesitate to remind citizens of their benefits and responsibilities. A democracy sabotages itself if it does not encourage an equivalent awareness.

Why are democracies slow to require the participation of their citizens? One reason is the dominance of economics over politics: the people of industrial democracies demand a productive economy, while accepting whatever apparent version of democracy delivers material well-being and the open playing field that rewards initiative. A reason more critical here is the confusion of character and role. Democracies are devoted to respect for the autonomy of persons (hence character) and are unwilling to compromise it by the imposition of unwelcome roles. Yet democracies are self-subverting if they neglect a condition for two things they prize: namely, the elaboration of character in their citizens and the state's own existence. The condition for both is the set of reciprocal relations that make citizens responsible to one another and to this corporate entity, the state. Neglecting this point is a persistent nominalist error, the one of denying the reality of relations and the duties they imply. This error is most consequential in democratic states that carelessly ignore their citizens' public duties. This is self-defeating, because the state is responsible for fulfilling such duties, and because it ceases to exist—as a democratic state—if the duties are not performed by the reciprocally joined citizenry. What is better: not to perform the tasks, have them performed poorly by people (whether mercenaries or bureaucrats) who feel no responsibility for them, or have them done well by citizens (*qua* citizens)? Who has more interest than a citizen (again, *qua* citizen) in the performance of those acts of self-regulation that express the defining aim of a democratic state: government for and by the people? How long can a democratic state survive while one of its political parties constantly repeats that government, the agency of public self-regulation, is the enemy of the people? America sometimes tests the limit.

How is this political error represented in our cognitive-affective postures? Its site is the place where affect supersedes understanding, where significance overrides signification. Think of Fourth of July celebrations, or of flags displayed on bumpers or porches. Such symbols and the reverence they inspire are less critical for the well-being of the state than the citizenry's respect for public duties, and the learned aptitudes for satisfying them (by serving on juries or holding public office). But evidently, acquiring these virtues cannot be left to luck or impulse. Citizens do not typically have or care to use these skills, unless we organize to learn and apply them.

There is also this final point. Persons are animal bodies with specially elaborated insides (cognitive-affective postures) and a complementary, self-created outside, one of families, friendships, work places, and government. Accordingly, *person* signifies systems that are uniquely elaborated, not a unique, ontological type. This is a richly honorific word, one that implies standards for treating other humans and standards for understanding ourselves. The moral it expresses reminds us of a question that is unresolved in this section and the one before: Have we done justice to ourselves as persons if we fail to engage one another in reciprocities that are sustaining in the case of family and friendship, productive in the case of work, and self-regulating in the case of civic virtue and government? Is it good enough that we be self-sufficient and socially marginal (as every one is, if atomists have their way), or does personhood imply the obligation to support other persons by participating in reciprocities that nourish them as well as ourselves? Neither strategy can be justified merely by a "conceptual analysis" of the word *person*. We do better to take our directives from the accurate appraisal of what we are and may be. Which of these options describes conditions for more ample personhood? The issue is considered again in Chapter Four.

5. Myth

Symbols and significance may suffuse our thinking about the state, but eventually the pragmatic use of signifiers overtakes us. Our notion of family may be dominated by the obligations of ancestor worship; but members also communicate about matters of everyday concern—food and shelter, for example—so that signifiers, not symbols, are critical for family discourse. There are many such examples, and all of them encourage us to expect that actual circumstances and the words used to signify them will break through the haze of valorizing stories. This doesn't always happen, because perception is often warped by our culture's answers to two questions: namely, what are we? and what is our place in the world? Both questions barely disguise the hope that what we are and do is important in some enduring way. Is there, perhaps, an ample narrative that confirms our value by making us the pivot in its story about the world? Science also asks these questions, but its answers are disappointing, because it suppresses or eliminates the obsession with personal value. Astronomers and biologists may believe without discomfort that we humans have no greater value than mosquitos from the perspective of nature at large. Others are scandalized. We want firm evidence of our worth. Where scientific inquiry fails to supply it (because it distinguishes facts from values, and restricts itself to testable hypotheses about facts), we resort to myth.

Myths are odd stories. They tell of powers and events for which there is no evidence but the myths themselves. Why believe them? Why, in particular, should the mythmaker believe his or her own story? The author's confidence would sag if everyone hearing a myth were to scoff. But confidence soars when the myth is believed and retold so that the mythmaker hears a richer, more compelling story from those to whom he told a simpler one. This is causal reciprocity as it creates communities bound by a shared interpretation. Mythmaking sometimes infuses family, friendship, work, or citizenship with glorifying histories, rationales, feelings, and affiliative attitudes. Or it creates distinctive religious sects that incorporate all or part of these other systems. Participants are guaranteed the elevated self-esteem that derives from membership in a self-valorizing community: we know our importance in the whole. This sometimes resembles Rousseau's exultation when he described the ascent from barbarism and the state of nature to civility and the social contract. More often, people joined and valorized by a myth are less certain of their worth or place. Wanting a rationale for who, what, and where they are, they seize on a myth and the social system it promotes, be it a religion, a state, or a cult.

Many of us participate, by choice or chance, in one or another of these communities, so we have a criterion for distinguishing ourselves from outsiders. Each member's self-regard is enhanced, because the esteem of the members is conditional and reciprocal: I value you for believing as I believe and for valuing me. Our self-esteem may also vary in proportion to our hostility toward those who are excluded: nonbelievers are pariahs; we, the community of believers, are ennobled. (Think of heaven, then of the beliefs and practices required for going there.)

This way of reassuring ourselves is open to everyone. Where any two people can join to tell a story that interprets the world for them, where each can reinforce the other's security and esteem by retelling the story, we have the possibility for myriad stabilities. Systems of this kind—including collusive friendships and alliances nourished by exaggerated hostilities and fictive histories—are especially rigid: reality testing is too dangerous for them. Living within a myth, remaking their physical circumstances in ways it prescribes, the members punish, defy, or ignore their skeptics.

Such systems encourage the confusion of character and role. Tell the members that their characters are separate from such roles; tell them that having roles within such groups is no guarantee of virtue; and you make them fearful and angry. Allegiance to a football team, a faith, or a politician sets us apart by making us different and better than "them"—better, too, than our everyday selves. These loyalties are the angry, despairing reaction to a self-perception: we lack conviction of our personal worth or of the worth of our deeds and associations, though we respond vehemently to these doubts. We solve the conflict by engaging our humble selves in something grand, something whose myth-sponsored values may be visible only to the believers. We are bigger and better than we look.

IV. SELF-IDENTITY

Self-identity is complex, because each of us prepares for several or many roles. We are not surprised that some people are multilingual; this is (merely) a complicated cognitive skill. The integration of disparate roles (like the multiculturalism of contrary practices) is harder to explain, because it may require that a person's psychic posture accommodate itself to values that are mutually exclusive. The good father and neighbor is a professional hangman. His world is multicultural; his cognitive-affective posture is partitioned in ways that are appropriate to his roles within these several domains. Are his attitudes disconnected and cocooned? Is he oblivious to the contrariety of his values? The partitions in him are (presumably) repressions, so anxiety, rigidity, anger, self-disgust, and guilt are likely concomitants to keeping the attitudes separate. Cognitive-affective posture is, plainly, no harmony of parts. Yet, this man seems coherent and steady, not crazy or chaotic. He has a particular psychic shape and tone, despite the anomalous parts. What holds him together? It may be two things. First is the integrity of his cognitive-affective posture. It was achieved when successive accommodations and habits were established in him over the course of his developmental history. Second is the satisfaction experienced in his different roles. We know they stabilize him, however contrary they seem to us, because he begins to disintegrate if one or other is denied him. Character, this confirms, is distinct from one's roles, though roles are end points in the progressions that must be achieved if character is to be stabilized.

One wants to say (I do) that cognitive-affective balance is character, but why say it if the more accurate statement is that one's character is the psychic posture stabilized by one's roles? The first is not shorthand for the second. Still, we can say the first while intending the second, by analogy with the progression that terminates when cells, tissues, and organs are stabilized within bodies. Each of these intermediate stages has a structure and is a system without regard to the higher-order system in which it is a proper part. Yet, the integrity of these structures is provisional and conditional. For no structure intermediate within a progression is stable short of the highest-order system—the terminus—of the progression in which it is stabilized. (We ignore the possibility that a tissue is frozen or preserved in formaldehyde.) Character, this implies, requires socialization: it is not formed or consolidated apart from its roles in systems.

Roles supply the information, attitudes, and skills that are constitutive of character. Renouncing my roles, I suffer in two ways: first by losing whatever content and identity they provide, second by separating myself from people—the fellow members of systems—who confirm my worth. They may regard me as a renegade and an enemy, or—worse—as no one. How can I sustain my identity if all its contents derives from beliefs, attitudes, and behaviors appropriate to roles I abjure?[16] This dialectic—capitulate to others or choose a sullen isolation—seems unresolvable, though it is not. The distinction of character and role does not require that each of us be able to separate him or herself from every role: everyone declines many roles; most of us renounce roles we once accepted. Still, we cannot absent ourselves from every role, because character is acquired in a succession of roles, then exercised, sustained, and embellished in them or others. Many roles are imposed, not chosen, so that much of everyone's identity—as child to these parents, man or woman, English speaker, or citizen—precludes choice. It doesn't follow that we are victimized by such roles or that we cannot make them our own by embracing the tasks they enjoin, as we master a task or skill. The opposition of character and role is deflated whenever roles are sought or seized. Indeed, their apparent contrariety is merely the product of the analysis that sets one against the other. It is the complementarity of character and role, not their opposition, that distinguishes the acquisition of self-identity.

Character may have specific features in the absence of roles—as infants have distinctive personalities—but not content or direction. The roles that supply character's aims and content are, conversely, dominated by it. This is apparent in the distinctive way that roles are satisfied, in the significance that any role has for the person enacting it, in the resistance or pleasure that comes with filling a role, and in the relative priority that one ascribes to his or her roles. (Character's domination of role does not imply that one dominates a system's other members.) These considerations promote a balance: the character determined by its roles integrates, interprets, and enjoys them on its own terms.

Descartes and Freud have taught us to believe that self-reflection alters us in desirable ways, so that we are less well formed if we do not introspect. Yet character's domination of its roles does not presuppose an altering, or merely observing self-reflection. For there may be little or no reflection when the information, attitudes, and skills appropriate to particular roles are acquired, or when constellations appropriate to disparate roles modulate one another within us. Like the weight-bearing structures of a building, these separate constellations pull and strain until a (usually) viable equilibrium is achieved. Some people—small children, for example—accept and integrate their roles without reflection; they may ignore the tensions generated by having to satisfy the opposed demands of disparate systems. Still, reflection clarifies attitudes, aims, and priorities. It helps us to distinguish roles from one another and from the systems that obligate us. It sometimes enables us to dominate our roles merely by affirming them, or to separate ourselves from inimical roles by altering or extinguishing the attitudes that provoked affiliation. Reflection, in either case, is deliberation that takes one's intentions, commitments, and values as its topic. Character is hereby exposed, articulated, and consolidated. We may be liberated or reconciled; or we despair, because circumstances oblige us to renounce a duty, with consequences we deplore.

Remember now the self-perception that Descartes used to establish the self's priority over socializing thought and feeling: I am, I exist, each time I pronounce or mentally conceive that I do. What am I? A thinker whose character is prior to, and independent of, anything I conceive or intend.[19] Atomists agree. They would have us use Descartes' argument to establish the priority of character—thought—over role, including thought's aims or affiliations.[20] The atomist strategy is faulty, because it misidentifies the inception of personality. For there is the difference, remarked above, between the terminal state of a human body having mental functions (it has progressed from cells, tissues, and organs to body) and the terminal state of a socialized mind (from an infant's psyche through the successive stages of its socialization). Having thought is an act or power of human bodies; it does not entail having character. Character is the achievement of the second progression cited above. It comes with the information, attitudes, and skills appropriate to one's roles. Accordingly, self-reflection testifies to the existence of an agent, but not to its power for reflecting on itself prior to the time of having roles and acquiring character. The empty, purified ("transcendental") self is a myth.

Atomists persist. Doesn't each of us sometimes distance him or herself from every role, while appraising them and him or herself? This often happens, though its implications are misleading: failure to participate actively in a system is not evidence that a role is rejected or that the thinker is not still constituted (in part) by the information, attitudes, and skills that qualify him or her for the role. Self-identity is fixed by cognitive-affective structure, including the meanings, values, and intentions that qualify one because of the systems that engage him. Turning on myself, I find these intentions (and whatever reaction they provoke in me). Fidelity to one's roles (hence reciprocities with other people) are rooted in the aims and duties they sanction, so that ruminating on them is evidence of a socialized self-identity. It is incidental that one is sullen or indifferent to one's roles: even the *Meursault* of Camus' *The Stranger* has no identity apart from the roles he rejects.[21] This is what he has become. Or as he should say: this is the I that I have become.

Consider, too, that roles give us sanity and self-esteem, whereas isolation makes us inconsequential and morose. Locate us in systems, add their power to our own, and we may become something grand. Forced to choose one side or the other—isolation or affiliation—we are depressed or elated. We need both sides, each moderating the other, if we are to avoid the extremes of this schizoid self-perception. A character displaced from every role is self-deflating and unstabilizable. How shall we promote well-being in creatures who know that they live briefly in a universe that is oblivious to them? Morale is all the more precarious if we owe nothing to others and get nothing from them.

What does reflection reveal about me? Principally, it exposes the virtual reciprocities in which I participate: including the values, meanings, and intentions appropriate to my roles, whether real or ideal. No matter that my roles are crippled or intact, rejected or affirmed. The separability of bodies is misconstrued as the separability of selves from their every role. Each of us locates him or herself within a network of affiliations.

Chapter 3 Sociality

Human societies gather and connect their members. A family, a friend-ship, a culture or religious sect, a company or school: these are stable systems. Each has a structure—proper parts joined by reciprocal causal relations—appropriate to its one or many tasks. Each relates to others, including systems that are independent of it and those to which it is related reciprocally, by nesting or overlap.

I. AFFILIATIVE BEHAVIOR

The parts of houses, animal bodies, and cars are joined mechanically, with cement, blood vessels, or bolts. Such connections—in a car's power train or between heart and lungs—make a system's reciprocities easy to see or understand. There is no comparable mechanical interac-tion in most human systems. The members' bodies are typically set apart. Their reciprocities—as in speech—seem ephemeral. Atomism gets much of its leverage from the observation that interacting humans are physically separate. Its next inference—that separability implies self-sufficiency—is mistaken, because people require the advantages of their mutual relations, as infants need their caretakers. Still, there is a point to answer. What glue turns an aggregate into a system, joining humans to one another? The principal factors are shared or complementary needs and interests. Discovering the personal advantages of reciprocity, we establish the relations that support or satisfy us. All this is obvious, but incomplete, because it doesn't explain the generation of our bonds. This is a question about *affiliation:* namely, how is it achieved?

Imagining a social world of people who are effectively but quietly joined, one recalls a Spanish saying: God creates them, and they find one another. This is not our world, where systems rely heavily on the chatter of gestures and words. One thinks of the many ways—including sighs, winks, smiles, embraces, and words—that people signal their needs, wants, or intentions. We are eased into our respective places by such expressions of feeling or desire and by words that appease, intimidate, flatter, or inform. We may eventually be bound by reciprocities made habitual, so that affiliation seems routine; but first comes the binding mix of affiliative language and feeling.

Affiliation is not usually thought to be one of the principal effects of linguistic usage. It is, because language overcomes our physical distance, by reducing our isolation and disguising our vulnerability. Affiliative uses of language—including tone of voice and the ideas expressed—are vital information to prospective companions. They help us to see others as desirable and safe, then to cooperate with them in ways that satisfy common or complementary wants and needs. Performative uses of language[1] should be seen in the context of our various affiliative behaviors. For performatives are a particular genre of affiliative behaviors. The relationships they structure are likely to have foundations that were established by other kinds of affiliative language: promising requires mutual trust between promisor and promisee, trust created by speech perceived as sincere and true. Performatives are likely to fail if these other words and gestures are absent.

II. ORGANIZATIONS AND ASSOCIATIONS

Systems having humans as their proper parts are created when people do together what they could not or would not do alone. There seem to be just two kinds of stabilities. Systems of one sort, including businesses, athletic teams, universities, and orchestras, are designed for specific aims. Call them *organizations*. Systems of the other kind are generated by the members' affinity for one another, or by their dedication to an objective or beliefs they share. Societies of this sort are *associations* (or *affiliations*). Mixed forms, including political parties and religions organized to propagate their beliefs, are a complexity that is mostly ignored here. Equally, nothing is said about classes of people, including consumers, students, and housewives. Such classes are often stable, but they are not stable systems in the respects considered in Chapter One: they are not stabilized by the reciprocal causal relations of their members.

Human social systems of both kinds have all or some of these ten features:

1. Causal Reciprocity

One may assume that societies are created as their laws are formulated and applied, as people assemble where the rule of law establishes their mutual rights and duties. This legalistic persuasion overlooks the many systems that are created merely because common interest or need drives people to take up and sustain their reciprocities. It ignores the productive activities that are undertaken voluntarily (in tyrannies as well as democracies), without laws to urge them along. Systems are the sites for these activities: better, reciprocity in the conduct of these activities creates and sustains systems.

Systems of both kinds—organizations and associations—are constrained by limits on the mutual accessibility of interacting causes and by those limits on size that are fixed by the available energy or by conditions for its efficient use. Equally, these two kinds of system are susceptible to the same failings. There may be a lack of balance between mutual duties and rights: one side is obliged, the other is exempt. Or, one of us is able but unwilling, distracted, or incompetent. You say "Go!," but I don't understand or move. A system survives if its reciprocities are mostly unproblematic. It disintegrates if reciprocity is confounded because a system's parts don't respond to one another.

2. Purpose

Organizations have objectives that are specific or determinable. Winning games is one; governing, as realized variously by cleaning streets or raising an army, is the other. The aim of associations is the fellowship that enhances the well-being of their members. This is the mutual mirroring of friends or the affinity of people who defer to powers invoked by their shared beliefs—a god, for example. Organizations cease to exist when their task is accomplished; they behave as before, though the need is past, or they find some other aim: the charity that raised money for a disease now cured supports a different, still dangerous ailment. The aims of associations are realized merely by their existence. Let religion be our example. Its interpretations and rituals sacralize the lives of believers, though other interests sometimes overlay this one, as happens when believers, coupling association with organization, work to convert the heathen. Their passion hides an anxiety: beliefs that others doubt may not be true. For remember that associations are formed and secured when each member is stabilized in his or her beliefs (and more fundamentally his or her self-esteem) by the agreement, appreciation, or consent of another. Nonbelievers are virtual heretics, because their failure to believe is a tacit rebuke to those who do. Believers in some cultures easily tolerate dissenters. Others are uncomfortable until nonbelievers are hidden or removed.

We may believe that systems succeed or fail because of the quality of their aims or because circumstances are more favorable to good aims than to bad ones. But nature precludes only contradictions (there are none); it tolerates malign objectives if they are cleverly managed. Expensive aims are purged—no strawberries grown on ice floes—because effective reality testing discourages systems from adopting aims they cannot achieve at reasonable cost.

3. Design

Organizations, but not associations, have designs appropriate to their aims, as restaurants are organized to serve their customers. Members—workers—have differentiated roles; the system's aim is achieved by coordinating their work. Design precedes the organization, as in Plato's *Republic;* it is discerned and used regulatively after a time of trial and error; or the members are oblivious to the plan that organizes them. Either way, a design should not be inefficient because of roles that are not well differentiated or well-ordered. It should not be self-defeating, because one effort cancels another. It should not be impractical, because confounded by its circumstances (for example, any plan for a transatlantic highway). Compare the serenity of associations. Reciprocity in them is the mutual confirmation of believers or the empathy of friends. Their inertia is evidence of their efficiency. They are hard to divert.

Associations are more amorphous than organizations, because the efficiencies of a well-calculated design are irrelevant to systems that have no aim but the one of fellowship or shared commitment to a belief or practice. The members of a religious sect may be happy in their homogenized tens or millions, whatever their apparent disarray. Fan clubs intensify the feelings of their members because of a shared idealization, not because they are well organized. Or think of a crowd that passes from disorder to the solidarity that shouts with one voice. Some of us turn cold, because we dislike the suspension of judgment and reserve. The pressure of bodies, rhetoric, or song makes other people delirious. This is their only role: each provokes the others.

4. Role

Each of a human social system's participants—proper parts that are individuals or social systems—has, in effect, an in box and an out box, one for demands that others make on this member's time and skills, the other for his, her, or its demands on them. These two—specific duties and specific rights—define the role of each participant in a reciprocity. An organization's members have specialized, complementary functions appropriate to the system's aim, roles such as parent and child or short stop and first baseman. An association's members have the same function: each is to the other as the other is to oneself. This homogeneity of function is especially notable within communities of believers. Imagine that two people, each one passionate in their common faith, discover one another. No skeptical doubt distracts them; each one's pleasure is magnified and confirmed when the faith is shared. Each is the mirror in which the other sees himself. These may be the fans of a team, collectors of postage stamps, or people whose lives are explained and valorized by a creed or cosmology. Interests differ among systems, but members of an association have the same function: one encourages another by valuing the same things. There are many societies of this sort, including Democrats, royalists, and the practitioners of scientific method. Each member sees his or her attitude, practice, or belief confirmed by the allegiance of other members. Liking this displaced image of himself braces his resolve.

5. Circumstances

No system is self-sufficient without regard to context, because each one derives its energy and material from sources distinct from itself. Organizations are shaped by their circumstances when their aims require that they make a difference there, as farming is different in Iowa and the Garden of Eden. Context is more incidental to many associations, because their purpose is limited to the mutual effects of the members. They may be altogether indifferent to their circumstances, even to the point of imagining that they derive no material benefit from them: we say that friendship survives altered circumstances, and that eternal love is self-sufficient.

This distinction between organizations and associations may seem badly formed when some associations are dedicated to changing their circumstances. The societies one is likely to have in mind—Greenpeace or the ASPCA—are organizations by the criteria proposed above, not associations. These are instances of a mixed form, both organization and association: they are designed for a task, but there is mirroring, hence its stabilizing effects, among their members. Families are another example of this kind. As organizations, they are subject to context (the schools available to their children, for example); as associations, they may be bound affectively without regard to circumstances.

6. Officers

Some organizations dispense with directors, as when the NBC Symphony named itself the Symphony of the Air and carried on without a conductor after Toscanini died. Reducing managers may enhance a system's efficiency. Too little management encourages inefficiency or stasis: the leaderless orchestra was best when playing familiar music. Administrators are vital to complex organizations, though leadership is more ideal than real in systems that are choked to death by manager-barons: one thinks of university deans. Associations that have no ulterior aims—religious fellowships and friendships—dispense with administrators.

7. Passion

Organizing provokes the instrumental thinking that most of us do well. Given a problem, we solve it by coordinating the relevant pieces or people. We may appreciate the efficiency, though we reject the aim. Associations seem mysterious, or irrational, by comparison. Passion for the solidarity of common meanings and feelings is their motor. This is an oddly inflected energy, one that is always recognizable to those who share it. No wonder associations have a life and persistence independent of rationally calculated means. The efficacy of most plans seems feeble when compared to a power that magnifies as it passes among the initiates. All of us know these passions and the self-confirmation one feels when having them. Only their expressions—family, friendship, or Nazi rallies—are different.

Associations are stabilized by the intensity of these feelings. Reasons may be given for joining an association, but feelings convince new members. Sour the feelings, and the membership falls away. Yet affiliations may persist for generations, centuries, or millennia. Think of the guilt and self-alienation of members who no longer feel the inherited loyalty. Why are these affinities so much deeper than the calculated loyalty of an organization's members? Because organizations are "merely" effective. Affiliations are expressed as resolve, perhaps joy, certainly as an intensity that appears to exceed its reason or cause. Religious fundamentalism has this quality: reason and argument are incidental to it. Not sharing the feeling, one is baffled by the persuasion, though no one prudent discounts the resolve of an association that organizes to promote its views. Some associations are unwieldy and hard to organize, their organizational structures weak and inefficient. Others include Maoist China, Khomeni's Iran, and the IRA.

An association's criteria for choosing its officers may be obscure. Do candidates qualify for positions because they know how to pursue an association's objectives in the style of organizations? Or do they earn selection because of passion for the beliefs or practices that bind the members? One thinks of saints, especially those in whom the members of an association discern the apotheosis of themselves. Compare an organization's managers. Efficiency is their principal virtue, though efficiency is a measure of technique. There is no mystery in it, and no reward beyond the emoluments required to win the manager's loyalty. He is revered as long as the job is well done. Doing it badly, he is fired. No one laments that our sun is dimmed; no one waits nervously to announce the coming of an inspired successor. We advertise for a replacement.

Associations are less practical and effective when seeking leaders, because the task is ambiguous—is one leading an association or an organization? It may be this confusion that makes associations so vulnerable to official abuse. The members affiliate because of their hope for fellowship or a shared idealization. Their enthusiasm and commitment are, they believe, the best part of themselves. They never expect that honest feelings may be turned against them, as they are when officers responsible for propagating a faith hijack it to enrich themselves. We get self-interested bureaucrats where there should have been holy men. Alienated believers reclaim the community in the name of its original ends; or they leave it.

8. Needs

Aims of all sorts, good and bad, are often thwarted, so that organizations come unstuck. This foundering is consequential if the defunct systems satisfied basic needs such as those for food, health, leadership, and defense. Their members reorganize, because the original vulnerability is unaltered. Thoreau couldn't do everything for himself: he went to Lenox for nails and other things he couldn't make.

Associations, too, are founded in the mutual needs of their members, though now the issue is solidarity in belief or feeling, not differentiation, purpose, and efficacy. Frightened when alone, we gain courage when our beliefs and feelings echo in the faces of our friends. This need endures, so that associations are less vulnerable to failure than organizations. They survive because the members recognize and bond with one another. Religious communities, with their valorizing morality, rituals, and cosmology, are a principal example. The heightened esteem of believers sometimes resonates in the magnified worth of their everyday reciprocities: what was done out of need becomes an activity sanctified by a higher purpose. Practical affairs are now re-perceived as expressions of a devotion. Life may come to seem empty without this orienting persuasion, as though no value deriving from family, friendship, work, or citizenship could justify a member's commitment in the absence of this orienting belief.

9. Loyalty

Members of both organizations and associations are loyal to their systems, though loyalty has a different character and conditions in the two cases. Loyalty to an organization is contractual: members require that the organization satisfy its aim, and that they be rewarded in money or prestige for contributing to it. Members may also have a deep affection for an organization, but their empathy for one another and their idealization of it are then evidence that this system has acquired the distinguishing features of an association. This other loyalty is less calculated, more simple and direct. Members have come to feel that a principal condition for their willing participation is the mutual acknowledgment of their fellow workers. These values are all the more apparent in friendships or religious communities. Members enjoy the open gaze of their fellows (whether loving, respectful, or forgiving) or the mutual confirmation of believers in a creed. Tasks seem extraneous to these commitments, or we use them to express our loyalties.

10. Access

Systems of both kinds may be open or closed to new members. Public libraries are open: they exist to educate and serve a large public, so members need only satisfy minimal requirements. The Society of Librarians is closed: it limits the size of its membership for reasons of competence, status, or economic advantage. Families and nations are typically closed. So, too, are some religions: outsiders cannot usually solicit membership.

III. THE WORK SYSTEMS DO

Stabilized systems of both sorts do work and have effects. Organizations are designed for specific, often utilitarian tasks; associations intensify or support the feelings or beliefs of their members. The effects of an organization are often experienced by people or systems external to it—buyers or patients, for example. The effects of associations are experienced principally by the members—the meeting of friends, for example.

Success of both kinds presupposes work of a different sort. It requires energy, information, or materials to sustain the system's parts and relations, thereby enabling it to satisfy its primary aim.[2] The difference between these two kinds of work may be costly, as when the difficulty of raising children while working to pay the bills is a reason that families are abandoned by people who cannot do both. This suggests a measure for the efficiency of systems: is system-sustaining work separable from its primary tasks, or are the two mutually reinforcing? A system is most efficient when the work sustaining it is also the work that accomplishes the system's primary aim, as hearts in good order are required for walking, and walking is good for hearts. Everyone whose work is his vocation intends this result: the activity we enjoy should also pay our bills. This ideal is not easily generalized, because much work that is system-sustaining is not directly relevant to an organization's defining task, as firing the boiler is incidental to selling milk.

Emphasizing a system's tasks without regard for system-sustaining work is sometimes described approvingly as *functionalism:* meaning that we specify a task while ignoring the conditions for its realization, as radios use transistors or tubes. Social systems and their members do not have this luxury: they cannot perform their tasks in the absence of the work that sustains them. Any disparity between the two kinds of work is expensive or frustrating: costly health care sustains elderly people without giving them pleasure or power in the lives thereby prolonged; a parent works long hours to support a family he barely sees. This discrepancy is less problematic for associations, because the work sustaining a friendship is the very activity that fulfills it. (The individual friends must also sustain themselves; but this is work appropriate to a system's parts, not to the system itself.)

Work has a third focus, too. After a system's task and the activity that sustains it, there is the work of endowing members' lives with significance. Organizations satisfy this need with positions, honors, or badges: one is an adored grandmother or a captain of industry. The power of associations is more surprising, because it is simpler and everywhere close at hand, as happens when organizational work is motivated by the interest of an association. War—a kind of work—is an example. It requires organization, and is sometimes undertaken to defend a society's self-regard.

This example is typical of associations: they intensify values, feelings, or beliefs, hence self-conviction, in their members. This effect is familiar in one's family and friendships: we feel better in the company of those who like us, or merely with those who are like us. But sometimes we need more. We want to be, or feel that we are, important on a larger scale—more important than other people, or important to God: we are, by our estimate, made in his image. (An inverted argument for God's existence is inferred: he must exist in order to valorize us.) The paragraphs that follow describe examples of this affiliative work, from simple affirmations of mutual regard to grand myths vindicating claims that we are special. Why call this *work?* Because it is a social undertaking that alters the self-perception and relations of those who do it.

Roles in a family—when the family is an organization—are differentiated by the tasks assigned to the members. Each one contributes to the economic and vocational well-being of its members, as child-bearer, wage-earner, or student. The affiliative relations of people in a bar are simpler: they require only that each be made to feel good about himself because he is welcomed by others. These are often people who resemble one another in a salient way: they are working men, people who are lonely, veterans, or fans of a local team. Visitors are unwelcome if they differ in the relevant respect. They are intruders in the circle where self-esteem is reinforced in the absence of significant difference. There are, of course, bars of another kind. These are sanctuaries for everyone who reciprocates in a generous way; a newcomer's idiosyncrasies are overlooked when he quickly perceives and responds to the affective conditions for participation. Everything alien is suppressed or ignored: everyone bathes in the simpler expressions of mutual affirmation.

Religious feeling has similar foundations when the faithful revert to an early expression of doctrine or worship, in order to associate themselves with simpler, "purer" feelings. If the original message was uncomplicated, let us have the warm feelings of that plainer devotion. There are insuperable obstacles to knowing that our feelings are like those of earlier congregants, the original, true believers: the feelings have perished with the faithful. These obstacles may seem to vanish if we re-create their sentiments by telling their stories or imitating their practices. For we suppose that certain feelings only are appropriate to these rites. We propose to recover the direct, affecting intuitions—the intensifications of feeling common to those who lived in the presence of the thing adored—by placing ourselves in the original situation. Our devotion to the old stories explains our feelings and justifies us in thinking that a community of feeling and belief joins us to the original believers. Changing doctrines is dangerous, because it would disrupt this continuity: a different story may provoke different feelings. Where changes have occurred, in doctrine, clothing, work, location, or worship, fundamentalists would have us reestablish the old ways, hence— they suppose—the authenticity of feelings which, circumstances being the same, must be close to the feelings of the original believers. "Give me that old-time religion," says the song: ignore its meaner successors, the more to feel as old-timers did.

Associations are forever searching for credible self-affirming sentiments, in order that these may be used to dilute or suppress bad feelings about our selves, situations, or estrangements. Many affiliations—new friendships, for example—have no history, so that religious fundamentalism would seem to be irrelevant to them. But the difference is superficial: we regularly re-create friendships having an affective quality that duplicates prized feelings from our past. These are not the utilitarian bonds that change with our needs. For friendships of this other sort revive feelings that gratified us before. These are buttons we push, forever wanting to restore a feeling-state that was once self-affirming. I have the memory of people coming singly or in twos and threes from a Roman gelateria, each one preoccupied by the nearly auto-erotic pleasure of the ice cream. Walking together, people were nevertheless alone, each one dominated by the intensity of this self-perception, each one feeling whole and satisfied. Associations give us some degree of this feeling. Their reciprocities make participants tingle, each one confirmed in himself by the meanings he shares with others.

The first and third of these three kinds of work (that is, tasks to fulfill and significance felt and believed) are sometimes a point of chronic friction between organizations and associations, one as it appraises its aims and actions pragmatically, the other as it nourishes its myths. A balance is sometimes struck between them. Friendships and families accept disruptions caused by work or school. Some religious communities make similar accommodations, though theocracies and orthodox believers often do not. They would like to dominate social life, as sometimes they do. Are we fated to go in cycles, where pragmatic solutions, then affinities of feeling and imagination, succeed one another? Are there discernible moments when the cycle begins to repeat itself? Here is one mark of a change to come: organizations breed a reactive movement in the direction of associations when their pragmatism has stripped life of all "superior" meaning, or when the kinds of work available to many citizens produce too little security or satisfaction. People leading mean lives are restless, then rabid in defense of self-esteem and the craving for something better. Associations are subverted—the contrary tendency—when passion for their aims makes them reckless about the security and satisfaction of their people, or when organizational, bureaucratic features so pervade an association that members reject it as a perversion of their shared passion. Any manipulation that is too conspicuously utilitarian poisons feelings or beliefs. Forsaking the passion, the members demand a well-run organization that serves their needs, until having it feels mechanical and meaningless. This cycle is hard to stop.

IV. EDUCATION

Members of an organization need skills, attitudes, and information appropriate to their roles. They also want information about other members and roles, and about the circumstances in which the system carries on, the better to coordinate the one and exploit the other. Compare the members of associations. The information vital to them is not (usually) different from member to member; there may be no corporate effects apart from the association itself and no concern about the system's circumstances. The learning that prepares us for associations is harder to direct but more elementary, because their aim is the intensification of feelings, beliefs, and relations in and among the members. Imagine anxious friends talking in the rain. They go on talking, though their clothes are soaked. Passersby speak to one or the other, but they are ignored. Intensity of feeling, but nothing learned in school, explains their mutual concern. Systems of this sort are founded in preliterate needs. Feeling vulnerable in ourselves, wanting the support of others, needing evidence of our significance (the third kind of work described above), we learn to recognize their beliefs and feelings and to convey our own. These conditions are satisfied universally, usually without special training. People find one another and bond, in friendship or shared belief. The associations they form resist argument, evidence, or criticism.

The special training for associations is a warning that our views about education are usually too narrow.[3] Learning French requires that one learn its vocabulary, grammar, and pronunciation; but this is less than all that is required to speak it. For imagine someone who speaks French but doesn't know how to address other people: he talks in a low voice, with his back to them, interrupting every phrase with a song. This is unlikely but not tendentious, because it reminds us of skills that are critical for every cooperative endeavor. Children learn them by playing together. Crews of fishermen or miners know them too. Bonding of this sort is typical of associations, but a point it illustrates generalizes to organizations. For the thinking appropriate to systems is an orienting power, one that bends us to the requirements of the system at hand. This is thought— the navigator and steersman—as it directs our engagements with other people, whether for specific aims or shared feelings and beliefs. Systems of both sorts test our preparation for affiliation, though Dewey emphasized that the facility for accommodating oneself to diverse associations can be taught.[4]

A different sort of education—for language—is common to every human social system. Baseball players may play well despite being illiterate and mute, but language facilitates the give-and-take of social life, so everything is more complicated if they cannot read line up cards or speak to their coaches and one another. Wittgenstein is curiously silent about those uses of language that facilitate the creation and transformation of systems. The "language-games" he describes are routinized: you do it, I do it after you.[5] These are games without play. Nothing that Wittgenstein says of them illuminates the experiments that conversation provokes—"Shall we have lunch?"—or the collaborations thereby established. Perhaps we ignore these affiliative uses of language because they are fundamental to the point of being invisible. Lost in the rhythm, doing the steps, dancers don't think about patterns. Nor do we think about affiliative language—whether regulative or constitutive—as it gives voice, form, and moral edge to our social practices: "Did you remember your mother's birthday?"

It is also relevant that speech seems ephemeral—indeed, too feeble to connect the speakers. We are disinclined to extend the notion of thinghood to systems that are sustained by the efficient and formal causality of human speech. This bias is a symptom of the tacit distinction between bodily connections (deemed natural) and mental ones (deemed conventional). The basis for this prejudice includes the belief that minds are complete, so the speech of others adds nothing essential to us. This is odd when human character is altered by information we receive and by relations established because of words we exchange. Speaking—thinking—freely, we transform ourselves and create associations that include the Republic whose Constitution acknowledges and defends this founding practice. One may discount the special status accorded to speech as a bit of florid rhetoric, one that mistakes a metaphorical cause for a real one. But speech is a natural cause (as sound waves are natural), however arbitrary the signs used. Individual speeches come and go, but speech is not abstract, fragile, or ephemeral. Words—written or spoken—are a nearly incessant tide moving through and among us. We participate in the tide, first as we listen, then as we deliberate, finally as we speak or write. Apes socialize without these skills, with the result that their systems depend barely or not at all on signs and mental intentions. Verbal undertakings, written contracts, literature, and the rule of law are nothing to them. The difference is culture: education that teaches the affiliative uses of language is its condition among us.

V. BEING ALONE

Each of us is sometimes alone. In the midst of other people or at night, content or terrified, we satisfy the atomist perception that relations are accidental. Sociality may seem remote, ephemeral, or mythic at such times. Are we spoiled by too much socialization, needing time and separation to restore the confidence that our inner bearings are reliable and sufficient? Could it be true instead that we are anxious rather than pleased at the opportunity to recover our singularity? Why do we shiver if being alone is our natural state?

Some things—the feel of one's body—are available principally or only to introspection. Equally personal and private are the memories, feelings of anticipation, satisfaction or guilt, plans, and the *soto voce* commentaries that pour through us. Are we alone? Our physical isolation—at least our separability—is real. But do these features of mental life confirm our self-sufficiency as thinkers? Notice that socialization is assumed when we describe such reveries: the people so described were never feral children, deprived of discourse and care. The blank stares and gaping mouths of such children intimate that something important is missing. Compare monks or nuns in orders that limit conversation. They are keenly aware of the mutualities in their lives, including conversations that are all the more important for being rare. Or think of elderly people, the lone survivors of their generation, or of prisoners in solitary confinement: each retains a window into the social world, and sanity, by talking to imagined friends.

One learns to enjoy being alone. But we do it by exploiting the gaps in our times with other people.[6] For being alone is a sporadic event in most lives. We don't lose our beliefs, attitudes, and skills—the tools of socialization—merely by withdrawing from contexts that require them. Someone drowning is too busy for other concerns. Let him pull himself out of the water, and he thinks of family, friends, or creditors. Sociality in him is virtual when it is not dominant and real. We know that it is, because character is acquired in the course of our roles. Thinking of ourselves, we can hardly fail to think of them.

VI. SOME RELATIONS AMONG HUMAN SOCIAL SYSTEMS

Chapter One describes four possible relations between or among systems: systems are mutually independent, though this does not bar their interaction; they establish the reciprocal causal relations that create a higher-order system; one is nested within another; and one overlaps another. These relations translate into more specific terms: namely, indifference, competition, dependence, cooperation, amalgamation, subordination (four kinds), and engulfment (two kinds).

These relations are ontologically significant. They qualify the impression that things are bound tightly as systems or loosely, either as aggregates or by rare, casual, or sporadic interactions. Several of these relations create sustained, effective connections.

Indifference and *competition* (sometimes) are expressions of mutual independence: systems do not interact, or they affect one another without establishing more than incidental or sporadic relations: phone calls from a tele-marketer are an example. Competition is also familiar in overlapping systems that vie for control of a shared part, as happens if both countries send draft notices to a dual national.

Cooperation is mutually supporting interaction. It creates higher-order systems that have the cooperators as their proper parts: one thinks of marriages, schools, work crews, and ecosystems.

Dependence occurs when one system draws sustenance from another. This is a relation that may endure without reciprocity, as happens if one takes while the other derives no benefit from giving. This is a first example of the sustained, non-reciprocal relations mentioned above. *Mutual dependence* is the obverse of reciprocity. It too may last indefinitely, if each takes from the other something that is ample or cheaply replaced. Imagine that a blind man pushes the wheelchair of one who sees for both. This is reciprocity (cooperation) that creates a higher-order system, not the mutual dependence that drains the participants without supporting them.

Subordination, in one of its versions, is the control of one system by another. The subordinated system is not independent of the one that controls it, though the controlling system may be independent of the one it controls (as when a church dominates a state). Subordination of this sort is another example of relations that are sustained, but not reciprocal. Subordination of a second kind is a version of nesting. It occurs whenever a lower-order system is altered to some degree by the norms imposed by the higher-order system to which it is responsible, as state laws are superseded by federal laws. Subordination of this second kind does imply reciprocity, because the higher-order system exists by way of its lower-order constituents: the American federal system is composed of its states, commonwealth, and territories. Subordination of a third kind mixes the reciprocal relations of a system and its parts (subordination of the second kind) with the system's relations to things that are independent of, and external to, the system: think of cults that mediate the relations of members and outsiders. Finally, subordination is evidence that one system has mastered another by bringing it within its domain, thereby making the subordinated system one of its parts. It happens, for example, that a state subordinates a church by appointing its bishops, or a company by appointing its officers.

Engulfment has two versions, each identical with one of the alternatives left ambiguous in the fourth version of subordination. For there is this question: does the subordinated system retain its identity when it enters the domain of the subordinating system? Is a church reduced to a compartment of the state's bureaucracy—hence all but defunct as a system in its own right—if its bishops are state-appointed? Or is engulfment the more commonplace relation of nesting, as when churches subject to all a state's laws retain their integrity?

Amalgamation is easier for associations. Organizations are designed for the functions appropriate to an aim. Those having different aims—or the same one—may have anomalous designs. Effective integration is precluded if their respective parts and functions are not complementary. An association's tasks are simpler, its members less differentiated by their roles. Indeed, every believer may have the same role: he or she confirms, by mirroring, the beliefs of others. Amalgamation occurs as two systems are joined: churches merge when the mirroring of fraternizing members has blurred any doctrinal differences among them; political factions coalesce as members discover their affinity.

All these styles of relation are available to associations: they may cooperate without merging, though this implies a degree of organization within and between the cooperators. All the styles but amalgamation are available to organizations. They often merge, but can't amalgamate because doing that would require the absence of differentiated functions within them.

We may assume that some styles of relation are good, while others are bad. Yet each may be good or bad, depending on the circumstances. Dependency is sometimes disparaged, though we encourage it in children and people too feeble to provide for themselves. We encourage cooperation, though not collaboration, with a hated regime. Is indifference or competition always, never, or sometimes a good thing? There is no formula to help us decide. Circumstances and the interests at issue are determining: we may cooperate with kidnappers.

VII. REWORKING SOCIETIES:
THEIR DETERMINABILITY

Systems are malleable and deformable: their character and relations are determinable. *Atomism, communitarianism,* and *holism* are three recipes (theories used as ideologies) for giving them determinate form. We can push and bend other systems and ourselves until we resemble the ontologies they prescribe. But are we satisfied by the alterations thereby created: meaning the particular character of systems that are made or remade to the specifications of the ideology applied? Let ecology be our example. A sustainable balance of nature is often a benchmark for the complaint that we exploit our material circumstances without regard for the damage done. Could our recklessness be the effect of using a flawed or false theory to organize our social world? For atomism—the ontological and social theory that dominates thinking about the world and ourselves—is oblivious to systems in general, and heedless in particular of the network of systems that supplies a niche for us humans. It is hardly surprising if some effects that result from using this (or any) theory to shape our determinable circumstances are odious or destructive.

Using ideologies to rework human relations has had four remarkable effects in the modern history of societies, especially those influenced by political developments in Europe from the Renaissance in northern Italy to the French Revolution. *First, the rule of law* replaced rights that had been a function of one's place within a system or class (that is, one's status as prince or commoner). It abstracted individuals from contexts wherein status was the basis for rights, giving the same protections, rights, or duties to all a society's members (in theory, if not practice). *Second,* dominions that were once the near-possession of their rulers—satrapies—became *states* whose sovereignty derived from the will of the governed: namely, individuals—citizens of the state—who were protected by the rule of law. *Third, free-market economies* replaced systems where the exchange of goods was protected and monopolized by royal families or merchant oligarchs. Governments that guaranteed stable currencies also enforced laws that protected contracts against the nonfeasance of the parties engaged. Status could no longer guarantee control over goods and services when anyone having the purchase price could buy the goods presented for sale. *Fourth,* the combination of marketable skills, money, and the rule of law enabled ordinary people to challenge the traditional centers of value. *Secular values*—meaning tastes and morals that originated in the talents and inclinations of ordinary people and their systems—displaced values that carried the imprimatur of royalty and the Church. These creators of new values—principally the emergent middle class—could not ape the higher classes without introducing commercial or populist values of their own. Was credit a bad thing if markets (like churches and states) needed it? Churches, which had banned usury, changed their views. The credit that lubricates modern economies and the lives of modern consumers is an accommodation to the idea that money is a commodity whose use earns a rightful profit. Innovating people were emboldened. The courage to act on one's values expressed confidence in one's rights as a citizen, including rights that accrue under the rule of law (*habeas corpus,* for example) and power that accrues to people who earn and spend money.

These consequential changes were inspired by Jewish and Stoic thinkers, then propelled by Luther, Calvin, Machiavelli, Descartes, and Hobbes. These are some principal sources for the atomist thinking that reduces systems to the aggregates composed of self-sufficient, autonomous thinker-actors. Atomists want us to believe that the uncontested benefits of their political program certify their ontology. But the lesson for ontology is different. These changes exhibit the malleability (the determinability) of social systems. Such systems can be remade, within limits, to satisfy the prescriptions of all three social theories: atomism, communitarianism, or holism. Which of these recipes best represents the material character of things? Which one's recommendations least distort their character?

VIII. REGULATION

Many human systems have negative feedback. Each of them has an internal economy that is self-regulating: meaning that the behavior of the parts is turned on or off, then maintained within limits established by their relations to other parts. Self-regulation in human systems has additional features, including intentions, rules or laws, bureaucracy, and politics. It is only human systems that concern us, hence the importance of these features in the discussion that follows.

Imagine that trucks, buses, cars, carriages, bicycles, and pedestrians compete for space on unregulated roads. Trucks become tanks, as diversity is reduced to the few viable alternatives. Or we regulate traffic, by educating ourselves as drivers and by making laws. This is agreed self-regulation. It redirects salient activities while promoting mutual responsibility among the agents regulated. Conflict is not eliminated, but it is reduced. The agents of self-regulation, in this example, are individual drivers and their government, a system that provides services useful for other systems. Governments regulate when the complexity of the interactions among individuals and their other systems exceeds the control that might be exerted by the aggregate of individual choices: drivers try to avoid accidents but have no rules to regularize their actions.

Governmental regulation is just one expression of a feature that is pervasive in human social systems: every efficiently managed system organizes itself to create opportunities and reduce conflicts (whether internal or external), thereby stabilizing the system. Self-regulation—whether by individuals or by their organizations and associations—is achieved by tuning or reconfiguring the reciprocal relations that create them. Regulation has four aims. *First* is self-control, because systems are unsustainable if uncontrolled. *Second* (a reason for the first) is the reduction of conflicts within and among systems, including persons, families, neighbors, companies, and jurisdictions. Members should practice the self-restraint that is mutually securing, as happens when people pass carefully on a narrow path. There should be effective, secondary defenses—including policemen, prosecutors, and courts—when restraint is not practiced. *Third* is the deliberation that identifies and ranks a system's values (including its objectives), so that the means and discipline appropriate to achieving them may be taught and applied. *Fourth* is the planning and execution of particular initiatives.

These four expressions of self-regulation may be distinguished as *self-control, mutual restraint or governmental regulation, values,* and *planning. Procedural neutrality, minority rights,* and questions about the universal application of a society's regulative principles—*inclusion or exclusion*—are three subsidiary points.

1. Self-control

The simplest self-regulating social system has two members. Self-regulation occurs when each of the partners alters what he or she gives the other in response to what is received—affection or respect, for example. These reciprocities stabilize the system. If one person is inattentive, the other expresses displeasure or behaves similarly, until the one distracted is attentive again or until the relationship dissolves. Communities of believers regulate themselves in a similar way: lapsed believers are encouraged to reaffirm their beliefs lest they be denied the fellowship of those whose belief is firm.

Accordingly, we intensify the feelings and confirm the beliefs of members, in order to maintain the steady state for which the members aim. Doing this is routine in established associations, because each participant has learned reliable habits for connecting him or herself to others: we enjoy our relations to them without always having to think about the terms of engagement.[7] But sometimes this reflection is urgent, so that self-regulation within associations adds self-scrutiny and self-controlled interventions to the reciprocities that create and stabilize them. Self-control is more complicated in organizations, because they often require machinery that is additional to the complementarity of a system's roles. The members of a string quartet play together without a conductor, though ensembles as small as chamber orchestras usually have them. The administrator-manager-director inherits the specialized task of controlling a system, somewhat as Plato argued that reason controls a person's appetites, and philosopher-kings regulate the state.

2. Mutual Restraint, or Governmental Regulation

Self-control is commonplace within individual persons, where the parts are mutually dependent: impulse control is one of its expressions. Control is harder to achieve in human social systems, where the parts are relatively autonomous. Control of these systems requires self-control in the members, their mutual restraint, or the regulative force exercised by a higher-order system, be it a family, a school, or a government.

Sometimes, when conflict is mutual and uncontrolled (lacerating spouses, for example), the cure is mutual restraint. This can be monadic, as each party controls him or herself; but it can be coordinated and reciprocal, so that each is appeased as much by the other's behavior as by his own. Regulation of this sort is often informal and plastic: the people having an argument sit down to talk. This willing self-scrutiny and accommodation is especially desirable among the members of systems, because it establishes habits or procedures they may exploit again, and because it averts the intervention of laws, regulators, and penalties. Yet many systems and aggregates—stock markets and traffic, for example—do not regulate themselves successfully. The density of the social world and the ramifying complexity of social relations guarantee that many more cannot regulate their effects on other systems, as war, traffic, and trade do not. We who hope to regulate them form alliances that compete for the power or right to organize and control a social space. This is politics construed generally, not only for the purposes of government. For it happens everywhere that the power to command the activities within a space is achieved by allied power-seekers. Teachers compete with administrators for control of a school. Husbands and wives may compete for power within a family, making alliances with children and other relatives. Competition evolves in either of two ways: into accommodations that are brittle and unreliable (members are joined by nothing but their aversion to someone else) or into alliances that are flexible but stable. We get factions or systems. The members of systems are mutually supporting; each one's efficacy reinforces the work of other members. The members of factions are mutually suspicious (even of one another) and reactive. Their quarrels are hard to regulate in the absence of a third party, one empowered to dictate the terms of a resolution.

Politics is urgent business when the power to regulate is a government's authority to make laws that govern the behaviors of systems within its domain. The communitarianism I favor welcomes this intervention. Social atomism encourages the terror that government will intervene against us (for its own benefit or for that of a competitor allied to government). Governments sometimes justify this fear. Yet our dread of them is exaggerated by misconceptions, as when atomist ontology affirms the reality of individual persons, while supposing that governments are jerry-rigged expedients whose one legitimate aim (police power) is inevitably perverted by the ambitions of their officers. This is theorizing that defends and magnifies an aversion.

There is a prudent and viable alternative: we say that *government is one system among others,* that its authority is explicit and limited, and that its functions are critical for the welfare of other systems. Do fishermen want to fish? What boats and nets shall they use? What fish shall they catch? Imagine that competition among fishermen turns nasty, or that the scarcity of fish arouses states that depend on fish stocks for food. We urge governments to settle these issues, though they cannot do so effectively until there are answers to questions of three orders: constitutional, legislative, and practical. Constitutional decisions are foundational. They settle questions about the origin, legitimacy, and aims of state power, including the kinds of activities that may be regulated, the sanction and authority of the regulators, and the range and depth of acceptable intrusions. The virtual system prefigured by a constitution comes to be realized as a government having limited authority to regulate other systems within a domain, usually a territory. A domain so governed is a state. Its legislators make laws within the parameters established by the constitution, usually after negotiations that hear and consider the competing interests of citizens and higher-order systems. All the participants in these negotiations are a system's members, its citizens, though governmental systems may differ, as there are democracies and monarchies, parliamentary and presidential democracies. These are differences that express the various resolutions of ancient quarrels about the uses and limits of authority. They remind us that using regulation to reduce conflict is an old practice for which there are competing strategies. Some states, mired in tradition and fear, still use power to suppress conflict. Dewey's solution is better.[8]

He shared the liberal theory of Locke, Rousseau, Hume, Kant, and Mill.[9] They postulate a domain—the *public*—then credit it with two wondrous powers. *First* is the power to endow participating persons, described as citizens or rational agents, with inalienable rights. Every participant is inviolable in himself, hence exempt by right—free—from damaging, or merely unwanted, intrusions by other members of the public. Participants are also free to do such things as suit them, short of damaging others. Notice the paradox that inalienable rights are not unconditioned: these are rights that qualify members of the public, meaning one or another democratic society.[10] Equally, these rights are not universal and necessary: they do not obtain in every possible state or world. They are coterminus with citizenship (or mere residency) in a democratic state, so having them is a contingency. Rights survive, this implies, only as we participate in the reciprocities that establish and sustain states. Where the rights at issue are democratic freedoms *to* and *from,* they survive, because we establish and sustain democratic states.

We extend these rights to every person—describing them as universal rights of mankind—by adding the proviso that all who satisfy a minimal standard of rationality and self-control may participate in democratic society. The rights hereby created are civil. They qualify us to participate in acts of social self-regulation—governance—and they limit the intrusions of government into our private lives. Citizens are equal under the law, though equal civil rights create an anomaly, because roles in other systems—families, schools, and the army, for example—often make us unequal. How shall we reconcile civil equality with inequalities that dominate the lives of workers and employers, experts and their clients, recruits and their officers?

Democratic rhetoric strongly favors equal civil rights to the disadvantage of unequal roles. This is apparent when it encourages us to assimilate civil rights to character (by way of attitudes), as happens when we emphasize freedom and equality, but minimize duty. This is the effect when authority and duty are perceived as temporary or accidental liabilities consequent on time spent in a role (teenager or employee, for example). The authority of roles (with their inequalities) is hereby pushed to the margins of moral consciousness. Democracies consolidate this effect by assimilating entitlement rights to civil rights: public policy affirms that the state has an interest in seeing each citizen exercise his or her freedom, so it empowers citizens by guaranteeing a least standard of nutrition, housing, and education to everyone. This saves many people from having to enter systems where roles are unequal—low-paid jobs, for example.

These are some expedients that use civil rights to cover, without hiding, the inequalities of our many roles. Marx, hoping to minimize the difference, proposed that workers should govern, and that machines should relieve them of unequal burdens. The anomaly would remain, because some roles inevitably introduce inequalities into the lives of people filling them. Atomism disguises this conflict by denying the reality of systems, though it is mostly our roles in families, schools, businesses, religious communities, and armies, not our civil rights, that occupy us. We may invoke political rights to ease the damage or wrongs (assaults to dignity, for example) suffered because of our roles in nongovernmental systems; but this strategy is superficial if it fails to acknowledge that these systems, with their unequal duties, dominate most lives. We may rethink every such system, wanting to reform it so that the dignity of personhood (extrapolated from civil rights) is satisfied within it. Still, we are confounded, because roles and duties within systems other than the democratic public and state are typically differentiated and unequal. Excessive emphasis on the equality of civil rights—affirming that they define personhood—is false to many of the systems that engage us.

The systems that create civil rights are themselves established by the mutual respect—the respectful reciprocity—of the members. Such systems are associations (though they acquire the administrator-officials that are characteristic of organizations because of their size or complexity). States of this kind are an evolutionary development in the lives or histories of reflective people: they do not exist in perpetuity or from the beginning of time. Starting in other systems, whether families, religions, or clans, we bootstrap ourselves to the realization that life is better for everyone when a public is created.[11] This doesn't happen at once. The public, with its freedoms to and from, is established over the days, years, or centuries when prospective members negotiate the terms of association.

The public is also important in this other way. The rights with which it endows us are potent defenses against abuses we may experience within other systems. For these rights, to life and liberty, may arguably supersede duties that fall to us in families, clans, or commerce. Finding these rights violated, we have a counterweight to systems that insist on our responsibilities to them and their members, however inimical they are to us.[12] People intoxicated by their democratic rights or afraid to lose them sometimes decline to participate in systems that temper rights: marriage is an example. Doing this is not equivalent to alienating oneself from every system. It implies only that people minimize their commitments to systems other than the one that creates these rights, as big-city anomie is an attraction.[13]

The *second* power credited to the public was apparent already in America's Constitutional Convention (and maybe in the thinking of the barons who wrote the Magna Carta). No one formulates it more clearly than Dewey. His views about governmental regulation extend the liberal theory that government's principal task is its use of police power: government intervenes only to restrict or punish those who damage the bodies, liberties, or property of others. *Private* behaviors, he said, are those occurring between or among persons who pursue common aims by forming associations—families, for example. Dewey's *associations* are systems: they are established by the reciprocal causal relations—the affiliative behaviors—of their members. Dewey supposed that each person should be free to enter into associations of his or her choice, while steps are taken to insure that the playing field isn't constricted or closed by the actions of groups that are excessively powerful or heedless of others. He prized initiative for consequentialist reasons: individuals enjoy their lives best if they are free to pursue their aims with companions of choice in circumstances that are not encumbered by other people's business; the productive activity of all is often beneficial to each.

Dewey's *public* is the citizenry organized for self-regulation.[14] The public emerges as citizens meet to consider the adverse effects that associations have on one another. For we wear two hats: one private, the other public. As private persons, we join with others to satisfy our aims. As members of the public, we legislate solutions after considering the unexpected consequences of self-interested behaviors (noisy parties, for example) and the predictable effects of aims that are malign (subordinating other people or systems, monopolizing a market to eliminate competitors, for example). We also anticipate future difficulties, making rules to avert them. Our attitude as regulators is practical and tentative. There may be several ways of preventing, diverting, or altering a practice. Knowing that particular solutions may not work, we are ready to amend them. Finding a viable solution, we don't suppose that it will always work. We may be less tentative about the values that direct our regulative proposals, but we acknowledge that they too must satisfy a consequentialist test: namely, do they promote both access to the playing field where associations are initiated and the health, good sense, and freedom of the individuals who participate in systems?

It was important to Dewey, in the spirit of Hegel, that citizens should rise to the consciousness of their responsibilities as members of the public. Each of us struggles to overcome self-interest in the name of our shared interests. It is better not to hide this struggle or to pretend that altruism and the public interest always dominate us. Creating and sustaining a public is a fragile achievement, one that cannot be glossed or assumed.

John Rawls averts attention from the struggle by supposing that a constitution institutionalizes the prudent altruism of his "original position." This is the imagined situation where each participant wants reasonable conditions and rights for all, because he does not know how they shall be distributed to him. A constitution that guarantees "fairness" is to be prescribed and enacted, thereby freeing subsequent generations of citizens from having to understand and resolve conflicts of self- and public interest. This is risky, because citizens who take their democratic rights for granted may thoughtlessly ignore them (by selling public power to private interests, for example). Jürgen Habermas objects that Rawls begs a central question for democratic societies: *how to assemble and sustain* a public.[15]

Rawls rightly emphasizes the advantages of having an established constitution with the rights it guarantees. Yet, one suspects that his preference for a settled agreement is too much the effect of talk about an "*original* position," as if a constitutional convention might permanently establish inviolable rights and procedural justice. Won't rights, law, and justice atrophy, because citizens treat them casually? Should we ever forget that these are the precarious, but renewable achievements of a people who learn that public self-regulation is a principal condition for the well-being of individuals and the social systems they create? The rhetoric of an "original position" too quickly becomes an anti-democratic soporific:

> When the prophet had thus spoken . . . the drawer of the first lot at once sprang to seize the greatest tyranny. . . . He was one of those who had come down from heaven, a man who had lived in a well-ordered polity in his former existence participating in virtue by habit and not by philosophy, and one may perhaps say that a majority of those who were thus caught were of the company that had come from heaven, inasmuch as they were unexercised in suffering.[16]

Justice, rights, and the public are the products of reflection and negotiation. They are emergent, not original.

The *public,* as Dewey conceived it, is the elementary government of citizen-lawmakers dear to Aristotle and the Enlightenment. Such governments are voluntary associations of men and women who convene to regulate the behaviors of all. Such regulations include laws, rules, and procedures, whether formalized or tacit. These are agreed ways of reducing conflicts, including calculated attacks and the unintended effects of group behaviors. Our critical starting point is the realization that every person and system is responsible for regulating him, her, or itself, both internally and externally: we suppress impulses or choose our words. Conflicts are often terminated or averted because people who are self-controlled alter their behaviors after perceiving their effects. Other times, nothing is settled without discussion, though negotiations are informal, as when people resolve the frictions between them. It also happens that people or systems are stubborn, because altered behavior doesn't satisfy their interests. These are occasions when we need the intervention of third parties. Ad hoc legislatures with shifting memberships—neighbors—convene to solve local problems—

disruptive neighbors. Legislatures, issue-centered elections, and referenda are reserved for problems that affect many or all of a jurisdiction's members. For these are tasks that exceed the authority, attention span, or inventiveness of town meetings. Is taxation complicated? We elect representative officials to make appropriate laws. We intend that some of them should be experts, or that they hire people who are, though we know that experts, too, may be corrupt or mistaken. We—the public—take care that our authority is not reduced to a formality when experts tell our representatives what the rules shall be. We fear such abuses and limit the power of the institutions formed to regulate us: government is not empowered to make families or friendships or to organize the citizenry for the production and distribution of goods and services (with qualified exceptions such as prison labor and munitions factories). It should not sponsor religions or propagandize on behalf of favored ideologies. We drastically curtail its interference with the right of association or with the legitimate systems thereby formed: we encourage families, not criminal conspiracies. These are private spaces where regulation needs special justification (for example, child abuse).

Government is, all the while, the permanent, formalized, and powerful expression of the public. It is responsible for scrutinizing the complex of systems, then for passing legislation that averts or repairs the effects that accrue when systems damage one another or their members while pursuing otherwise legitimate aims. Do factories pollute? Are cars or the food chain unsafe? Are factories or hospitals inimical to their workers or patients? Do businesses suppress competition? These are occasions for regulation. Systems should regulate themselves; but they are not self-regulating on many occasions, because their effects are not perceived, or because some other consideration—profit, for example—makes self-regulation onerous. Inheriting a task that other systems cannot or will not assume, speaking for the public, government intervenes.

We, private citizens, are to suppress our personal interests when we meet as the public. Reflecting on the effects of conflict, whether intended or not, we— or our representatives—enact laws or procedures that regulate behavior, without prejudice to the systems regulated or advantage to the regulators. This is ideal. Is it also simplistic? Doesn't this outcome depend too much on a high-mindedness that we rarely achieve and never sustain? Suborners and monopolists are not ideal candidates for the public-spirited citizenry. Why would they participate in the public, if not to pervert it for their benefit? Did Dewey believe, rather like Socrates, that everyone desires the good, so that an evildoer is diverted merely by pointing out the effects of his actions? What if this information doesn't change his mind? What if self-concern disqualifies many or most people from participating in the public?

The obstacles to having a self-regulating public are apparent. But Dewey's reasoning was simple. Valuing the freedom to associate, profiting from many systems that other people create and sustain, we encourage initiative. Yet uncontrolled ambition has confounding effects. Nothing moves; or one or a few systems acquire power at cost to every other. Freedom makes regulation incumbent in a world of scarcity and crowding. But who shall regulate us if we will not regulate ourselves? The argument goes in a circle, unless we break it by creating an agency—a regulator—that is distinct from the parties needing regulation. We make ourselves corporately responsible for self-regulation. We do it—in a way that abstracts from the interests of contending systems—by creating the public. We may fail to convince dominating people or their systems that they too have an interest in promoting restraint; but then the public lapses or never forms. The powerful few dominate the rest of us for a time, before they are superseded by people or systems more powerful than themselves. Accordingly, Dewey's public is an exercise in prudent self-regard. Failing to create it, we risk Hobbes's state of nature, or the cynicism of governments that do the work of tyrants or oligarchs: those described by Thrasymachus and Marx.

Dewey must answer the charge that governmental regulation is itself a danger if it fails to guarantee the neutrality of regulators or to prevent their meddling in domains where they have no authority. There is also the reasonable fear that order may become our principal social objective (with bureaucrats to enforce it). We want a clearer idea of our social priorities.

Freedom and the initiatives it sponsors are one priority. Yet initiative breeds conflict in circumstances of scarcity, crowding, and complexity, circumstances intensified by the reciprocity, nesting, and overlap of systems. The public's role as regulator is also, therefore, a priority. Indeed, it makes little sense to value the freedom of choice, if we do not also value the regulative oversight that averts stultification and conflict. These two values—initiative and regulation—are sometimes contraries, so care must be taken when both are realized: we don't want to stifle initiative and diversity in the name of control.

Some Americans believe that we live on a greased slide to despotism, because our state tolerates an imbalance of real power between individual initiative and governmental control. This impression of powerful government but weak subaltern systems and a weak citizenry is (*in theory*) exaggerated. Governments of the sort that Dewey described—such a government as we constitutionally have—are coordinate with, not superior to, individual citizens and the private associations they form. This crude parity is evident when public officials are turned out of office because dissatisfaction has percolated through hundreds or thousands of individual households, businesses, or churches. How do such governments compensate for their relative lack of authority? Dewey's answer is that of traditional republican thought: governments don't need vast power over their people, because the people's civic-mindedness is governments' principal power. People who want to be self-regulating submit themselves to the law and procedures formulated by their representatives. Private wills are shaped by this common aim, for government is *our* act of self-regulation. Its officers are citizens. Its policies are formulated and enacted in our name. We, who sometimes forget that political entitlement entails civic responsibilities, should reclaim them from bureaucrats, legislators, lobbyists, and monopolists who gladly fill the spaces we vacate.

How big must government be in order to regulate other systems? Regulation is suspect wherever statist power overwhelms the civic interest in self-scrutiny and self-control. More than clumsy, this power murders initiative. No opposition—no alternative center of efficacy and imagination—is allowed in states such as these. Nothing flourishes, because every other system is bent to the requirements of the state. Deflation, depression, and stasis are everywhere; families, friendships, businesses, and affiliations wither. Or the effects of regulation are more seditious: bureaucracy suffocates every initiative under a blizzard of rules and penalties. Nothing moves. Government becomes, by default, sponsor and agent for whatever is done.

Regulation's critics emphasize this threat,[17] while neglecting the offsetting burden of unregulated conflicts provoked by competition, scarcity, crowding, imperfect information about the plans and behaviors of others, and the unexpected consequences of interaction. These critics rightly point to the evidence that governments often interfere and destroy in the name of regulation. They rightly dread the corporate state. Fearing alternative, subaltern centers of power, it extinguishes difference, thereby creating the static, forced harmonies of death. But this is not the only, or most likely, outcome in states that regulate. There is a viable, democratic alternative. It encourages systems to reduce their inimical effect on one another by regulating themselves. Conceding that systems cannot always perceive or control their effects on one another, it extends the idea that government is a night watchman: government regulates conflicts that would otherwise damage bystanders or the systems engaged. This point of view sees initiative and regulation as permanent, competing goods. It acknowledges that regulators too often have the upper hand, because state power usually dwarfs the power of the systems regulated. Still, the confrontation of producers and regulators can be softened, if public overseers understand that regulation is not control, and if the systems regulated accept and anticipate the need for public oversight. Regulators in states of this sort do not lust for power. Their authority to regulate systems they do not create or command is power enough.

This program risks mistaking its idealized virtues for achievements: the objective is not the reality. The public of republican thought is unachieved, and was never closer to achievement than the pallid versions of our time. Reformists have yearned for its perfection in American life since early in our history (Dewey's interventionist views were influential earlier this century). But government is clumsy and wasteful, so we inherit the backlash of those who say that intruding governments usurp the rights of the governed. These critics misconstrue the aims of public self-regulation, often because important thinkers have interpreted it autocratically. Rousseau and Hegel, writing for nations that were fragmentary or dispersed, favored states that incorporated lesser systems into a unifying whole. A government that expressed the people's will for unity was to be their unifier. There is also the example of garrison states, where every other activity is subordinated to the aims of aggression or defense. Such governments supervene on other systems for purposes of state, be it unity, defense, or glory. Regulation isn't enough for them: they suppress or direct other systems.

The difference between regulation and control is not always apparent in the tokens of governmental authority, including officers, buildings, budgets, and the respect of those who defer to power. Nor is this difference apparent to corrupt regulators, or to governments inspired by ideas of the corporate good. Yet nothing in these confusions justifies the presumption that government should exceed regulation on the way to direction and control. Government is a service to its citizens and the higher-order systems they form; it reduces their conflicts by facilitating movement within society at large, as when traffic is regulated and contracts are enforced. Autocracy is a perversion of public self-regulation, because government, as regulator, is usually incompetent to do the things it regulates. Families and schools, workers and management, may do their jobs poorly—they may need help. But they are not done better if government does these things itself, or if it commands subaltern systems—families, for example—to do them in a style that government prescribes.

Dewey, like Mill, was suspicious of governments that suppress the many associations of persons for the benefit of a state's corporate aims. Such governments quash initiative by emphasizing duties to the state. Character is reduced to the role of responsible citizen. Nothing could justify this but an extreme, immanent, and (hopefully) temporary threat to collective well-being. There is no evidence (short of such crises) that totalizing control is better for us than the mere regulation—by traffic laws, for example—of systems that choose their objectives. Nor can a democratic government usurp the right to fix these aims. For government is derivative. It is the set of offices and procedures created to oversee the public in whose name it regulates. Government cannot nullify the rights that citizens claim for themselves when they organize as a public.

There is also the material, empirical fact that government's competence as regulator is no guarantee of its ability to do the work regulated. Fruitful activities are initiated and sustained elsewhere, in families, friendships, or business. Eliminate this difference of role—between producers and regulators—and the power to regulate becomes the demand for authority in matters where it is inappropriate or incompetent. We avert this risk by regulating the regulators. We—the public—require that governmental regulation have reasonable aims and vigorously enforced limits. Excepting only some national emergencies, we prescribe that no governmental system or office-holder should confuse oversight with the right to assume control of the practice regulated. We don't quash regulation, because government's power to regulate is an enabling lubricant, one that promotes initiative and productivity by limiting the disabling, demoralizing effects of conflict.

Regulation is prudent management. It satisfies a consequentialist test: What happens when we regulate? Are things made better or worse? We intrude to make a useful difference, without being certain that the difference made will be the one foreseen. For there is no effective alternative to that of careful, revisable intervention, if we care to avert the aggregated consequences of unmanaged complexity. The effects of centrally organized, command economies—strangled initiative and stagnation—are sobering but inconclusive. The former Soviet Union is not the only example of a regulated economy. Other states, including prosperous democracies—Germany and Switzerland, for example—have tighter regulative standards than America. Initiative is not suppressed merely because businesses are made responsible for their effects on workers, clients, water, and air. Systems that demand exemption from all regulations should be carefully examined: what do they do when left to themselves? Concern to defend their profits is already a discipline in businesses that are careful to avoid liability for the damage done to others. But there is not enough foresight—whether self-interested or public-spirited—to justify saying that self-control is the only viable regulation. It is estimable and true to say that every system is responsible for its actions, hence answerable to the private civil actions of neighbors or competitors who claim to be damaged by it. We don't use this as an excuse to eliminate traffic laws and traffic policemen, so that drivers can press their personal claims against one another. Where conflict is imminent or endemic, the public intrudes. How much interference can a society tolerate? Let there be judicious experiments wherever an activity has severely distorting effects on other, vital, human interests.

Regulation resembles gardening. Both credit other systems with autonomy. Both require intrusions that are particular but normative, and less than comprehensive. Skirmishes between regulators and the people or systems regulated are chronic. Even sensitive regulators make contestable judgments. But their touch can be light. Remember, too, that every system is (to some degree) self-regulating. Making systems responsible for themselves relieves government from having to be their oppressive, alien regulator. Does this imply that government's regulations may hinder us no more than traffic laws? That hope is ludicrous to anyone who prepares a payroll, runs a farm, or markets pharmaceuticals. Some governments are perverted irremediably by the bias and ambition of their officers, by their personal or class interests, or by the incompetence that needs power to hide its mistakes. Add that regulation is difficult to achieve in states of great size and diversity. Wouldn't it be better to dispense altogether with governmental regulation? Leave the conflicts that promote it to the systems thereby engaged. Let each of them be more deliberately self-regulating, as airlines that never trade safety for profit can manage themselves. Now consider. Which is the more egregious fantasy: that governments cannot regulate honestly and effectively or that competitors such as businesses will regulate themselves in ways that make them coherent internally and safe for the rest of us?

This formula has an additional provision, one that softens the hard edges of police power by emphasizing a kind of regulation that is complementary to the effect of rules and laws. Dewey described this other control when he wanted to offset the sober intellectuality of the deliberating, lawmaking, republican legislature—the public. What other bonds might citizens have? Surely not the ones of familiarity, intermarriage, or tradition, because America in the 1920s—when *The Public and Its Problems* was written—included unassimilated, former slaves and forty million recent immigrants. There was mutual hostility and suspicion, but little shared tradition that could reduce these antipathies. America could sustain the practice of freedom—averting the conflicts that would subvert it—only if a public were formed from citizens newly baptized into its democratic ways. Yet Dewey perceived that such a public would be subverted by the merely formal relations of its members. Deepening their affinities required the warmer, effective relations that would transform the public into a community of mutually respectful, sympathetic citizens. This would happen, Dewey hoped, when Americans became familiar with one another through working together within schools and businesses, or as legislators. No one would know everyone, but each of us might have our fears appeased by working with sample members of unfamiliar cultures. This would usually be a good experience: few people would act badly; fewer still would betray the faith of those who counted on them. *Sympathy, mutual respect,* and *affection* would become regulative sentiments. They would steady us for the task of making the laws that reduce our conflicts. Civic virtue—participation in the public as it exercises the imperative of self-regulation—would be easier now, because damaging people we like would be no part of our aim.

This fellowship is the recommended substitute for a super-state that deters conflict by prescribing what citizens and subaltern systems shall do. Dewey hoped that respect, responsibility, sympathy, and accessibility would accumulate everywhere within the public. This was his version of Hegel's concrete universal: meaning deliberation meliorated and focused by feeling. There should be evidence of our mutual esteem in the discipline of individuals and small systems, in the efficiency of our public self-regulation, and in the thoughtful scrutiny of our common interests and aims. Working and legislating together should make each of us better than we would otherwise be. These are the messianic, leading principles—the secular parable—of American life. They fail, other reasons aside, because the size, diversity, and energy of America confound this deliberative, generous style of self-regulation. We pay for our heedlessness, in crime, waste, and mutual incomprehension.

3. Values

Values are critical parameters of action. They include the objectives (however diverse and idiosyncratic) for which human systems organize themselves and the norms—the general rules or procedures—used to direct and appraise their actions.

The scruples of individuals—each of us has values that prescribe moral boundaries for acceptable actions—are a helpful point of reference for thinking about the regulative use of values in social systems, as values direct schools and businesses. Still, the analogy is imperfect, because an individual's deliberations, however much they resemble a colloquy, differ from the conversations of a system's members. Individuals, deliberating alone, rank their aims in accord with their values. A desire for coherence (threatened by contrary aims), available energy, and opportunities restrict a person's choices. The members of a system, deliberating together, want accommodations that enable members to satisfy their disparate, private aims by way of their corporate aim.

Mutual accommodation requires that members coordinate their actions, given their shared or complementary aims. Negotiations are often informal yet effective: we get things done. We are more likely to fail if there is confusion about a system's aims or rules or if new members don't understand the affiliative, valorizing stories that explain the loyalty of older members. Systems stagnate or dissolve when there is no consensus about pertinent values, because reciprocities—and self-regulation—lapse for want of agreement about right actions. Churches avert this result by declaring their values at the door.

Every system needs to simplify and integrate its values, so that all participants can know and apply them. But how are a system's values taught to its members? How are these values ratified or revised? How do we organize to satisfy them? These are the achievements of social deliberation. We often participate in communal reflections—during family crises or the discussions that precede elections—such that we modulate our values in the course of working with members having different values. We know too little about this process (partly because our ritual atomism encourages the belief that deliberation is always and only personal and private). What, for example, are the limits on difference within a system that achieves its aims? A clamorous democracy often tests the limits to viable discord without knowing what they are. Labor negotiators and savvy politicians do better: they discern boundaries, barriers, and overlap in the values of their clients or constituents. Most of us don't see as well, though everyone's effectiveness within systems depends on knowing the divergent values that restrict the pursuit of common aims. This is conspicuous when the associates in a project are nation-states. Their accommodations are fragile, because their aims and norms diverge. Joint action is difficult for them.

What mechanism fosters deliberation within a network of systems, so that shared or complementary values may direct the actions of the systems engaged? Here is a place where Dewey's public acquires an additional task. Originally it bestowed rights and mediated or anticipated conflicts among systems. Now the issue is more elementary, because conflicts are sometimes the expressions of contrary values. Regulating conflicts is easier if there is tolerance for different values, a procedure for airing and justifying one's values, or a style of negotiation that produces agreement about overriding, mutually reconciling values. There may be accord, for example, with Mill's principle: that every system is free to pursue its aims up to the point of damaging others. Systems that espouse this principle are more likely to reconsider objectives or behaviors that are inimical to the welfare of their neighbors or competitors, as monopolizing or restraining trade is inimical. Dewey's public becomes a forum where systems learn to distinguish their individual objectives from the aims and procedural values they share. Each participant comes to agree that the steady application of these norms is an overriding objective.

What is this forum? How is it assembled and conducted? Assuming that alternative values are expressed, how do they come to be ranked in ways that are acceptable to all or most of the participants? What agency represents the many participant systems by formulating and enacting policies that express the values agreed? Democratic societies answer that the forum has no settled place or membership: it is established by the many sorts of discourse that prosper within democracies. Discussions crystallize at different places, with effects that ramify from those centers. And sometimes they eventuate in public policy. For there is an agency—government—that brings some of these diverse views to the point of legislative decision. Still, government, as the public organized for self-regulation, is not all of this democratic forum, or even its apotheosis. Talk about values—what to do, what to be, the procedural limits on doing or being it—is pervasive. This is the steady buzz that occurs as people and systems reflect on their aims and the effects of pursuing them. The initiatives of private persons and systems provoke conflicts that are to be resolved by these very people and systems meeting as the public. Manageable conflicts are usually resolved informally when the parties engaged step back to mediate their own quarrels. Occasionally quarrels are suppressed because courts or legislatures impose their solutions. Though now interested persons or their systems talk again. Do the new rules ease disputes or complicate them? Are they fair? Conversation resonates with these questions, because the tension between initiative, conflict, and regulation is perpetual.

People who don't like this tension want to dispense with one side or the other. They would have us abandon regulation for the advantages of unencumbered initiative, though doing this would reduce the forum where conflicts are discussed and regulated to the muttering of victims. Or they propose that we scrap the forum for discussion and decision in favor of edicts that decide objectives and procedures—emphasizing uniformity and discipline—for all a society's systems. Rejecting the extremes, we acknowledge the ineliminable tension in the middle: regulation—meaning self-control and social regulation—is the constant, necessary antidote to initiative in circumstances where there is crowding, scarcity, and competition.

How shall we manage this task in a society that encourages diversity? For difference creates mutual unintelligibility and distaste. Why would you want to do such things, each of us asks the other? This is the state of affairs for which Dewey formulated his program. All systems, his associations, are to commit themselves to the value of an open playing field. Every system is free to undertake whatever objectives its members choose, subject to only two requirements: systems must not damage one another, either directly or by monopolizing the space, resources, personnel, or information that others require to achieve aims of their own; and there must be rules, fairly administered, for adjudicating whatever conflicts arise among them. Freedom, self-control, and mutual regulation are to be our cardinal virtues.

Dewey did not have much to say about ontology. But the associations he emphasized distinguish his version of diversity from one that is better known in our time. "Postmodernists" promote variety by saying that individuals or cultures create their own "worlds." A swelling entitlement should pervade every system as it creates a world appropriate to its aims; for each system, like a Cartesian mind, exists in a space where it has neither partners nor competitors. Each should think itself unbounded, limited only by its power to generate the resources—including the intelligibilities—that sustain it. There is no standpoint, given postmodernist thinking, from which any system can see the ensemble of systems, each one spinning its web. Nature, the common matrix that binds these worlds, is unacknowledged. No provision is made for the norms to which all do, or should, defer. This persuasion is dangerous. It implies that systems may annihilate one another without guilt or blame, merely because they are mutually unthinkable, hence mutually invisible—all this, because each one's constitutive, organizing structure is the function of values known only to its members. Postmodernists are idealists: the problem of other systems—like that of other minds—is endemic among them. But this is an oddly hermetic result. For the mutual oblivion of the world-makers they describe is intolerable (and implausible) in systems that are mutually independent (but interacting), reciprocally engaged, overlapping, or nested. Systems having these relations are richly entwined. Power—war—may eliminate some of the conflicts among them. But there is a better solution: tolerate difference, then formulate and apply the regulative, procedural principles that promote sustainable freedom-in-difference: who goes first at four-way stop signs?

The tolerance for difference—acknowledging another's freedom—is one of the hierarchy of values that determines the shape and quality of life within a society. Health, safety, education, sociality, privacy, piety, and initiative are some other decisive values (perhaps, its "ultimate goods"). These values are a system's highest-order regulators. Their integration establishes a lattice of directives for social practice. Changes of every sort are moderated or directed to satisfy the more or less crude balance of values established within this framework. Every society has attitudes about each of these factors; but their attitudes are different, for historical and circumstantial reasons. Attitudes sometimes change, with implications for their relations; but usually the hierarchy of values is stable.

Dewey's *public* cannot do its task—regulate conflict—if it does not reflect upon and identify these values. For it cannot know the limits of tolerable difference if it is blind to the sensibilities of the society it regulates. Articulating these attitudes would appear to be easy when every participant in the public has a more or less crude sense of the society's values. Yet members disagree about particular values or their limits, so the public must encourage reflection on its own value hierarchy: what do we value, corporately, and why do we prize it?

Answering is difficult, because there is no set of societal norms distinct from the values of individuals. We may liken a society's norms to the aggregated social effect of the members' disparate sensibilities. Molecules have an average effect—pressure—and equally, we may speak of a moral average, calling it a *norm*. The analogy is imperfect, because individual molecules may have any energy state, though a person's values are not counted as part of the moral average if they fall outside the norms of the society concerned. Individuals learn and express their system's norms in singular ways: the mix and balance of values is idiosyncratic and private. Yet members of a community are morally intelligible to others and themselves because of having learned the norms. We learn them thoughtlessly by rote: you do it, I do it after you. Or we discern attitudes in ourselves that were acquired without reflection; we formulate other people's norms by deciphering their actions; or private, self-concerned deliberation is made social and self-conscious, when cooperation requires that we adjust a plan or behavior to make it cohere with the aims and actions of other people.

Indeed, the rote learning of norms would come to little or nothing but for the mix of discourse and reflection that eases our accommodations to one another. Morality is the effect of reciprocity. It is produced when a system's members deliberate together about their aims, scruples, and plans. This conversation is repeated wherever people are allied by shared aims, and wherever they or their systems risk colliding because they act in a shared place. It often happens that norms which work for individuals—truth telling—prove to be equally viable for these systems, so that the range of a norm's adherents moves out and up from the centers of personal reflection until it is broadly shared or challenged by competing norms. Reflection turns dialectical when this happens: contrary norms are considered and defended until there is rough agreement and viable uniformity, or until a legislature formalizes one set of norms, establishing them as laws.

Laws (but also rules, mores, practices, and procedures) are the expression of values used in the service of social regulation. Dewey's public reduces conflict by making laws that repair or avert it. Yet the public must articulate its values before it can know which conflicts to interrupt or the terms for resolving them. For the public's intrusions are intolerable if they do not satisfy norms that are acceptable to its constituents. This implies (as above) that norms have crystallized in the conversations occurring within and among the many systems, and that they are shared by agencies that give formal expression to the public, including its legislature, executive, and judiciary.

A familiar, contrary view proposes that legislators are the moral leaders who prescribe values to people of cruder understanding and sensibility. It is assumed that values, like truths, have standing independent of thought and that we, the mob, need morally perceptive leaders to serve as our public vicars. These refined intellects perceive decent values before teaching them to the rest of us. Suppose, however, that norms are rules of practice, not truths; that they vary among societies; and that the reasons for espousing some norms rather than others is circumstantial and experiential, as nudity is less favored in colder latitudes.

There is no place for moral edicts in the life of the public. Never supposing that norms might be merely proclaimed, it encourages deliberation in the individuals and systems that formulate and defend their versions of social norms. Their conversations are, ideally, a regular feature of social life, so that the form and justification of commonly held values are widely known and agreed. We typically formulate—declare—the norms we adhere to when this is so. We reasonably assume that legislators will apply these norms when making laws, even at cost to a legislator's personal interests. For there is often a discrepancy between private interests and public norms. Indeed, the public is not established if there are no occasions when private interests are overridden in the name of public norms.

Knitting a public from the conversations within and among disparate people and systems seems less urgent in homogeneous societies. With less variety among their people and systems, there is less disparity between social norms and individual practices. Order may be everyone's priority. But here too, the appearance of homogeneity is deceptive. Idiopathy—difference—is a universal feature of persons and systems. We vary from one another, whatever the regularizing practices and norms that disguise our differences. A regime's ferocity is sometimes the best evidence that it fears our private differences and the resistance they incite.

The order required in repressive societies is also taught and respected in the homogeneous societies where freedom is a value, though order in them is evidence of an effective public. Conversely, order is hard to establish in societies that encourage initiative and diversity, for there individuals and systems risk losing touch with one another's values. In America, where initiative is encouraged and conflict tolerated, we need a public (that meets informally in the conversations of neighbors and abutting systems, and formally as the legislature) to devise and teach the norms that make free choice a viable social practice.

Autocracies aim to declare, then freeze, a society's norms. But this is always a deception, one that founders on the resistance of people and systems that continue to amend their values as opportunities and circumstances change. Even core values shift, as attitudes towards euthanasia have changed with the belief that human life is not divinely sponsored if we humans are machines. The drift is usually slow, though it may accelerate with opportunities that seem benign. There are, for example, the radio and television evangelists who convert churches into commercial enterprises. Having a product to sell, they behave like other businesses. Such churches argue that access to their flocks is protected by the Constitutional separation of Church and State. Competitors say that piety should compete in the market with other goods, and that churches selling it should have no special advantages—no exemption from taxes, for example.

Altered perceptions are volcanic and threatening to societies that owe their coherence to the static relations of constituent systems and to norms prescribed by autocrats. Yet well-managed systems, eager to exploit their opportunities, perpetually challenge the norms within their societies, however rigid. Societies that encourage initiative should expect that some undertakings—we don't always know which ones—will challenge core values. Is this dynamism self-subverting: how shall a society cohere when there is flux in its regulative principles? This is not usually threatening in a complex society, where the stability of most values has consequences that much exceed the effects of change in one or a few others. Still, most changes are subtle or slow, so they are not perceived by a system's members. Should we expect the variations to accrete, so that eventually all core values are significantly altered, unnoticed by anyone but historians? This too may be characteristic of all societies, however punitive their response to altered values. Could all a society's values change abruptly? This is least likely, short of a cultural or environmental disaster that makes old values life-defeating.

There is ample change in the regulative values of American life; but this is not grist for the fatalist prediction that core values will change whatever we do. We can resist or advance these changes in the ways described above: distinguishing the public from the private, we can militate for the conversations, inquiries, and reflections that give us some control over the drift of core values. The distinction between the public and private is itself one value to debate. We would not want to alter this procedural norm without the deepest consideration. For this is a value having myriad advantages, including the one afforded to people and systems that regret changes in other core values, changes they cannot prevent. Think of people who dislike the permission to pursue secular values—in speech or education, for example. The public defends these values but never obliges individuals to adopt them in their private lives.

The tension between private systems and the public is the source of a powerful and barely suspected social energy. Like the movement of continental plates, these two are in motion, sometimes at the same pace and in the same direction, sometimes in opposition. There is stability in the network of systems when the shift in public values alters apace with changes in private values. There are spasms, rifts, and buckling surfaces when principal systems go one way and the public goes another. We avert disintegration, or reduce its effects, by perpetually weaving a conversational web within and among systems. We talk about values, so private aims and behaviors are tempered by procedural norms and shared objectives. Confidence in ourselves is enhanced when the free expression of difference helps us to formulate and defend our choices (if only to ourselves). Learning to abide values different from our own, we perceive that mutual tolerance is a critical social value.

4. Planning

Planning is regulation with foresight. Expecting we shall have a future, we resolve to control some part of it. Planning has five aims, including two that are prefigured above as self-control and mutual restraint: *First,* systems plan to do such things as will give them control of themselves: individuals go to school, families buy insurance, companies secure credit and supplies. *Second,* valuing initiative, we are careful not to impede or punish the activity of (most) systems. Intervention is urgent if the playing field (where associations form) closes down because of monopoly, intimidation, or inefficiency. Anticipating conflict, we reduce or avert it—by way of traffic laws and divided highways, for example.

Third is concern for the people who join to create social systems. There is too little initiative (there are too few productive systems) if they are too enfeebled to pursue shared or complementary aims. We plan in order to assure the health and skill of the people. *Fourth,* we organize or create the resources—including space, water, and currency—that are commonly required if systems are to form and sustain themselves. *Fifth,* sharing a common space, having common needs, we formulate and rank our shared values. These five aims are permanent topics for deliberation, irrespective of the ways we satisfy them.

Responsibility for these tasks is widely diffused throughout the network of systems. Individuals, families, and governments have the primary responsibility for health. Education falls to individuals, families, churches, or governments. Planning is never effectively centralized, because there is no plan of more than modest complexity that is appropriate to the different circumstances, members, postures, or aims of the many different systems. Traffic laws—Drive on the right!—parking rules, and schedules for picking up refuse are often standardized, but they are simple. There is a general rule that prescribes the orderly conduct of people on dance floors—don't step on or hurtle into other dancers—but there are no detailed rules, because the dances are different, and because dancers interpret particular steps in varying ways. Universal planning—rules that prescribe the same conduct everywhere—would eliminate these differences in the name of predictability or control, hence uniformity.

Friedrich Hayek feared coerced regularity and opposed economic planning, because it required that planners should know more than ever they could:

> Far from being appropriate only to comparatively simple conditions, it is the very complexity of the division of labor under modern conditions which makes competition the only method by which such co-ordination can be adequately brought about. There would be no difficulty about efficient control or planning were conditions so simple that a single person or board could effectively survey all the relevant facts. It is only as the factors which have to be taken into account become so numerous that it is impossible to gain a synoptic view of them that decentralization becomes imperative. But once decentralization is necessary, the problem of co-ordination arises—a co-ordination which leaves the separate agencies free to adjust their activities to the facts which only they can know and yet brings about a mutual adjustment of their respective plans. As decentralization has become necessary because nobody can consciously balance all the considerations bearing on the decision of so many individuals, the co-ordination can clearly be effected not by "conscious control" but only by arrangements which convey to each agent the information he must possess in order effectively to adjust his decisions to those of others. And because all the details of the changes constantly affecting the conditions of demand and supply of the different

commodities can never be fully known, or quickly enough be collected and disseminated, by any one center, what is required is some apparatus of registration which automatically records all the relevant effects of individual action and whose indications are at the same time the resultant of, and the guide for all the individual decisions.[18]

No planner can know all the factors pertinent to the circumstances of individual buyers and sellers, so that any plan imposed on them as a routine or rule compels some or many to act in ways that are contrary to their perceived interests. Buyers and sellers rebel by declining to act as the plan prescribes. It fails, but not without disrupting the production and distribution of goods and services. It is better to let buyers and sellers express their different intentions in contexts where factors independent of their differences—Hayek's "apparatus of registration"—are steady. He supposed that a stable currency and prices fixed by supply and demand are aspects of this apparatus. It enables buyers and sellers to translate their subjective preferences into an objective medium: they buy or sell, or decline to buy or sell, at market prices. Prices rise or fall as there are more buyers or sellers, but the excess of one typically brings the other into the market, so prices are stable and roughly predictable (allowing for seasonal or other deviations). Hayek's aversion to planning allowed for exceptions, as war requires them. But exceptions are costly, as Britain required decades to recover from the distortions of two wars. Discount these special circumstances, and nothing justifies intrusions that devalue currencies while destroying the market's capacity to establish prices—the common measure to which every participant defers—for whatever goods are bought and sold.

Hayek feared that a little planning is a greased slide to ever more of it, hence to distortions that ruin markets. Is his fear justified? Consider the work of the American Federal Reserve Board's Open Market Committee. It controls the money supply in ways that minimize inflation while averting deflation. It considers trends, sometimes making veiled warnings before acting decisively. Should we suppose that its actions are capricious? Isn't it usually or always true that this committee calculates and alters its policies in light of its economic objectives? The Open Market Committee has managed American economic growth with remarkable success in recent years. Here is evidence that planning is not always bad: all this in a milieu where planning is anathema.

Hayek's antipathy needs qualification: bad planning sabotages us; judicious planning may be good for us. Even he agreed that planning is sometimes appropriate:

There are, finally, undoubted fields where no legal arrangements can create the main condition on which the usefulness of the system of competition and private property depends: namely, that the owner benefits from all the useful services rendered by his property and suffers for all the damages caused to others by its use. Where, for example, it is impracticable to make the enjoyment of certain services dependent on the payment of a price, competition will not produce the services; and the price system becomes similarly ineffective when the damage caused to others by certain uses of property cannot be effectively charged to the owner of that property. In all these instances there is a divergence between the items which enter into private calculation and those which affect social welfare; and whenever this divergence becomes important, some method other than competition may have to be found to supply the services in question.[19]

Hayek cites roads and pollution as matters that reasonably fall under a governments' jurisdiction. One would expect him to agree that an efficient government meets these responsibilities by planning roads, reservoirs, or sewers, by building granaries for the seven lean years, or designing corporate structures to encourage the use of new technologies. Planning of these sorts would seem to be judicious, good sense. Private interests may do more than was once anticipated, as they run prisons or supply water. But they won't do everything we need. Government inherits responsibility for planning and acting in circumstances where a general interest makes profit irrelevant (schools), or where private interests decline the work (putting out fires).

We require that government do these things without affecting private initiatives. This happens, for example, when planning eventuates in a system that directs traffic flow. The plan reduces conflicts while facilitating actions that drivers initiate for themselves: government merely regulates traffic; drivers decide where and when to go. Examples like this contrast with the tasks that actual governments assign themselves (with Hayek's approval), as when a government supplies water or energy to factories and households in regions where no one else will supply them. The costs are substantial: government inherits the task by default. Many people or higher-order systems benefit, including families and businesses that profit directly and companies that are later enriched by investments in the newly improved regions. Planning for government investment implies a "mixed economy"—some enterprises are sponsored by individuals or private systems, others by government. When government cannot withdraw—because the activity is generally desirable though not commercially viable—we double the occasions for planning: government plans in order to regulate other systems and for activities inherited when private businesses refuse a task that serves a particular sector of the population or the people at large. A government that does both inevitably seems greedy and pervasive: it competes with other systems for opportunities and resources while making and enforcing rules they follow.

Purists object, because government hereby compromises the (ideally) rigid demand that it must not act in ways that favor one or another private interest. Government was to be the public's neutral organ for regulating its members: planning that exploits or provides resources is nowhere anticipated in the idea that we plan to solve or avert conflict. Governments sometimes try to recover their status as neutral regulators by privatizing government-owned businesses. But this strategy has its limits, if there are desirable or necessary services that no commercial system will undertake. The result is a mixed blessing: the competitor is also the self-interested regulator. Governmental planning is never convincingly disinterested in these circumstances. One thinks of business taxes raised to supply the capital needed for government projects, and of fire departments that compete with private companies for trucks.

What explains this perversion of the idea that government is the public organized to regulate conflicts? Government's power to satisfy needs would be sufficient to explain it, even if there weren't the added factor that power is hard to restrain as it fills and dominates every social task and space. There is also a different explanation, one that is implicit in the five aims for planning listed at the beginning of this section: namely, planning for control, planning to reduce conflict and encourage initiative, planning to endow people with the power for initiative, planning to exploit resources, and planning to formulate and rank shared values. Government becomes focal to planning, because of its role as the public organized for self-reflection and self-regulation. Reflection and initiative begin when persons and systems affiliate themselves with others to control their common future. The neighbor becomes a partner. But then difficulties slow the process: we can't agree about a shortlist of priorities, or we do agree but can't organize to achieve them. A government having the power and means to build as it chooses breaks the impasse by crystalizing public opinion: meaning only that it chooses and acts in the name of the public. Government comes to be identified, half mystically, with the will of the people, though this formula is ambiguous: does it imply that the public is the forum for expressing public concerns, or that tasks are publicly debated so that the government can solve them? A government organized to regulate conflicts soon finds itself struggling with other systems for the resources needed to satisfy high-priority interests—housing, education, or defense, for example.

This evolution offends thinkers who favor a simpler division of labor: initiatives and self-regulation to people, families, businesses, and schools; conflict resolution to publics organized as governments. Never let government intrude in other domains, they say, because doing this muddies the distinction between regulator and producer. We are past the time when these other tasks could be distributed without alloting some of them to government, as Hayek agreed. It is critical, nevertheless, that we not lose sight of the structural relations that bind government to other systems: government, however distended, is one system among many. Originally designed to plan for other systems—the better to regulate them—it now plans for itself.

Remember too that the emphasis on government's role as regulator is the feature of one theory of government, and that government has usually done or been many things this theory deplores. It is not surprising that government exceeds this limited role, or that social life resists the directives that issue from theories. Think of the effort required to keep a garden or farm from reverting to wilderness.

5. Procedural Neutrality, Minority Rights, and Inclusion or Exclusion

Preventing harm, encouraging initiative, and achieving consensual goods are alternative, sometimes mutually exclusive, aims. Pollution control is a familiar example: it restrains the initiative of manufacturers. Societies may differ in their ranking of these values. Americans sometimes hesitate to regulate all but the most urgent conflicts, because of supposing that freedom from regulation is a condition for the freedom to act. Or we retell other people's histories to justify our fear that a tyrannical state may oblige us to do or believe abhorrent things. Regulation, we imagine, is forced conversion to deplorable aims, beliefs, or practices. This is shortsighted, if the state—the public organized for self-regulation—cannot disavow its responsibility for regulation, given the concomitant effects on initiative and conflict. What features of regulation make it tolerable to those it controls? The neutrality of the regulators is one principal factor: the state created by our need for self-regulation should have procedures that are blind to the interests it adjudicates, as traffic laws apply universally, without respect to drivers or their destinations. Compare individual systems, such as families and businesses. They rise (ideally) to a neutral posture as participants in the lawmaking public, while their private aim is that of securing or satisfying themselves. Kant required that participants in the kingdom of ends use the categorical imperative to test every maxim, but he never doubted that each thinker would test and use maxims useful to him or herself.[20] We fear this bias in officers who may abuse their positions for the advantage of themselves and their friends. Accordingly, neutrality has complementary implications: laws are to be neutrally formulated and applied. Abstracting from irrelevant differences in the domain to which a law applies, we are careful not to invoke such differences when applying it: tax laws, for example, are to be applied without regard for political loyalty or gender. The law, we say, is blind. Neutrality is liberating to regulators: they look for the common denominator targeted by the law, not for irrelevant differences (political enemies, for example).

The demand that we abstract from difference in the name of fairness is odd. What can *fair* mean if not that each system is considered in the fullness of its specificity and difference? For surely, it is not fair to the system of differences that is Paul if we ignore his specific motives and context to the point that he could as well be Peter or John. Neutrality requires that a law's applications ignore differences that are incidental to the grounds for invoking it. But why is it fair that applications be coarse-grained, without regard for distinguishing differences within the domain of the law? We justify this policy by recalling the motive for regulation: interaction has consequences that are deleterious to some or all of the systems engaged. Do cars move at the regulated speed in the orderly way prescribed? This, not their colors, shapes, or makers, is the matter regulated. Are some cars overpowered for city driving? Let their owners know that qualities they admire are incidental to the social value served by the law.

Challenges to the neutrality of a law's applications vary with this difference in the use of laws: some laws enjoin behaviors that have effects we want; others deter conduct whose effects are undesirable. Regulation expresses these complementary attitudes: we scan the effects of interacting systems looking for opportunities to improve either systems or their relations; or we look for damage. Preventing harm is less contentious than choosing among competing lists of goods, so we are less apt to notice breaches of neutrality when harms are ranked, as sickness, war, and death are odious to everyone. Allegedly positive goods—affirmative action and redistribution of wealth, for example—are often disputed, so that formulas reconciling the aims of competing individuals or systems are hard to negotiate. Regulating for positive aims is mostly restricted to goods, such as fresh air, that are undisputed.

Governments that are aggressive on behalf of contested goods are perceived as doing the work of special interests. We recall Marx's belief that no state can be neutral until divisive economic interests are resolved (by proletarian control of land, labor, and capital), so that governments can rule in the interests of all their citizens. No government currently is, or will foreseeably be, neutral in this respect, given that ruling parties typically represent the economic interests of dominant classes, cliques, or companies, whether they address foreign powers or their citizens. There may be no way to avert the chronic favoritism of governments, though it should be possible to identify, and sometimes to justify, their biases. Failure to do this—failure even to declare a government's priorities, hence its justification for favoring one or another interest—reflects the public's inability to organize itself as a forum for discussion of the people's business. We don't want to know a government's biases; or monopolistic interests sabotage open discussion. Either way, the public is crippled.

Marx is nevertheless misleading when he argues that economic power is the only factor subverting neutrality. Ideological objectives, whether military, political, religious, or secular, often supersede economic interests, as they did in Sparta and do more recently in Iraq and Iran. Economic power was not the decisive factor in struggles for political power within Marxist states, including the former Soviet Union: the Communist Party, not industry, won those disputes. Neutrality is overwhelmed in all these ways. Governments have less of it than they require for organizing the public's deliberations and expressing its will.

There is, at best, a generous neutrality regarding issues that are not central to the economic, political, or other interests that dominate state power. For there is consensus (if not unanimity) about a shortlist of urgent goods, including education, public health, clean air, and water. Should we defer from organizing to achieve objectives such as these because regulation violates the freedom of persons or systems who do not acknowledge the goodness of their effects: should we decide not to fluoridate public water supplies because of those who decry the effect? We pass from the safeguards of procedural neutrality to those of *minority rights*.

The contest of values may be innocuous when disputes are restricted to words; but it turns consequential when regulators enforce behaviors that express particular, contested values. Hence the problem of minority rights: how shall we defend the interests or values of those members of the community who are threatened by particular laws, because of penalties or other discriminatory treatment. One solution is a set of constitutionally sanctioned procedures—vetoes—that defend minority rights. These are limits on the power of a majority to establish penalties, restrictions, or values by way of the laws that regulators apply. Regulators, such as community policemen, need to know these limits so that exceptions made for particular systems or their members—exemptions because of religious scruples are an example—are not seen as advantages that are bought and sold.

How ample should minority rights be? Three considerations are primary. First is the realization that diversity among the persons and systems regulated makes it likely that each of them will be out of sympathy, occasionally, with the majority view. The interest in establishing minority rights is, therefore, universal. A second, offsetting point is the need for regulation and neutrality. Exceptions to the law diminish its credibility and efficacy. Taking care that no law crushes a minority's reasonable concerns, we aim to establish laws that apply to everyone within the domain established by some least common denominator. A third consideration is each state's perception of its power. Imagine a state so weak that every individual or system has a veto on government's intervention, or a state whose actions are unconstrained—it does whatever it likes. Citizens and the systems in which they participate are usually unwilling to approve either extreme: a veto in the hands of every system guarantees public paralysis; a state's unconditional power is a license to abuse everyone. Minority rights are claimed in the middle, where private and public interests compete.

Minority rights are typically understood as claims made by individuals or groups against the majority or the state. Yet it happens sometimes that a public interest opposes the attitudes of systems it oversees. Should we familiarize ourselves with the religious views of other people, thereby encouraging respect or tolerance for them? Or should we refuse to inform ourselves or our children about ideas that are anathema to us? Which interest should dominate when the parochial views of one faith are set against republican ideals that favor an informed citizenry, one whose citizens know the distinguishing practices and ideas of the society's constituent systems? We answer by considering the demand for personal self-regulation. It requires that one control him or herself in relation to other people; and that one participate in public deliberations where ideas are mooted, values are ranked, and laws are made. Both tasks require that we be familiar with the people and systems of our state. For one will not do either very well if ignorance about other people and systems compounds our hostility to them. This consideration is decisive when a society educates its members so that it—as the public—may be self-regulating. American courts typically affirm this value: they rule that education for the role of citizen is more important than the risk that one may be seduced or perverted by hearing views different from one's own.[21] (This judgment assumes, though it is incidental to the public's role, that our convictions are strong enough to withstand hearing other views.) We also provide an alternative for the frustrated minority. Those who dislike the feared liberality of public schooling can enroll their children in private schools having a clientele restricted to people like themselves. Corporate self-regulation would be confounded if everyone made this choice. But this is a viable way of assuaging the minority; it releases people or systems from their subjugation to the public and its rules.

These two strategies have similar effects: we make room for persons and systems having different aims. Either way—by mutual recognition and tolerance or by promoting minority rights—we reassure one another that we are safe companions. None of us would seize the powers of state, using them to install and defend the interests of one person, cabal, organization, or association. Still, there is a difference between the two solutions. The appeal to minority rights is defensive: it expresses the anxiety that persons or their system are threatened. Acknowledging this perception—invoking minority rights to appease it—implies to the minority that their fear is legitimate. It confirms to them and others that fear (justified or not) is a reasonable basis for public policy. Much more daring is the strategy of learned tolerance, with its implication that mutual fears would be ill-grounded if mutual anxiety and hostility were quashed. Notice, too, the confirmation that government is often benign, not invariably oppressive. It sometimes secures other systems in their private spaces.

Last (under the heading of *regulation*) is this question about *inclusion* and *exclusion*. Civic virtue is the concern shown by each citizen and system for the maintenance of the public. This virtue extends each person's moral purview beyond the range of the several systems that engage him or her to the network of persons and subsystems whose relations are regulated by the state. There is a moral trajectory in the evolution of our awareness: from self-concern to concern for the systems in which one participates, then to all the systems whose relations fall to the oversight of the citizens or societies organized as the state. Every public administrator is better equipped to distinguish public from private interest, each with its prerogatives, when this trajectory is emphasized in the education of citizens.

Is there also a further step, from the people and systems engaged within our state to all people and perhaps all systems, whatever their state of origin? Universalism is problematic. Citizens often resist it. Why should they agree that individuals, associations, or organizations native to other states—Egyptian brotherhoods or Canadian families—automatically deserve the treatment accorded to individuals and systems in our state? What explains or justifies a difference in the treatment accorded to the people or stabilities of other states?

One primary reason is the essential locality of practical life. Impinging on one another, learning about our differences, we reduce friction by adjusting our relations. Doing this over many years, we create a web of local laws and practices.

They are often similar among venues, because the problems and conflicts of human systems are similar everywhere. Yet laws and practices may vary considerably from place to place, because of different circumstances or histories. This is the commonplace that farming, fishing, and mining occasion different sorts of regulations, and that a society comes to be formed in distinctive ways because of such practices.

Should anyone receive the protection of local laws upon presenting himself within their jurisdiction? Which is more reasonable, the attitude that universalizes or the one that construes morality and self-regulation locally? Ontology supplies evidence for both sides. It remarks, on the side of locality, that people are sensitive to their partners and neighbors. We typically adjust our behaviors because of their idiosyncrasies. Morality of this sort is discerning; it satisfies the particular character and interests of the people involved. Or we promote universality because we discern similarity in difference. No matter that you seem unrecognizable to me; closer inspection reveals our affinities. Valuing myself and my neighbors, I value you. Why make this extrapolation? Because I cannot justify a difference in behavior or law where there is no significant difference in fact. The localist says that there is a difference, for this is not someone with whom I am normally engaged, someone with whom I share a history. More, treating him as I treat those who are better known to me requires that I behave in ways that he may not understand: there could be no reciprocity between us. The universalist responds with counterfactuals: this alien would respond appropriately (albeit in a style unfamiliar perhaps to me) if he or she were convinced of my good intentions; there could be trust between the members of disparate communities if the near universal fear of difference were allayed by the realization that most differences are incidental to the interests and problems we share.

This opposition is intensified by two additional, mutually offsetting considerations. One side speaks of causal reciprocities and the systems they generate. There are pen pals and telephone friendships; but these are extended versions of local phenomena that are sustained by mutual accessibility and regular contact. The "global village" fills people's heads with the same "information." It may create similar attitudes; it doesn't usually create reciprocities or systems that supersede local ones. The other side emphasizes a value that abstracts from the material circumstances where systems are generated and sustained. Universalizers propose that our moral sentiments and principles should apply to everyone, hence to people with whom we have no history or mutual reliance and sympathy. We have Kant's dictum that contingencies of feeling or situation are irrelevant to morality. Or we generalize Hume's claim that one sort of moral feeling—

sympathy—informs our attitudes toward people we do not know: we can feel their distress as keenly as we know the pain of those who are close to us. Here is affective content for moral extrapolations beyond the circle of one's friends.

This opposition is not easily solved. Morality is local, at its inception, for most of our relations. Life in large, complex societies requires that we extend the domain of our moral concerns to people or systems that engage us only casually or mediately. Relations to many people whose work is critical for our own are rarely more than polite. We would think favorably of their interests if we knew them, or knew their contribution to our work; but we do not. People more remote, in thought or space, fall outside our network of moral concern. Not going out of our way to run over a stranger or his bicycle, we are much less concerned for him than we would be for someone close to us. The idea of moral universals doesn't easily cohere with the localization of moral practice, though the domain of our sympathy is extended by newspapers and television. We are quick to help friends; we care about the barbarisms committed in many places; but the energy we bring to the one contrasts with our torpor in the other. Too bad, we say; it's not our problem. Locality strangles the impulse to universalize.

Should we strive to achieve a universal moral demand for recognition, reciprocity, and sympathy, as in Dewey's Great Community? Should we solicit help for schools, plagues, or merely everyday annoyances in other places: Idaho or Eritrea, if one lives in New York; Brooklyn or Ecuador, if one lives in Boise? We sometimes ameliorate these problems; but more often, we ignore them. The issue is joined more dramatically when refugees cross our borders. Here they are—at our door. What should we do? Never pretending to answer the question, I suggest a criterion that limits what we do. Considering the economy of our society (to the degree that it can be distinguished from the global economy) and the economies of its constituent systems, we ask this question: how many people can we integrate into our systems before our reciprocities and resources are irreparably damaged or deformed? This is a criterion that limits inclusion without implying that anyone in particular is excluded. It is a criterion vastly more liberal than the one currently applied by most states when refugees ask for asylum.

6. Summary

Regulation is implicit wherever a system is formed in the mutually modulating, reciprocal causal relations of its parts. Systems are self-sustaining or self-transforming when they regulate something within themselves by repressing or promoting it. They are mutually coordinating when they alter the reciprocities that join them. Regulation of both sorts is involuntary and mechanical in systems that are pre-human—molecules and cells, for example—but voluntary and conscious (though often reduced to habit) in humans and the systems we form. Getting control of ourselves, modulating or redirecting the systems in which we participate, we shift relations within and among systems to our supposed advantage. Interventions are most effective and least costly when the range of their effects is small. No wonder that personal self-regulation—self-control—is everyone's ideal. Public self-regulation—whether economic, political, or ecological—has complexities that sometimes exceed our understanding and control: we risk affects that are less predictable and hard to repair. These are some conditions, benefits, and costs of our corporate well-being.

IX. ECOLOGY

Plato and Descartes (equivocally), then Kantian idealists (dogmatically), require that mind keep its distance from nature. It cannot, because every stable system—we humans included—lives in the midst of Kant's things-in-themselves as one of them. Are there pervasive natural processes? If so, they occur within us. Are there universal laws of nature? If so, they apply to us. New properties are introduced into nature by the formation of higher-order systems, as consciousness and valuation are distinctly animal or human activities and properties. None of them is extra-natural: they emerge when reciprocal relations are established among a system's proper parts, where each of the parts is a system or nest of systems having elementary particles as its least parts.

Do all these higher-order properties fall within the ambit of physics? They do, in the respect that higher-order systems are composed of particles in space-time and are subject, therefore, to the laws and processes appropriate to elementary particles. They do not, insofar as higher-order systems and the new properties thereby generated supply special domains for other disciplines. Chemistry is distinct from physics because of the emergent properties of molecules. Biology and literature are all the more remote from it. For no matter that the pervasive properties and processes important to physics are constitutive of books and authors; words and authorial intentions are the evidence of emergent entities and properties, rules, regularities, or symmetries. Nothing in this implies an extra-physical status for systems and processes that physics cannot describe. Knives are different from forks, and both are different from chopsticks, but they and their uses are only physical.

Locating ourselves within nature, then affirming that everything about us is physical, vindicates the basic ideas of ecology: we humans are an animal species that occupies a niche within the physical world. Our locus, with all its species-sustaining resources, is the space established by the many systems that impinge on us. The biblical story—that these things were made for our use and pleasure—confuses their utility with the conditions for their being. For we find ourselves in the midst of things we shape but do not make. (Molecular engineering will somewhat change this balance.)

Concern for these other systems may have either of two roots. We may be anxious for the environment because it supplies energy and materials we need: using it effectively secures and satisfies us; carelessly running it down is shortsighted. Or the risk is immediate: poisoning resources affects us, too. (A third possible root—that natural systems have intrinsic value, hence rights—is considered in Chapters Four and Eight and discounted.) Either way, sociality is extended, because both alternatives imply that human systems are located in the midst of richly overlapping and nested physical systems, each one having extensive and critical effects on some or many others. Ecology is sometimes dismissed as a passing fad, one that foolishly reifies nature. For isn't nature merely a "transcendental object," one to which we ascribe extra-experiential reality, though nothing other than mind and its experience can be known to exist?[22] Acknowledging this Kantian conceit, I suggest this other interpretation: the veneer of human constructions overlays, or lies within, systems we shall never change. Knowing and accommodating ourselves to them is simple, (Stoic) good sense.

X. CHANGE

It may seem that my description of stabilities makes them oddly static, like clockwork. Motion is everywhere, but all of it is routed and controlled. Defective parts are repaired or replaced, so that everything goes on as before. This misdescribes reciprocity, motion, and change. It is also false to social changes that are irregular, unforeseen, and beyond our control. Here is, first, a characterization of social change, then a specification of its principal conditions, and finally some remarks about its control.

1. Characterizing Change

Change, the noun, signifies the altered state or position of a thing. *Change,* the verb, signifies a process having this altered state as one of the moments in a sequence of movements or transformations. Change is perpetual, as movement is perpetual, in the geometrized, dynamic spacetime where systems assemble and stabilize or dissolve. A comprehensive metaphysics of nature would describe change and its relations to the other categorial features of nature, including matter, energy, and spacetime. It would likely say that particular changes are moments in the overlaid patterns of change, some linear or nonlinear but deterministic, others random. It would consider the idea that change is illusory and the belief that pervasive change implies a reference to something unaltered.

My focus is simpler: namely, the assembly and stabilization, disruption, and disintegration of systems that are bound by the reciprocities of their parts. This includes the emergence or dissolution of properties, hence the fixing of determinable property values by determining conditions. These effects—emergent systems and emergent properties—typically occur as one. Not knowing what to think of something—my views are determinable—I speak to you. My uncertainty is resolved as we talk: with you as determining condition, I come to hold a specific point of view. You in turn are bound to me, because something I need or say holds you. Such reciprocities stabilize relationships, so that a system and one or many properties, including conviction and trust, emerge. Changes are not always this productive: they may disrupt rather than stabilize, so that systems repair themselves or dissolve.

Assembly, transformation, and disassembly, whether sputtering or continuous, are pervasive in nature. Changes therein are heated to a rolling boil. Some things are lifted in the froth to an order they sustain for a time before breaking up. Many others dissolve into turbulence, where their parts churn for a time before establishing new, sustainable relations, either to free agents like themselves or to systems already formed. A dynamic steady state is (metaphorically) a pause, one achieved in some region of a soup in which disassembly and disorder are more common than stabilizing reciprocity.

It is an odd choice of examples, given this point of view, when thinkers as hard-headed as Plato and Augustine think that the orbits of the planets and stars are the proper model for such changes as occur in social systems. They approve of change only if it is circular, hence regular and predictable. Wanting social control, they idealize circumstances in which change has stopped, though it never does. There is, however, something canny in their dream, for it is not true that every aspect of human societies must be perpetually coming together or falling apart. Stability in reciprocity is possible, because there is a decoupling of orders within a hierarchy of nested systems: changes at one level do not entail changes at every other. Consider a nation whose stability is enhanced by the absence of rancorous neighbors—Iceland, for example. Its practices are typically stable, though its citizens are regularly replaced by the cycle of births and deaths. One imagines that societies may be stable over many hundreds of years, though all their members change and though many of the constituent intermediate sub-societies—families, ships' crews, and schoolmates—have come and gone. Disassembly at one level is consistent with long-time stability at other levels: lower-order stabilities—healthy people—supervene on the metabolic processes whereby some cells die while others are generated. It is even true that stability at a higher level may require chronic instability at one or several of the lower levels. A productive human society would be impossible if its citizens never died: there would be too many people to feed.

There are, principally, three changes that concern us: the formation of systems, the routinized motion within established reciprocities, and alterations occurring within individual systems or systems of systems. Each of these kinds of change—call them *formation, routinization,* and the *sustaining of viable complexity*—has its distinctive features, limits, and conditions.

2. Formation

Systems form when causal reciprocities bind their parts. This is sometimes the mutual accommodation of things that mesh with one another and sustain their reciprocity. There are, for example, generous neighbors who look after one another's interests without regard for the benefits to themselves. The binder at other times is negative feedback: each cause regulates the other, or each is regulated by one or more others within a network of reciprocally related causes. Systems are not formed unless the reciprocal causes have a source of free energy, and unless their constituents are mutually accessible. I suppose that things are disposed, or not, for causal reciprocity; but I agree that questions about the detailed physical conditions for their affinity or incompatibility are better left to mechanics, chemistry, and molecular biology. There are, however, some considerations to which philosophical views are pertinent. *First* is the error implied by Hume's principle that anything may follow anything else. Applying this principle to prospective causes entails that any two things can engage one another reciprocally. This is surely false. Most things cannot participate as reciprocally controlling causes within particular negative feedback systems: there are no conversations with ventriloquists' dummies. *Second* is each cause's response to the action of another: is it impaired or enhanced, inhibited or excited? Some interactions provoke mutually controlling cycles of excitation and inhibition: B's response to A (and the reverse) provokes A to behave in a way that sustains B's effective relation to *A*. This is the mutual control of negative feedback—the structural, dynamic spine on which human social systems are founded.

3. Routinization

Change is routine when the energy exchanges that stabilize a system move through established causal relations. Routinization is selected, so to speak, over the course of a developmental history in which random actions and reactions— someone speaks to anyone within earshot—are replaced by the orderly exchanges of a negative feedback system—a conversation. Making and sustaining reciprocal relations is not a necessary or, perhaps, even a probable outcome: action and reaction might always dissipate. But there, in a large sample of interactions, some mutually controlling reactions do occur. Actions that would disrupt the newly established reciprocities happen less often in neighborhoods where these systems are formed; or the modularity of emergent systems makes them resilient when disruptions occur. Sustained reciprocities, then extended networks and layered orders of stabilized reciprocities, are the result.

Their achievement is evidence of the free energy required and exploited by the causes, the system's parts. Each part establishes (from some energy reserve) such reciprocities as supply its system-sustaining energy. The niches of a biosphere illustrate the predicament and its solution. Each niche is defined by its energy needs and products. Neighboring niches may have needs and products that are inversely complementary: the oxygen and carbon dioxide, respectively, eliminated and metabolized by plants are metabolized and eliminated by animals. A system is stabilized—its reciprocities become routine—if there is free energy to fuel each cause as it acts on the other, and if the additional energy required for breaking these relations is greater than the energy required to sustain them. Disruptions come in various ways. Conflict between a system's members extinguishes their reciprocities, perhaps by exhausting the energy required to sustain them; or the members are impaired by sickness, distracted by other duties, or destroyed. Systems recover from assaults like these if they secure a supply of energy, material, or information, so that members or relations may be replaced or repaired. Otherwise, the systems lapse.

4. Limiting and Sustaining Complexity

Why do systems stop growing? Why are there limits on the elaboration of networks and hierarchies of systems? One answer is the absence of free energy sufficient to feed ever burgeoning systems: a rose bush doesn't bloom continuously.

This is a limit on growth, one that assures the collapse of systems that outrun their energy supply. Parallel answers concern materials and information: great builders run out of bricks; military operations fail because significant information is lost when communications fail. A different reason for limited growth is the mix of defensiveness and grandiosity in some human social systems. Single individuals may be asocial, because of fearing they will be overwhelmed in the company of other people. Friendships close around the few friends, each one afraid of losing the others to competitors. An organization's members fear that their sense of purpose or affiliation will be superseded by a different one, thereby reducing the importance of their commitment to the system. Its managers fear the loss of authority that would come were the system to welcome new members or affiliate itself with others. Resisting change by isolating a congenial system—turning it into a lifeboat—we defend ourselves from the new members or affiliations that may undermine us. Compare disciplines that thrive to those that wither. One grows in many directions at once, exploiting opportunities that extend the work it does, welcoming new members. The other is reduced to shards: isolated members tell self-justifying stories.

Is there a single, "principal" cause for social change? Or are there always many causes? Marx supposed that such changes are always the effects of economic organization. He was often right about the economic determinants of effects he cited, but wrong about the uniquely privileged role that he claimed for economic causes. Marx's error was stubborn emphasis. No one perceived more clearly than he that the world is a network of systems, some independent, some overlapping, all of them nested within various hierarchies.[23] Change, tumultuous change, may be instigated at any of these sites or levels. Changes occurring at one level of a hierarchical system ripple through it, with consequences for some or all of its constituent levels: lead in the water supply poisons members of every family, bringing down every system; or the layered and extended system of systems collapses because of incompetent generals or inept procedures for distributing credit or food.

Extended networks of overlapping and nested systems exhibit an odd coupling of strengths and weakness. Like the neighborhoods of a large city, there is modularity but interdependence. Each system may have multiple bases of support, but telephone lines or avenues facilitate the spread of decay. It is unlikely that weakness or strength at any level or site will be augmented and propagated throughout the network of systems, but this does happen. Witness the influence of Moses, Jesus, and Mohammed. What theory would have predicted them? Marx would have said that his own theory explains the hopelessness of the poor, hence their susceptibility to religious myth. The nuclear family, the capitalist state, and so many other changes are consequences, he would have said, of economic organization. But this is false to the complexity of systems that have several or many functions and several or many vulnerabilities. Poisoning or disease, or health and well-being, promote some changes. The accidents of friendship or family, language, technology, or religion promote many more. Obeisance to a single cause ignores the interdependence of these many factors. Plato described the decline of the ideal state by emphasizing the incremental loss of its two cardinal virtues, specialization and self-control.[24] But Plato ignored myriad other possible causes (a workers' revolt against didactic music and poetry, for example). Marx's tunnel vision is equally constricting. A laterally extended, multiply layered system can change in many ways. It is likely to be changing in several ways at every moment.

5. Vulnerability

The systems of a network are especially vulnerable to change at four sites.

First, a freestanding system falls apart—let binary stars be our example—if changes within a proper part disable it for the reciprocities that bind the system; if the distance between the parts is altered so that the efficacy of their causal, gravitational relations is reduced or increased so that one star escapes the other or is drawn into it; if an agent external to the system interferes with the parts or their relations by capturing or destroying one of them; or if a system more powerful than this one—a black hole perhaps—annihilates it. Human social systems are richly connected to their circumstances, so these vulnerabilities are also common to many of them. Either of two friends may die or tire of the other; opportunities or obligations may force one to leave for a distant place; one may suffocate the other; or circumstances—war or unemployment—may overwhelm them. Every freestanding human system is vulnerable in all these ways; none is vulnerable in *only* these ways.

Second, change is almost guaranteed where nesting occurs, because the economy of a higher-order system is imposed on its parts. A storekeeper runs his own affairs: he determines prices, inventory, product quality, and service. Let him become a franchise-holder, and he becomes responsible to a higher-order system for the standards it sets. The situation is more complicated still when higher-order systems compete for jurisdiction over the same part. Every difference in their demands is a basis for conflict and change in the part.

Third, overlapping systems perpetually risk instability, because the part overlapped is responsible to systems whose aims may conflict, systems that may compete for the loyalty of the part. The child's relation to his or her parents is unproblematic if parental child-rearing styles cohere and if the relations of the parents are good. But there is always a difference of styles and affinities, so the child comes to have a distinctive relation to each parent. Children are vulnerable to conflicts that arise if the relation of the parents is disrupted, or if the child exploits differences in the two systems: he asks one parent for permissions the other would refuse.

The possibilities for instability and change are multiplied when an individual is the part common to many systems at once, as happens if one participates in a family, friendships, work, school, and state. Limited time and resources deter anyone from satisfying his or her responsibilities to each of them even when duties cohere. But often they do not, so each system's economy is disrupted by someone who fills all his roles inadequately, with consequences for each system's relations to others that share this common part. Or suppose that a city's ethnic communities—each one a network of systems—overlap one another (because of intermarriage or shared spaces). You want quiet in the park we share: I like noise. Or there is conflict between organizations and associations: think of women engineers living in the West but wearing veils. Organizations often adapt to changes, thereby enhancing their efficiency for achieving their aims. But opportunism is often anathema to associations: they intensify feelings or convictions without regard for other aims. The first pulls us along in a direction we agree to go; the other is our center of gravity. Affiliations rivet us, we like to believe, to more important realities. They anchor us in stable places where practical questions are ephemeral and incidental to our feelings or beliefs. Opposed affiliations may coexist uneasily in people or systems that find ways to satisfy both claims. But tensions are not always so easily managed. Something snaps within people who integrate these contraries. Organizations having secular aims are suppressed; or members liberate themselves from associations whose attitudes are deemed simplistic.

Fourth, the members of a system, whether subaltern systems or persons, are responsible to the system, hence to one another. But this responsibility is no bar to competition: member teams of athletic leagues compete with one another, though all are bound by certain practices. Competition for opportunities or resources is all the keener among persons or systems that are unconstrained by membership in higher-order systems. International treaties and parliaments limit the behaviors of states; but they don't eliminate power relations, piracy, or change. Indeed, we, who prize loose bonds and ample freedoms, wouldn't agree to eliminate the competition that creates change.

These four points confirm that change is routinized or redirected, but not stopped, within stable systems. They also imply that the stability of extended networks and hierarchical nests of systems is precarious. Conflict—the tension that ruptures systems—is pervasive. Instability is commonplace, because of contrary aims or competition for resources. Change—to diminish conflict and recover equilibrium, or to form new, more compatible systems—is chronic.

6. Managing Change

Managing change is a complex skill, one that is all the more difficult because it frequently requires that we alter ourselves. Ranking objectives, appraising a situation, revising a faulty plan in mid-course, we shape circumstances to satisfy an aim. These managerial skills compare to factors within us that oppose change. They include information, skills, and the developmental history that shaped us, for these are the elements of our (mostly) fixed capital: we don't stray far from them. There are also some deeper stabilizers: namely, attitudes. They cannot be stubbornly opposed to information that our circumstances are radically changed, as by flood or war; but attitudes are strong conditions for stability, given reasonably cogent information and skills and stable circumstances. The recruiting of Marine sharpshooters is a useful example. Information about one's interest—higher pay—is opposed to attitude—don't kill. How should we understand the volunteers (there are often more candidates than available places)? Do all have attitudes that qualify them for this sort of work? No, some are enticed by the higher status and salary. We should worry about recruits who take the job for these rewards, contrary to their attitudes. They will be less stable—when military service is ended—than volunteers who like the work. The former have managed change badly, because of misperceiving themselves.

Managing change effectively is ambiguous in respect to a manager's objective. Is he concerned to produce an effect that satisfies values supplied by someone else; or does he intend that change should satisfy his own values? Should we (can we) disengage information and skills from attitudes, hence values, in order to make ourselves useful to those whose objectives are different from, or inimical to, our own? How neutral a tool can deliberation be? Everyone who earns a salary by serving other people's objectives is evidence that this dissociation occurs; but how does this square with the stabilizing, conservative effect of our attitudes? This happens in any of three ways: we are mercenaries who do work that coheres with our attitudes; or our attitudes are pliable; or we disengage ourselves from the work done in order that we not be offended by its effects. Deliberation has effects that vary as attitudes are engaged or not. Chapter Five considers this point in more detail.

XI. ONTOLOGY

Deliberation without constraining values is dangerous. Deliberation without a social ontology is merely clumsy: the practices it sponsors are blind to the character of the processes and systems altered. Not having an accurate theory to represent the structure of the human social world, we risk ignoring systems in which we participate, systems that are critical to what we are and want. We get changes that were unintended, given our interests and attitudes. The ontology proposed should be testable; there should be empirical evidence of its truth; and it should not be useless for practical decision making through being too abstract. Does the ontology described here meet these conditions? Does it justify my claim that metaphysics is vital information? What follows is a recapitulation of the issues discussed so far. Using atomism as a foil, the discussion is dialectical. Applications are stressed.

1. The Atomists, Aristotle, and Hobbes

Atomism supposes that the complexity of systems is the configuration of their simplest parts, so that layers of complexity reduce to particles that are related spatially and temporally. Particles may also be related dynamically, but then the only changes occurring in them are assumed to be changes in the values of their few, constituent properties: namely, altered mass, velocity, position, or charge. Wittgenstein's *Tractatus* proposes that relations among particles are merely additive, not dynamic. Wittgenstein's *objects,* his atoms, are presumably tiny things having the scale of elementary particles. Configurations result when objects are joined spatially or temporally.[25] (One thinks of Tinkertoys, the models of molecules, or models of the Sun and its planets.) Stability is, presumably, the persistence of configurations. It results when objects hold their places; or, more generously, if one object is replaced by another having the same internal form. Stability cannot result, even in part, from the efficacy of objects configured, because efficient cause (and reciprocity) is nothing but configuration: meaning spatial or temporal relations only.[26] This implies that the character of objects (like that of Aristotelian primary substances) derives from the internal forms of objects, not from their relations to one another.[27] This formulation is an odd mating of Hume's rejection of efficient cause with a version of Aristotle's formal cause. Color is said to be a relational property consequent on the spatial relations of objects having the appropriate internal forms: red emerges when properly disposed objects are configured, as the *gestalt* of a face emerges when its parts are joined.

This characterization of objects—internal properties qualify them for se-lected places within configurations—also applies, I infer, to us humans and our social relations. Each of us is a complex configuration, such that the relations of our elements makes no difference to their character: configuration does not al-ter them. Equally, the relations of humans to one another, as in families, make no difference to the character of the persons related. Nor is one configuration, a family or friendship, affected by its relation to other systems of objects, in-cluding employers and landlords. These are some paradoxes that limit our use of the *Tractatus* in contexts where social and psychological issues are the matters at issue.

Aristotle supposed that causality does make a difference to things, though its effects are superficial in the respect critical here. For each primary substance has a character, an essence, that determines its internal form.[28] Causal relations can only realize a thing's form, change its accidents, or destroy it. Hobbes agreed that bodies are essentially independent of one another, as when interaction causes a change of direction without otherwise altering the things that interact. He thought that social order is the result of fear, not of reciprocity, as when coer-cion restrains unruly impulses. For then, fear changes the aim, hence the char-acter, of a person's actions.[29] Causal reciprocity would have implied for Aristo-tle that things are mutually affecting, though the self-sufficiency of primary substances entails that such effects—altered qualities, quantities, or relations—are accidents. Causal reciprocity would also have had no implication for Hobbes, beyond the mutual repulsion of colliding bodies or the standoff of mu-tual intimidation.

Aristotle and Hobbes are the primary sources for naturalistic ideas about causality. Their neglect of causal reciprocity largely explains its near absence from philosophical sensibility. This oblivion is a disabling mistake, because re-ciprocal causal relations are a necessary condition for the construction of sys-tems. The effect ramifies when reciprocal relations establish successive orders of stability, hence the network of overlapping and nested systems, each one a "thing" in its own right. This is the trajectory when the basic ingredients of me-chanics, but nothing magical, supply everything required for the emergence of systems, their hierarchically organized networks, and their properties. We start with particles. (Particles may or may not be systems—see Chapter One, section I.2—but we assume for the expository aims of the next three sentences that they are not.) The values of their constitutive properties are fixed by mutual deter-mination and by the determining action of circumstances that may include great heat, velocity, and the spacetime in which they are embedded. Systems form when each of several particles is captured by its relations to one or more others, because of the stabilizing causal relations between or among them. Every higher-order system has equivalent constituents and conditions, though subaltern systems substitute for particles.

Imagine a baseball team, its members lounging in the dugout while their team bats. Uniforms apart, this gaggle of individuals doesn't look a team. Yet disorder in the dugout obscures design in the order of play. Baseball encourages the idiosyncrasies of its players, but this is all the while a corporate activity: each player fills a role geared to the other eight. Is the team distinct from its players? This question has one answer during games, and a different one when the members are dispersed. During a game, when each players does his part, the team is the relationship of its players, not their aggregate. It includes its members, while being distinct from them. But, you say, the team assembles only moments before going to work; each member goes his separate way when the job is done. Why acknowledge the emergence of a system distinguishable from its members? There are two reasons: because the coordination of the players establishes a system, however ephemeral, where each player exhibits his skill; and because this team plays other teams, both of them systems. A triangle is distinguishable but not separable from its three line segments. So are these partnerships distinct from their members.

Outfielders don't run in to do a catcher's work. Violinists don't pirate the cellists' part as their own. Atomists explain these constraints by saying that workers are well trained. This is right but simplistic, because atomism conflates two abilities, or emphasizes one while ignoring the other. First is the skill required for doing a task; the other is the talent for doing it in ways that relate to the abilities and tasks of fellow workers. Each has distinctive powers that are turned on or off by his perception of the task at hand, and by each one's causal relations to his fellows. These relations limit a worker's role (and the expressions of his or her talents) within the larger enterprise. Skills and interests are put to the service of a corporate aim. The array of mutually conditioning agents is a system, not an aggregate.

2. Systems

There are many questionable cases, as when reciprocities are unachieved because people or systems are inept, distracted, or hostile to the aim that would bind them. How good must coordination be for the creation of systems? There is no general answer, given the differences between the three kinds of systems created by a balance of forces (Chapter One, section I.5): namely, static systems and those created by positive or negative feedback. It happens only occasionally that human systems are static or that they are established by positive feedback: one thinks of states that do no trade, though each is secured by the other's recognition of their common border, or of gold-rush towns where every new arrival attracts others because of finding more gold. Nonhuman static systems are usually established almost at once, as arches are completed by a capstone. Static human systems may require a stabilizing history: it may take years before each of the contiguous states can acknowledge that it profits from its respect for their common border. Systems established by positive feedback are, by nature, temporally extended, as gold-rush towns grow. Negative feedback systems are established over the course of two cycles (described in Chapter One, section 4). A cycle has two moments: each party affects the other; the other then replies with a controlling response. Human systems having negative feedback require two of these cycles, for there may be no system until each person or higher-order system registers the other's response, then confirms that the response was controlled by his, her, or its act. There is no conversation, for example, if my parrot answers me cogently, though she cannot do as well the second time around. Accordingly, we require the second cycle to confirm that a system is established. This use of *confirm* is not equivalent to *verify:* the demand for two cycles of interaction is only superficially epistemological. Better: an affirmative answer to the epistemological question—does each of us have evidence that he or she is understood by the other?—is a necessary and sufficient condition for the truth of the factual question—is a system established? This is so, because confirmation is also consolidation: the second, confirming cycle secures the connection. So *B* twice responds cogently to *A*'s remarks by saying something to which *A* twice responds cogently. Their conversation is launched, as my talk with the parrot is not.

The precision for which I am aiming is more elusive in many phenomena that combine a balance of forces, positive and negative feedback: weather systems are an example. The "moment of transition" from aggregate to system is too exact for them.

There are awkward cases of a different sort when people do not seem to engage other people or systems. So, shepherds work independently; though independence of the sort that concerns us—freedom from reciprocity—is more apparent than real in them. The Fuller brush man, too, is (was?) part of a system. It is irrelevant that we don't see the other parts or the reciprocities that bind them. They do obtain, as the salesman gets nothing more to sell if he fails to pay for goods previously sold and delivered. Equally, there is nothing decisive in the objection that systems dissolve and reform, as partners marry, divorce, and marry again. Here, as before, the integrity of the parts does not preclude their sporadic participation in higher-order systems.

3. Independence, Reciprocity, Nesting, and Overlap

No less commonplace than the formation of systems is their mutual independence, reciprocity, nesting, and overlap. Every system has little or nothing to do with most others, gravitational relations apart. But every human system is multiply connected by overlap and nesting. Members who locate themselves by looking up and down as well as sideways see responsibilities to others, whatever direction they look. Members are saved from overload or vertigo, because each one also perceives his place within a module—a subsystem—of fellow members. There are rules for ranking one's duties, with priority usually going to duties owed to the other members of the group. Independent systems devoid of overlap or nesting do exist, as a family farm may be isolated and self-sufficient. But even this farm is sometimes captured within a network of reciprocally related, overlapping, or nested systems, as when distant farmers use mirrors to signal one another of foxes and tax collectors.

Consider these four kinds of relation: mutual independence, reciprocity, overlap, and nesting. (See Chapter One, section I.9h.)

Mutual independence: Systems often interact though they are not reciprocally related, overlapping, or nested: billiard balls collide, one buys a used car, the local church hires a band. One feature characterizes all these interactions: neither party captures the other in a sustained reciprocity.

Causal relationships sometimes take a long time to develop. Causes assemble and interact, so that each is changed; but this alone is not evidence of reciprocity (gravity apart) or feedback in the relations of the causes. Volcanic eruptions endure without creating a stable system, though fumes, rocks, and lava interact. Compare the reciprocities of systems: they route energy, material, or signals (hence information) between or among the causes, so that their interaction is regulated and sustained. Mutual control (sometimes with the mutual modulation of negative feedback) qualifies the independence of interacting causes by creating the higher-order systems that engage them.

Reciprocity: Humans often capture one another in sustained reciprocal relations, including friendship, conversation, work, or marriage. These relationships are often consuming. We may come to define ourselves in terms of the rights and duties that accrue to us within them, thereby forgetting that character is never reducible to role. For never mind that we would survive, however wounded, if separated from roles we prize: our passion is evidence that the reciprocities engaging us have an ontological integrity of their own. We locate ourselves—physically, psychologically, and morally—within the systems they create.

Overlap: Suppose that the Channel Islands were to fall under the jurisdiction of both France and Britain, or that Maryland and Virginia were to share jurisdiction over Washington, D.C. The relations of these sub-societies to their higher-order societies is the more complicated one of overlap: the part falls within two (or more) higher-order systems. How would New Jersey and New York manage Liberty Island if both had jurisdiction over it, given their different laws and practices? Or are questions of this sort already resolved in the case of entities such as the Port Authority of New York and New Jersey, a system that already falls within the jurisdiction of both states? The Port Authority is evidence that overlap is common, encouraged even, as when divorced parents share custody of their children. We would have something similar were Britain and Eire to share sovereignty of Northern Ireland.

These expedients typically settle into either of several forms: systems compete for control of the part they share; they alternate in controlling it; or they coordinate their practices or laws in order to minimize conflicts over the shared part. Competition between higher-order systems is often destructive for the part and for both systems, because competition uses scarce resources and because of consequences on all sides. Periods of alternate responsibility make everyone dizzy: from whom does the contested child ask permission this weekend; which authority collects taxes this month? Coordinating practices or laws is likely to be the most efficient of the available choices, though the hardest to achieve.

The difficulty of managing a shared part sometimes has the odd effect of inverting power relations: the part may come to dominate the systems that share it. So two or more nations coordinate the administration of a common harbor or mine, in order to share its revenues. First describing one another's citizens as *visitors,* later as *dual nationals,* each comes to accept the other's people as its citizens. This incremental fusing of jurisdictions is sometimes sponsored by multinational corporations. Such companies suffer if conduct that satisfies one country's laws is illegal under the laws of a different host. They do better when states harmonize their conflicting laws, and better still when the need for investment and taxes provokes governments to let international companies make the rules that apply to them. Such states may come to be unified, economically at least, by the superior interest of the company that was originally their common part. Opposition to the common markets created by such arrangements is often excoriated for being reactionary: why worry about our traditional national currency, our laws and routines, our kilts, their beer? We worry because we value autonomy. Some people or states may not prize their independence; some others don't want it violated by a common child.

Overlap is not always so problematic. There are church buildings shared by two denominations, and the multiple families or subfamilies created by polyandry or polygamy. These expressions of overlap are sometimes affiliating and stabilizing. Their articulations of social space are much richer than those of self-isolating, nuclear families. But they make us uncomfortable. Here as in so many things: *separable if distinguishable* is our social policy.

4. A System's Relations to Its Nested Parts

Two considerations are primary in the relation of a system to the individuals or subaltern systems that are nested within it as proper parts: they are constitutive of it; it has regulative force over them.

Saying that a higher-order system is composed of its subsystems is insufficient, because it implies that the higher-order system is the aggregate of its parts. More accurately, systems are composed of their reciprocally related parts. This is problematic if *identity* is construed as identity over time. For a system is identical, at any moment, with its reciprocally related parts. But parts may be replaced, so that the character of a system's reciprocities may evolve. In what respect is the American presidency self-identical over the past hundred years, given that the office-holder and his relations to Congress, the courts, and the electorate have changed many times? Philosophers tie themselves in knots when essentialist notions of identity oblige them to locate a core of features that are unchanged. We do better to say that reciprocities that engage any current president have evolved from some that engaged his predecessors. We concede that butterflies do not resemble caterpillars, DNA apart, and that any stage in the history of a system may differ considerably from remote predecessors and successors.

Ignoring this historical dimension, I suppose that a system is identical with its reciprocally related proper parts. These parts may include individual persons or the subaltern systems composed of reciprocally related persons. An orchestra includes sections that are organized as systems, the violins, and single instrumentalists, the one tuba player. Cities are a richer example. New York is not a single system supervening on all its parts (except governmentally), but rather a network of hierarchies, each sharing parts with some others. There is also the qualification that city systems are not identical with all the people or systems currently present in them. Extraneous people or systems fail to establish even briefly sustained reciprocities with any of the city's parts. Passengers in transit at its airports and people driving through it are some examples.

Now reverse the perspective: put aside the question of a system's constituents, and consider its regulative force upon them. A city that lays down rules of practice for its parts is a higher-order system regulating—legislating for—itself. Most conspicuous is the act of making, then enforcing, laws. This power is complementary to the responsibilities of a system's members. For a higher-order system is stabilized and sustained only as members fulfill their responsibilities to one another and to it. These are obligations to behave in ways that are appropriate to the roles of citizens or subsystems. Such duties are expressed in work or civic behavior. They determine the character of the reciprocities that bind the system's parts. For the city is, from one point of view, a patchwork of reciprocal duties, some that apply to every participant, others that apply to some of them.

The downward pressure of higher-order constraints has many simpler illustrations. Imagine a family that works a farm. Every member over ten years old has significant responsibilities for one or several chores, hence responsibilities to the family and to its other members. Personal relations among family members are warm and trusting; but the parents impose strict rules of personal conduct on their children. Never posting the rules or threatening, they exhibit these standards in their own behavior. What do the children think of these rules? We hardly notice, they say. Never doing the things they proscribe, we never suffer the penalties. Regulative principles are often enforced this way: older members are controlled by having to imitate one another; newcomers learn a system's norms from the behaviors of older members.

Atomists respond that norms are merely the preferences or behaviors of a system's inventive or powerful members. This is sometimes true but irrelevant: it ignores the role of norms within systems that are established and/or sustained because the members apply them. A different example suggests that power is not always, or even usually, the condition for propagating norms. Consider an accent that starts in the speech impediment of a king. His accent is disseminated and standardized by a system's reciprocities, when everyone learns to speak as he does. Those who do not imitate him are corrected or ridiculed. Children learn the accent from their parents; foreigners learn it from any or all the local speakers. Speak to us that we may understand you, we say to them: speak to us as we speak to one another. Norms of this sort no longer rely in any way on those who established them.

Higher-order systems constrain their proper parts—a family's members—in three ways. *First* are the attitudes and interpretations that are taught to members. Certain things are picked out for approval or disapproval; everything else fades into an unvalorized backdrop. One also learns a story that makes coherent sense of the world and one's place there. Attitudes and interpretations are first brought into families by husbands and wives, later by their children. Parents reconcile their different points of view somewhat before children are born. Later, attitudes and interpretations evolve, especially as the reciprocities of children, parents, and other family members create a perspective they share. *Second* are laws, incentives, and punishments. They regulate us, either by facilitating action or by deterring it. *Third,* some systems—organizations especially—sharply differentiate the roles of their members: one is hired to play shortstop or to manage the accounts, not usually both at once.

These constraints have different effects on a system's members. Members' attitudes and interpretations are constitutive of their cognitive-affective postures: they are hard to change. Compare the behaviors sanctioned by laws. Changing laws that are prescriptive and utilitarian usually makes no deep impression on attitudes or interpretations. No one feels changed by amendments to the tax code or the traffic laws, though a law requiring all Americans to drive on the left would necessitate wholesale retraining. Proscriptive laws—don't kill—are deeply inscribed in our attitudes and interpretations, such that most of us could not torture a child. Resistance to change also applies to skills that qualify us to fill particular roles within systems. An orchestra advertises for a cellist, not a tuba player, never expecting that either has the skills required of the other. We who have learned the attitudes, interpretations, and skills appropriate to our roles within systems are properly skeptical of those who advise us not to lose the flexibility that would enable us to assume different roles in other systems. For systems often require that their members behave (for years) in strictly determined ways. People who have been shaped by and for systems having sharply differentiated functions are inevitably unprepared for new ones after war, unemployment, or divorce.

Atomists can make little sense of the claim that each of these three constraints is a means for imposing the standards of a higher-order system on its parts. They explain social order by citing the character of individual agents, or the laws that regulate their behaviors. They have nothing to say about the process whereby a system's members learn its attitudes and interpretations (they may have been passed on for generations). Equally, they say nothing about the changes that occur when reciprocities within a system modulate inherited attitudes and interpretations. We should acknowledge these two things: that higher-order systems have no reality apart from their parts, and that such systems do, nevertheless, establish norms that are satisfied by the parts. This is no mystery: both are explained by the causal reciprocities of the parts. Coming into situations where reciprocal relations are already established, we learn the steps. But then circumstances or initiative prompt some of us to try variations. The norms are modified when others step as we do.

5. Holism

Someone who considers the last three of these four considerations—reciprocity, overlap, and nesting—while ignoring the first—mutual independence—may suppose that we are forever entangled in networks of relations, never able to cut ourselves free. A suffocating holism will seem to be our fate. Is there relief from the higher-order constraints that systems impose on their members?

America is big, so big that it once seemed possible to avert conflicts by moving down the road. This perception (if not the spirit it expressed) was already outdated when Dewey argued that freedom of association and action implies an offsetting responsibility for the unexpected and damaging effects of our actions.[30] This is a global responsibility, one that engages all a system's participants as each assumes the perspective and authority of the whole: we regulate for all, hence for ourselves, without benefit to or prejudice against anyone. Though notice: it is particular wholes—individual systems or assemblies of systems, not the entire human society—that concern us most of the time. Families, friendships, and sects of all kinds legislate for their members. This is the freedom in modularity: each system legislates for itself. Participation in higher-order systems—states, for example—invites or assures regulation; though even these rules or norms may be interpreted in ways that are appropriate to the specific differences of the member systems. And usually, higher-order systems—democratic states, paradigmatically—have nothing to say about some of the behaviors of their parts—whether individuals or systems—so each of them is free to make some of its own rules.

Our fear of drowning in the whole is intensified by the idea that there are public interests, meaning interests of the whole. We are paralyzed by this suggestion, because it implies that the whole may use its power to suppress subaltern interests out of regard for its own. This is premature. For the principle public interest is concern for an open society. Regulation—mutual restraint—is a secondary interest, one that has no point and no domain if subaltern systems do not form and interact. The freedom to join with others in pursuit of common aims is, therefore, an urgent public interest. Such activity is good in two ways:

it satisfies the participants, while generating effects that benefit others. Conversely, we care that the open playing field not be perverted or polluted by systems grown so powerful that they do not cede space to competitors. And because free association requires it, we suppose that information regarding available resources and the behaviors of other groups is widely disseminated. No one, no system, is to be deprived of information that is vital to initiatives it may take.

Each of these policies is liberating in its intent. Yet each is also a constraint that the whole, the system of reciprocally related individuals and systems, imposes on its parts. Each of us could struggle for open space, intimidating others or monopolizing information to get it; but Dewey's public (after Rousseau's general will) resolves that the conduct of its members shall be restrained. Why? Because we shall not be able, in the resulting free-for-all, to avert the disintegrating spiral to which it leads. Prudence counsels that we do these other two things instead: join for mutual advantage and meet as a whole so that private citizens can organize as a public, thereby creating a government to regulate themselves.

Atomists may concede the virtues of Dewey's formula, while denying that any of it justifies reifying the whole. Their fear is misplaced, because Dewey's public is not the shadow of Hegel's Absolute. It is not the God that Leibniz and Whitehead evoke to unify "monads" or "actual entities." Neither the public nor the Great Community is a tidy whole; nor is either reified, though each is the secularized, pluralized heir to Hegel's community of spirits. What is the whole? It is not the state, for that is merely one higher-order system among others: the one formed by individuals and their higher-order systems for the purpose of self-regulation. The whole lies elsewhere, in the network of systems that are mutually independent, reciprocally related, overlapping, or nested. Every resident of a big city knows the difference between this whole and the government. He knows it when the city's people seem to fill every space, though its government is overwhelmed and invisible, or merely incompetent. Accordingly, it is not holism that threatens us, but rather our ability to manage ramifying systems and our places in them.

6. Alternative Explanations for Conflict

There are myriad difficulties as we regulate ourselves while pursuing our initiatives. Many are expressed as the incompatible demands that are made of democratic governments. Guarantee our freedoms, we say, so that we may establish the systems of our choice; mediate our conflicts, whatever the cost to the freedom of our competitors. Chronic conflict would not have surprised Dewey or Kant. Do what you like, they would have said, only take care that your behaviors do not subvert the very conditions for the openness presupposed by your actions; otherwise you subvert yourselves. Recognize the network of systems in which you participate, then act in ways that acknowledge the interests of other persons and systems. This is a condition we can satisfy. It is our fault if public officers are not obliged to distinguish personal from public concerns. It is our fault if shallow differences (of race, for example) become seismic. It is our fault if tax policy magnifies the differences between rich and poor. These are failures of perspective and deliberation, failures to distinguish narrowly calculated personal advantage from the benefit of living in a system where productive individuals and the systems they form are mutually supporting. Granted that the network of self-correcting, self-stabilizing relations—an effective state—is hard to establish, any particular democratic society has nothing but itself to blame when the systemic character of social life is not acknowledged and effectively (self-) regulated: other societies do better. Knowing this leaves us pawing the air, for the democratic society which fails to achieve its own objectives cannot delegate the task to a prince. The weakness is internal, constitutive, and sometimes irreparable.

Atomism abhors the idea that constraints originate in higher-order systems or that responsibilities conflict, because the person having them participates in overlapping systems. The atomist account is simpler: there are only individual persons and groups of them, their contractual relations, and the laws that regulate behaviors and these contracts. Traffic jams may supervene on cars and their drivers; but these are aggregates, not systems. Individuals—whether stationary, colliding, or freely going their self-interested ways—are the only realities. Equally, the duties that constrain us have no source but the laws that regulate our behaviors. We inherit the duties because we act voluntarily in ways that bring us under the law (as happens if we marry or drive), not because we participate in systems having their inception in reciprocities that create duties to the other members of a system. Let individuals make such mutual arrangements as minimize conflicts in their contractual duties. There is no domain of systems to which we must accommodate ourselves; no clash of systems generates conflicts for prudent individuals. Some systems—governments—are vastly swollen and falsely entitled. Individuals who use them for personal advantage have persuaded us that these systems have a reality and rights that set them against individual persons; but this is a moral fiction and an ontological error. Cut away this fiction (and its bogus obligations), so that individuals may be free to choose their contractual duties. Prudent men and women choose duties that are fulfilled without conflict.

This atomist creed makes individuals responsible for the coherence of their duties. But this is a coherence that no one can guarantee, however prudent his or her choices. Conflicting duties are often the sign of unreconciled roles within disparate systems. Family, work, and citizenship make opposed demands on me. Should I prudently abandon some two of them? There are duties to one's children and duties to one's spouse, duties to fellow workers and duties to one's employer, duties to elected officials and duties to law. Is it always evidence of bad choices when these duties collide? Systems engage us all around, because we cannot live without them, not because we are self-indulgent and heedless (though this happens too).

Ascribing all conflicts to the muddled choices of individuals is an error described above: it confuses character with role. We blame individuals or their training for conflicts that may derive entirely from whatever is mutually exclusive in their roles. There is no justice—no harmony—for someone in a job that is wrong for him or her. Where characters are formed in ways that anticipate the roles to be filled, there is also the near certainty that preparation for some roles makes one unsuitable for others. Yet people regularly occupy roles for which they are unsuited, with cost to them and to those reciprocally related others who suffer because the role is badly filled. Systems, as much as characters, are unyielding. A beekeeper on a fishing boat is probably an unhappy sailor and bad companion.

7. Autonomy and Constraint

Free-marketeers will dislike the idea that work is dominated by systems: doesn't this imply a maze of constraints on production and trade? Remember that Congress passed antitrust legislation early this century to eliminate cartels that controlled the production and distribution of principal commodities. Such constraints are no more popular now than before. Anything that implies them—systems, for example—raises hackles. This hostility is our response to every impediment to our freedom of action (though we do accommodate ourselves to some constraints, as no one bridles at the laws of motion). Systems—some that are mutually independent, others that are reciprocally related, overlapping, or nested—are another constraint upon us. They are a permanent feature in many venues, including production, distribution, family life, and friendship. Taking the measure of our circumstances, we trade the perception of ourselves as autonomous agents, each one having merely incidental relations to the others, for the more accurate persuasion that our very individuality is the consequence of our roles within systems. There are, or ought to be, limits to the demands made upon us within these roles. Contracts establish these conditions and also the circumstances for taking up or leaving a role. But contracts are a limit on the terms of engagement. Engagements in family, friendship, work, and the state were not invented with the inception of contracts.

Do we compromise autonomy, hence moral and political freedom, by acknowledging that we humans are systems who participate in higher-order systems? Four reasons justify saying we do not. *First* is the modularity of systems. Each is established by the reciprocal causal relations of its parts and has, therefore, an inside and an outside. The relations constitutive of its inside are its principal determinants. Autonomy is, in part, the vigor of these self-determining processes. Higher-order systems often supervene on their parts, sometimes penetrating a system to the point of assuming control of its internal economy. Thought control is one effect, though some systems, humans especially, resist this intrusion. Humans and other modules typically survive disengagement from higher-order systems, on the condition that these parts are terminal states in finite orders of complexity, as described in Chapter One, section I.11: it is whole persons, not tissues or organs, that are sustainable systems. *Second,* a system's routinized causal relations are consistent with degrees of freedom in the persons or systems that are its parts. The principal site for this freedom in us humans is cognitive-affective posture: each of us is both liberated and constrained by our feelings, information, and skills. *Third* are the degrees of freedom consequent on filling a role (the many ways to teach a class, for example); and sometimes freedom to disengage oneself from a higher-order system. Disengagement is often costly: we lose advantages that were prized. But the system may tolerate losing us, either because it has substitutes or because it re-forms in ways appropriate to its reduced parts. *Fourth* is the measure of freedom that accrues to someone in proportion to the complexity of his or her situation. A man (or woman) alone in the universe has nowhere to go: underdetermination deprives him of freedom. He may whistle or yawn, but not much more. Someone who lives with others finds himself connected, unforeseeably, with many people and systems. He chooses reciprocities from the position of having to remove himself from some in order to do justice to others. Critics say that we suffer an excess of socialization. But our ailment is often the reverse: too many of us suffer for want of it. Too few systems engage such people; the ones that do are impoverished: they distort information and require feeble or pernicious skills; they encourage attitudes that are more fearful than generous.

The aversion for systems and fear for human autonomy come together in the ontological atomism and political views of Aristotle and Hobbes. Aristotle believed that no other material thing has a form as rich and layered as our own. Every living thing is internally regulated, but we are unique in being self-regulating, as reason controls appetite. Hobbes shared Aristotle's individualism. But he was not convinced by our claim to moral autonomy—he doubted our powers of self-regulation—because appetite causes us to resist every law that is not imposed forcibly. Where each of us would be a law unto himself, thereby creating perpetual war among us, there can be no peace without a prince who subordinates us to his will in the name of our common good. Aristotle would have responded that reason is common to all, and that (ideally) each of us subordinates appetite to laws we make for ourselves. This difference between Hobbes and Aristotle is significant for their politics, but incidental to their shared aversion to any entity—any higher-order system—that supervenes upon individual substances. The society each described—the *polis* or Leviathan—is an ennobling aggregate of complementary parts or a forced convention, not a system. Aristotle and Hobbes are the antitheses who define our political conversations. One favored a state in which each citizen is the apotheosis of a type: public man, supportive woman. The other preferred a captious equality where the sovereign enforces order. No wonder we think it unproblematic that atomism is the correct social ontology. What remains to dispute when all sides agree that reality is the aggregate of material particulars?[31]

I suggest this answer. We need to talk of stable systems: meaning the organizations and associations formed by routinized, reciprocal, causal relations. Relations binding people to one another are not different categorially from the ones that sustain the organization of single human bodies. Spatiotemporal, causal relations are the only glue in both cases, though we add that the pertinent causal relations are the reciprocal loops characteristic of systems having negative—self-regulating—feedback: citizens who drive pay taxes that go toward the salaries of policemen who stop our cars for speeding. The implication for social policy is direct. Autonomy and constraint are often (*not always*) coterminus; some kinds of autonomy—of husbands, wives, first violinists, or presidents—do not exist outside the systems where freedom is the latitude for initiative in a role. This is, equally, the autonomy that comes with information, attitudes, and skills, the autonomy-in-constraint of cognitive-affective postures.

8. The Atomist Response

What should be said to those who deny that individual well-being is founded in reciprocities that fulfill our responsibilities to one another. Mill is emblematic. Freedom to unite is his third region of liberty, one that comes after cultivated thought has chosen wisely among alternative tastes and pursuits.[32] For sometimes we need the help of others to satisfy us. The associations we enter into have specific, typically practical aims: work, for example. Participation carries limited responsibilities—one cannot sell oneself into slavery—so these contractual relationships do not qualify the essential autonomy of the contractors.

This atomist formulation is also a program: every relationship is to be reconceived in atomist terms. Work relations, marriages, and the relationships of parents and children or friends are to be reformulated (or remade) as the conditional couplings of parties defended by their contractual rights. It is no matter that some relationships resolve more easily than others (losing little or no efficacy) into their participants. For there is no tolerance in this atomist persuasion for the more tolerant view that some things are reciprocally related, overlapping, or nested, though others are mutually independent. Networks of systems, even individual systems, are perceived as cloying and obscure. Let every complex be reduced to its simple parts, so that distinguishable individuals are perceived as separable.

This has some distorting effects, as when businesses are regarded as aggregates of workers, or analogized as individuals, each one making its decisions in the style of Mill's solitary thinker: we are to imagine firms that go about their work independently, albeit interacting occasionally with their contractually related suppliers and customers. This is a story better suited to the businesses conducted by single persons—dentists or luthiers, for example. It has no relevance to businesses that make or control a product through the many stages of its production and sale, often in several nations at once. No personalizing advertisement converts Exxon into a larger version of the lady who sells the pies she bakes from fruit grown in her garden. Nor shall we understand individuals or companies until we agree that neither is legitimately extracted in thought from contexts where character is formed and work done.

Atomist views may prevail for generations or centuries. But they will not survive forever, because thoughtful people notice that atrophied social bonds impoverish most lives. We are implicated in the successes and failures of our social systems. They serve our purposes. We, in our reciprocal relations, are their necessary conditions. We should believe the message on those self-congratulatory billboards at civic building sites: society—not merely the presiding governor or mayor—is often good for us.

9. Acknowledging Systems and Their Interests

The distaste for systems is, nevertheless, visceral and ideological. Political atomism is a complement to the ontological kind, so that value, not truth, drives the policies that make systems invisible. Atomists decline to acknowledge systems intermediate between, or additional to, individuals and governments, because they refuse to cede them power. Organizations and associations must not vote; they cannot make laws that supersede or conflict with laws made by properly sanctioned political authorities; they cannot collect taxes. Lower-order systems are aggregates or fictions; only their members—they have bodies—are presumed real. We are told another time that a whole cannot be more than the sum of its parts—though all-star teams, an atomist's dream, are often outplayed by regular but mediocre teams. Atomists should find this hard to explain. Or they could cite the obvious reason and agree that the relationship of team members is a higher-order system, one that is distinguishable, though not separable, from the individual players.

It is only a matter of time before the reality of such systems is forced upon our political thinking. We may not like the claims they make of us; but can we ignore their demands for recognition? This is not an implied suggestion about the direction that public policy should take: *is,* rather than *ought,* is our consideration. Atomist liberalism is fiercely assaulted by a conflict it created when the public was installed (however imperfectly). For atomism denies the existence of intermediate systems, insisting that each is an aggregate, and that governments need respond only to their individual members. Individual persons—not systems—are members of the public. No intermediate power is to come between them and their government. Yet governments struggle slavishly to satisfy other, high-order systems. As "special interest groups," these systems lobby governments for policies that serve their interests. Some want a congenial regulatory climate. Others want public money, or the right to prescribe laws, curricula, prayers, codes of behavior, or a schedule of membership fees that would be deducted from taxes paid to government. Government taxes citizens in return for services, but these societies also provide services. Why not share the revenues, they ask the rest of us: some to government, some to subaltern systems, themselves included? Many of these systems already have power: they own businesses, communications systems, and schools. Some have numerous, committed adherents. Will these groups always feel that their political interests are satisfied because their members can vote for president and their representatives to Congress? One isn't sure. Nor is it certain that their political interests should always be ignored. Hospitals, schools, and corporations are engines of stability, well-being, and growth. Their lobbyists influence critical legislative, executive, and judicial decisions.[33] Is this the ideal way of bringing these intermediate systems into an open political system? Might it not be better to give them political responsibility—a vote or votes—while requiring that all of their activities be subject to the careful restraint which should limit the behaviors of every politically responsible citizen? One trembles to think of the senator from the National Rifle Association. But is it certain that we do not already have one or several? Why is it better not to know who they are, than make rules to regulate legislative authority of this and every other special interest?

The uneasiness this idea provokes is the symptom of a paradox in our perceptions of social reality. First are the many systems, each a center of activity. Second is the public, that eighteenth-century ideal of Greek and Roman origin. Atomist theory directed that individuals be abstracted from systems that engage them, in order to create a domain whose elements are these individuals. The state was to be the fellowship of individuals organized for self-regulation and defense. This solution was proposed when atomists rightly perceived that the contentiousness of systems would forever preclude the achievement of distributive justice under simplified laws that apply universally. Legal rights and identity were, previously, a function of the entitlements or attachments acquired by virtue of one's status, a condition determined by family, church, or occupation. Societies that were transforming the bases for commerce—northern Italy in the sixteenth century, Britain in the seventeenth and eighteenth centuries—needed rules of a different sort. Political theorists encouraged them to strip away this tangle of disparate interests, so that justice could be founded in properties or powers, such as reason and self-discipline, credited to everyone, irrespective of status. This was the atomist program, and its achievement.

There is, however, a counter tension. The public originated as an idealization treated as a reality. Systems were demonized. They were said to have no reality apart from the individuals that compose them. This persuasion deprived systems of standing within the ontological and political theories that dominated political thinking and practice. States inspired by the atomist creed—revolutionary France, for example—tried to eliminate or enfeeble them. Systems were called "factions," implying that they were marginal and subversive. The *loi Chapelier*, issued by the Committee of Public Safety in June 1791, decreed that there are no interests but those of individuals and the community of Frenchmen, meaning the state. Every intermediate system was hereby disestablished, or reparsed as an aggregate. Yet systems are not aggregates, and they continued to exist, all the while engaging their members in the families, schools, villages, commerce, and farms that supplied life's context and values. Nothing of this has changed in our time. Systems engage us, form our characters, and ask that we promote their special privileges or exemptions from a government which speaks, in principle, to and for its individual citizens, not for "private interest groups," not for systems. Hence this problem: the public assembly of citizens is to make laws for all of us; no legislative powers are reserved within it for systems. They supply much of what is good or bad in our lives, and they may be heard when we deliberate, but systems don't vote on laws that affect them. And, most baffling of all, the ontology we profess doesn't acknowledge that systems exist.

This is the conceptual and practical tension that makes us uneasy when systems vie for power. We participate in many systems; they often dominate our lives. Yet systems are disenfranchised. Having no reality in atomist ontology, they are unacknowledged in the political theory sponsoring legislatures that regulate their affairs. This leaves government as the one obstacle to individual autonomy—though atomists prefer that it too disappear, or that we acknowledge it as an administrative reality, but an ontological fiction. For atomists believe that we should not make ourselves responsible (in theory) to higher-order systems for behaviors that we have not prescribed for ourselves (though we frequently defer to such systems in practice). Systems respond by subverting legislative practices. They enter through the back door, as lobbyists, while we, speaking with the voice of atomist authority, make decisions for them.

Why is it odious that individuals should have duties to the systems in which we participate? Why should systems have no representation—not merely a right to be heard—in the councils of the public? Why should we deceive ourselves about ontology when the principal concern is, historically, practical: namely, the fear that acknowledging the reality of higher-order systems encourages their designs on political power, thereby adulterating the powers of citizens and government? The motives for this attitude are plain, and admirable: the Enlightenment created a political space in which overreaching systems—religions, for example—were denied the power to interfere in public policy. This is a vastly consequential achievement. But why should our ontology derive from our antipathies? Political atomism—individualism—misrepresents the material world. It says that reality is composed of separable particulars, though the causal reciprocities that establish the integrity of human bodies are also the basis for the unity of other systems, some that are less complex than we are, some that are more complex. The ethical and political theories deriving from atomist ontology may satisfy our self-interested self-perception. Yet theories that misrepresent us will inevitably misdirect us. We shall want to do things we cannot do, or fail to do things we need, or should want, to do. No one supposes that a traveler is more likely to find his way if he starts with a map that misrepresents the terrain. Chapters Five, Six, Seven, and Eight describe particular issues—deliberation, free speech, structural conflicts, and ecology—where the maps of atomist theories almost guarantee that we shall take wrong turns, making choices that misconstrue our circumstances and interests.

We do better if ontological atomism is acknowledged as a false hypothesis about us and our situation. For we are perpetually socialized, having participated since birth in a variety of systems. *Robinson Crusoe* is a myth consciously embellished to test the limits of possibility: what will a social creature do if removed from every role? Crusoe saves his wits and dignity—behaving as though he were still responsible to others—until the day when he has a companion, hence reciprocal pleasures and duties.

Could we repudiate every duty, hence all responsibilities to the systems that engage us? Is the agreement to participate in any particular system made from a position external or prior to every system? These questions misconstrue our situation. For we choose to participate in one system from our perspective in another one. We augment our duties—by choosing to accept an additional role—or we substitute one role for another. No one chooses his contractual relations from a standpoint (transcendental or merely aloof) that is disengaged from every higher-order stability. We think otherwise because generations of philosophers have turned the ideology of individualism and unconditioned freedom into a sacred truth. They encourage us to imagine every undertaking as though we were free to take or leave it, as though one could forever stand at the door or turn away, declining to participate in every social system.

10. Freedom

Is freedom therefore a delusion? No, *freedom to* is the power to explore new behaviors, hence new roles in unfamiliar social systems. *Freedom from* is more equivocal. Do we invoke it to avoid coercion? Or is it used to justify relief from responsibilities to others, whether inherited or chosen? Some duties are odious. Others are reasonable, whether or not we chose them. *Freedom from* is sometimes a slogan that expresses our desire for exemption from every duty. This is not feasible, unless we excuse ourselves from every social system, including family, friendship, work, and the state. No one does that; no one believes that participation in every system is a kind of indentured servitude. There is often a degree of freedom within systems (one cannot do one's work without it); and often we leave them. Still, the liberty promoted by this slack should not be misperceived. Children leave home; friendships end; governments are turned out of office: these are a few of many ways to reorder a social life which remains social. The rare hermit, like the feral child, is marginal or mythic. Social life is plastic; but there is no power to withhold ourselves from all of it.

There is often good reason to resist some of it. The libertarian passion for *freedom from* or *to* is, sometimes, a reaction to the experience of being victimized by regimes or cultures that asphyxiate character in favor of role. How should we liberate ourselves? Descartes is a deep source of atomist legitimacy. He proposed that we rethink our circumstances. Discovering that I am, that I exist when everything else is dubitable, I question the legitimacy of the demands made of me. For I am a complete thinker and moral being, without regard for the systems that engage me. No longer defined or conditioned by my roles in them, I affirm myself before choosing my affiliations. My choices are unconditioned by external circumstances, including systems that already obtain. I may decide not to participate in any one, present or prospective.

This is the combination of self-reflection, reaction, and self-invention that enables us to imagine ourselves stripped of every responsibility to others. Having no duties to distract us, we are free to do as we like. But this ideal is a fantasy, one we claim to achieve only as we repudiate the substantial responsibilities to others that burden but valorize our actual roles and circumstances. For there could be an unrestricted freedom to do as we please only if there were no higher-order systems that engage us, hence no responsibilities to them and their members. Some of these duties—those of slaves to their masters—have no status apart from the coercion that enforces them. Others, to families, work mates, and friends, are not so easily dismissed.

11. Public Control, Private Power

I agree that duties are limited, and that one volunteers for many of life's roles. But (i) many systems—families, friendships, commerce, religions—have a reality that antedates the contracts that refine the conditions for our participation in them; (ii) fulfilling our duties to these systems is a condition for their efficacy and stability; (iii) we choose some of the systems that engage us, but no one can opt out of all systems, thereby achieving a freedom unencumbered by duties; (iv) promising too much—that we start from a position abstracted from all roles and duties—we shouldn't be surprised that people are dismayed to discover themselves in roles they cannot reject, roles freighted with responsibilities to others. Having some degree of freedom within each role, we are not exempt from every one.

This cannot be the last word, because the structural conflicts of systems, in competition, nesting, and overlap, damage systems and their members. Relief from these conflicts—at least a foothold in neutral ground—requires that we cleave to the public that atomism created because of its hostility to the politics of systems. For what are the alternatives to the legal, moral identity that atomism helped install when it postulated that each citizen is the sovereign member of a public? The alternative, theological answer—that God created us equal— expresses a hope unconfirmed by empirical evidence or plausible inference. The public is a better, though troubled choice. For we have all the evidence of democratic governments that are ineffectual, because everywhere confounded by systems determined to protect their interests. Needing a public, we must do these two things: liberate it from the control of systems, all the while finding a device that allows systems to express and pursue their legitimate interests—legislative interests included—in ways that do not corrupt the public. Fail to do this, and we shall have, as now, the rhetoric of public control and the reality of private power.

Chapter 4 Value

The members of human social systems are forever having to choose between cooperation and conflict. Accommodating ourselves to one another within systems where each has a distinct role, we learn that other people, or the system itself, have aims that are not perfectly reconciled to our own. Plato's solution is detailed in the *Republic*. Character is perfectly shaped by the requirements of role; work is specialized. Individuals do not have conflicting duties, because competition for their services is eliminated. This is Plato's *ideal* state. The conflicts he wished to reduce are still the everyday noise and tension of our lives. Character does not neatly elide with role: responsibilities to the different systems that engage us are often opposed.

This chapter has four emphases: (i) the two bases for value are self-affirmation and the instrumentality of things that are good or bad because of their effects on things we prize; (ii) individuals and the networks of independent, reciprocally related, overlapping, and nested systems are the natural—appropriate and material—setting for questions about value; (iii) individuals and systems may be reshaped to satisfy the value-driven theories used to direct public policy, because they are determinable—plastic; (iv) the variability of individuals and systems is saved from relativism, by a norm immanent in causal reciprocities. These four points are elaborated over the course of fifteen sections.

I. SELF-AFFIRMATION

We experience ourselves as the resonant centers of our respective "worlds." Saying *yes* or *no* to whatever things impinge on us, we rank their instrumental values. Their worth is conditional: they are good or bad as they have good or bad effects on us or other things. *Our* value is fundamental, for we discover and value ourselves: we are, by self-election, good unconditionally. This is Nietzsche's contention: we humans are self-valuing in a world where other things have value only because of their utility.[1] Having and using them, we exhibit our power and declare our value.[2] Yet self-affirmation alone does not secure well-being. Living among competitors, we struggle for advantage (Nietzsche and Spencer were contemporaries). Doing this doesn't reduce us to the primitive level of other animals, because we fill the void with our works and projects. Some secure and satisfy us. Others, art and great buildings, exalt us. The goodness we ascribe to them is a reflection of our worth. Those who believe in a moral God loathe this arrogance; but it does rightly describe us when we doubt that our worth is assured by a God who values us. Other creatures don't know that they have no intrinsic value. We who know it would despair if we did not value ourselves and the things we make.

Self-discovery and self-valorization are delayed a while; infants are slow to do either one. Still, each of us eventually discovers an immediacy, depth, and intensity that sets us apart from other people and things. Descartes' half-surprised, half-exultant, "I am, I exist" is a declaration we all make, one that affirms our self-declared value and existence. There may be some people who despise themselves and all the systems that engage them; but this is unusual. All or most of us can be counted on to value him or herself and some, at least, of his or her affiliations.

There are two directions to go as we elaborate these observations. First is our self-regard, with the implication that any other thing is good or bad as it impinges on us in ways we favor or reject. The value of other things is their utility: we, by comparison, are self-declared goods-in-themselves. Second is a question about our identity: is it character or role that supplies content for a person's self-perception? Which of them do I affirm when affirming myself? The answer is critical for the interpretation of our answer to the first question. For what is the thing whose value I affirm: is it myself alone, or is it myself as systems and their other members engage me? Are these systems and their members mere utilities for me, or do they share my status of self-declared good-in-itself? This second question is also critical at moments of self-appraisal: what is the ground of our value at moments of success or failure? Is it character or role?

Plato wouldn't let us prize character from role. They are not separable, or even distinguishable, in the ideal state, for breeding and education supply us with a character appropriate to the work we do: cognitive-affective postures comprise information, attitudes, and skills, all of them distinctively social in respect to origin, utility, and vector. They embody the common languages used to formulate and communicate information, the attitudes that anticipate and prescribe our relations to other people, and the skills that locate us within a society of workers. No one qualifies as a third-baseman in the absence of teammates and an opposing team: the skills are learned by playing the game. The separability of psychic postures from their roles is, therefore, qualified: every character derives from and anticipates its subject's relations to other people. How tightly is character joined to role? There is no tension between them if someone doesn't participate in a system, doesn't want to, and has no information, attitude, or skill that would qualify him for a place within it: someone blackballed by the Philatelic Society doesn't collect stamps. But is one's character equally separable from the roles he fills? Everyone past the first hours of infancy has character *and* a role. What is more, there would seem to be no way of having either without the other, because we acquire character in the midst of our roles. This last remark implies that character and role are so mutually implicative as to preclude all but a crude distinction between them. This would have significant moral consequences, if true. For then, all the rightness or wrongness of one's behavior might be explained by citing the role in which one has acted, for good or bad. Individuals could always defend their actions by denying personal responsibility. "The role required this of me," or "I had conflicting duties," would be universal excuses. But is one's cognitive-affective balance inseparable from one's roles? What part of psychic posture—including all one's information, attitudes, and skills—is not a qualification for one role or another?

Consider the psychological relation of parent and child. The parent's beliefs and values are focused by the child's need for care. The horror of losing a child is the void of a care that has lost its object and objective. yet neither parent nor child reduces to the role that each assumes for the other, because each qualifies, now or later, for a diversity of roles. Unpack these roles, lay out the qualifications for each, and there is nothing left to distinguish individuals from the roles for which they qualify.

This perception of us explains certain of the moral duties, failures, and conflicts that are entrained by our participation in systems. Each of us sometimes neglects duties and has to be reminded, then cajoled or coerced to satisfy them. This hectoring is morally complex, because each of us has several or many concurrent roles; there is often competition among systems for a member who has roles in two or more of them. Family or career is a familiar example. Citizen, but member of a pacifist church, is another. The conflicts implied by these examples—time and effort in the one case, contrary attitudes in the other—are chronic strains in everyone's psychic posture. Reducing us to our roles does not cure them.

There is, however, an offsetting integration within many or all such postures, one that we discover when we reject a role that has defined us. The career soldier who becomes a pacifist, the elderly nun who loses her faith: they, especially, challenge this alleged inseparability. Plato, recounting the myth of *Er*, describes the first person to choose a life for his next incarnation: "He was one of those who had come down from heaven, a man who had lived in a well-ordered polity in his former existence, participating in virtue by habit and not by philosophy."[3] We first learn virtue in the context of our roles. Later, we may learn to separate it from them, making ourselves responsible for what we do. Plato made philosophers the kings of his ideal state, because (among other reasons) he believed that their capacity for distinguishing virtue from role is evidence of their wisdom. This capacity develops early in some lives; there may be only hints of it in some others. Many are careful to take their morals from their roles, because of prudence, fear, or no imagination. Having roles that make contrary demands, they try to satisfy all of them, each in its time. But this won't work when the roles are concurrent, leaving accommodationists incompetent, embarrassed, or exhausted. Someone having moral autonomy does better. He, too, cannot do contrary things simultaneously. But he doesn't shun hard decisions. He asks that his duties be revised in systems that compete for his time, or he withdraws from one or both. Never trying to do the impossible, he shows and reaffirms the moral integrity that distinguishes him from his roles.

The perspective of the self-affirming center is everyone's point of view. It implies that interpersonal conflicts are not resolved morally (they are often resolved by power) until the belligerents perceive that their conflict is generated, in part at least, by each one's claim that he or she is the center of value about which everything else turns. Atomists—"rational decision theorists"—believe that no one acknowledges a self-valuing center different from him or herself, unless obliged to do so. "He would be mad," if he did, is Plato's helpful gloss of their view.[4] Is this so? Family members, friends, work mates, fellow believers, and citizens regularly give and die for one another. Atomists explain that people sacrifice themselves because, one way or another, they are getting something from it. No matter that the benefit is often invisible to everyone, atomists included. Why do we sacrifice? For a reason implicit in the fact that character is acquired as we engage ourselves in systems, learning to value ourselves as we value them and their members.

The self-valuing slaves who rowed Venetian galleys would have preferred doing something else; it was unimportant to them that the boat moved briskly while a duke and his friends enjoyed their lunches aft. These slaves could not project their self-love onto the systems that engaged them. Such idealizations express a member's anticipation and hope that a system will satisfy aims and ideals that he or she brings to it. Sometimes partners in the system (or the system itself) justify this projection by proving that they (or it) are instrumental goods for the member. Evidence that this is so comes by way of the reciprocities that establish the system: one is sustained and encouraged by the other members. It is easier in these circumstances to extend one's self-affirmation to them and this collaboration. For systems are foci for value. At the best of times, all of a system's members valorize it with a passion that derives from their self-love. Families, friendships, organizations, religions, and states profit from this investment. Their members flourish in the warmth and energy of it. Someone who encounters a system of this kind is startled at first by the ardor of the members. They like one another and what they do together. These are feelings one has in good times; but they often carry over to situations where things go badly. Loyalty then is an expression of gratitude for help intended or received. Or loyalty endures, in parents, friends, and soldiers, despite atomist incomprehension, because each perceives him or herself as an instrumental good in the lives of others. Circumstances are not always so benign. Enthusiasm deflates, and loyalty fades, if a system's members disappoint or betray one another. For loyalty is earned in systems that deserve it. Systems sometimes sabotage themselves for the benefit of a short-term advantage: think of businesses that convince workers to accept reduced salaries by encouraging fears of redundancy. They miscalculate.

Atomists won't like the claim that the worth of systems may be confused with one's own. This would be, for them, the category mistake of confusing a secondary value—the contract I make—for a primary value—myself. Isn't the affirmation of my worth free and clear of every such encumbrance? Don't Luther, Calvin, Kant, and Mill imply as much? They do, mistakenly. For contrary to them, autonomy is learned in the course of having and satisfying one's roles, as children acquire it in relation to their parents. Childhood is a kind of purgatory from the standpoint of the atomists; they say little or nothing of the intellectual and moral growth that do not occur in the absence of reciprocities that are commonplace in families. Atomists describe adults who were born for autonomy, though this persuasion is an unnecessary apriorist myth. For the adult is no less autonomous for having been a well-cared-for child. It is no paradox that autonomy is the product of reciprocity and dependence.

Character is, nevertheless, distinct from the context of its development, and distinct from the roles that later engage it. Distinguishing—separating—character from role restores the tension that lapses if the only moral claims upon an agent are directives that affirm his duty to perform as a role requires. For now, each of us discovers a ground for moral judgment that is distinct from duty: namely, his or her self-interest. General Motors is a source of many goods, given the pleasure derived from the cars it sells and the lives supported by the salaries it pays. But how shall I, a production line worker, resolve the demands upon me? Driven to distraction by the noise and speed of the work, I cannot bear the idea that this is my fate until retirement, death, or defeat. Recovering authority for the course of my life, I want to separate myself from this role in order to reclaim the dream of my peace on my terms. But what will my wife and children say? Do my responsibilities to them offset the responsibilities to myself? I may be trapped and paralyzed; but I am not a passive witness who docilely goes along, repeating to myself, "my station and its duties." What conceptual resources enable us to solve moral dilemmas such as this? There is no formula for deciding the greater good, that of a family that includes me, or my own. There are rough measures—five of us, one of me—but no algorithms. More to the point is the assumption that makes the dilemma real: I have a character and a moral identity that are distinct from the demands of my several roles. For absent that separable character, there is no one to profit from leaving the job, hence no offsetting center of value to balance the deleterious effects on my family.

How do we find this agent? By turning on ourselves. Set against our socialization is the autonomy of our psychic life. We sometimes disguise and hide from this autonomy; but hardly anyone resists it entirely. Each of us discovers and values him or herself. Does it follow that we are valuable in ourselves? Yes and no. Our worth is not an objective, intrinsic value—one bestowed, perhaps, by a god.

Our value is self-bestowed. Discovering myself within one or another of my roles, but able to distinguish myself from it, I want the best—or merely something better—for me.

Can these self-affirmations produce nothing better than the narcissism that atomism promotes? Plato had a solution for the moral opposition of character, freely determining itself, and the roles that constrain us. Should I favor myself or others? These two goods are not easily separated: alienated from others, I am angry with myself. Must these values compete? Satisfy both, says Plato: find work that pleases you while contributing to the well-being of pertinent others. Valuing myself, I also value them. Plato neatly tailored character to role. His ideal state is meant to avert their collisions. But the opposition is real, and not so easily dodged: pleasing one side may thwart the other.

This perpetual opposition—character or role—should confound the assumption that each person's self-affirmation entrains his or her possession of certain rights. This is mistaken for several reasons: first, because there are no entitlements that come from declaring one's worth; second, because this notion of rights wrongly supposes that they are acquired in some asocial way, rather than negotiated, then legislated or otherwise acknowledged; third, because it assumes that individuals are the bearers of rights irrespective of their roles. These three assumptions converge in the idea of natural rights, meaning rights acquired at birth or acquired because of our volitional, rational, or spiritual nature, without regard for our roles. But there are no rights of this sort if all rights are negotiated between or among us humans, as the rights of citizens are the products of a negotiation. All that survives of natural, unnegotiated rights are the claims or demands we make of others.

There is also this last point: it may seem inconsistent that an ontology of systems ascribes primary value to subsystems of a very low order: namely, ourselves. The anomaly is superficial. I am not suggesting that we humans are primary values, merely that we declare ourselves to be goods-in-themselves in a universe that is otherwise value-free, instrumental values apart. (See section II.) Our self-valorization is an expression of animal will, the determination to survive, or the pleasure we take in ourselves. These are some aspects of an emergent property or power, one that expresses the systemic complexity within us. This power is fruitful. Good things derive from it, including our insistence on the rule of law (as it acknowledges the equal primacy of individual persons) and the public where we negotiate (ideally) as equals. Moreover, our self-preoccupation isn't surprising, given our internal wiring, the competitive spirit that drives us, and the moral code that makes us responsible for ourselves. It can't hurt if we balance the score, conceding that we are small wheels in bigger ones.

II. INSTRUMENTAL VALUES

Something is useful or not, good or bad, for some end. Artifacts especially are created for a purpose. We perceive them correctly if we understand their use: bombs as well as bottles are good if they serve the purpose for which they were designed. A thing's function is therefore both the final cause of its creation—it was created to perform in this way—and the basis for understanding it. Imagine mechanically minded people in a culture that has electricity but no radios. Presented with a radio, they are mystified until someone notices the electric cord, then the volume and tuning dials. It is more plausible now that this thing has a purpose. Speculating that its form is appropriate to its function, they experiment until it performs as designed. Or they never decipher the radio, because they don't discover its design and purpose.

Plato argued that the proper organization of the ideal state is useful to the well-being of its citizens. However, Plato exceeded the reach of his argument when he said that the Good is the highest Form.[5] For if radios are good for transmitting signals, what is the end, beyond Being, for which the Good is a value? The likely answer is that it is good for all of Being; and that the good for Being is achieved within Being itself, not beyond it (as would be impossible) in nonbeing. What good is intrinsic to Being? Only the harmony of its parts, as a well-ordered soul is engaged harmoniously with the other parts of the state. Extrapolate from this image, and we have the idea of a harmoniously ordered universe. We humans are to accommodate ourselves to our place within it.[6] But this is facile, because the offsetting goodness—the instrumentality—of some things (bacteria and penicillin, for example) precludes the harmonious composition of all the parts of Being. Plato's story is, nevertheless, half the truth about value. For utilities of every sort are good if they produce effects appropriate to an aim declared by us self-valorizing humans, bad if they damage or frustrate us.

Notice these two aspects of instrumentality: things interact, affecting one another; and *we* label some effects good or bad as they interest or affect us. We may believe that the first consideration is sufficient to justify calling an instrument good or bad, as water is good for fish whether or not the difference to them is favorable to us. But this is a mistake, one promoted by too casual a use of *good*. For goodness or badness are introduced into contexts such as this by our judgments, not by way of the intrinsic goodness or badness of instruments or their effects. A lake is drained when a new dam diverts its water, killing all the fish. We describe the situation, without assigning a value to the outcome. Or we project our concerns onto fish, imagining that this fate is bad for their predators, or bad for their health, hence bad for them because they, too, want to live.

The structure of valorization is plainer now: it requires both the instrumentality of things, their effects on one another, and their effects on a thing or things specified as primary goods. Plato rightly emphasized these materially based utilities. Aristotle helped to clarify them by distinguishing efficient and final cause.[7] Together, they supply the basis for the consequentialism I favor: no utility is good or bad, right or wrong, except as it affects things deemed good or bad in themselves.

Joining consequentialism to the previous remarks about primary goods, we strip our moral theories of slogans and incantations, acknowledging only these four considerations. *First* are the more or less generalized expression of self-regard that elect the primary goods. *Second* are consequentialist estimates of the effects that instruments have on things chosen as primary goods (as laws, virtues, and justice are instruments, while persons and their societies are primary goods). *Third* are criteria for evaluating the effects of utilities on competing primary goods (including self, systems, or other people): what is better for us, apples or oranges; what is worse, hunger or fatigue? Such criteria are also appraised consequentially: are primary goods served better or worse by applying them? *Fourth* are consequentialist strategies for maximizing benefits and reducing harms for the primary goods. If education is good for us and tobacco is bad, we pursue the one and shun the other.

These principles are not an algorithm for resolving every moral question in ways that satisfy all the primary goods. Complexity, irresolution, and conflict abound—as there are self-regarding and other-regarding virtues. Add that we are often stymied by having to rank too many effects that are pertinent to too many aims; and by having to do all this while balancing perspectives in which self, systems, or other people are competing goods. The practical difficulty of applying consequentialist principles is often daunting.[8]

A theoretical issue is easier to resolve. For this sketch of a moral theory precludes the objection that consequentialism is faulty because utilitarianism—the greatest good for the greatest number—sometimes has morally unacceptable consequences—torturing one for the greater benefit of others, for example. This objection conflates utilitarianism with consequentialism, though the difference between them is plain: utilitarianism is consequentialism *plus* a stipulated good:

namely, the pleasure or well-being of the greatest number of people. Distaste for utilitarianism is, more accurately, distaste for its primary good, the greatest number (the undifferentiated mass of humanity). Such disputes about primary goods (fetuses or pregnant women, for example) are chronic. What principles dictate or justify our choice of them? There seem to be no such principles, religious doctrines apart (as man is said to be made in the image of God). Lacking demonstrable principles, we rely on other resources. They include each person's self-valorization—with valorization of systems and other people that engage him or her—and our recognition (more or less acute) that every other person values him or herself. Damaging some people for the benefit of others is never an option, if our primary good is the self-affirmed value of everyone—though we may prefer to shrink the domain of primary goods. Like Polemarchus, we may restrict care and help to friends, while ignoring or hurting enemies. Consequentialist calculations are appropriate to both choices. Either way, we appraise things for their effects on us and the other things valued as primary goods.

The choice of final goods is also complicated in this additional way: we (who are normally self-affirming ends) sometimes choose a role as instrumental goods. This happens whenever we help to establish and sustain a valued system. We usually expect that our benefit to a system or its other members will redound to our advantage. But this doesn't always happen and isn't always expected, as we know from the parents, soldiers, and friends who sacrifice themselves for the benefit of the system. Their sacrifice is no less admirable for being secondary to a different virtue: namely, the cooperation that establishes social systems. This is the premier, instrumental, social value, though it presupposes the other utilities required if systems are to be established and sustained, including language and efficacies of all sorts.

III. TWO KINDS OF SOCIALITY

Morality, as I am describing it, is a regime of behavior appropriate to four considerations: each person's psychic identity, with its values and priorities; the systems in which one participates, each making demands appropriate to itself; the values, often expressed as laws or rules, that regulate the behaviors of individuals and systems; and the constraining effect of the material world as it limits the character, behaviors, and relations of the individuals and systems that are its parts.

Ought does not derive from *is*. But nothing we ought to do is precluded by what we are, while everything we ought to do is something whose consequences are favored because of what we are. Accordingly, we need information about our-selves and our situation before we formulate moral rules. One question directs us: namely, what is the character of human sociality? Are we socialized because of using rules or laws to organize our behavior? Or is socialization achieved as we establish reciprocity in our relations to other people? The focus on laws ab-stracts us from our material circumstances; reciprocities locate us within them.

We emphasize the role of laws because of the Jewish emphasis on the Ten Commandments and because of Kant. He said that plans for action should be formulated as maxims, and that candidate maxims must satisfy the categorical imperative, the principle that no rule should direct action unless every rational agent could apply it without contradiction.[9] Lying violates this formulation, be-cause of the effects that would accrue were everyone to lie: no one would believe anyone else, with the effect that no cooperative work could be done because no information would be exchanged. The liar's self-subversion is an example to the rest of us: no rational agent should will contradictions, because doing this sub-verts the conditions for effective sociality.

Kant's kingdom of ends postulates a domain of moral agents. Each is re-sponsible for insuring that its behaviors respect both the autonomy of the oth-ers and the cooperative activities on which all depend. Laws—maxims that are acceptable to every agent, because none is contradictory—establish the para-meters for moral relations among these agents. This is the atomist alternative to Plato's ideal state. Yet something in this formulation is missing, something whose absence is easily parodied. Imagine the one survivor on an island that has a working traffic light. This single pedestrian stops invariably when the light is red. It is, he says, his social duty. A contradiction would result were he to do oth-erwise, for many or all might be killed were everyone to cross on red lights, with the effect that none would survive to do it. A rational agent, one whose will is self-consistent, stops at the light. No matter that there are no other pedestrians and no cars. These contingencies are incidental to the categorical imperative: *"act as if the maxim of the action were to become by thy will a universal law of na-ture."*[10]

Kant would reject my story, because it confuses two contingencies: inclina-tions and circumstances. He was more concerned with the first than the second, though the example features only the second. Kant distinguished categorical from hypothetical imperatives, in order to found morality on a principle that abstracts from each person's inclinations. For it was familiar to him that each of us wants his or her own good, and that inclinations move us toward one or an-other alleged good.[11] Desires are different and opposed, so that realizing mine may preclude realizing yours. This is the conflict that justice and morality should obviate. Kant's solution overrides self-concern: "*So act as to treat humanity, whether in thine own persons or in that of any other, in every case as an end withal, never as means only.*"[12] Reason and morality require that we restrain the inclinations that would have us use other people as means to satisfy personal desires. Equally, reason and morality enable us to acknowledge that satisfying my inclinations is not better than, and should not come at cost to, other people's desires.

It is this aversion to prejudicial inclinations, not Kant's disregard for the peculiarity of our circumstances, that explains his universalizability principle, and his distinction between hypothetical imperatives—do this, given your desire for that—and the categorical imperative. Contingent circumstances are sometimes elided with inclinations, as when we plead circumstances to justify actions sponsored by desire. Yet there are times—the parody above—when the appeal to circumstances is not a disguised appeal to inclination. It is mistaken to suppose on these occasions that the distinction between the categorical and hypothetical imperatives is unexceptional, as though circumstances are never relevant to maxims that satisfy the categorical imperative. For no one acts in circumstances that are stripped of all character; no one can decide what actions are feasible if he has not considered the details of his situation: Is it raining? Is this peace or war? It is not the indeterminate Everyman living Anywhere who proposes to act, but rather I, in these circumstances, who considers doing this or that. Ignoring significant details of my circumstances would be flagrantly irrational. These are some reasons for saying that rational agents are not obliged to abstract from the *salient* details of their circumstances so as to rid a maxim of all tacit appeals to inclination before testing it for consistency. Where there are no cars and only one pedestrian, stopping at red lights is foolish, not virtuous.

Kant himself was not always clear about the relevance of a distinction between inclinations and circumstances. Never lie, he said, whatever the circumstances. Yet many of us would think ourselves moral if our lie frustrated the murderous intention of an other. Kant's appeal to contradiction is easily turned against him to support this persuasion: it is a contradiction to hope that other rational creatures will prosper while piously revealing their whereabouts to killers. Circumstances are relevant to the maxims tested by the categorical imperative, when inclinations are not.

An analogy from pure to practical reason is clarifying: Kant never supposed that the categories of understanding—quality, quantity, and relation—are sufficient to generate experience. We also need empirical schemas: rules for organizing sensory data to produce empirical objects of specific kinds.[13] Equally, the categorical imperative alone is insufficient to direct our behavior: we also need maxims appropriate to our situations. For his imperative is plausible only as it bars rules biased by our inclinations, not maxims that are appropriate to our circumstances. Kant would protest that this is an open door to confusion. It justifies the backsliders who appeal to their special circumstances—whatever provokes this terrible urge—to justify their immorality. But this dodge is usually transparent: we quickly perceive that the contingencies alleged to justify conduct are the inclinations Kant feared, not circumstances. Special cases—the cannibalism considered by people adrift in boats—are more difficult, but they are rare. Such examples test a moral theory at the limits of its application. They are not the examples we use to formulate it.

These details are incidental to Kant's notion of socialization, except as they emphasize that material circumstances are relevant—and typically critical—for our moral choices. This is not a point one would garner from Kant. Moral behavior for him is the act of bringing one's will under the law, meaning rules that satisfy the categorical imperative, irrespective of circumstances. It is not so silly, from this point of view, that I stop at red lights though there are no other cars. The absence of traffic is contingent; the moral law is necessary and universal.

This is Kant's restatement, in formalistic terms, of Plato's distinction between appetite and reason. Appetite risks being asocial or antisocial. Reason civilizes appetite by bending passion to a rule. This is often good sense, as when impulsive drivers reduce accidents by obeying traffic laws. The problem comes as we abstract from complex circumstances to say that sociality derives only from our obedience to law, for then—as my single pedestrian confirms—this notion of sociality is empty. Perhaps no thoughtful Kantian is deterred by Kant's rigid distinction between hypothetical (circumstantial) and categorical imperatives, so none would endorse the irrelevance of circumstances to the application of laws. Still, the Kantian emphasis upon law is usually construed as a reason for abstracting from—or ignoring—circumstances. One is social, on such an account, merely by virtue of shaping one's behavior in the ways prescribed by a law or laws. This is the point that invites application to worlds inhabited by single persons.

Has Kant ignored the material sociality of people who are richly connected, people who press against one another on streets or trams, at work or war? Would he have been surprised by a Brueghel painting? No, his abstractions make a different point. He, like Plato, insisted that everyday life be infused with the ideal, and that we judge it adequate or not by testing for the presence of the ideal within it. Life together, in the absence of wills shaped by the categorical imperative, is deficient. Such lives fail to achieve the ideal sociality conferred by living under the moral law. Kant may never have said that this condition is sufficient as well as necessary for sociality; but this implication suffuses the Second Critique. One infers that life is otherwise degenerately social and imperfectly real, as Plato supposed when he imagined people dominated by appetite rather than reason. The ideal condition—willing the categorical imperative—becomes, by comparison and implication, the only condition for sociality, or the condition for the only estimable sociality.[14]

This conclusion dominates the views of deontological moralists. It cannot be right, because something critical is ignored when the condition for an idealized sociality—all of us will the categorical imperative—has become the necessary and sufficient condition for any sociality. Kant has ignored the character and material conditions of the moral agents, including the muscular reciprocity of people who live and work together. The reciprocity he encourages is different. It is established if no maxim willed by either of us damages the other (whether we apply the same or different maxims) because each of us has shaped his will in accord with the categorical imperative. Reciprocity of this sort is lame: it implies safe passage without interaction.

Compare the reciprocities that join us in families, friendships, work, citizenship, and prayer. There are often no laws regulating these relations, though moral values suffuse them. Social dancing is a model for all of them. There are steps to learn, but good dancers work out variations for themselves; or dancers improvise, with order in freedom. This is paradigmatic for many of our reciprocal behaviors: we agree on a task while experimenting with ways to do it. Prescribed steps—rules—are a helpful guide; but each of us must feel both the rhythm and our partner's way of moving to it. Often dancing together, we come to do it better. Sociality is like this for spouses, friends, parents, children, and fellow workers. There is sensitivity to one another's idiosyncrasies and a shared devotion to the task. There are mismatches and misunderstandings. There is sabotage. But many of these relationships are moral and effective, for reasons that have nothing to do with Kant's formal conditions for sociality. Causal reciprocity—including the regulation of mutually respectful agents—is their condition. Kant agrees that morality is vital in a crowded world; but his moral theory ignores the reciprocities and systems that are one focus for moral action. Indeed, Kant's moral theory is tailored exclusively to the needs of the other focus: namely, the relations of mutually independent people and systems. His social ontology—the kingdom of ends—has blinded him to one principal feature of social reality.

I agree that the social relations of mutually independent agents are familiar and important. Sitting on a bus with people one doesn't know—where habits supported by laws are the conditions for civil, uneventful rides—is also a social act: self-control, rather than mutual control—reciprocity—is the operative factor here. Encounters such as these invoke Kant's rule—don't do what you would not have others do—but they are not examples of the sociality that concerns us. Nothing fruitful happens, merely because no one is jostled. Productive social activities are, almost invariably, the effects of causal reciprocity, hence the work of systems.

IV. ATOMISM, COMMUNITARIANISM, AND HOLISM

We add the distinction of character and role to the claim that reciprocity is the principal material condition for the morality and sociality appropriate to stabilities. This is more elaboration than addition, because one needs character of some sort in order to act at all, and because engaging one or more people reciprocally implies that one thereby enacts a role. Now this question: How does reciprocity illuminate moral questions that arise with conflicts between character and role or between roles?

This notion of sociality, with its emphasis on personal, reciprocal relations makes rules marginal. Proscriptive rules—don't murder or steal—only come into play when people do, or are about to do, what most of us don't do. There is, however, a point that is common to the sociality of reciprocity and the sociality sanctioned by universalizable maxims: namely, the expectation or demand that associates will be responsible to the other members of the society they share. Thrusting a foot toward an approaching friend looks more like a kick than a greeting. Standardized expectations are the rules of engagement known to people in families, friendship, and work. The differences between these two kinds of sociality are, nevertheless, more conspicuous than their similarities. Rules that satisfy Kant's criterion are rigid: they tolerate no exceptions, because universalizing exceptions entails contradictions. Rules that govern reciprocities are often loose, permissive, and sensitive to the variety of circumstances and partners to which they apply. They are similar in this respect to the pliable rules of speech: either may be described equally well as normalized expectations or as rules. Indeed, many of the rules governing reciprocities are counted among the rules for performative uses of language, as there are expectations, hence rules, appropriate to greeting and parting. Each partner's expectations express the anticipation of, or desire for, a modulating, reassuring or controlling response from the other. Friends embrace; people quarreling do an elaborate walk as each avoids the other. Yet expectations are tolerant. Familiarity with our partners and their many roles makes us forgiving when an expected response doesn't occur. We merely chide them for disappointing us, if the regular exchange of reciprocities is otherwise sustained. These are informal solutions to conflicts of character and role, or to conflicting roles. No law or rule is easily generalized from them.

Is there a rule for deciding conflicts that are not resolved by informal accommodations? Such a rule would be enormously helpful if it resembled a procedure for untangling a knot without cutting it. For such a rule would identify routes that reduce or avoid conflicts without costs to the conflicted parties. Candidate rules are disappointing. The categorical imperative is costly to the frustrated inclinations of people who cannot satisfy themselves by acting on maxims that are not universalizable. A different option—one that sometimes avoids harm on all sides—requires that no one do anything: unable to divide something indivisible, we agree that no one shall have it. But this too is not a universal solution, because it often happens that declining to act damages one or all of the parties. We infer that no rule averts every harm, and that any rule formulated to solve conflicts that are not solved informally may exaggerate the harm suffered by one or several of the parties concerned: laws that award or deny leave to pregnant employees damage employers or the women.

A stronger conclusion is close at hand: morality is never reducible, simply, to actions that accord with rules. An example makes the point. Organized murderers at Birkenau or Srebenica are not culpable merely because they broke a law. It is their systems, characters, aims, and the consequences of their actions that are deplorable. What is more, we know that such things are evil without needing a law to inform us. Guards or soldiers at either place may have refused an order to kill because character in them was inimical to their role. Did their morality derive from laws they observed; or did the laws ratify what character already prescribed?[15]

Assume that laws are not a sufficient foundation for moral behavior. Can we locate firmer ground for our moral choices? Is there a more supple but concrete moral ground, one sufficient to determine—morally justify—our actions at times when choice is exigent but available choices are contraries? There is an alleged ground of this sort, one that is said to trump every other: namely, the self-impelled directive that each of us choose him or herself. Let everyone give priority to his or her interests (as they are self-perceived), so that conflicts of character and role are always settled to the advantage of character: meaning the person who fills the role. This is a possible strategy, but not the incontestable one that egoists suppose. There are, for example, the lieutenants in combat units whose self-love is equaled by the intensity of their commitment to the troops they lead. They can't make the choice this principle prescribes. There are also parents forced to choose between the interests of two children, though nothing in the circumstances justifies favoring one over the other. What does choosing oneself imply in such contexts? Does it merely prescribe that we walk away from forced choices that affect the well-being of other people or their systems? It is better to concede that this ("incontrovertible") principle is irrelevant to many of the circumstances where choices are made. Worse, egoism makes the foolish and false assumption that self-love is detachable from one's valorization of other people and the systems that join us to them. It supposes that I may justly abandon them for my advantage, though I would think very little of myself were I to do such a thing.

What shall we do—what is actually done—when no single principle obviates conflicts without punishing costs to some or all of the parties concerned? Having real conflicts to solve, but no transcendental principle by which to settle them, we show our inventiveness by invoking either of three ontological theories to interpret and resolve these conflicts. Each theory describes our circumstances in a distinctive way, and each alleges that its norms are justified by the circumstances it describes.

At one extreme—*atomism*—priority goes to individualist versions of democratic practice. The individual is said to be a storehouse of rights—freedoms from and freedoms to—that defend him from the demands of others (whether individual people or social systems). His relations to them are merely contractual and voluntary, says this alternative. *Holism,* with its emphasis on an integrated system of rule-governed roles, is the other extreme. Holism alleges that individuals are intelligible to themselves and other people because of the duties inherited by filling a role or roles. This strategy's preferred examples are organisms or machines: each part is calibrated to the others, while having no value apart from its contribution to the whole. The corporate state is an example.

In the middle—*communitarianism*—are theories that ease the opposition of the two extremes. Like atomism, they say that character does not coalesce with role: meaning that character develops within roles while having an integration (hence integrity) that distinguishes it from its roles. Like holism, such theories emphasize relations. They affirm that talents languish apart from one's roles, so that individuals deprived of every role are desiccated husks. Like actors who come alive only within a movie or play, we risk losing our self-understanding if we have no roles and relations to fill. This middle option shuns the narcissism of the one extreme and the other's fusion of character and role.

Figure 2 represents the three theories graphically. Figure 2a shows atoms that move independently, but sometimes in association with one another. It also shows trajectories of conflict, and, by means of wavy lines, laws introduced to proscribe some behaviors (murder, for example) or prescribe others (as traffic laws facilitate movement). Figure 2b represents two of the many possible arrays of systems that are mutually independent, reciprocally related, nested, or overlapping. One is flat, the other is steeply hierarchical. Figure 2c represents a network of relations in which each node is a role. Additional facilitating laws are extraneous, because the network and roles already prescribe each role's conduct, though innovation (automobiles, for example) would require additional facilitators (traffic laws). Proscriptive laws that enforce the order prefigured by the network are assumed.

Each of these theories—atomism, communitarianism, and holism—may justify itself by appealing to an a priori principle or ground, but doing this is always a sham. For these three are strategies, not eternal truths. Human social reality is plastic and determinable. It can be shaped, sometimes even remade, to satisfy an ideology. Each of these theories may be used as a recipe that emphasizes one feature of social life, while de-emphasizing or suppressing some others. The communitarianism I favor is guilty of this distorting effect when it ignores the many things that are mutually independent. Still, the choice among the three theories is not arbitrary. The middle way describes us better. There are five reasons to prefer it:

(i) This is the ontologically more accurate hypothesis. Parts are not abstracted from the systems in which they participate; nor are they merged, inseparably, within them. Character does not reduce to role; but characters without roles are empty or aimless. Conversely, a social system's parts lose their energy and initiative, if the characters of the persons filling them are obliterated in the web of their interactions. The degree of freedom within systems varies from role to role; but there are relatively few roles which reduce the activities of the part to the narrow space of the role: one thinks of army recruits, the citizens of despotic states, prisoners, slaves, bureaucrats, and too many laborers of all sorts. There are many people, but not many roles. They contrast with the variable spaces established within systems that tolerate or encourage the initiative of people who fill their roles.

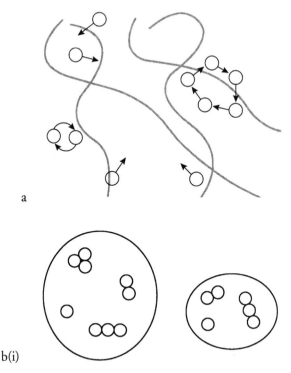

a

b(i)

Figure 2. (a) Atomism, with independent agents, some in contractual relations, some colliding, with laws that facilitate movement or reduce conflict. (b) Communitarianism, with two variants: *i* is flat; *ii* is steeply hierarchical (deeply nested). (c) Holism, with individuals—*a* and *b*—at nodes that determine their roles.

(ii) The middle way's perception of individuals is different from that of the extremes. Atomism affirms that each of us is morally, intellectually, or materially self-sufficient, and that we engage other people from one or more of these three positions of independence. Such engagements are always defended, when states are well-ordered, by laws of contract. Mill assumed this when he described his third region of liberty: we are fully formed—capable of independent thinking and able to choose our tastes and pursuits—when we engage other people. Co-operation satisfies a common interest; but the bond is temporary because we are, effectively, self-sufficient. Children are an embarrassment to this formula. It was once believed that adulthood is preformed in children, so that children relate to adults as potency to actuality. Childhood dependency was explained away as the process of realizing this potency. This is half right: childhood is a passage to adulthood; but children are not incipiently autonomous, as if adulthood were

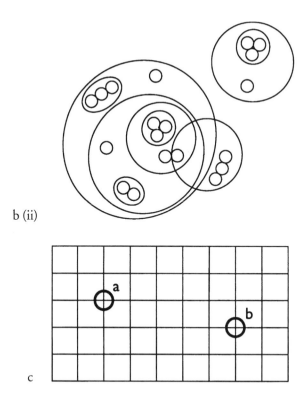

b (ii)

c

achieved already, but only potentially, within them. Nor is the dependency of children explained by saying that potential adults are temporarily housed with their actuators. Children evolve into adulthood because they have actual properties and powers, as well as specific roles within families, friendships, and schools. Speaking only of their "dependency" disguises the reciprocities and systems that atomists prefer to ignore.

Holism argues, from the other extreme, that individuals are ciphers, apart from their roles in complex systems. Our distinctive, self-directed aims have otherwise lapsed; psychic identity is feeble or lost. Holism exploits our mutual dependence and the considerable evidence that we are altered dramatically by our roles within systems; but then it reduces a system's parts, including their cognitive-affective postures, to their several roles. Compare the middle way. It acknowledges three decisive features of individuality: each one's distinctive developmental history, his or her cognitive-affective posture, and the distinctive way that a person fills his or her roles. Someone else would fill the same role differently.

(iii) Individuals have disparate aims, though there may be considerable agreement among them: all may favor a productive economy, neighborliness, public health, and a particular style and standard of education. Atomism acknowledges the similarities and differences without explaining them; or it regards them as the converging or diverging expressions of individual choices. It fails to remark that many interests are acquired only when one participates in systems. This is apparent when employees, team, or family members discover their aims by learning that something is good or bad for the systems that engage them. No supersystem can integrate the many aims, because some of them are contraries. The interpretive stories of the many religions are an example. Their incompatibility may seem to be no problem, because one can line up the books of contending faiths on a shelf: we have our choice of creeds. Holism is less tolerant. It requires that the many be bound by internal relations such that each is accommodated to every other. It binds the creeds forcibly or suppresses all but one. Contrariety in every domain of practice and belief mimics contentious religious views. For it often happens that we have no criterion for determining that one practice or claim is good or true, while the others of a domain are bad or false. The want of such criteria precludes the forced harmonization of practices or ideas, or the arbitrary choice of one to the exclusion of others.

Diverse objectives are best served by the open playing field that Dewey advocated: let everyone associate with like-minded people to pursue shared aims up to the point of damaging other people or systems. We are productive as we join ourselves with others, thereby forming the extended networks and hierarchies of systems where related activities are nurtured, supported, and performed. We do these things in contexts where certain rules of conduct have been decided. We submit ourselves later to the oversight that may require adjustments to subsequent behaviors and to these regulations. We never submit, early or late, to the universal accommodation and compression of a corporate state. Initiative and efficacy would expire if we did.

(iv) Relations within the networks and hierarchies of systems may be rigid, flexible, or something in between. Flexibility is maximal for freestanding individuals: they may have considerable psychic and physical space in which to move. Freedom is reduced by the reciprocity, overlap, and nesting of systems. These constraints are not only material and causal, but also moral: people are bound by their responsibilities to systems that engage them and to their fellow members.

Atomism and holism push these factors to their opposing limits: they promise inalienable autonomy or the security of comprehensive and constraining internal relations. Communitarianism avoids both extremes. Acknowledging that degrees of freedom are appropriate to every character and many roles, it supposes that the kinds and degrees of freedom required are functions of the work to be done. Artistic and intellectual activities require a loose fit; commercial pilots are more tightly constrained.

(v) What do material and pragmatic considerations imply for choosing a form of government? Should it be the minimal state of atomist theory or the internally ordered whole preferred by Plato and Hegel? Neither solution is appropriate to systems that may be mutually independent, reciprocally related, overlapping, or nested, for no system is entirely independent, and none is the container of every other. Communitarianism supposes that regulation is intrinsic to every system and complex of systems, so that there is considerable self-regulation short of the time when individual members, or members and their systems, join to create an additional system—the public, hence democratic, government. It adds corporate regulation—by the public—to the self-regulation of individual systems.

Government is one system among others. Yet government is an anomaly among systems, because its power to regulate makes it intrusive and intimidating. The need for regulation, nevertheless, multiplies when systems proliferate. Government grows to meet this need. It may interfere everywhere, though too often in ways that are ineffective, destructive, or corrupt. We tire of government and want it reduced to the police power; or government captures every other system within itself after misconstruing regulation as the principal aim of social life. How should regulation be reduced to a *service,* one that is respectful of other systems while facilitating appropriate behaviors but inhibiting others?

One solution requires an alert citizenry that monitors and controls its government. Citizens in efficient democracies too often suppose that government doesn't need their attention. We turn away from the things governments do, depending on probing journalists, elections, and good luck to save us from incompetent, arrogant, or corrupt leaders. Vigilance and participation in forums of all sorts are a better defense against incompetent government. It helps if regulative authority is clearly labeled and divided, so that successive orders of systems—cities, counties, and states—can regulate themselves, thereby preventing the concentration of regulative power in a remote central government. We need this mix of activism and organization to assure that the regulative tasks of government do not operate at two levels: one apparent—elections and legislative debates—the other hidden—influence peddling and bribery.

These five points illustrate the different directions that thinking can go when material and pragmatic issues supersede the ideological ones of atomism and holism. Atomism emphasizes the benefits and harms to individuals; but it hides much that is beneficial or harmful, because it does not acknowledge the systems that are helped or harmed. Holism makes both harms and benefits all but invisible, because every effect is attenuated or turned ambiguous as it spreads throughout the system of ramified, internal relations that makes a one of the many. Atomism and holism misdescribe the world, then direct practices that distort it to our cost. Each justifies itself by emphasizing its good effects, but neither concedes the damage it does. We who are remade to satisfy these theories see clearly enough that corporatist policies are ruinous. There are always totalitarian states, but few people who promote holist strategies. Atomism is longer-lived, because its effects—including the public, the rule of law, free markets, secular values, personal freedom, and the minimal state—are conspicuous and desirable. Still, it too has costs, including anomie, mutual hostility, disintegration, and waste. We continue to prefer it, because we like the freedoms it promotes, and because the holist alternative is unendurable.

Communitarianism almost disappeared when the Enlightenment agenda required that individuals be empowered, that government be diminished, and that there be no intermediate systems to mediate a government's relations with its citizens or to share power with citizens and their government. Why give constitutional recognition to such systems if atomist theory denied their reality, construing systems as aggregates? It was enough that such systems were sometimes protected from governmental interference by dispensations implied, for example, by freedom of religion. Citizens were to move freely in the spaces vacated when intermediary systems were purged or ignored. Government was to be nearly invisible. It would discipline the occasional vagrant, while keeping an eye on barbarous foreigners.

This atomist story still dominates our thinking, though government (now large and powerful) is co-opted by systems, including transnational corporations, irresponsible political parties, and organized minorities, that dominate political or economic life. The public's inability to regulate them is another of its consequences. Atomism empowers individuals by endowing them with personal and political rights. It also makes them morally and legally responsible for their conduct and regulates their conflicts. Yet atomism reduces systems to aggregates, so that their moral responsibility reduces to the responsibility of their individual constituents. Where aggregates misbehave or conflict, their parts—individual people—are to manage them better. Yet individuals cannot do what atomism requires of them, because the things called *aggregates* often prove to be systems, and because human systems do not reduce to their self-disciplined human parts. Atomist theory has disarmed us. It doesn't acknowledge the ontology of organizations or associations that subvert and cripple the only system that might regulate them: namely, the public.

Does this characterization of social paralysis give too much weight to the role of atomist theory? Haven't the governments it inspires approved and applied strategies for regulating other systems, including laws against monopoly, pollution, and child abuse? This is true but not a solution, because these responses have created a tissue of ad hoc defenses and gestures. Policy is enfeebled, because the dominance of atomist theory obscures our situation: it supposes that aggregates should have no more power than the sum of their constituent parts, though systems typically have powers that are greater and different from those of their members. How should we regulate them?

The public is more effective when we have a more accurate description of our circumstances: meaning a more accurate ontology than the one that atomism provides. Such an ontology is help of two kinds. *First,* it doesn't tell us which side to favor in every particular dispute; but it does exhibit the character of some conflicts, thereby enabling us to find particular solutions. A husband denies a rupture with his wife; we then discover that he has wives and families in three cities. This man is a victim of overlap. Atomists talk of bigamy laws. Holists squint to see the beauty of this additional complexity within the whole. The middle way is the better representation of a conflict's structure. It makes viable solutions plainer. Sending the bigamist to jail reduces all his families to penury. Let him work to support them. *Second,* we are better able to construct and defend the public if we acknowledge its actual circumstances. We can think better about the extraordinary anomaly created when atomist theory contrives to set individual humans apart from the systems that engage them, thereby securing the rule of law, free markets, and secular values. For we need an answer to the question mooted above: How shall the interests of systems be represented within a public that is composed only of individuals? Failure to answer guarantees that systems will find ways to inveigle the public on their behalf. Lobbyists will continue to pressure legislators. Too many of them will succumb. This is a structural problem—not only one of character. How shall we reconcile the public that regulates for the community of individuals with the systems in which we participate, systems that achieve all or most of what is valuable to us? Denying the reality of systems is not an answer.

A different answer is more useful and probably true. The public's inability to regulate other systems effectively is the permanent consequence of the aims and circumstances that prevailed when it was established to regulate individuals while endowing them with rights. Creating the public, while denying the reality of systems, construing them as aggregates, exalted individuals while defending them from dominating systems. This would have been unproblematic if (somehow) systems had disappeared. But they didn't, so the public's inception was, at once, empowering and enfeebling: the individuals it ennobled were rendered unable to conceptualize or contend with the systems it disestablished. We do better to acknowledge the reality of the systems that everywhere engage us, then to rethink the public so that it may regulate them better.

There is also this cerebral consideration: how shall we explain the deontologists who affirm that one or the other of these three theories—atomism, holism, or communitarianism—is a necessary truth? Could it be that their assertiveness is a reaction to the uneasiness of the ideologists who preceded them? Deontologists are vocal wherever a social theory seems to be true because a state of affairs has been reworked to satisfy the theory.[16] These apologists intuit or derive prescriptive rules that everyone should observe, lest we violate logic, our rational nature, or God's decree. The form of their arguments is a priori, but the deontologists' task is cosmetic. Joining the discussion after the important work is done, they promise incontrovertible justifications—window dressing—for rules and procedures that are never better than practical, imperfect, and contingent. The ontological middle ground—systems that are mutually independent, reciprocally related, nested, or overlapped—is the safer, empirical basis for prescriptions that direct social practice.

V. CONTRACT LAW: A TEST
OF ONTOLOGICAL THEORIES

Theories that can be used as recipes (or ideologies) to shape sociality have instrumental value—the results are good or bad—for the people affected. There are several ways of using ideas to alter or remake social life, including education, rhetoric, and laws. Make laws, convince people to behave as they prescribe, and one has (over time) a population that thinks of itself as the laws prescribe.

We distinguish two kinds of laws. Regulative laws organize phenomena whose character and existence are already established. Others laws—they are regulative and constitutive—create the domains to which they apply. Laws of the first sort enjoin people to do as they have done, or they modify an established practice. So traffic laws reorganize roads and rights of way in order to facilitate the movement and interactions of cars and pedestrians. Laws of the second kind are more powerful, as the rules of chess create the structure of the space in which the game is played and the pieces that move within it. The effects of regulative laws are less dramatic but more reliable, because established states of affairs are material levers that legislators can manipulate to achieve their aims. This contrasts with the uncertainty that prevails wherever lawmakers create a domain by writing its laws. Let there be this or that, they declare, as the banking system or World Court are conjured; let such things act in the manner and within the boundaries these laws dictate. Lawmakers may pretend that they are refining systems whose character and efficacy are well known—the "well-behaved" market—though they invent as they tinker. The entities thereby created may behave as the laws require, but their effects may be largely or altogether unpredictable. Legislators are pleased if the new game works; they amend the laws for the benefit of those who speak loudest if it does not. Compare lawmakers of the first sort. They resemble gardeners, who accommodate their designs to a terrain and its growth. Declining to cut and burn, they reshape the established growth. Lawmakers of the other sort more nearly resemble gods: they prescribe the world's form.

How do atomists and holists compare with lawmakers of these two kinds? Atomists suppose that individual persons are the only social realities: everything else is a quality or aggregate of persons. Being (ideally) self-controlled, fully formed, and self-sufficient, such people may decline to enter into relationships with anyone. Atomists may almost convince themselves that contract lawmakers must inevitably stake out new domains for human activity. For never mind if there were casual or occasional couplings that predated these clarified associations: they were mere shadows on a cave wall compared to these substitutes. The jurisprudence of contract law is reminiscent of the clarified reformulations of Descartes' *Rules* and Locke's *Essay Concerning Human Understanding:* acknowledging obscure, antecedent ideas, we replace them with something intelligible.[17] Less than gods, we are gardeners in the French or Italian style. Atomists agree that their laws are stipulations calculated to satisfy the best interests of the individuals who make contracts. Holist legislators have a different aim. They appraise every relation for its contribution to the harmony, coherence, or beauty of the whole. This requires that laws governing contracts be more than conventions: we should discover, rather than make, these forms, in the way that reconfiguring the furniture in a room reveals one or another of the many possible symmetries, all of them present but previously unrealized.

Both atomists and holists invent some of the problems they solve. Most associations are not created by the statutes or principles of contract law. Nor are they immanent but unrealized until laws prescribe a form that brings them to light. Marriage has been construed for the past centuries as a contract. But marriage was not invented by contract law; nor would it pass into limbo if all the laws relevant to it were annulled. The couples preoccupied with their pre-nuptial agreements would be rattled by nullification of every law pertinent to them. Most others would carry on as before. What sustains marriages of both sorts? Just the reciprocities that establish and support stable systems. Why would some marriages collapse? Because partners in them were deceived by the idea that marriage is a contract. Ignoring or suppressing reciprocity, they honored the terms of a relationship created by their legal agreement. They shared expectations that were appropriate to the agreements sanctioned by laws designed to stimulate activity in domains newly opened by the mix of technology, initiative, and law, as Internet marriage will not resemble any known before. How will its spouses respond when they understand that their bonds have no glue but legal formalities and fictions? Expect the surviving partners to work hard for marriages founded in reciprocity, not only in law.

What does contract law achieve for systems that are already established? One benefit is their recognition by a government empowered to protect the interests of their participants. Marriages generate wealth and children, both of them important to governments that need tax money and prospective taxpayers. Recognizing marriages in law is also good for the self-regard of the spouses, for partners who are deserted or needy because of a spouse's death, and for spouses treated like chattel labor. These effects are mostly changes in the legal and perceived status of marriage. None of them results from the law's interference in the reciprocities that establish marriages, though we get this other effect when laws diminish a *de facto* marriage by refusing to acknowledge reciprocities that already obtain. Laws forbidding miscegenation, marriage between siblings or cousins, the marriage of minors, or same-sex marriages are intended to damage or discourage established reciprocities for one or another "good" reason. No contract, we say, can be made between parties who are disqualified on one of these grounds. No matter that the couples at issue have been together for a time, sometimes for decades: marriage between them—legal marriage—is barred. Never mind, some of them reply, we shall do as we have done (unless one or both are jailed).

Marriage is more often a domain in which contract law accommodates itself to realities it does not create. Marriages are made and sustained by material reciprocities, not by the abstracted, conceptual forms that are dear to atomism and holism. It is the variability tolerated by these reciprocities, not the imaginations of lawmakers, that establishes their parameters. We learn to prize the values favored by law; but this is equivalent to preferring a trained voice to that of a woman who sings from conviction, not from refinement.

VI. IMMANENT NORMS

What factors constrain us as we make laws? What keeps our intrusions from churning capriciously as interests or circumstances change? There are two stabilizing factors.

One is our steady concern for human flourishing. We want to be secure and satisfied, whatever *security* and *satisfaction* signify within a culture, given its technology, circumstances, and imagination. Conditions for human flourishing include health, work appropriate to one's talents, fellowship, civil order, and the absence of arbitrary authority and war. Additional, desirable conditions include the development of physical and intellectual skills, the cultivation of sensibility, and a network of sustaining social relations. We acknowledge, by citing fellowship, that flourishing is more than personal. No one prospers if things go badly for all the systems that engage him or her.

Isn't the freedom grounded in rights—including exemptions from interference and the power to choose and act as one desires—another condition for flourishing? This is the question of people who believe that democratic rights are the *sine qua non* for human well-being. The answer is not so plain as the question implies. Someone having the advantages cited in the previous paragraph has, thereby, the power and opportunity (hence freedom of one kind) to enact the plan of his or her life. This freedom is the capstone to many satisfactory lives. Freedoms grounded in democratic rights (i.e., freedoms we have because we live as citizens in democratic states) are not a necessary condition for flourishing in every life, unless we suppose that no one who lived without them—the vast majority of people, past and present—could have flourished. Why not say that there are alternative, variable conditions for human flourishing, conditions that may direct us in one direction or another, so that adding them gives a particular flavor to life. Spirituality and the circumstances that enhance it are one such condition. The civil rights we treasure are another. They are critical for the unencumbered lives we prefer, though inimical or incidental to the lives of some priests. Never wanting to lose our civil rights—partly because they are fundamental to the self-regard of those who have them—we concede that this is a historically and situationally parochial view, one that is not incumbent on every one.

This first stabilizer—concern for human flourishing—is not much disputed, though we disagree about its character and conditions. The second is contentious. We identify it by way of three features that obtain where laws (including rules) apply: these circumstances are material, plastic (i.e., determinable though having specific values at any moment), and normative. Plato's notion of justice illustrates all three points in the context of human beings and their state. There is materiality in the constitution and causal reciprocity of each system's parts: we are well trained, mutually engaged and regulated human beings organized to secure and satisfy ourselves. There is plasticity in the diversity of organizational styles and aims to which we are adaptable. Plato's ideal state is only one such aim, though it is, he believes, the best guarantor of our well-being. There is normativity in the behavior of the parts, for stability is established and sustained when each part satisfies its responsibilities to the system and its other parts. The principal expression of this normativity is justice. There is justice in the person if each of his parts sustains the well-being of the whole because of its reciprocal relations to his other parts. There is justice in the state if each person does the work for which he or she is qualified, work that needs to be done if the state is to be self-sufficient and defensible.[18] My concern is the normativity in human flourishing.

Plato's idealization of justice is our point of reference. He wants us to agree that justice is ideal but natural, and that it is realized when reciprocities are established among the parts of the soul or state. This ideal prefigures a society where individuals are educated to realize their talents, then given work that is suited to their skills, work that satisfies them while it contributes to the welfare of other citizens. Plato would have us create civic harmony, within the limits appropriate to the interests and abilities of people and their life-sustaining systems. The ideal is general, but not so vague that we cannot imagine material conditions for achieving it. Nor is the ideal controversial: no one admits to believing that other people should not be cooperatively, fruitfully, and happily employed.

The idea that there may be norms immanent within nature is, nevertheless, annoying to some philosophers. Didn't philosophy discover long ago, when Hume distinguished *ought* from *is*,[19] that ideals are only the projections of human interest? It should follow that "natural norm" or "natural ideal" is an oxymoron—though it is not. Let me show the plausibility and utility of this idea in several steps, starting with its advantages.

Remember the determinability of properties: each may have either of two, several, or many expressions. Is any value of any property good for us? Or is our welfare better served by limits on the variability of relevant property values? The answer is plain, as each of us has an ideal range for his or her body weight. Similarly, we know the sorts of work that please us and the acceptable limits for violence in our social relations. These are ideal values immanent in the homeostatic processes of our bodies or social interactions. Merely knowing these ideals, whether or not we tend to realize them, would have dramatic effects on learning, planning, and lawmaking. For we would then want our actions directed by habits, procedures, rules, and laws that are calculated to satisfy immanent norms.

We need a more accurate and ample conception of the particular norms that operate within the lives of people and their systems. We identify them by asking what people want and by observing what they do. We discover that people want many different things, and that we organize ourselves in many different ways to get them. How do we interpret our survey? Where is the gold in the dross? We look for the evidence of clustered behaviors, wants, and aims. Some of these may be fads, though a careful reading of the evidence should enable us to distinguish them from immanent norms. For norms are the common, hard-to-divert adaptations to our material circumstances. Do a patient's jaws fail to meet? His dentist imagines the proper fit while adjusting bridgework and overbite. Is there a relation between delinquency and a lack of family, education, and work? Improve family life and schools, provide employment, and notice the effects. The glut of differences resolves itself into a smaller set of specific questions about the conditions for physical, mental, and social well-being. We look for ideals like Plato's justice that are immanent within material conditions, while being measures of the integrity, integration, and efficacy of things. We are careful not to blind ourselves by confusing persistent desires with immanent norms.

What are the abiding norms that regulate human systems, including human bodies and social systems? *Health* is a norm of this sort. Disparate bodily systems and the body as a whole are healthy if reciprocal causal relations within and among the parts stabilize it, thereby maintaining its relative self-sufficiency while enabling it to participate in higher-order systems or to nourish itself.[20] Compare disease. It disables a system's parts or alters their relations, thereby reducing or shutting down their reciprocities. Either effect may disable the system and prevent it from sustaining relations to its sources of nourishment or to other systems that engage it. These changes may be sudden or slow, reversible or mortal.

Each of the body's parts and cycles sustains, and is sustained by, some of the others, so that their equilibrium within a range of values (health is the variable) implies direct or mediated reciprocity in the relations of all the body's constituent systems. Equilibrium may be sustained for a time when values fall outside this range, though disruptions and failures then become more or less imminent. Equally, we may perform our roles satisfactorily for a time when sick, though we don't do so for long or as well. That pertinent reciprocities (internal and external to a system) and the ranges of values for specific parts or systems are subtly different from person to person is apparent. That some parts of a body may be healthy while others are not—healthy lungs, bad heart—is consistent with the modularity of a system's parts. That we speak loosely of health—healthy but for a headache—is incidental. For the essential notion is plain: health is the dynamic condition achieved when the property values of a body's parts and systems are maintained (within ranges specific to them) by the causal reciprocities of its parts. Health is an immanent, self-sustaining organic condition and norm.[21] Nothing vital to it is imaginary or conventional: people and systems that depend on us worry if we lose it.

There are three characteristics, any of which justifies the use of *health* when speaking of activities or systems. *First* is an evaluative use, as accurate accounting practices are said to be healthy. This way of speaking implies nothing additional about the character or relations of the system whose activity is approved: they are already described as *accurate*. *Second* is the intimation that the system at issue has an internal economy, one founded in the reciprocities of its parts and the efficacy of its relations to other things—healthy airlines, for example. *Third* is the fact that humans are included among the parts of systems called healthy, as we speak of healthy companies, but not of healthy star clusters. Or the parts called *healthy* are human parts (eyes, for example).[22] These characteristics are generous enough to establish an ample penumbra around the human systems that affect or engage us: it is individual humans, families, schools, businesses, and governments that may be healthy. The normativity of health is founded, for examples such as these, in either the causal reciprocities that establish the system or sustain its parts, or in the stable, effective relations that join one system to others: the healthy business.

Health is apposite, principally, to plant and animal bodies. These same considerations warrant the ascription of *functional integrity* to systems that have none of the three characteristics cited above. Such systems also embody reciprocal relations that restrict the values of pertinent properties to ranges that sustain the relative self-sufficiency—the integrity—of the system. Let a bog be our example: it has functional integrity, because reciprocal relations among the occupants of its niches maintain each one within a sustainable range of variations. Each is a module that maintains its internal economy. Each has a barrier to things external to the system. Each filters the effects of these other things through the systems' internal relations, thereby interpreting or otherwise using them in a style appropriate to it. Functional integrity, like health, requires this mix of homeostatic autonomy and selectivity. It presupposes that qualifying systems reliably nourish themselves by virtue of their relations to other things. Indeed, health is an instance of functional integrity.

Should we invoke health or functional integrity when describing natural systems? Those who doubt that norms are anywhere present within nature will deny that we can or should. But this is odd. Is it alleged that *health* is merely stipulative when applied to living things? For this is not a question about conventional designations, as when someone is called "healthy but for a cold." The issue is factual and empirical: is there a range of values such that a system is self-maintaining within this range, but unsustainable when values fall outside it (as in bankruptcy or brain death)? Thinkers who ignore the empirical evidence are guilty of a fierce, conceptual prejudice. They believe that nature is the aggregate of sensory data that Hume described, an aggregate whose bits and pieces are connected by no relations more binding than space, time, and resemblance.[23] Causal reciprocity is contiguity in space and time. "Immanent norms" are projections of human interest or desire, or nothing at all. How shall we describe this Humean view in the presence of falsifying evidence that includes energy transfer, control, and mutual control as regards causality, function and dysfunction as regards health? Call it dogmatism.

Suppose we ignore this prejudice. What things are appropriately described as having functional integrity? Is it widely or narrowly founded in the systems of our world? An inventory of them is beyond us. A limiting condition for functional integrity is more easily stated: namely, the limit to effective modularity, hence to relative self-sufficiency. This limit is achieved at the point (different in every case) where extended systems cannot secure their internal reciprocities. They may be sustained for a time, because of supportive (or undisruptive) circumstances, but eventually they fragment or dissolve with effects that include distended galaxies, the final years of the Roman Empire, and companies whose parts are out of touch. Less extended systems are less vulnerable. The health of families, for example, is less secure than the health of individual members, because of the complex resources required to sustain it, and because the complexity of its parts and relations makes it more susceptible to disruption. The health of capital markets is all the more uncertain, because markets have so little internal structure, because so much that is critical for their internal relations is contingent on factors beyond their scope, and because the "health" of markets is a partly honorific notion, one inflected by the interests of the speaker. Is it healthy that interest rates be high or low? Healthy for whom? We say, as before, that health generalized is stability in the reciprocal relations that establish and sustain a system; but we concede that these conditions may be hard to identify, sustain, or control.

This characterization of health and functional integrity may seem objectionable because of implying an essentialist standard for the functioning of things: it requires that bodies, companies, governments—or, by generous extrapolation, cars and solar systems—work in standardized ways. But electric cars don't work the same way as cars that have combustion engines. Doesn't this prove that the idea of functional integrity risks being falsely Procrustean? We avoid this error if we are specific whenever we need to be. Something has functional integrity, whatever its parts, if the properties of the system are sustainable within a range of values, given these parts, their reciprocal relations, and their relations to other things (including an energy supply). Any monster, not merely systems having a standardized (desirable) form, is healthy if the reciprocities of its parts create a stable system.[24]

Remember our point of reference: how is human flourishing to be achieved within the systems that engage us? The determinability of systems entails their variability as we use a succession of theories to direct social policy. Because the ontology of stable systems somewhat restricts these variations, we wonder if there are specific navigating lights—immanent norms—within these systems to direct our policymaking. Health is an immanent norm and usually a necessary condition for our well-being. A healthy family, for example, has a stabilized internal economy. It is stable because the parts are intact and because of the reciprocities among them. Is this the immanent ideal that can focus our lawmaking? Not yet, because too much is vague. Families can be stabilized in many ways: they can be nuclear or extended; the wage-earners may be men or women, both or neither (if social welfare pays a family's costs). Families that are healthy by the standard proposed above—they are sustainable in themselves and reliable as partners within higher-order systems—may embody terrible abuses of both adults and children. We cannot predicate laws on the immanent health of systems if health disguises abuses that laws should regulate.

Is health (or functional integrity) therefore useless as a directive for lawmaking? No, health is important in systems, as in persons, for either or both of two reasons. *First,* no one flourishes in isolation from systems. This is all but guaranteed when character is formed by one's place in systems, so that isolation—alienation from others—is a punishment. Families are the primary sites where characters are made. Their health (by the value-neutral criterion proposed above) is no guarantee that a family's members shall flourish, but families are principal examples of systems in which individuals *can* flourish. Knowing the conditions for their health, we hope to regulate them in ways that enhance the well-being of their members: we encourage employment and regulate abuse. *Second,* every system may be prized for its instrumental value, hence for its effects on other things. The stability of healthy systems makes their effects, for better or worse, more predictable. It then falls to us to choose among them. What are our aims? We choose our instruments accordingly. These are some reasons for thinking that health, the immanent norm, supplies leverage for lawmakers who think in consequentialist terms.

These benefits are easily perverted. Ignore for the moment the skeptical regard of thinkers such as Hume, for whom nature is the oddly coherent aggregate in which there are no internal constraints. More embarrassing is the support his argument gives to people who are grateful for the opportunity to press their essentialist remedies for physical, psychic, or moral health. I have been supposing that health is the natural condition of systems: stability is the evidence of their health, because this is the effect of causal reciprocities that fix property values within sustainable ranges. This is the natural condition of systems, one we discover by inferring and observing the conditions for their perceived stability. These details seem arcane and incidental to people who like the notion of health for different reasons. They recommend one or another style of behavior, each one called *healthy* by those who favor it. Can a family be healthy if it lacks the traditional structure? Is it bad for health that I read particular books or refuse to believe certain "truths"? Health as an immanent norm becomes the banner for contending moralists. There is a saving distinction.

The norms immanent within systems were to save us from the variations introduced when legislators tinker aimlessly, or when the aims of successive policymakers wash back and forth between atomism and holism. We want to avert circumstances in which systems are successively remade to satisfy one theory, then the other. Functional integrity deters these intrusions by convincing everyone willing to recognize it that there are intrinsic conditions for the stability of systems. But, critically, functional integrity is limiting, not Procrustean. This is so because of the two kinds of variability it allows. One is the variability of a system's parts paired with the constancy of its function, as radios may have tubes or transistors. The other is the variability of functions paired to constancy in the parts: families that fish or farm. Those who talk about the "essential family" are keen to prescribe unique conditions for its health, including constituents, organization, and behavior. Zealots of a narrow, moralizing essentialism ignore these two sorts of variability, though health is consistent with both. We may recommend, for reasons of our own, that systems be restricted to one style or another; but we cannot defend this choice by citing the immanent norm.

VII. LAWS AND IMMANENT NORMS

How shall we legislate in ways that are sensitive to immanent norms? There may be several of these norms, though health (hence functional integrity) is the only one suggested here, because this one is fundamental to the very existence of stabilities. Its basis is material: the parts of living bodies are so related that they and their collectivity—the body—are sustained. Such systems are, or can be, effective in their relations to others. We seem to be making progress: boundary conditions expressing natural laws (meaning constraints immanent in nature) may be favorable to reciprocal relations that establish the functional integrity of human bodies and, perhaps, many kinds of higher-order human systems. These laws might be versions of least-energy principles, each one an attractor for reciprocal causal relations, hence for systems of a kind. Legislators might hope to infer the bias of these immanent natural laws before formulating their regulations. There might be two kinds of evidence for such laws. First is evidence of the internal economies of systems, especially the conditions for their functional integrity. These include the character of the parts, their reciprocal relations, and the range of sustainable property values fixed by these relations. Second is information that other things have instrumental value for the functional integrity of the system at issue: they are external determining conditions for the values of its variables, hence conditions for its stability. With this information in hand, we may legislate in support of actions that damage or support the systems that concern us. Hence this other question: Which of the systems we may affect have good effects, bad effects, or no relevant effects on us or matters that concern us?

Answers are less straightforward than the question implies, because of a difference, cited above, in the status of systems covered by our laws. Do the systems at issue exist already—families and schools, for example—so that laws would modify their current, possibly well-known behaviors? Or is their design and existence conditional on our having laws to direct their construction, as chess is the creation of its rules. Legislators considering laws that regulate families or businesses have the advantage of knowing something about them, including the range of their variations. Compare Medicare and Medicaid. What is a *healthy* social welfare system? Does it support its clients forever, making them reasonably content? Or does it return most of its clients to active independence? Not knowing what to say, we thrash about. This is an instance where *health* is an external criterion used to appraise conduct, not an immanent norm. Our irresolution is evidence that different values pull us in contrary ways. We may decline to legislate, thinking it better not to affirm a new rule if it is no better founded than the one already applied. Or we abandon the issue, because we despair of fixing it, or because we are distracted by collateral issues (the budget, for example). We steady ourselves by remembering the two kinds of laws. One is well-founded in systems that already exist to be studied, as there are successful programs for returning the Great Lakes to ecological health; the other is more speculative, because such laws are used to construct systems that are not well understood. Shall we trade reliable effects we favor for speculative effects we cannot insure?

How do we balance our concern for stable well-being with our concern for initiative and the advantages, often unexpected, that it brings? We start by declaring that the cost of speculative goods must not compromise our *core interests*. Core interests are universal; they abide because of our material nature as human systems, meaning bodies with cognitive-affective postures. We need food, clothing, and shelter; care, fellowship, education, work, and protection. Our needs aren't different from those Plato described, however different and various our ways of satisfying them.

Still, the implications of this formula are sometimes vague. Is medical treatment a core interest? The answer varies. In what country and century do we live? Effective care of any sort was unavailable until recent times. It is still unavailable in many places. But we value life, so medical procedures that were once unimaginable are a core interest when available. How much education is core? Every culture educates its members to some degree for the tasks important to survival. What of literacy or high culture? Does the taste for Schubert or ballet make a difference to psychic health, hence to moral choice? Are these core interests? Such questions embarrass the point I am making, because health is not a trustworthy norm beyond core interests of a basic sort. There—in personal health, families, education, friendship, productive work, and citizenship—its prescriptions are reliable. Active people need to consume 1,800–3,000, not 10 or 10,000, calories a day. Children learn better when active conversation is part of their everyday family lives. These simple remedies are effective in systems known to everyone. Legislation is safest when it supports the determinable, but steady-state, rhythms of systems that are local and familiar. We have no detailed theories that explain these phenomena (they are complex, whatever their familiarity), but nor do typical mothers understand the physiology of the children they feed. These are systems we know how to support.

More complicated systems, or those we invent rather than discover, elude this easy regulation. We legislate for them as we do for systems that are better known; we extrapolate from things we know, modifying established procedures as new circumstances appear to require; or we legislate for invented systems as if there are no precedents, designing them to our tastes or interests.[25] Only the third alternative encourages us to do as we like, without regard for the constraining effect of circumstances (actual or prospective). Legislators are typically cautious, so this option is rarely chosen. They often prefer the second strategy, but only because they are unable to conceive a new behavior in terms appropriate to the first. For lawmakers have a conservative and reasonable respect for the systems they know. Valuing certain core systems, they legislate by extrapolating from familiar systems and behaviors that satisfy core needs. Are there markets where corn is traded for cloth? Construe capital markets as developments from them, with equivalent protections for buyers and sellers.

We make these decisions with the advantage of understanding the reciprocities of systems that are critical for well-being. Processes that create and engage human bodies, families, production, exchange, and traffic flow are not mysterious. We readily analogize, extrapolate, and generalize from them. Are there too many cars and too many careless drivers? The speeds are slower, but sidewalks too are often crowded. Knowing some useful rules that reduce the press of bodies, we alleviate the effects of overcrowding at higher speeds by applying them here. Should cars stay several lengths behind the ones they follow? Extrapolate to airplanes, and let them be separated by thousands of feet. The variables differ; the principles are the same. Trouble comes when the analogies are lame. Legislating for systems we don't know, or for systems conjured, we make clumsy laws or laws having consequences we rue. There is, nevertheless, a smoothing that operates as we legislate, for we knit the systems we know—those that are vital to our core interests—to systems that are less well known. Joining peripheral interests to the core extends the core, as analogizing the Internet to telephones and libraries makes it a core interest.

What progress do we make when our understanding of systems is grounded in the recognition of immanent norms (remembering that health is our only candidate norm)? Discerning them is our window into systems that are well established, viable, and familiar. Knowing that dividing families weakens or destroys them, we don't pass laws that have this effect. The norms operating in familiar systems are, equally, a useful window into cultures different from our own. For the core interests of any human society are likely to have parallel expressions in others. Cultural variability is less bewildering and frightening where this is true.

Yet, we need to take care if another culture's practices violate sensibilities that reflect our core interests (hence our perception of the immanent norms that organize us). Conflicts of this sort are fraught with the likelihood of exaggerated reactions (for example, disgust at the things other people eat). Other times— when the wholesale abuse of some people is the provocation—the issue is not so easily burked. Americans suppose that everyone wants information about the life-preserving, life-enhancing practices that profit a society's members. We forget that each culture tells itself regularizing stories that interpret its place in the world, stories that justify such elementary practices as the treatment accorded its members. What should we do when other peoples reject our advice: they continue to mistreat some of their people for what they suppose are good reasons? Remember that core interests are shared. They are a basis for communication, without the guarantee of success. Remember, too, that systems such as families are viable under a variety of circumstances, so that reproduction and effective child rearing carry on in circumstances that may repel us. Accordingly, health— functional integrity—is too meager a norm in these circumstances. It is too easily satisfied. It supplies too little leverage for appraising systems and practices different from our own.

We are not completely disarmed if we recall the basis for all value: namely, our self-valorization and the instrumental value of things that are good or bad because of their effects on us and the systems we approve. Does the culture at issue allow each of its people to valorize him or herself and the systems that engage him or her? Cultures that withhold this freedom from some of their members are guilty of an elementary incoherence: their dominant members believe that suppressing the voices of others is testimony to their own worth. There is no self-affirming voice, they suppose, in those whose voices are suppressed. These are offensive errors, because they reveal that people having power are ignorant of the fragile basis of their own value: merely their self-affirmation. This act or propensity—Nietzsche described it as the will to power[26]—is universal among humans, and the only ground for the judgment that each of us is a good in him or herself. Denying this power to some is bad for them, because it is contrary to their principal core interest. Seeing this failure in other cultures or our own is different from changing it. Customs are deep as the differential permission to be self-affirming are tightly bound to a culture's practices. Forcibly changing this attitude—by legislating against it—causes unexpected distortions elsewhere within a society. For many of its constituent systems are organized to exploit the assumption that some people are rightly self-affirming, while others are not. Altering this assumption and the roles of people who make it disrupts the reciprocities that sustain these systems. We, foreigners, cannot legislate for them. It is war, not our laws, that would alter them.

Partial successes, mistakes, and frustrations are not peculiar to communitarians. Atomists and holists are fellow travelers in the trial and error of legislating for systems known or proposed. They rely on the same experiences and gather evidence by using the same inductive principles. But they ignore, minimize, or exaggerate reciprocities that generate systems and their interactions. This makes a difference when legislators convene. What will they say, for example, about child abuse or same-sex marriage? Atomists may condemn abuse of any sort, but their generalized opprobrium loses sight of this particular offense: namely, damage at the hands of those—one's parents—who have a principal role in determining one's character and identity. Holists are more likely to dismiss the effects of abuse as a kind of incidental noise, when other relations—generational authority, property, deference—are more critical for the unity of an imaginary whole (the folk, for example). Atomists are perplexed by same-sex marriages: these are two individuals who cannot be joined. Atomists are sometimes reluctant to hear that such partnerships are already formed, so that the issue is their legal recognition, not their existence. Holists who oppose them are likely to say that unions of this sort are anomalous in the whole they commend: they are alien, for example, to the community that renews itself by bearing and raising children. Claims of both sorts are a priori stipulations: they tell us what cannot be in the face of what is. This is the communitarian advantage: it doesn't struggle against the character of things as experience shows them to be. We are not obliged to like every reciprocity, though we shouldn't forget our legislative aim. The issue for legislators is human flourishing: its styles, impediments, instruments, and costs. Should we despise amity in a same-sex marriage, punishing its partners for a kind of well-being that all of us know and admire?

Communitarianism is also more effective than its competitors when it legislates for domains that are new, fragmentary, or evolving, though now its advantage is much reduced. For it may not help to interpret a practice we do not fully understand in terms of one that is better known. We don't know the effects of laws that regulate genetic engineering, because we don't know how this technology will alter us or how we shall appraise the changes. Suppose that human sexuality becomes dispensable because artificial breeding is more effective in several ways: the results are more predictable; the babies are healthier; and women are saved the nine months of pregnancy. We might be encouraged to engineer such changes as make sexuality otiose. But then the very basis for the reciprocities of family and many friendships would be sabotaged, with the likely consequence that these reciprocities would dissolve. Should laws save us from these effects by prohibiting these experiments? We don't know what to legislate, because we don't know well enough where we are, or what is best to do. The conditions for healthy systems are variable in the two respects mentioned above— same function, different parts; same parts, different functions—but they are not infinitely variable. How much of us will be preserved, if such changes are sanctioned and encouraged by legislation? Having identified ourselves for too many centuries with abstract ideals of moral, mental, or spiritual autonomy, we do not resonate deeply enough with the information that human nature is material and systemic. We are plastic, but not formless. The conditions for our health are constitutive of our identity as humans. They will not survive every change.

VIII. ATTITUDES

Discussion has moved from our self-valorization through socialization and the search for constraining norms to the interest for which we legislate. The remaining sections of this chapter go back to the start, providing a different point of reference for a parallel evolution.

What is the basis within cognitive-affective posture for our values? Is it cognition, attitude, or a mix of the two? *Cognition* is shorthand for an array of processes that require powers of observation and inference (both hypothesis and deduction). Using these powers, we discover that health extends life while making it enjoyable. It would be foolish, by comparison, to say that terrible illness has these effects. Does the perceived difference between sickness and health entail that health should be pursued? Someone whose habits destroy his health may remark the difference but persist in his ways: the perception doesn't alter what he does, or even what he thinks he ought to do. Noticing a difference is a cognition; approving or not is an attitude. Attitude is the valorizer. Yet attitude incorporates cognition. For attitude alone is inclination without an object. Cognition supplies attitude with referents, as one is angry at someone, not merely testy. This focus transforms a passion into a point of view: we approve some things but condemn others. Health is approved. We prefer it to the point of acting to get or sustain it, even passing laws making people and companies liable to damages for their effects on health. Cognition alone could not have this effect, because cognition alone is directionless: it informs us without prescribing a direction. Valorizing attitude does that.

The numerous attitudes within a cognitive-affective balance are organized in a system that may be described as federal, meaning that there are disparate centers of relatively autonomous attitudes, all of them more or less efficiently coordinated under a smaller set of dominant attitudes. Changes within this complex may occur in the way that a change in the weather moves across a continent: everything is disrupted a little, some things a lot. This figurative talk is partial evidence for the great obscurity of attitudes, individually and in their relations to one another.

Clarification is forthcoming as we specify the cognitive component within attitude. For there are two places where cognition is relevant. First is the provision of objects or objectives for inclinations or feelings. Second is the alteration that sometimes occurs in attitudes when information is revised. This second point is troubling. For information doesn't shake everyone: some attitudes are unmoved by information that confutes them. Two people having the same information may use it to support different attitudes. This independence of attitude from information is evidence that attitudes have a relatively autonomous developmental history: prejudices learned early are hard to override, whatever the evidence. Information shared in later life may not supersede our disparate histories, because we construe information in ways that confirm already established attitudes. This formulation suggests that my first characterization of attitudes is incomplete: it isn't enough to say that attitudes are passions or inclinations that acquire objects when information is supplied. For something additional explains the rigidity of attitudes confounded by information. This factor may explain the choice of objects or the attitude taken in respect to specific ones. It may affect the development of attitudes, so that we need a more ample characterization of our primitive affective states during infancy and childhood. We should expect, as we find, that attitudes acquired during childhood are not easily changed by new information.

Such attitudes crystalize at a time when vulnerability and satisfaction are dominant, but precarious, affective states (one speculates). For we are sensibly vulnerable and only temporarily satisfied. The degree of anxiety within us—it may be high or low—determines many, most, or all of our juvenile attitudes. Expressing our pleasures and fears, attitudes appraise our circumstances. We like pleasurable states and things associated with them; we don't like discomfort and its apparent sources. Quickly learning to look beyond the present to things anticipated, we express our likes and dislikes as hopes and fears. Experience tests one side or the other, augmenting or reducing particular expectations. An attitude hardens when the child who fears a voice is hurt by something the speaker does. This may happen many times, so that the dominant quality of the child's anticipation spills over into every attitude. Such children perceive the world with unfocused anguish: everything encountered looks threatening. The creature that roared and snapped is remembered for being scary, not merely for being a dog. It provoked fear, so fear abides, focused or defuse, as an organizing condition for action, feeling, and belief. Or something that frightens me is reassuring to you, perhaps because I often failed or barely succeeded in situations where success seemed effortless for you. Or I did succeed, but always because of converging circumstances, none of which I controlled. I feel powerless now and full of dread that luck will be against me next time. I tremble, but you—convinced that you can turn anything to your advantage—are full of delight.

Attitudes acquired during infancy and childhood cannot be the whole story about us, because we also learn the attitudes of our families, friends, and coworkers. Every such person expresses his or her personal attitudes, often with nuances that distinguish us as a culture. One may perceive a culture's attitudes as an insider or as an observer. Insiders express the intentions, values, and valencies of the members. Observers see a people's attitudes as its intellectual, emotional, and moral accommodation to impinging circumstances.

Culture interprets and reconciles us to them. It tells us who and where we are, what is required of us, and how to do it. We imagine (this may be fantasy only) that individuals were the apotheosis of their culture's dominant attitudes in simpler times. Now, when many of us live in several cultures, we embody their differences. The effect is overdetermination and conflict within us. For every culture is a tissue of standards and values. Each one imbues us with attitudes favoring this, reproving that. Discrepancies between the attitudes of divergent cultures are sometimes dramatic, as they are when Western-educated women are veiled at home. We may resolve such conflicts by favoring attitudes that mimic those of companions or by surrendering ourselves to attitudes that reinforce our dominant anxieties or points of view. Still, forced accommodations don't always work. Conflicted attitudes are sometimes crippling, so that we do nothing without guilt or confusion. If my father doesn't like the neighbors, while I fear a beating from their children, I won't like them either. But then one of their daughters fascinates me. We are tortured and reduced to near immobility; or we do awful things.

Personal history and culture usually supersede information and truth as conditions that fix attitudes formed early in life—*primitive* attitudes, I shall call them. Imagine two groups of people, one whose members are rich, the other poor. Some people in the first sample—perhaps a majority—express satisfaction with their lives, though many admit to being dissatisfied and insecure. This difference is observed among people whose actual circumstances are similar in most or every apparent respect. But oddly, people in the other sample have attitudes that vary in roughly the same proportion. Some feel secure and satisfied, despite their plain lives; others, in similar straits, are much less satisfied and secure. The proportion of people expressing positive attitudes is likely to be lower in the poor group than it is in the rich one, but the difference is not as much as we would expect if a correct reading of one's circumstances were the decisive condition for one's attitudes. I infer that information acquired later is not sufficient to affect attitudes formed early in life.

This is an imaginary survey; would an actual one confirm or confute it? Consider a case for which there is evidence: let everyone think of those shifts in his or her own moods and attitudes that do not correlate with the weather, the economy, family life, or one's prospects. These changes of attitude come and go, though nothing in our circumstances is changed. There are likely to be endogenous—hormonal or metabolic—explanations for them; but then it also follows that knowing truths about our extra-somatic circumstances is not their cause. Information does change primitive attitudes sometimes, as information about the effects of segregation in America changed the minds of some people. This is uncommon, because attitudes are mostly fixed by one's history and culture. This surmise is confirmed when people having different cultures but similar developmental histories discover affinities and anomalies in one another's attitudes. Each may be puzzled by this inconsistent mapping and be unable to predict where contrary attitudes will be succeeded by accord. We may try to use information to overcome these differences, but this doesn't usually work, proving again that attitudes, once formed, are independent of, and resistant to, refuting information. It is no matter that things that frighten us are not dangerous. Having started with the wrong bias—we are recklessly optimistic, or excessively fearful—we are slow to adjust ourselves to the moderate circumstances in which many of us live.

Human accommodations to the world would be much less viable than they are if this were the last word. Some attitudes do change, but most of them have developed in later childhood or adulthood, when the deep core of self-defining attitudes is settled. For now less is at stake. There are times (adolescence, for example) when we are vulnerable all over again. But mostly, the attitudes and information now acquired rest more gently on us than the ones formed early. There is less risk and more slippage when attitudes are susceptible to the revisions that new information provokes.[27] Indeed, these two—information and attitude—are, in later life, mutually determining. This is apparent when attitudes decide the kinds of evidence we seek or the sorts of inference we make and also when information shapes our attitudes. Expecting the worst from people of certain kinds, I observe that many of those known to me behave better than I expected. Or I give up smoking—both the habit and the attitude that supported it—when I learn its effects.

How do we explain these examples of plasticity? By distinguishing among attitudes, and by inferring that there is a hierarchy such that the attitude favoring health and fearing vulnerability is more effective (as inferred from its control over behavior) than the one that favors the habit. How is this hierarchy organized? Attitudes learned during childhood are its base and center of gravity. Culture—especially the culture of one's family—is almost as deep. These primitive attitudes organize, cull, and control all or most of the attitudes acquired later in life, though attitudes learned later are often the ones that other people first notice about us. New friends don't see the congruence of a new attitude—our enthusiasm for a political candidate, for example—with core attitudes. What makes this candidate so attractive? He addresses the fear or confidence that defines us.[28]

IX. MORALITY AND ATTITUDE

What determines that concern for oneself should count more or less than concern for our roles and duties within the systems that engage us? Power may decide the issue, as happens if systems coerce us. Suppose, however, that power is discounted. What explains the judgments, plans, actions, and loyalties that remain? Attitudes explain them. When applied to matters of judgment, they prescribe conclusions. When applied to desires, they determine our choices. When applied to alternative plans, they decide our actions. Attitudes direct us one way or another, when our participation in systems is perceived as gratifying, safe, and good, or dangerous and bad.

Citing attitudes resolves one uncertainty about the relative priority of character or role. Previously, this was a question about the separability of character from the roles and context where it is learned and exhibited. Now the question is obviated in circumstances where primitive attitudes are acquired, for character and role are not distinguishable during infancy. We begin to distinguish them only during early childhood. For then we begin to experience the symptoms of their difference: we don't like the available roles; we may perceive the freedom to take or leave them.

Why are roles taken or rejected? Decisions at any age are rarely or never principled choices only, though we may give high-sounding reasons for them. We do what our attitudes prescribe. We join, or are captured by, systems that are congenial to our attitudes, or we resist them. It follows that attitudes determine our choice of roles and the comfort with which we fill them. Find a rebel, examine his attitudes, and notice that they do not jibe with the attitudes of people who dominate the system.

Does attitude also testify to the morality of our acts? Is it the guarantor that action shall have a particular moral signature? Surely not, you say: sociopaths have attitudes, but they aren't moral. Where is the alternative, plausible intrapsychic locus for morality? Kant nominated reason, though he agreed that most people do not consult it when making moral choices. This would entail (contrary to their self-perceived responsibilities and to the expectations of other people) that such people are amoral or pre-moral. What is the site of morality within us, if it is not reason? Where cognition is perception, hypothesis, or inference, there is nothing but attitude to supply our moral standpoint, as Hume spoke of moral sympathies.[29] Deliberation, this implies, is more than clarification or inference: we decide what to do by surveying information through the lens of attitudes. This is the truth in Aristotle's claim that an internal determinant, not an external one—character, rather than law is the necessary condition for morality.[30]

Founding morality in attitude may seem disabling, because it risks conflating each person's moral basis with his or her fervent and idiopathic expressions of self-interest. How can it be plausible or safe to identify perceptions of my moral duties with attitudes that are founded in childhood pleasures or fears and the culture of my family? It isn't safe, as many horrible deeds testify; but there is no alternative and only this defense: hierarchically organized attitudes include the ones just mentioned and also attitudes acquired in friendship, school, work, religion, and the business of government. There are multiple opportunities in every life to overlay the idiosyncrasy of primitive, core attitudes with different ones. Each of us internalizes conflicts of attitude, and most adults usually suppress the primitive ones.

We see the dialectic of attitudes in the nuanced reflections where valorizing intentions—attitudes—regulate the balance of demands between selves and their roles: who and what must I consider? what should I do? What do we do when attitudes compete? We elevate cognition to the role of reality-tester. What are the consequences, we ask, if one attitude or another determines our conduct? Cognition estimates the likely outcome, and we make a judgment. What attitude constrains us to make this judgment? One that is affirmed individually and supported by the rhetoric of our culture: we value ourselves and the flourishing of people and systems who are important to us. Sometimes we extend this self-love to the well-being of all. Giving priority to this self-valorizing attitude and its implications, we inhibit attitudes that would encourage us to damage those others. We confirm hereby that moral tension is not only monadic. Morality passes beyond every narrowly focused self-concern. It balances the demands among selves, or among selves and the systems in which they participate. Attitude is the vehicle for personal morality; thus attitudes are materially consequential for the actions and effects of people engaged.

We may disclaim an interest in the attitudes of others, in order to satisfy an atomist standard of civility: we worry about someone's actions and their effects, not his motives, because motives are private and no proper topic for our appraisal. This is polite, but wrongheaded. Nicely averting attention from someone's motives is equivalent to ignoring the preparation of students whose work is deficient. Teachers don't tell these students that we care only for what they do, not for the skills or information that would enable them to do it better. We should also care about attitudes, because these are the sponsors and triggers to action. We sometimes excuse our disregard of them by remarking the legal implications: should someone be indicted for his attitudes, or only for behaviors they promote? Atomist morality sagely errs on the side of tolerance: you may like or dislike what you please, it says, up to the point of acting in ways that damage other people or their reasonable interests. This concern for law enforcement is separate, however, from the regard for morality. We acknowledge this difference when passive sympathizers in murder or torture are themselves condemned. We say, in effect: not doing the things you approve saves you from punishment, but not from immorality. Equally, we insinuate this difference when rearing children. Not wanting them to do bad things, we teach them attitudes that are appropriate to morality, attitudes that inhibit some actions and impel some others.

This is the point of entry for the moral authority of laws. Laws have two effects: they coerce people having recalcitrant attitudes—don't kill—and they establish rules of the game where attitudes are not sufficient to direct us, as when they are baffled by genetic engineering. Laws of both kinds have the advantage of a foundation that is independent of attitudes: namely, the interests of the people and systems at issue. Finding a discrepancy between a member's attitudes and the stabilizing interests of systems we value, we try education, flattery, or bribery, then laws and coercion; or we expel him from the system.

X. MORALITY AND SYSTEMS

Locating morality in the attitudes of individual persons cannot be the whole story, unless we are prepared to say that higher-order systems—including families, corporations, and states—are neither moral nor immoral, because they lack the condition for being one or the other. Expecting a system to behave morally would commit the fallacy of composition: we would ascribe to the whole a property reserved to the parts, as soldiers, but not any army, march on their stomachs. How shall we justify treating systems as moral agents?

Atomists believe that we should not credit morality to systems in any but a derivative way. Let the members of a society organize a civil government; let that government choose appropriate laws or policies for dealing with members and nonmembers. These are, we suppose, laws or policies that acknowledge the integrity of individual persons while sanctioning no behaviors that cause them uncompensated harm, wars or catastrophes apart. Such a government's laws and policies express the attitudes of some members—the majority of elected representatives sitting in this government's councils or the majority of citizens voting in referenda—but not the moral posture of a distinct entity. Morality writ large is just the morality voiced by individuals, then ratified by the organizations they have created to regulate their affairs: namely, the public and the state. It is no fault of this democratic program if governmental policies in badly organized states express only the attitudes and interests of those in charge. For the idea of democracy is ideal in the way that health is ideal: we use it to specify what should be, or should have been, done. This atomist theory inspired the Nuremberg war crimes trials. Denying that there was an entity properly denominated "the German State," they averred that the crimes of World War II were the actions and effects of individual war criminals and the system they corrupted. Ideas of tribal or national guilt are odious to a theory that perceives systems as aggregates.[31]

Is there a cogent way of making systems, not only their organizational apparatus and members, morally responsible for the things systems do? Think of a barge or a blimp: both are slow, clumsy, and hard to stop. But they do have a direction, and they can be controlled. Systems are also in motion, and they have effects. With them, as with individual persons, these effects are the flash point of morality: one's motives and aims may be horrific, but usually there is no legal sanction until the act is done, because only then is some one or thing harmed. Equally, systems are found to be moral or not because of their behaviors. The preparation and purpose were already immoral, but this finding is based on the prospect of the effects intended. Why make a system rather than the members responsible for them? Because the reciprocity of their relations gives the system an efficacy that members do not have alone. Each of them is responsible for choosing to participate in the system (if this was a choice); but they are not responsible for its corporate effects: a single musician is not responsible for the harmonies and sonority of the orchestra in which he or she plays.

This reference to corporate effects does not imply that systems, like their members, have attitudes or, *a fortiori,* that the morality of systems is founded in their attitudes. There is nothing exceptional in this, for it often happens that systems lack some or all of the properties of their parts: bodies have DNA or metabolize sugar only in the respect that cells have the one and do the other. Equally, systems don't need attitudes if their members have them. There is often accord among a system's members about the attitudes that should dominate their interactions. All have the same attitudes, or they negotiate a directing attitude when there are differences among them, so that reciprocities exhibiting these attitudes appear to express the attitude of the system: we infer its attitude from its actions and effects. But again, there is no justification for ascribing attitudes to systems. Systems perform as the reciprocities of their members determine. This is apparent in the behaviors of families, schools, businesses, and the army: each is directed by the attitudes of someone charged with responsibility for them. The bias changes only as we go from aims to their implementation. Something valued is sought; but the mechanism for pursuing it is the mutually modulating effect of a system's reciprocally related parts. There is the appearance of intentionality, but no corporate attitude (or corporate mind) to direct it.

A contrary argument affirms the doubling of attitudes, ascribing them to both systems and their members. It extrapolates from Descartes' *cogito.* Leibniz and Hegel (following Descartes) argued that God or the Absolute is an infinite mind.[32] Finite minds are said to be moments of consciousness inscribed, somehow, in an infinite mind, so that there is nothing in us that is not in God, our cause and ground. Attitudes in us are the guarantee of attitudes in both the Absolute and the state. For the state is but the expression of divine unity in the relatedness of its individual members. Where atomists suppose that the state has attitudes because its members have them, this holist theory reverses the order of priority: the Absolute has attitudes, so states and their citizens have them too.

One thinks of Leibniz's monads: each has some degenerate degree of intensity—consciousness—because God has it. And, we say, "Man is made in the image of God."

This way of providing for attitudes and morality within systems is appropriate to subjectivist, mentalist ontologies; but mentalism is implausible when mind is known only by its acts, and when all but a few of them—the luminous awareness of qualities such as colors, for example—are mimicked by machines that add, subtract, solve mathematical theorems, win chess games, and write music. Locke's surmise, that God could create matter that thinks, is confirmed. God could also equip human bodies with the means—attitudes—for behaving morally. Our question is here: How are human systems (families, schools, businesses) moral, given that they have these individuals as their proper parts, while themselves lacking the attitudes that are the ground for individual morality?

Consider the two bases for morality cited above. First are the attitudes of individual persons: they favor some things (themselves, for example) and oppose others. Individuals can be relied on to coordinate the expressions of attitudes they share. This is the point that atomists exploit when they favor mechanisms, such as elections, publicity, and education, that select among competing values, hence attitudes. Second are laws that restrain the behaviors of people whose attitudes resist certain practices or aims. Systems don't need attitudes, because individuals have them, and because laws, a common culture, and similar developmental histories regularize some principal attitudes in us. Human systems qualify as moral agents despite having no systemic attitudes to ground their morality, because these systems comprise individuals whose reciprocities are suffused by their moral attitudes. Such systems, like flocks of birds, only need a mechanism to select the attitudes that will lead and direct them. Election is a useful analog: this is a procedure for choosing a president; citing the procedure saves us from having to say that the state elected him.

One other consideration is critical if systems are to behave morally: they must consider their effects on other things. Reality testing—collecting, disseminating, and evaluating information—is critical for systems, because they cannot steer themselves effectively or morally (with sensitivity to their consequences for other things) without it. Information is critical for the collectivity of individuals and systems organized for self-reflection—the public—and to subaltern systems, such as businesses that perpetually test their markets.[33] Individuals need it too, lest they fail to correct a wandering course by testing their beliefs and attitudes against reality. Have I now made the error of compensating for the lack of attitudes in systems by crediting them with a different power that belongs only to their parts? No; testing a system's ambient world is also a function of its parts and their reciprocities. It is the pilot and computers, not the passengers, that correct a plane's trajectory.

A system's reciprocities express the moral attitudes of its members when the conditions just cited are satisfied: attitudes are regularized when laws are invoked and reality is tested. Such systems have a corporate purpose. Their actions are consistent with relevant laws. They revise their behaviors to minimize the harm they do. Think of any business, school, or hospital: we require nothing more to justify saying that one of them has behaved morally.

XI. DIVERSITY AND TOLERANCE

Granting that systems should do no harm, does their morality also require that systems should do some good? There is little disagreement in principle, but trouble comes as we spell out the details of the good to be done. Some people espouse a regime of goods that all should pursue. Every faction that likes this idea knows, unqualifiedly, what it is good to do, as in the phrase "doing God's will." Why should we accept one or another of their recommendations? What harm does difference make, accept to those who are offended by it? Why not let human flourishing be construed in any way that people please? They will usually come to solutions that fall within the ample range of variability wherein individual persons and human systems are stabilized and secured. Distinguishing the bizarre from the deadly, we can be all but certain that few of us will choose a style of behavior that makes us unsustainably worse rather than better. Mere difference, however exotic, threatens no one who is not compelled to practice it. Let those who enjoy their preferences tell us whether they flourish because of them, only supposing that they cause no harm. For flourishing is not like absolute pitch: there are different perceptions of it. The one reasonable demand is that everyone should acknowledge these four considerations: that we value ourselves and the systems and people to whom we are joined; that sustained stability—because of functional integrity (health)—is an immanent material ideal for individuals and for systems; that systems have effects that are harmful or benign for other things; and that laws directing or restraining the behaviors of individuals and systems are required when some are adversely affected by others. These four conditions are the moral environment for the pursuit of human flourishing. There are many ways to exploit these conditions, hence many feasible practices and mores. We should expect the diversity we have.

None of this is perplexing to theory, though it must be confusing to anyone who lives in two or more cultures, or wherever cultures collide. Such people are saved from moral chaos, because these four points are common to every culture, and because certain proscriptions—against the murder, mutilation, and abuse of fellow members, for example—are constants across cultures (though there are diversities of interpretation: "mutilation" to you may be "religious rites" to me). Education, family integrity, shared objectives, and civility are everywhere prized. All of us have gleaned this much about the conditions for human flourishing, though our perceptions of it may be shallow or deep. That little else is shared is no reason for alarm. For morality is not a universal algorithm. Think of the variations in national or regional styles of cooking. All of them aim to nourish and satisfy; all use similar ingredients. But the styles of cooking and the things made vary considerably.

Should we who enjoy these differences also tolerate different moral practices? Every society narrows the array of plausible goods to one or a few of the contested contraries. It then declares—in laws, religious dicta, or generally accepted mores—that certain aims and practices are good, others bad. A British landlord once told me (during dinner) that the American way of using a knife and fork is barbaric. This is tribal morality, and it is all of morality for all of us, most of the time. But we do, or can, distinguish life-defeating evil from plausible variation. Morality of a deeper sort is joined only as we identify the unconditional goods worth defending, including ourselves and our life-sustaining, life-enhancing associations. These are values we defend. The rest is anthropology, or a walk down Broadway.

XII. WHAT SYSTEMS OWE THEIR MEMBERS

What is proper—what is just—in a social system's treatment of its members? There are various, often unrelated issues.

Consider the uneasy balance of character and role: there may be too much latitude for autonomy, or too much authority to role-sponsored discipline. Are precisely programmed roles bad because they cripple individual initiative? Is too much freedom bad because it promotes a breakdown in the reliable reciprocities of commerce and civil life? Both charges are persuasive in some circumstances; but these opposed emphases—discipline and freedom—may also express a different way of doing a culture's business, as in Japan or the United States. Neither style is objectionable in itself.

When do systems abuse their human parts in generic, rather than particular, ways? When the system's aim is anathema to a member; when there is no place in the system for his or he talents; when there is no escape or relief from its reciprocities, no time for one's responsibilities to others, no time to breathe; when the form or pace of a system's reciprocities is crushing; when enmity has displaced respect in the relations of the parts. These are occasions when the gap between character and role is visible, welcome, and enabling. It helps us to separate ourselves from poisoned systems.

Suppose that none of these abuses obtains, leaving us to address this other question: Where is moral priority, on the side of a system or its members? Holists ascribe it to the system, atomists to the part. How could we justify one claim or the other? Atomists remind us that there are two kinds of value: we are self-elected goods; instrumental values are founded in the relation of cause and effect. It should follow that moral priority lies with the primary goods: systems that secure and satisfy us have instrumental value only; they should never trump the claims that members lay against them.

This is too simple, for two reasons: first, because it mistakenly abstracts character from the roles in which it forms; second, because it elides the difference between roles in character-forming systems and participation in systems that are more incidental to character (yesterday's bus ride, for example). Character-forming systems, including families, schools, friendships, and some jobs, are more than instrumental values. They are closer to being final causes, in the respect that self-valorization embodies our idealizations of them. Having been made on behalf of their aims and because of their structures, we may spend our lives trying to achieve ideals they taught us. Many of us never separate ourselves from them—despite their demise and whatever grievances we had as their members. This leaves the many other systems in which we participate, each of them having little or no value but the instrumental one of helping us to satisfy and secure ourselves. These other systems also have interests and aims. They give something in return for our participation; but they need to take care: for as each of us may say, I am not any system's creature. I am distinguishable and separable from even those systems in which I was formed. The suppression and perversion of character in the interests of systems having merely instrumental value is, therefore, intolerable. We think with honest pity of everyone trapped in social relations they cannot evade—though equally, there is terror for the first astronaut lost in space, with ample food and oxygen.

What do systems owe their members? Space to be themselves, including the opportunity to use relevant talents; recognition in salary or respect for a member's contribution to the system's aims; the fellowship of other members; the opportunity to share in the system's idealization of itself; acknowledgment that members have duties to other systems; exemption from abuse and circumstances that debase the members, as hard work is different from work that debases people who do it. Many systems are all the things they shouldn't be. Members who can, should leave them.

XIII. MAKING LAWS

What laws should regulate the many systems in which humans are engaged, given this characterization of us and our roles? I assume that governments should not prescribe the constitutive practices of systems that are established because of our human needs for security and satisfaction. Families that need help raising their children will not usefully get it from the state, short of the safety net of family courts. Schools or medical facilities supported by tax monies are not evidence to the contrary; the government that pays for these services is not required to decide their content. Let doctors formulate minimal standards for medical practice, before states pass licensing laws that embody these standards. Families that require intervention to prevent abuse are a different matter, one appropriate to both the regulative interests of every person and the regulative powers of the state, as expressed, for example, in child labor laws.

The state's regulative power expresses itself in laws of two kinds.[34] *Prescriptive* laws are largely facilitating, either directly or instrumentally. These include laws that finance highways and laws that establish property rights: they facilitate the use, control, or transfer of property. We make *proscriptive* laws when there is evidence that certain practices are harmful. There is a shortlist of things we dread—including murder, bodily harm, dishonesty, want of access to needed resources, theft, breach of trust, loss of freedom, and monopoly. Regulators can never assume that all harms are known: our initiatives are forever creating new circumstances that require laws of both kinds.

Declining to prohibit a practice or prescribe its character is not the same as refusing to oversee it. For oversight—vigilance—is implied by the injunction that we be self-regulating. Yet perceiving a conflict of interests or even pernicious behavior—pornography, for example—may be insufficient grounds for the state's intrusion. Is abortion a practice of this sort? This is a hard case, because some human is harmed whatever the choice: fetuses are killed, and women are demoralized; or women are obliged to carry fetuses to term at cost to themselves. Weighing these harms is daunting. We do it more effectively by supplementing our information about the two candidates for harm. For it makes a difference that abortion averts the birth of an infant whose self-valorization would require more than preliminary stages in the development of a psychic posture, including participation in some of the roles that bind us to one another. A living body is a necessary, not yet a sufficient, condition for the value ascribed to human life. Adult women satisfy all these conditions: they value themselves, have roles, and distinguish benefit from harm. Does this entail that people's suffering from Alzheimer's disease are not centers of value because they, too, cannot value themselves? It does have this implication. However, such people are valued by extension, because they were once self-valuing or because we value them. Could we also value fetuses by extension? Yes, we could; though valuing them does not override the priority given to adult women.

Unease about abortion also makes this other point. We are slow to proscribe an activity whenever a strong case is made that the effects of freedom are less harmful than those occurring if freedom is limited. This rationale applies generally, as when we defend free speech and individual choice knowing that speeches are sometimes vicious and that decisions sometimes have effects we rue. These are atomist priorities. Communitarianism shares them, but adds another: resist creeping intrusion, first into the deliberations of people wanting to control themselves, then into the workings of the systems they form. Respecting the freedom to affiliate, encouraging the initiatives and systems it promotes, we don't intrude.

Granting now that a government should not use its legislative power to prescribe aims or organizational structures for a society's other systems, does it follow that government should also decline to legislate special protections or burdens for systems of particular kinds, including privileges for families, costs for gambling casinos? The temptation to use law in defense of valued systems is a two-edged sword. Vital systems are defended; but initiative is blocked. How shall we defend important systems? In either of two ways: secure or elevate them with special privileges or exemptions; or legislate against the systems or behaviors that damage them. The second policy is wiser than the first, because establishing a system's privileges in law is likely to make it less effective at the elementary tasks required to manage and sustain itself—including self-care and self-regulation. Systems are healthier—their functional integrity is enhanced—when the primary responsibility for their well-being lies with them. We don't want to re-establish the medieval system of entitlements and burdens. The warren of rights and liabilities it created enfeebled the systems it protected as well as the ones it repressed. This is a trap to avoid.

This aversion to interference should have among legislators the status of the Hippocratic oath among doctors. I assume that the dignity and worth of patients are independent of the services doctors render, as systems form whether or not there are laws that acknowledge them; and that both doctors and legislators have authority and skills that can subvert the subjects on whom they practice. Still, the analogy is imperfect because doctors do not usually control the context in which health is secured, though legislators are responsible for laws, both prescriptive and proscriptive, that facilitate affiliation. These are laws that endow us with rights of association, and rights to the goods instrumental to it, including free speech and information. Equally, these laws imply punishments for behaviors that interfere with the rights of, or conditions for, affiliation. In America, these laws are Constitutional. They include the articles of the Bill of Rights, though its right of assembly only hints at the conditions for association. Subsequent labor and business laws supply the missing detail. Together, these laws supply the context in which systems are formed and sustained. Such laws express a core interest: they convert a natural inclination and practice into a state-defended right.

The ideal public (and representatives who legislate in its name) would clearly distinguish its power from the responsibility of each person and system to regulate him, her, or itself. Still, one imagines other systems of regulation. Laws proscribing harm, for example, can be introduced without a public by a wise despot. Some may believe that this use of power is reasonable in a complex world of systems. Why give so important a responsibility to a querulous legislature that (eventually) passes toothless laws? Let the principal officer of the presiding system have the authority to make and enforce such laws as the society requires. One objects that tyrants make mistakes and may be corrupt. But there is also this better reason for objecting. Laws express our recognition that we live in complicated circumstances where, typically, there is scarcity, crowding, and conflict. Facilitating laws help us to secure and satisfy ourselves. Proscriptive laws express the discovery that each of us values him or herself, hence that none of us wants to be harmed. Let these self-perceptions rise to law as expressions of our common understanding and will: let the public constitute itself.

XIV. THE GOODNESS OF THE WHOLE

Consider the entire social order: meaning the array of individual persons and the network of systems in which we participate. Remember that Plato's Good is not good for anything beyond itself; its goodness is fulfilled, perhaps exalted, by the harmony of its nested parts.[35] But, contrary to Plato, there is no harmony in which we do or may participate. We are more destructive than useful for the other things of our ecosystem. Worse, we cannot remake ourselves to purge all the conflicts among us. Some of them are the frictions of mutually independent but competing systems: they are sometimes reduced but not eliminated. They compare to the intractable conflicts of overlapping or nested systems. Overlapping systems struggle for control of common parts; higher-order systems subjugate their stubborn subaltern parts. Harmony in these relationships is often no better than prudent accommodation: we make peace in circumstances where the alternative is greater conflict.

Plato implies that we acquire cosmic importance by participating in the whole: our misbehavior would sabotage its harmony. Discount the possibility of cosmic harmony, notice our place near the edge of a medium-sized galaxy, and you understand the sobriety that reconciles us to a less exalted role. We are important, principally or only, to one another (by way of the systems we share) and to ourselves. This is qualified only by the harm or benefit we do to systems that share our ecosystem. Our welfare depends on them. Thinking of our well-being, we also think of them.

XV. AWE

Systems are frequent causes of aesthetic feeling, as theater, architecture, literature, and music provoke it. Many such feelings are effusions of pleasure. One—awe—has a different tone. It couples perception with surprise. Awe, on such occasions, is our shocked reaction to the perception of complexity.

Consider the three systems of religious practice centered in Jerusalem. Each has its sites, rituals, and believers. Each has an interpretation that makes it the apotheosis of virtue, understanding, and desert. Imagine that one goes from the Dome of the Rock to the Western Wall to the Church of the Holy Sepulchre, each time entering, if only aesthetically, into a system that is seen as if for the first time. The response is awe: awe at the complexity and scale of the practice, awe in the presence of a complex that is different and complete.

We respond with awe to many things, from basketball players to the starry heavens. We are awed because impressed, attracted, or intimidated. But here, where systems are the point of reference—whether landscapes, buildings, or snowflakes—awe is our response to discerned, but unfamiliar, complexity: we are awed by systems perceived as strange, but accessible, wholes. This is an infrequent experience: we may not see the whole because of focusing on a part; or we see nothing distinctly, because of a preoccupation in us. More, such responses are ephemeral. They pass with familiarity (though they may be renewed). One is awed by the virtuosity of a musical performance, but this is not the wonder and surprise of first perceiving the complexity of the music.

Now extrapolate to any occasion when doors open into a system that was previously unknown, or known only partially. Invited to dinner with the family of a friend (not necessarily an exotic friend) we observe its members in their complexity and difference. We have many impressions; but one dominates the others, however briefly. We are awed: we look at them, see what they do, see the ways they relate to one another. Moving from system to system, sideways, up, or down, we may be perpetually surprised.

XVI. PREVIEW

The four chapters that follow apply the conclusion of the preceding chapters to specific issues in a succession of domains. First is deliberation, an activity appropriate to individuals and, by extension, to systems—societies—having us as members. Next is free speech as it concerns individuals who are engaged in systems and are responsible for their effects on these systems and their other members. Third is conflict, especially as it results from the disparate relations of systems that are mutually independent, reciprocally related, overlapping, or nested. Last is ecology and the consideration that every human system is nested within an array of others. Are these other systems merely a support and a resource for us? Or do we have a responsibility to them that supersedes our human interests? These last four chapters test my claim that the ontology proposed here illuminates, though it does not always settle, particular factual and moral questions.

Chapter 5 Deliberation

New properties are generated by the establishment of new systems; this is a point argued in Chapter One. Sometimes new properties are distributed within a higher-order system, as distinctive forms emerge at many places in a painting. Other new properties are corporate; they qualify—supervene upon—entire systems. A painting's structure is a corporate property, one that emerges with the integration of its parts. Awareness, too, is an emergent, corporate property, one that baffles us because we cannot yet tell how the brain (or some of its parts) generates it, and because the only words we have for specifying it are metaphorical: consciousness, we say, is a kind of phenomenal light, presence, or presentation.

The generating conditions for deliberation are also know incompletely: we describe it as a system of functions, not as a system of material parts. We know that hierarchical assemblies of neurons do it, but not how they do it. The social deliberation described later in the chapter is an analog to this intrapsychic activity.

I. DELIBERATION AS A COLLOQUY

Deliberation occurs when action is inhibited while alternative hypotheses, strategies, or behaviors are considered, then reduced to the single one chosen. The process seems reasonable and effective, but the word signifying it has the ring of middle age, as if no one who is resolved and competent should need to deliberate. Think of the tennis player who decides a shot by playing it: he hasn't time to ponder. Intelligence in him has almost achieved the mechanical perfection of robots or computers. They, too, do many things that we count as intelligent; but most of them don't deliberate. Any pause between input and output is only the time required to route signals between a keyboard and a monitor or a mechanical sensor and a robot arm. There is no facility within most of them for choosing among alternative strategies. This speed and the cogency of the output—the well-aimed shot, the accurate calculation, or inference—make deliberation seem slow and clumsy. Worse, deliberation—like self-directed mental intentions of all sorts—often produces conclusions that are false, immoral, or clumsy. Think of Wittgenstein's waiter: he concentrates on balancing his tray, only to drop it. Isn't this evidence that all such conscious states are a kind of impotent mental chatter? Why not ignore studied forethought when habits or other mental machinery assure better results? This chapter is an answer.

Reducing deliberation to habit would not so much save time or avert errors as cover over and resolve questions which are better kept open. For deliberation is a colloquy among four distinct factors: an interest or need, perceptual data, conceptualizations (interpretations), and attitudes. It terminates in a judgment or a plan of action. Any particular issue may be settled; but deliberation is never finished, because altered circumstances or irresolution provoke it again. Altered circumstances may include a state of affairs disclosed to perception or auto-perception, the shifting priorities of attitude, or the judgment that changes in our circumstances require altered behavior: no credit at the bank. Or the salient consideration is moral: more debt would be imprudent. Deliberation is the intrapsychic version of a town meeting: several or many voices are heard before a policy is endorsed or the meeting ends in irresolution.

Why do I assume that deliberation is effective: that it terminates in a judgment or in a plan that directs behavior? I believe it, because I have seen you thinking. You read relevant material, asked pertinent questions of me and others, then, after telling us what was decided, you did it. Or I believe that deliberation preceded your actions, though you reflected silently, because of the care you took before acting, or because you tell me afterwards that you considered your options. Why shouldn't I believe you, when reflection tells me that I often do the same thing?

How do we identify the participants in this colloquy, including an interest or need, perception, conceptualization, and attitude? In three ways: introspectively; by confirming physiologically that there are separate, though connected, sites for these four factors in the brain; or behaviorally: seeing that you are pensive, I wait to see what you will do. Why do we trust the introspective reports of our mental states? For reasons appropriate to every auto-perception—toothaches, for example: they are common, repeated, and reliable bases for discerning our condition, then for predicting what we will do,[1] or what a separate investigator, a dentist, would find.

The following remarks about deliberation are a hypothesis supported by my self-inspection, with some casual reliance on reasonable physiological assumptions. I do not suppose that deliberation is usually or always, let alone necessarily, accompanied or conditioned by the awareness that one is deliberating. We often ruminate, deliberating best when we let a problem incubate, without special, self-conscious attention to the alternatives. But sometimes awareness is a decisive control on the direction of deliberation, one that alters the result.

My assertive manner will seem shameless to anyone stymied by the dilemma of having to confirm that one is deliberating when there is no self-perception of it, and no action it provokes. My justification is the behavioral and physiological evidence that perception, conceptualization, and attitude continue to direct us, whether or not we attend to them. Consider the many occasions when forks in the road require drivers to make decisions for which there is no introspective evidence. Who will say that these decisions are harmlessly random, or that deliberation did not occur, however quickly.

II. THE FACTORS WEIGHED

Empirical data, understanding, and attitudes are reconciled under the pressure of a demand, sometimes urgent, that we secure an interest, or satisfy a need, or formulate a plan. The price of newspapers goes down, and I reflect: shall I buy the cheaper one, though it has less information and fewer political views that offend me? Or I hear water dripping, but after a moment's reflection—is the annoyance tolerable?—I do nothing. Inhibition, as much as action, may be deliberation's effect. This too is an act.

Why is deliberation useful or urgent? Because habit-directed routine is disrupted in circumstances that are triply uncertain: we don't know significant features of our situation, the effective ways to behave there, or what we want to achieve. There is also the self-imposed requirement that there be coherence within us. Coherence is difficult to achieve when there are three relatively autonomous centers of information: perception, conception, and attitude. Each may dominate the other two or bend somewhat to them. Deliberation suppresses action until the inter-modulation of these three reaches a threshold that isn't easily formulable as a standard or rule, because it varies from person to person and within persons as situations change.

Two of the three factors we weigh are familiar; the third—attitude—is better known as valorizing feeling or intention. *Perception* supplies information about the state of one's body and about the external world: we distinguish perceived hunger from seeing a restaurant menu. *Conception*—interpretation—does two things: it classifies percepts and makes hypotheses that construe the data. There are hypotheses of two kinds. Some estimate that things exist or have a certain character, as seeing something round and red, I call it an apple. Other hypotheses are plans used to direct behavior or predict its outcome. (The plan directing me as I bite into an apple anticipates the likely effect and provides an alternative strategy if the outcome is different from the one anticipated: a rotten apple is discarded.) Hypotheses of the second kind presuppose the first: directives are useless if they do not embody maps of the relevant terrain or hypotheses about the causal efficacies relevant there. (We have a map of the tree on which the apple grows and a hypothesis about the likely effect of pulling a branch.)

Conception supplies alternative ways of responding to interests or needs. But which way shall I go? *Attitudes* winnow the alternatives, narrowing them to one: I make a judgment or initiate the behavior directed by a plan. Evidence of my attitudes was present already in the choice of topics for deliberation. For there are many things to ponder. The subjects selected from this array have passed the filter of approval. This filter is the assembly—the hierarchy—of attitudes: wearing a hair shirt is no excuse for complaint if attitudes disable me from acknowledging its effect. Do urgent personal or social interests bypass this filter? They may not: think of hunger strikers whose attitudes override their needs.

Attitudes are elusive, because they are rarely or never presented for direct inspection. We infer their presence and character from our feelings, surprised reactions, and unconsidered behaviors, as when fear or joy expresses them. Or we consider someone's patterned behavior. How do we know that he favors blue shirts? Those are the only ones he wears. Notice that appealing to behavioral expressions is not evidence that attitudes are reticent or disguised, as thought is not reticent because of needing language to express it. Still, the observer's perspective is obstructed: he or she doesn't see the confrontation of attitudes with percepts and concepts. How is each of them modulated by the other two?

The tentative answer is a surmise. Suppose that need or interest activates the system which engages perception, interpretation, and attitudes. Spurred by need and making a hypothesis that attitude favors, I remark that its application requires circumstances that do not obtain. I know this, because the hypothesis anticipates bright sun, while this is a moonless night. Or one attitude—expressed as passion—favors the thing perceived, but action is stopped when a hypothesis about its likely effects intervenes. Or my hypothesis about the circumstances is confirmed by perception, but attitude deters me from acting as planned. This is deliberation as a conversation among three voices, each one responsible to the others. Perception is responsible to hypothesis for the information that hypotheses construe, and to attitude for data that confirm its biases. Hypothesis is responsible to perception for an interpretation of the evidence that perception supplies. It is responsible to attitude for hypotheses and plans that express its values. Attitude is responsible to hypothesis for directing and selecting among its conjectures and plans, and to perception for valorizing its content.

My description of this colloquy, emphasizing behaviors promoted when judgments are made or plans are accepted and applied, is, so far, too narrowly intellectual and pragmatic. Deliberation also fosters intrapsychic equilibrium. This happens when any of the three factors is used to qualify or correct one or both of the others. Seeing your posture and gait, I recognize you despite your Halloween disguise: hypothesis supersedes percepts. Or I am convinced by the idea that the Earth is flat until I see the pictures being taken continuously from a satellite moving around it. Or my antipathy to foreigners is altered by the evidence of their kindness. These are causes where deliberation changes beliefs and attitudes. Hypotheses are quickly altered if they are not rigidly defended by attitudes: I won't like them whatever they do, is a familiar attitude. Attitudes are sometimes hard to alter, though change in them is possible, because perception, conception, and attitude are reciprocally related. No one, alone, is sufficient to direct action, and none can stand immobile against the contrary bent of the other two. This may be the reason that bias—an attitude—is so often truculent: it needs to shout down the contrary evidence of perception and hypothesis.

I infer that psychic equilibrium is maintained by a cycle of regularizing deliberations. Here, especially, deliberation is largely unconscious. Dreams are sometimes evidence of this process, as when the information and tensions of the previous day are digested and resolved. The hierarchy of attitudes is likely to be the decisive factor in making these adjustments. It surveys and responds to the day's events. What were the disruptions or challenges to one's material well-being, or to dearly held moral attitudes? What conceptual assumptions were falsified or confirmed? Which of the changeable attitudes is altered because of information that makes this attitude irreconcilable with others that are tightly held? This is deliberation as the engine of psychic coherence.

III. KANTIAN OBJECTIONS

My characterization of thought and perception may seem faulty because of Kant's objection that they cannot be separated: perceptual data, he said, are never unschematized, hence never available as empirical tests of the concepts or theories that have been used to differentiate and organize them. Deliberation cannot use percepts to correct concepts, because sensory data are unavailable to experience until they have been cut and shaped by one or another concept.[2] This is an *a priori* truth for Kant, meaning one that pertains to the transcendental conditions for experience. Such truths are said to obtain necessarily and universally: there can be no experience in the absence of its transcendental conditions.

Kant distinguishes two kinds of experience-making schemas, while claiming that every perceptual experience requires schemas of both sorts. A few schemas are transcendental:[3] they are rules for introducing quantity, quality, and relation into space and time, the forms of intuition. Other schemas are empirical:[4] they are rules for differentiating and organizing the sensory data that comprise our experience of, say, cats and dogs. Every degree of specificity in the character of an experience and every aspect of its internal organization are allegedly, products of schematization, so this is the condition and source of everything that is intelligible, hence thinkable, in perceptual data. This is the claim that justifies Kant's transcendental mechanics, especially its affirmation that mind's use of rules—categories and schemas—is the source of all the intelligibility within experience. The alleged inseparability of perception from conception is the price for accepting this claim.

Notice that Kant's argument assimilates recognition to schematization. *Recognition* implies that a thing or datum having a character of its own is perceived and classified. It does not imply that the classification is a way of prescribing character to things classified. The difference between schematization and recognition is, therefore, considerable. Are there examples of phenomena that are noticed or recognized, but not schematized? Experiences of pain, lightning flashes, and shocking faces seem to elude schematization, if only for the moment that occurs before they are overlaid with concepts or evaluations that tell us what they are or signify, or what they are worth.

Dogs, cats, and amoebas are also a helpful point of reference. Being irritable, they respond in specific ways to particular kinds of stimuli. Is it plausible that their percepts have been conceptualized—and schematized—even without a language? Or should we infer that they merely register, recognize, and respond to particular perceptual stimuli? Now revert to us humans, particularly to the artists among us. Is it alleged that we are permanently constrained by one or another conceptualization (one founded in a language or practice), hence incapable of perceiving color and shape without it? This is implausible, because we often recognize a vast assortment of things for which there are no schematizing rules: there are *gestalten* and names, but no verbal recipes for constructing faces; we discriminate the timbre of voices without words or concepts to direct us. That many things are recognized—the dog that bites you—isn't in doubt. Do we acknowledge their character, or create it by schematizing sensory data? These phenomena are evidence of recognition, not of schematization.

Still more powerful is the abductive argument that infers from perceptual evidence to the character of things, as we infer that apples have shape and texture apart from the bites we take of them. We reasonably infer that such things have character and relations that are independent of mind, and that information about them is present within us as we perceive them. (One thinks of "stimulus information"[5] and "the information in the light.") We concede that pure cases of separable data, thoughts, or attitudes are rare, given the mutual modulation—the reciprocity—of perception, conception, and attitude. But they are not impossible, as would be so if Kant's apriori theses were true: we see things without having made them.

The evidence of things recognized, not schematized, is all we require to save the integrity of percepts as they function within deliberation. For deliberation does not require raw, unclassified data. It does not even require that perceptual data are not overlaid by concepts or appraisals. Deliberation often progresses in either or both of two ways. Sometimes it embeds the data within a network of concepts (or rules) and values. A juggler looks at his hands and considers how to use them: is cleaning the lawn mower a good idea before tonight's performance? Or I regard my feelings suspiciously: aren't they inappropriate and distorted? Shouldn't I strip away one or more layers of self-justification? We don't want raw data for the purposes of this deliberation, because it is feelings overlaid by interpretation that require analysis. Deliberation is satisfied if its per-

ceptual data are independent of, or distinguishable from, a problematic interpretation.

Consider again the riddle that provokes this discussion: how is any hypothesis tested empirically if perceptual data do not stand against it, without having
been captured by it? Easy you say: the data have been shaped by another conceptualization; they falsify one hypothesis in the respect that they have already
been made to satisfy its contrary. This is odd. For assume with Kant that perceptual data have no character until schematized (or no surviving character
when schematized). Why does any claim suffer empirical disconfirmation when
it could vindicate itself by reconceptualizing the data? It should be possible to
use every concept as a rule that imposes its form on every datum, with the result
that no claim is ever confuted empirically (though contrary hypotheses cannot
both be true). Kantians may have an answer to this *reductio,* but I don't know
what it is. I shall suppose in the sections to follow that perceptual data are often
used appropriately as an independent test of concepts, rules, and theories.

IV. SELF-AWARENESS

The foregoing remarks are indifferent to the degree of self-awareness in the deliberating agent: he or she could be sleeping but for the diminished sensory input. Self-equilibrating deliberation carries on without it. Indeed, people working at a problem often report allusive dreams, or they wake with hypotheses or
resolve they didn't have the night before. We infer that deliberation is a complex
reciprocal relation among distinct cerebral functions, one that occurs during
sleep when memory supplies surrogates for perceptual data.

What difference does self-awareness make to deliberation? A comprehensive answer is unavailable until we understand better what self-consciousness
achieves. That will happen when we know its neurological conditions and their
experiential and behavioral expressions. Just now, we have introspective and behavioral evidence that self-awareness enhances the differentiation of perceptual
data, the specificity, consistency, and integration of hypotheses, the making or
amending of plans, the inhibition of action or its fine control, and the discrim-
ination, inhibition, and revision of attitudes.

One is less sure that we have all the design and detail of large projects before
us as we deliberate about their parts and relations (as Descartes assumed that we
may grasp all the steps of a proof at once[6]). The comparison of introspective evidence with behavioral and the scale of our tasks suggests that our sense of the
whole (whether the task is intellectual, artistic, or practical) is often no more

than penumbral. We have a feeling for the design and know our way within it, as we confirm by focusing deliberation on successive or otherwise relevant stages of it. This is evidence for the efficacy of memory. Unable to see all a design at once we rely on memory to locate us appropriately within the whole. It supplies pertinent detail, including information about relations to other parts. Sometimes this information about a design is stored within us; other times it is external: author and reader, alike, may need the table of contents to recall details of a long book.

Only one of deliberation's concerns is forever impeded by the difficulty of bringing the relevant material to self-awareness: namely, the amending of attitudes. They sometimes change without reflection, because of success or failure, encouragement or frustration. Or they are closely allied to information, so that rethinking our beliefs may be enough to alter them. Primitive attitudes—acquired early in life—are hard to change and hard to identify introspectively. Primitive attitudes that never get us into trouble may never get our attention. No experience alters them, because every one is construed in their terms. They direct us without our knowing what they are, or even that we have them. (Many attitudes are better known to a person's observers than to the person himself.) Attitudes that make us confused or unhappy (because of conflicts they incite) may get this attention, though discerning them accurately is difficult. There is only the hope that attention to the feelings they provoke may enable us to alter or extinguish them.

V. THERAPY AS DELIBERATION

Deliberation typically resets the timing or interaction of accessible mental functions. But now—in therapy—attitudes are the primary concern. They are ossified, conflicted, and an obstacle to effective behavior.

Therapy requires self-awareness, though repression disguises attitudes, and sleep sometimes helps us to evade them. Therapy progresses as we search for the evidence of attitudes in feelings, desires, and our interpretations of other people or things. Attitudes are often transparent in our interests, the bias of our conceptualizations, and our reactions to things perceived—faces, for example. Or they are disguised, but discernible in the rigidity of our beliefs and behaviors, the consequences we regret, or in feelings, such as anger and fear, that are signal flares of vulnerabilities camouflaged.

We initiate therapeutic deliberations (with a therapist or alone) because our encounters with other people and things provoke bad feelings, or because we chronically make choices or decisions that gets us in trouble. The suspected cause of our trouble is a discrepancy between the world itself and the attitudes that direct our encounters with it. Wanting a particular outcome, we are angry when it doesn't happen. Acting again in the same way, getting the same result, we despair. Why do we fail? And why are we slow to learn from our failures? There are several possible explanations: reality testing was faulty when the relevant attitudes were formed, so things are not as we thought them to be; or reality testing was good, but things have changed, without correlative changes in our information or attitudes; or the attitudes are justified, though the people judged don't like the judgment. We deliberate to discover and appraise the anomaly: are we maladaptive because of having inappropriate attitudes? or is the fault in the world, not in us? Satisfied that the fault is elsewhere, we may be fortified in our resistance. Agreeing that the fault is ours, we try to alter the balance within us in ways that are more than cosmetic or ephemeral. For these reflections do more than spotlight conflicting attitudes or prune anomalies. This is deeper, because we want to identify the attitudes and relations of attitudes that define us in the way an architect's plan prescribes the design of a ship and its way of riding the waves. Identifying our attitudes and reasons for holding them may enable us to release, somewhat, their grip on us. This doesn't make us spineless. It does repair some of the distortions that accrued during childhood and beyond.

How do we modify attitudes, some of them primitive and unchanged since they were acquired? We do it by playing on three of these reciprocally related factors—interests and needs, percepts, and interpretations—to alter the fourth, attitudes. Internal coherence and an end to anxiety or frustration are two such needs. Learning to recognize and interpret feelings or appraisals that confound our needs, then to suppress our habitual reactions to them, we remake ourselves.

VI. EXISTENTIAL ANXIETIES

Computers do think, sometimes in the parallel processing, patterned, and inventive ways that humans do. Yet current models are unsuitable as paradigms for the life of the mind, because computers only begin to deliberate: they begin to have revisable strategies and aims. Mind assembles and interprets information, while valorizing its data or hypotheses; it judges that something is good or bad in a respect; it prescribes that something be done, or not. Valorizing attitudes set all these parameters, but there are no attitudes in most computers, and only a rigid few in some others. Notice that the issue here is valorization, not instrumental value. Computers sometimes register the consequences of things and match these effects against template-like standards of adequacy, thereby discriminating good and bad utilities. But these instrumental values are distinct from valorizing attitudes. Worth-bestowing, thought-constraining, behavior-directing attitudes are all but absent in the current products of the engineers.

Deliberation is sensitive to the difference between instrumental values, including percepts and hypotheses, and valorizing attitudes. We dwell on one or the other, depending on the issue at hand; but no instrument is more salient than another until we have an aim. Someone who considers his future behavior may hesitate because of knowing too little about the appropriate means; but means aren't relevant until he has chosen a direction or style. The questions resolved are self-directed: what do I value? They are not other-directed: what shall I use?

This isn't yet a discernible difference for most computers. Few of them declare an aim. Fewer still vindicate a choice by affirming it as their own. People, too, surrender the autonomy supplied by self-valorizing, self-directing attitudes. We—like programmed machines—defer to other people's values, doing as they have done. This may seem to be good sense. Why would anyone deliberate about his choices if ancestral formulas or other people make the important ones for us? Are we sure to do better for ourselves? How could we justify such choices when we realize that all the values we affirm have no authenticating ground ulterior to the attitudes that impel them? It is true, as a matter of fact, not of attitude, that fish need water. Who can be as certain that the self-directed plan of his life is appropriate to him? Why deliberate about the course of one's life, or even about its daily obstacles? A program eliminates the need for choice in machines. Why not suspend deliberation in favor of rules that do as much for socialized humans?

Shall we be self-directing or safely programmed? One requires that we trust our self-affirming attitudes; the other commits us to the accumulated, homogenized values of other people. We may have recoiled from the first to the safety of the second, but leaving our choices to other people doesn't solve the problem of having justifiable values. For values are only instrumental or self-affirmed. Either I make the rules my own, affirming them as expressions of my aims, or I submit myself to others, making myself their instrument. People sometimes refuse to live vicariously as instruments for other people. Does rejecting such values guarantee that one flies in a void, without reliable constraints to guide him? No; it may express skepticism about every choice or value. One may prefer paralytic inaction to anything that implies the bad faith of having merely instrumental value for other people or systems. Other times, rejecting other people's formulas is the breath of fresh air that precedes one's self-affirmation. One declares values of one's own, principally one's worth. Deliberation struggles for leverage in a conflict of attitudes. Shall I be self-effacing or self-affirming? What is the hierarchy of attitudes within me, and how does it filter and appraise this choice and its likely effects? Do I wan to—can I—alter this hierarchy, the keel of my psychic being?

Imagine that a person acquires or recovers self-conviction. What makes him a responsible neighbor, not a careless egoist? He is one, not the other, because his deliberations invoke three considerations discussed above: namely, self-valorization, instrumental values, and a severe consequentialism. Each of us quickly discovers (by considering his choices or seeing the choices of others) that there are many ways to be, but some hard truths about each of them. We learn that the behaviors sanctioned by our choices intensify and justify the sense of our worth and the worth of persons and systems we favor; or they reduce our esteem for others or ourselves. We know this is so, because consequentialism is a psychological calculus, not only a philosophical theory: choosing a route appropriate to our attitudes does not expose us to an epistemic purgatory where nothing is certain or justified. There is abundant evidence for the effects of many aims and instruments. We use this stock of collective experience without believing that it will tell us what to make of ourselves. We prefer to deliberate, making a route for ourselves through contingencies that no one can fully anticipate. We do all this without forgetting the effects of our experiments on other people and things.

The limited choices—be an instrumental value or a self-affirming good in itself, be used by others or take responsibility for yourself—orient our deliberations. Emphasizing this choice is cruel, because circumstances may not be propitious for self-affirmation. Circumstances, including poverty, despotism, sickness, and tradition, often preclude our self-valorization, with the result that most of us live, with unrelieved frustration, as instruments for other people or their causes. Or self-affirmation expresses the vanity of people whose self-affirming attitudes were formed, no thanks to them, in childhood. Affirmation in them is entitlement, the expectation that others will allow themselves to be used as their instruments.

This is true but incidental, because deprivation and entitlement are (almost) equally disabling conditions. They are excuses or causes—instrumental values—not justifications. We can struggle against them to recover the space in which to affirm our corrective responsibility for our attitudes and for the effects of the actions they direct. We may refuse to do things whose effects are bad for us or for people or systems important to us. Alcoholics stop drinking; angry people learn to control themselves. Valuing ourselves, learning that we have effects on people and systems we also value, we make ourselves responsible for the things we do.

We also acknowledge the irony of this reflection. Self-valorization is an expression of cognitive-affective posture, hence of character. Yet character forms within systems, including the family, friendships, schools, and work. Self-affirmation is not monadic, because it implicates our partners in these systems. This is one reason for our sensitivity to the effects of what we do: we affect, thereby, people who are responsible for qualities we value in ourselves. Self-affirmation is not, therefore, the expression of monadic deliberation. We cannot be self-affirming without deference to the people and roles that helped to create us. Existential anxieties are essentially social: have we acquired a voice that differentiates us from others, even as it locates us among them?

My previous emphasis is apparently too stark. Nothing, I implied above, reduces the difference between values that are self-affirmed and those that are instrumental. Something that is valuable but not self-affirming is valuable as an instrument. these are the exhaustive alternatives: we can be one or the other, or both (self-affirming parents are instrumental values for their children); but not either by being the other. This last phrase epitomizes the error of supposing that these choices are mutually exclusive. No one is self-affirming without also being the instrument for all the systems in which he or she willingly participates. The reverse is also true: no one is self-affirming without having discovered his worth in the systems where he serves instrumentally. This explains the otherwise incomprehensible choice of self-abnegation: we are self-affirming when making ourselves useful to other people at cost to ourselves. Is this answer the merely veiled reassertion of our barely suppressed egoism, the idea that no one ever does anything voluntarily unless to please himself? This question assumes the sharp difference between instruments and self-affirming goods. We do more justice to selfhood by avoiding the alternation it assumes. For the self is thoroughly socialized: we learn and affirm who we are in the midst of our instrumentality. I want for myself what is good for the systems I value.

VII. CHARACTER AND ROLE

Deliberation is the more or less supple power that exposes our instrumentality when it reflects on our socialized circumstances and attitudes. Yet deliberation also confronts the urgency of self-affirmation when new roles are chosen or current roles are odious. Accordingly, it mediates between the interests of character and role. Each of us regularly decides between their competing demands. For I who affirm my own value also affirm my responsibility to the systems that engage me. We typically create formulas that settle the issue: so much to the system, so much for me; or satisfaction to me by way of my role in it. Success is elusive when character and role conflict.

Deliberation shuttles back and forth in the name of satisfaction, equanimity, and duty. Doing justice to both character and role is the ideal charge. But each of them may be shrill and uncompromising. Which side to favor when they cannot be satisfied at once is the practical choice. Closer to home is attitude: which responsibilities have priority, those to the system or those to myself? More remote, but equally pressing, are the system's demands on me: how urgent are they? It may not wait for me to deliberate; but I, wanting to affirm my interests, resist living as its instrument.

The conflicts of character and role that provoke reflection are sometimes excruciating. Self-affirmation is a luxury for those whose lives depend on filling unwanted roles. Decent social and economic arrangements are one solution; but they depend on high standards of wealth, mutual respect, and organizational skill. People who don't have this advantage—most of us—submit to our roles while trying to salvage a scrap of autonomy in the ways we sequence our obligations or the pleasures we take. Deliberation is sedulous now. It requires a quiet survey of the advantages and risks of making one or another of the available choices. For attitudes are fixed: information and skill are the critical variables. What is our situation? How can we exploit it? The choices are diminishingly viable: embroider and enjoy the small space cleared around us; suppress frustration because of fear or duty; bide one's time, with hope for a better day; or lose hope and self. The self-system all but shuts down in the last of these stages: deliberation there is slow, unsteady, and restricted to exigent practical choices. Nor is this only the constriction of mindful reflection: every deliberation—wakeful or asleep, engaged or in dreams—surrenders to rules and routine.

A few of us recover by mastering the machine. Seeing the array of a system's relations and effects, we intensify the sense of our power and worth by directing it. Deliberation in this context is oversight. Oversight with authority is management: we direct, correct, and sometimes create these systems. This is a familiar responsibility: every parent has it. The task is consequential and increasingly hard to execute as the system is large and ramified, with layers of overlapping or nested systems. The president of a company may set policies which alter its size, architecture, and direction. The mayor of New York, all the less the president of the United States, does not—probably cannot—do as much. Their private deliberations are, nevertheless, a centripetal source of organization and direction set against the centrifugal forces of complex systems, where reciprocal relations are increasingly attenuated.[7]

This last paragraph almost loses sight of the question raised. For I have let the possibilities for managing a system eclipse the earlier task of choosing between one's responsibilities to the system and oneself. This is not so much a loss of focus as an emphasis on one answer to the original question: people having to choose between character and role sometimes identify themselves with the task of holding a system together: the will and deliberations of the manager—his perceptions, plan, and attitudes—guarantee a system's reciprocities. Character and role are hereby merged in the manager's perception of his power. This style may work temporarily; but it isn't effective in the long term, because system-sustaining reciprocities require the participation of parts whose autonomy—their modularity—is frustrated by the grandiosity of the manager. Character is not role; nor does it become role merely because the manager (figuratively) embodies the system managed.

This is plainer when a system is known to be more than a set of offices with flowcharts, telephones, and people nearby who jump to attention when called. Imagine partners who live together, share the bills, speak occasionally, but hardly penetrate each other's calloused oblivion. It is usually a crisis, not deliberation, that makes them mutually responsive. Deliberators also pick their spots. Grateful for reliability in some reciprocities, mindful of the sheer otherness of the things engaged, they identify the places within a system where oversight would make a useful difference. They don't (or shouldn't) let oversight blind them to the fact that they are participants in the system whose relations they sometimes adjust. Managerial power doesn't cancel the opposition of character and role, or the task of locating and sustaining oneself in the midst of one's roles.

VIII. SOCIAL DELIBERATION

Deliberation is, finally, the legitimizing process of institutionalized self-regulation. Regulation is institutionalized when a patchwork of independent, reciprocally related, overlapping, and nested systems standardizes its constitutive relations in the name of efficiency and distributive justice. Self-regulation is valued and practiced wherever there are procedures for resolving disputes and for making decisions that commit the system's parts to common ends. Democracies regularize deliberation in two ways: (i) by establishing procedures for electing or choosing their officers, including judges and legislators; (ii) by arming these officers with information and with power to direct the execution of their policies; by establishing legislatures that gather information, discuss alternative aims and policies, and make laws; and by creating judiciaries that apply these laws, or scrutinize them for compliance with a superseding constitution.

Democracy is the setting for these remarks about social deliberation, because democratic societies mimic deliberation in single persons. Monarchy and tyranny do this too of course—and even more convincingly, because the deliberator is one person. Yet there is a difference. Democracies are the more interesting example, because they organize themselves for the three-fold task of gathering information (perception), generating interpretations (conception), and appraising the alternatives proposed (attitude). Order in them is achieved by the reciprocity of their parts. Compare tyrannies: information about the circumstances and attitudes of the governed are ignored, because they are incidental when relations are imposed.

It is this regard for different voices—within the state as within the person—that makes individual deliberation the paradigm for democratic deliberation. Oversight in a democracy is the perpetual task of enabling persons and their systems to pursue their aims with the least interference consistent with minimal conflict and the achievement of agreed social goods. All the interested parties should know what the issues are and each side's reasons for thinking as it does. Legislative and judicial deliberations should be mutually transparent: judges don't merely declare a decision; they write justifying opinions. Obscure these deliberations, and it is reasonable to suspect that a system's reciprocities have been tilted to the advantage of one party or another. Members begin to doubt whether they are fairly treated. Reciprocities atrophy as cynicism, slacking, and corruption emerge.

Where is the forum for public deliberation, the public equivalent of self-conscious reflection? This activity rises in all the places and ways that are constitutionally prescribed, but also in the relations of neighbors, the chatter of the media, the slower style of thinkers who have time to ponder before they speak or write. This informal network is the necessary condition for an effective legislature, because it permits innumerable people to clarify the available options before elections and before legislators crystalize the one, preferred solution. The manner of choosing legislators is therefore continuous with the activity of democratic, social deliberation.

What qualities should legislators have? First is the simple requirement that prospective officers separate public duties from private interests. Here again democracies are superior if we suppose that other systems promote managers—emperors or kings—whose self-interest dominates their political role. It is never surprising, but never acceptable, that candidates confuse public with private interests. Candidates who satisfy this condition must also show us their capacity for the deliberative style that is familiar to self-reflective people. Sensitive to perceptual evidence, interpretations, and attitudes in themselves, they should look for comparable levers in the issues that concern us: including information about our situation, alternative plans for public action, and the values that constrain our plans while limiting or fixing their aims.

We often suppose that elections have the single purpose of choosing officers, hence the agenda of the party they represent. This is a terrible mistake; for there is also another aim, one whose neglect almost obviates the benefit of the first: namely, the task of educating the electorate, thereby encouraging them to think about public issues. Elections are wasted on an uninformed public; or they are a show that hides the ritual manipulation of voters. An ignorant electorate cannot support or advise the legislators who win elections, though it will hold them responsible for choices they make. Educated voters are also vital to democracies for the reason that some of them may run for office. Short of having a class of "natural" legislators, executives, or judges, we want an electorate whose members are qualified by their information and values to serve as officers of the state. For every adult is a member of the public; the state is the citizenry organized for self-regulation. No one can afford to be ignorant of social priorities and lawmaking, given the momentous consequences of public self-regulation.

People who despise their elected officers, people who know little or nothing of the activities that require regulation, people who are confirmed in their cynicism by elections presented as vaudeville shows, have every reason to fear that their "democracy" is the creature of interest groups that buy elections and politicians for their own purposes. Their suspicion is reasonable: why exclude anyone, if not to manipulate, use, or abuse them? But then the effects ramify. Deliberation in systems that pervert public education becomes a mockery. Citizens who need to know their actual circumstances don't want to know them. They excuse themselves from responsibility by repeating, truly, that the agenda for "public" policy is established by the attitudes of principal lobbyists, not for the public interest.

It is a matter of utmost concern (at least to its citizens) that a democracy organizes its elections so that its electorate is uninformed, but "sold" on one candidate or another. Where is the failure when this occurs? The process itself needs reform; laws regulating it should be changed. Political parties are also responsible: they should inform but prefer to confuse. More visible still are the nominal sources of political information: they assume the stupidity of their audience and then debase it more.

What happens when electors are discouraged from informing themselves? They don't vote, because they have no basis for making choices, and because they distrust the people who are avid for political office and personal advantage. This alienation from the process is an early step in a vicious spiral. People who are uninformed by legislative and elective processes come to feel excluded from government. Excluded and suspicious, they begin to draw conclusions of their own, though inferences made from a distance and without information are likely to be fantasies or delusions. Uninformed but fearful, envenomed by the stories they tell themselves, these outsiders become enemies of the regime they have imagined. They must defend themselves against it or rally to overcome it. We have Americans who rail that government pollutes their water, reads their mail, takes their guns, threatens their lives, and plots against them. Government, say these worried citizens, is everywhere. But where is the evidence of this in a country where the mailman, infrequent jury duty, sporadic tax payments, occasional elections, and a voluntary army are, for most of us, the only signs of government?

Isn't our problem this other one? Government has taken little or no care to make us participants in the activity of social self-regulation. Worried principally about budgets, reelecting members, crises, and the appearance of power, it has become a remote and alien bazaar. There are several reasons for this, but none obviates the failure of the people to control their government. This is— ideally—a responsibility in every state, but it falls squarely on the people of democratic states. They allow government to separate itself from them. They watch as officers of the public remake themselves to satisfy their political friends, their bankers, and themselves.

Representative governments need unusual devotion to citizens and their private systems. Failing this, we lose the idea of the deliberating public and risk the prospect that government's purpose—social self-regulation and defense—will be diverted. Accordingly, it is not too much government that estranges the people who demonize it. Government has distanced itself from them, hardly caring to convince them that it is democratic, honest, and efficient. These citizens are also at fault. Refusing to educate themselves about government's responsibilities, imagining its abuses, they fail to participate in the forums where issues are considered and solutions are formulated and defended.

Why is there little evidence of an enduring public, one that engages the citizenry as it regulates itself? This is a flaw in the reigning ideology of American life. Nothing in our mantra—"life, liberty, and the pursuit of happiness"—implies reciprocities or responsibilities to a system. The French slogan "Liberty, equality, fraternity," captures them better. *Fraternity* signifies reciprocity, mutual support, and mutual esteem. These notions are sometimes implicit, but otherwise missing, in the idealization of the American community. Where should we Americans go to participate in fraternal discussions of issues that concern us? Talk radio or the Internet shouldn't be the only answer. Nourishing local government is a better one. We already have successive layers of nested regulation, in cities, counties, states, and the federal government. Too much of this structure is sclerotic and ceremonial. Money goes in, but nothing comes out. Why not revive local governments, with their restraining influence on governments of every next-higher order, as Jefferson proposed? Why not restore or create the public forums where issues of public concern are mooted. Legislatures will be alien, and legislators self-interested, until citizens demand the restoration of public deliberation.

IX. DOES DELIBERATION PRESUPPOSE A CARTESIAN MIND?

Have I exaggerated or obscured deliberation's effects by supposing that it occurs within the space of a Cartesian mind or transcendental ego? Fearing this inference, I want to rebut it. Talk about the colloquy of mental functions is a metaphor, until the time when these activities and their relations can be identified as the behaviors of neural assemblies in the brain. The grounds for social deliberations are known already: people, whether singly or allied, talk to one another within a context established by such rules as they make for one another.

Deliberation is not arcane, however little provision there is for it in computer models of human thought. Preoccupation with them should not make us forget that deliberation is a condition for self-control and for control of systems we create.

Chapter 6   Free Speech

We celebrate free speech, though we are slow to think systematically about its rationale and limits. Here in America that justification rarely extends beyond our deference to the First Amendment, perhaps with citations of Milton and Mill. We assume that free speech is a nearly unqualified benefit, though no good is unqualified, this one included. A more nuanced rationale for free speech—one that marks out its limits as well as its advantages—is my first concern. My second interest is metaphysical. Evidence for the effects of free speech is disguised by the ontology usually invoked to support it. I shall be saying that we do more justice to our circumstances if we appraise free speech against the backdrop of the substitute ontology supplied in Chapter One and summarized below. Having this plainer view of the domain wherein speeches are made, I consider three kinds of objectionable speech: speech that violates privacy merely in order to expose its subject, speech that is malicious and false, and monopolistic speech. I shall also suggest some prudent ways of deterring these abuses. All these remarks are focused by this thought: the idea of free speech has been decontextualized, so that the mere phrase "free speech" provokes our respectful approval, without regard for the effects or circumstances of that speech. Contextualizing speech, then considering the conditions and effects of particular speeches, is decisive for appraising it.

This chapter locates speakers within the network of social systems where speeches are judged by their effects on other persons and systems.

I. JUSTIFICATIONS FOR FREE SPEECH

We typically cite one or another of three justifications for the doctrine that everyone should be free to say what he or she pleases, excepting only seditious speech during war or speech known to be provocative or false and likely to be destructive (for example, "fighting words" or "Fire!" yelled falsely in a crowded place). These justifications are constitutional, transcendental (in a sense that may be religious or Kantian), and consequential. Let me characterize the first two of these rationales before dismissing them in favor of the third one.

The constitutional justification is too weak to carry philosophical weight on its own. This is so because the Constitution is a stipulation, not an argument. We ask that there be a justification—not merely deference to a rule—for whatever principles are expressed by the Constitution. The judicial arguments for a decision sometimes invoke transcendental or consequentialist principles, but these are extra-constitutional reasons. The arguments sanctioned by such principles must be transparent, not tortured: it must seem that the cases at issue fall "naturally" under the constitutional clause cited, as when defenses of free speech cite the First Amendment. It is the authority of the Constitution, not this principle, that we reaffirm. But again, philosophical understanding requires more than an argument from authority.

The transcendental justification supposes that every person, not only American citizens, has inalienably the right to speak freely. God, we suppose, has given us both the power for thought and the right to be heard as we express such things as we believe. Or the transcendental defense is Kantian, with the rationale that thought's products are appropriately shared by agents having intellectual and moral autonomy within the kingdom of ends. I ignore a transcendental rationale, in its religious or Kantian form, because the arguments are forced, and because we don't need this arcane justification for free speech if this right, like every other, has no origin but social calculation and practice.

Consequentialism is the principal justification for free speech when the constitutional and transcendental arguments are discounted. This is the idea that the value of anything is a function of its effects, or a function of its effects as we appraise them. The word *consequentialism* is, however, misleading, for the intimation that it is effects only that are significant for determining value. "Wear a coat," we advise; "It's cold outside." We imply that the person addressed is vulnerable to the cold and also that he or she is valued. "Consequentialism" is a shorthand way of referring to a doctrine that gives equal emphasis to four things: actions, and effects of actions, the things previously valued and now affected, and the criteria used to appraise effects. The first two—action and its effects— are means to an end. The third—things affected—is the end valorized. It is such things as these that deserve, by our estimate, to be enhanced or impaired. The fourth—criteria—are the considerations pertinent to deciding that particular effects are acceptable or not: do they enhance or diminish a subject that deserves one or the other? Let free speech be our example of an action. What are its effects? On whom or what? Is that person or thing valued much, little, or not at all? Are the effects appropriate or not to this person or thing, given this estimate of his, her, or its value? Notice the form of this argument: actions or things are good or bad according as they have good or bad effects on subjects valued as primary goods.

Consequentialism may also be understood by way of a different schema, though this second one is equivalent to the first in all respects but one. The alternative also emphasizes actions and effects, something valorized, and criteria for appraising effects. But now it adds a fifth claim: that the source of effects appraised as good because of their effects on things valued is itself a good. So free speech is an action having effects on things valued, and free speech is itself a good because of its beneficial effects on the things appraised as good—thinkers, for example. The difference introduced by this second schema is only rhetorical. Goods-in-themselves of the second rank—such as free speech—could as well be described as means. We elevate them to the status of primary goods because of the formal structure of the second schema, and because we suppose that they are reliable and effulgent sources of beneficial effects.

Both formulations hang on the assumption that something is a primary good-in-itself. What are these goods? And how is their intrinsic goodness confirmed? Surely, the argument for their value is not consequential, transcendental, or constitutional. It is not consequential, because consequentialism measures the value of effects for ends, without itself justifying the ends. It is not transcendental, because we don't need transcendental arguments if we can provide for a moral order in naturalistic terms, and because transcendental arguments, whether religious or Kantian, are logically spurious, empirically unverifiable, or question begging. (The kingdom of ends is all three: it violates Kant's strictures against paralogisms; it is transcendental, hence not empirically verifiable; it is the postulate of his claims about moral freedom, though it begs the question, are we free?) The ends-justifying claim is not constitutional, because, as before, the Constitution is a rule. Affirming it proves nothing but our determination to apply it. Yes, we do affirm it because of its good consequences. But why assume that the subjects for whom it has these effects are worthy in themselves?

What style of justification is left? I recommend this one. We *choose* the objects of ultimate value. Not surprisingly, we choose ourselves. We, by self-election, are good-in-themselves. This is a considered choice, one that is justified by experience and interest, as we value human beings and human flourishing for the good reason that we are humans who want to flourish. If we nominate other things to this community of ends, it is usually because they are human associations or products—families or paintings, for example. Their flourishing wins sympathy as an extrapolation from our self-concern, or because their well-being is a condition of our own. This last point will be critical below: valuing ourselves, we value the conditions for our well-being. That we may not know those conditions is incidental: discovering that these are conditions for our well-being, we who value ourselves should, logically and practically, value them.

II. PRIVACY

The consequentialist justification for free speech usually invokes the second of the two consequentialist schemas: we say that free speech (like health) is good in itself, because it is the bountiful source of effects that are good for us. What are these effects? One is the cultivation of each speaker's intellectual powers as he or she learns to explain and defend ideas formulated concisely. Suppressing free speech stunts this development by denying us information or criticism. Other effects are the acquisition of knowledge in communities where open debate is one condition for successful inquiry and enhanced efficiency wherever information is communicated, including work, family, and government. Government is sometimes tyrannical, so the open criticism of a government's policies and officials is also a consequence of free speech, and a principal reason for defending it.

A different reason for favoring free speech is distinct from our concern for self-cultivation, social efficiency, and honest criticism as a control on governmental power. This is the aim sometimes characterized as the desire for an "open" or "transparent" society. That is, I suppose, a society in which information about motives and values, as well as information about every other thing, is available to everyone, without privilege. Government has no exemption from the general requirement: it too is to do its work before the eyes of its citizens, nothing hidden, everything explained and justified in the language and in the spirit of rules that apply generally to all the society's activities. This is the ideal on which our democracy is nourished. Free speech is to be a principal means of achieving the ideal, so anyone who wishes to thwart free speech must be inimical to it, for motives of his own. The rhetoric is compelling, but the claim it defends needs qualification.

Consider the atomistic ontology that dominates the history of Anglo-American thinking about human societies. This is the view that there is no reality to entities other than individual thinker-actors, or, more soberly, no reality to things other than bodies that think. Atomists agree that information will have to pass among the individuals who cooperate for the purposes of education, commerce, and efficient social regulation; but atomism makes all social affairs visible by reducing them to the behaviors of the many individuals engaged. The intention is admirable: princes and plutocrats should have nowhere to hide. They should be amply described, and thereby seen. No Gyges should steal anything from the rest of us. But now the motives darken, as we fear that our competitiors may have secured an advantage that is denied us. For no matter that these are individual achievements, earned at no cost to us by way of personal sacrifice and hard work. Democracy as we have come to understand it is a leveler; and we want to know of—perhaps to suppress—anyone who has distinguished him or herself from the rest of us. Or, still in the name of our homogenizing democracy, we are suspicious of people different from ourselves. Heaven knows what they do or what they intend. We render them transparent by exposing what they do.

Imagine a great encampment on a desert plain. We see all of it from above, so every undertaking reduces to the visible behaviors of single persons. If there are tents or houses, imagine that this observer sees through them. This is a transparent society, one left exposed by the atomism which reduces all complexity to the behaviors of individuals. Everything is disclosed, as much to individual participants as to observers having a view of the whole. There is only the difference that elevated observers see everything at once, while participants move through the camp at ground level, gathering information piecemeal, comparing perspectives, then making tentative, revisable inferences. Everyone is free to move about the camp, so everyone may, in principle, see everything.

We retell this story, emphasizing the force of free speech, if we suppose that a society is open because all thoughts and feelings are subject to expression or interrogation, hence to full disclosure. We encourage people to talk, about themselves or others. As Justice Brennan said, speaking for the Court in *Time Inc.* v. *Hill:*

> The guarantees for speech and press are not the preserve of political expression or comment upon public affairs, essential as those are to healthy government. One need only pick up any newspaper or magazine to comprehend the vast range of published matter which exposes persons to public view, both private citizens and public officials. Exposure of the self to others in varying degrees is a concomitant of life in a civilized community. The risk of this exposure is an essential incident of life in a society which places a primary value on freedom of speech and of press.[1]

Complete disclosure is the demand that there be no privacies to obscure the facts about us. The right to unimpeded speech is the cutting edge of this demand: we reveal ourselves, or others do it for us. Imagine the effect when each of us is, for the purposes of disclosure, Caesar's wife.

We shall not get this effect from free speech alone. It is important that no thought or feeling within us is intelligible even to its bearer if it is not expressible in a language, and also that all of us think and speak the same language. Remember Wittgenstein's arguments against a private language[2] and George Herbert Mead's remarks about the "generalized other."[3] They believe that there is only as much intelligibility within us as we do or can express in the language common to the members of a linguistic community. Free speech assures disclosure if each of us is an obsessive talker or if others can make us think as they talk. For there will be nothing in us that is not intelligible to the others, and perhaps nothing in us that was not already broadcast by them.

The unqualified benefits claimed for free speech are less certain now, for this is not so much a defense against tyranny as a guarantee that no citizen shall have any protective distance separating him or her from surveillance, and eventually perhaps from control. Nor is this farfetched when we remember that television is a principal educator among us, and that the documentation and access promoted by computer record keeping is the basis for the control of credit, passports, tax reports, fingerprints, and voter registration. If the "open society" is too easily turned from the rhapsody of cultivated democracy to despotic control, free speech will have been one of the principles that was turned against us. What perversion of free speech could produce this result? Just the claim that free speech implies the right to discover and recount every fact about anyone and anything.

This abuse of privacy is the first of my three charges against free speech. Why is this outcome abhorrent? Because it perverts the ideal of a transparent society for either of several motives: jealousy, fear of difference, or a desire for control. The social determination to create this society is a guarantee of perpetual conflict. Why? Because of our proclivity to form the systems (hence the privacies) that are ignored by the reigning ontology.

III. ONTOLOGICAL CONSIDERATIONS

How transparent can society be? Here are two notions of social reality. One favors the view that society is, or ought to be, transparent. The other emphasizes association. It affirms that societies are, partly at least, irreparably closed.

Atomism is the doctrine that the elements of social reality are individual persons. Atomists differ about persons' aims: some, like Bentham, stressing pleasure and the avoidance of pain; others, like Mill, emphasizing the cultivation of thought and moral virtue. Atomists agree that freedom is the birthright of every person. Oppressive social relations are to be re-formed in ways that acknowledge the incorrigible separateness and freedom of the participants. There are *freedoms to* and *freedoms from:* the one as we have unimpeachable rights to do as we like, up to the point of hurting others; the second as we are, or ought to be, exempt from the intrusions or demands of others. Freedoms of both sorts distance us from other carriers of these same rights, as though too close a liaison would sabotage all of us. We may be joined again on the basis of mutual sympathy or expedient contract, but always in ways that respect our autonomy. Though notice the odd effect of joining autonomy to free speech. Free speech is the right to disclosure. We can talk about ourselves; or others can tell us everything about us. Either way, we are exposed. Add that there are no private languages, hence no incomprehensible communications about me by others or myself, and we have the further implication that exposure makes me fully recognizable to everyone who speaks my language. More than exposed, I am transparent. This is ironic given the concern for autonomy. For autonomy reduces to numerical difference, together with the freedom or rights to defend one's separability. How shall I defend it when I perceive myself and am perceived by others as having only the public and private identity common to everyone else? Is there a difference left to protect—separability apart?

What could have averted this result? Just that inner region—partly conscious, largely not—where each one evaluates choices and ideas in the terms of his or her affective and intellectual economy. Social demands may overwhelm the scruples that partly define this space; we may be swept away by a crowd. Still, this inner space may have an architecture and valences peculiar to itself. One may fail to cultivate these powers. They may be suppressed. But having them defends us from control of the sort that exposes and eradicates our intrapsychic differences.

Atomism may go either way: it may describe each of us as a blank slate needing others to fill and manipulate us; or it may emphasize, as Mill does, "the inward domain of consciousness, demanding liberty of conscience in the most comprehensive sense, liberty of thought and feeling, absolute freedom of opinion and sentiment on all subjects, practical or speculative, scientific, moral or theological."[4] Atomism in our time is skeptical or cynical about this private space. It suspects—with the support of Hegel's distaste for private languages—that we have nothing to hide.

The alternative ontology, proposed by thinkers such as Plato and Dewey, is systemic. It denies the atomist premise that individuals are wholly formed in their separateness. Social relations, it says, are not ties of convenience established as we satisfy passing needs. For no one, acting alone, creates a language, literature, economy, or state. There are frontiersmen and shepherds who do many things for themselves; but Robinson Crusoe stories are fascinating because they require that we imagine someone deprived of his accustomed place within a network of interdependencies. What would be left of us if these mutually conditioning relations were stripped away? How long would memory and fantasy serve us before the arrival of a Friday to reestablish the old connections? Atomism dismisses these relations, calling them accidents in the lives of otherwise separate, autonomous agents. The alternative responds that the individual person is like an ion or free variable: he or she has skills and values that qualify him or her for roles within one or many networks of interdependency. Each one's identity is merely virtual apart from the relationships where these talents are exhibited. Think of the pianist without a piano, or of baseball players perpetually on strike. The talents wither; the self-esteem they justify is lost.

These networks of mutual dependence and common purpose are irreducible entities. What distinguishes them from aggregates? Just the relations joining the participants. A crowd of musicians is not an orchestra; mutual strangers are not a family. The reciprocal, causal relations of the participants create a system that is different from the inventory of its parts. There are two points to notice.

First, consider the relation of two causes, each of them sustained in its effects by the action of the other. Students excite the teachers who educate them. Each sustains his relation to the other in part because of being held there by the other. This is negative feedback: each cause limits the range of variation in the other, because each is switched on or off when the other's effects upon it exceed a certain range of variation. Think of the furnace turned on or off by room temperature. Systems such as these are stabilized and sustained by their internal architecture and by the mutual modulation of their internal reciprocities. They would be sustained indefinitely if there were a limitless supply of energy, and if the parts—the causes—suffered no breakdown or distraction.

Second, consider two kinds of system. One is differentiated by the roles of its parts, as pitcher and catcher, heart and lungs, have different roles. Systems of this kind are organized for some effect, so that the parts and their relationships are instrumental to this end. Systems of the other kind are associative (that is, affiliative). Their members, too, are related reciprocally, and they, too, are irreducible to the reality of their parts. But there is this difference: affiliations do not require that there be functional differences among the roles filled by their members. Individual Republicans and Democrats, Hindus and Sikhs, participate in their parties or sects because of views or practices which are like those of their fellows. It is similarity or identity, not coordinated difference, that is the test of participation. This similarity is either inherited, as in the case of gender or race, or acquired as with shared feelings and beliefs. The similarity of inherited features is insufficient by itself, however, to entail association with people similar to oneself. It becomes sufficient only as we distinguish, with Marx, between the objective and subjective conditions for group loyalty: having a common property is not enough for affiliation; conscious solidarity with people like oneself is also required. Reciprocity, here, is a mirroring relation. You see in me the feelings and beliefs that I see in you; each one's intensity excites an answering firmness in the other. It is Hegel who speaks for associations. Agreement in feeling or belief is the Idea incarnate, as each member of a group or cult finds his or her identity in the persuasion shared by all the members. There is one Idea that prevails universally, or there is a plurality of ideas, each incarnation tolerated by the others—multiculturalism, we call it.

When Justus Buchler wrote of systems like these, he characterized them as "natural complexes." Mario Bunge prefers the single word "systems." I shall describe them indifferently as "stabilities" or systems. Doing so has the five implications described in Chapter One.

(i) Systems are complex, because each embodies a network of relations that are spatial, temporal, and causal. The new complex is sustained—stabilized—because the energetic bonds within it have established a particular equilibrium, one that will sustain this thing's integrity until some greater energy is used to destroy it, or until energy within the system dissipates. Think of an orchestra or of

Plato's Republic. Sonority and balance in the one, justice in the other, are corporate properties, meaning properties consequent on the functional unity of the system. Each of them, no less than an individual man or woman, performs as an integrated whole. So an apple, an ax, and a human being are stable systems, as are thunderclouds, garden parties, and some wars.

(ii) Every system has an inside and an outside. Each is a relationship of parts with an internal equilibrium and relations to those things outside from which the system draws material, energy, or information. The inside is constituted of the parts in their reciprocal relatedness. Energy or information is cycled through these bonds, so that every dynamic relation to things outside a system is mediated by its material properties and architecture, or by that interpretation of the outside created by this agent's synthesis of the available information. Its every response expresses, however obscurely, something of these systemic properties or products. Extracting energy or information from the things outside itself, the system metabolizes them in its own terms. This is its distinguishing privacy and integrity, but also its vulnerability. For each stability is generated and sustained in the nourishing sea from which it derives energy and substance. Think of an old city, with its alleys, trades, and secrets. It thrives on the wealth of its port or the surrounding farms until its income is depleted by silt or drought. No stability defends the privacy established within it past the time when its relations to external sources break down.

(iii) Every system has a developmental history. Each is generated as antecedent stabilities interact or evolve: they are transformed, eventuating in this new complex, or they give up matter and energy, thereby supplying material sufficient to establish it. Consider the development of any child. He or she is the successively transformed product of development, not the enduring matter that abides through change. Stabilities are sustained, stabilized processes, not entities somehow underlying change. Some stabilities are conscious of their histories, telling stories about them, reenacting parts of them. These are developmental histories defended as traditions.

(iv) Developmental histories imply a determined result, but not one that cannot be altered further. For systems are determinable—malleable—within limits, while being determinate in every respect at any moment: every one of the infinity of possible properties is or is not realized within them. Families, businesses, schools, and governments work a certain way; but they can be reshaped.

This plasticity makes it possible to recast individual systems or even a domain of them, as when our social order is remade to look atomistic.

(v) Systems relate to one another in one of four ways. They may be mutually independent, meaning that the character and existence of each are independent of the character and existence of the others. We have a limiting example of this independence when neither of two things is in the light cone of the other. People sitting next to one another in a bus or subway car may think themselves to be almost that independent and remote. Other stable systems are reciprocally related, thereby forming a higher-order system. It may endure for a long time or briefly, as Buddhists are one, and Scientologists the other. There is overlap when a member of one system is also a member of an otherwise independent system, as happens if a dentist is also a Mason. Overlap is an instance of nesting: meaning the relation of a system to its proper parts. Nesting is hierarchical, with lower-order systems nested within higher-order ones: the city of Wheeling in the state of West Virginia in the United States. Each lower-order stability is a complex of relations limiting the effects of the higher-order stabilities in which it is nested, though sometimes the determining power of a higher-order stability overrides the integrity of a lower-order one, bending that stability to its requirements.

These five characteristics are as common to organizations and associations as to the individuals once described as primary substances. Atomists chronically deny the integrity of stable systems because they suppose that it is the separability and endurance of matter, not the stability of relations, that explain the integrity of substances. Relations, on their telling, are adventitious connections among separable matters. This too often ignores the fact that nothing is fully formed without its constitutive relations—what Aristotle would have called its form. Many things less palpable than stones and human bodies are systems of sustained reciprocal relations; many of them, whether palpable or not, have relations that connect them to, or embed them within, other stabilities.

Is there empirical evidence for this claim about systems? The structure and efficacy of teams, families, corporations, schools, bands, and governments is one sort of evidence. Equally cogent is the experiential evidence of individual people. Each of us knows him or herself as both a privacy and as a participant in disparate associations: one is a family member, a citizen, an employee, and a friend. Every collaboration engages our thoughts, feelings, and skills, and each of these mental states is a vector pointing beyond us to our place within overlapping or nested stabilities. We are spiders in our separate webs, but our isolation is qualified, because each of has thoughts, feelings, and abilities that anticipate our connection with other things. They are the referents of our feelings and partners in the activities that require our skills. Does each of us participate in systems of which we are unaware? This is certainly true, as there is no sensibility of electromagnetic fields, and little or no awareness of the speech patterns and accent shared with the other members of a linguistic community.

The idea of the transparent society was a promise that policies such as free speech would dissolve the privacies, hence the privileges and powers, that defended favored classes and regimes. Yet something is wrong with the idea that stabilities can invariably be punctured or turned inside out, then eliminated. Stabilities disintegrate under pressures such as urban renewal, free elections, tax policies, and free speech, proving that societies are reformable. One can also eliminate extended families, replacing them first with nuclear families and eventually—when infants are raised like oysters on strings—with no families at all. But then the elements re-form; other associations—whether utilitarian and role-differentiated or affiliative—replace the old ones. This recurring process does not yield. Systems remain the stuff of social reality, except as debilitation enfeebles individuals to the point where they cannot engage others in reciprocal expectations and behaviors.

Every society above this threshold of despair resists dissolution into passive, exploitable openness. Its systems resist being turned inside out, losing viability as they are reduced to their individual members. Yet we stack the deck, favoring dissolution over stability when we legitimize free speech as a weapon. Idiosyncrasy is perceived as deviation, so individuals are exposed and punished if they do not conform. Other, higher-order systems respond in either of two ways. Reciprocal relations among members are intensified as they draw together, all the while testing and securing relations with allied systems. Or the system loses its internal coherence as individual members withdraw from one another in disorientation, fear, or shame. These are the effects when free speech is not the idealized, civilizing instrument of toleration, culture, and inquiry, but rather the blade that opens society by eviscerating its constituent systems.

IV. FALSE AND MALICIOUS SPEECH

False and malicious speech is a second abuse of free speech.

Imagine a family of circus roustabouts living on your street. Their hours and dress are odd by your standards. Their pets—chickens and lizards—wouldn't be yours. The children adore their parents, but they avoid your children. The parents are civil, but they avoid you. Could they dare to imagine that they are better than you are? The family's house is burned to the ground when one of the neighbors takes offense and says ugly things that are quickly passed around and believed. The family members are dead, injured, or dispersed.

It's a free country, you say. Everything up to the arson is regrettable but excused in the name of free speech. But speech has costs. Here are five, from the most to the least apparent: (i) family members are injured; (ii) their property is destroyed; (iii) one of the neighbors has been provoked to make himself a criminal, with consequences for him, his circle, and the criminal justice system; (iv) each of the family members is wounded in his self-regard and in his ability to sustain viable links with other people; (v) this was a family that nurtured its members. They, by their reciprocities, supported and improved one another. Some of the members survive, but they are impaired, as their children will be. The family is gone. But there is an offsetting benefit: namely, our ritual deference to two principles: These are first, the claim that everything distinguishable is separable, as starting or repeating gossip is different from starting a fire, and second, the principle that free speech is an absolute value, whatever its abuses.

Is the outcome different if we alter the example, substituting an association—a race or religion, Yankee fans or bingo players—for the utilitarian family? (Most families exemplify systems of both kinds.) Suppose that the members are slurred maliciously, for then the difference is plain: members recoil from one another when their affiliation has become an embarrassment or a burden, one that marks them as separate and alien. Self-loathing or aggressive self-affirmation are additional possible reactions. Where is the solidarity, the mirroring, that gave the association its identity, the members their strength? It dissolves.

There is a much commended remedy: let everyone learn to disregard the scurrilous things said of him or her, because these assaults do most of their damage when they simmer within us. Better, expose them to the light of day. We recover more quickly if we see them for the malign and stupid things they are. Make all of it public, including the act itself and one's feelings about it, then forget the provocations and their effects, as women learn to disregard catcalls and whistles. This response is tendentious, however well intended. The motive for it is atomist oblivion to the integrity and essential privacy of systems. Atomism dissolves the reciprocity of utilitarian systems and the solidarity of affiliations, leaving only the counsel that we should have a thick skin and the good sense not to strike back. There should be no rancor, the atomist assumes, because every member has mastered the situation by controlling his or her anger.

This remedy works by separating each member from the others, as each one is reduced to his or her defenses. It is only later that members may find support within the stability they share. Indeed, associations like these are, at such moments, almost defunct. They stop performing as systems, because affiliation shrivels when there is mortification rather than pride in shared properties, practices, or beliefs. This is the intention of the seductive claim that a slur is not intended for you or me, but only for the group at large. What effect do such attitudes have on the persons or stability insulted? It may have none; the members may ignore it. But they may be scared and diminished, or thick-skinned but angry and alienated even from those who are like them. A complex, higher-order system is hereby reduced to the fears or defensiveness of its members. Speech has made them independent of one another, destroying their solidarity and their society. For remember that it is the subjective conditions for group loyalty, not only the objective condition—race or gender, for example—that secures reciprocity among the members.

"Sticks and stones may break my bones; but names can never hurt me" is a child's rhyme, and also the posture of those who agree to be insulted for the greater good: meaning free speech. We should know better. For if some people are able to consider ideas with a firm neutrality, taking no position in regard to them until the supporting evidence is appraised, most people cannot do that. Ask an advertising agency. Do its ads speak to reason and prudence, or to attitudes? Is it trying to inform the one or influence the other? The nineteenth century—with Mill as its liberal example—supposed that intellect could usually or always suppress attitude. Our century, with lots of experience to support it, concludes that attitudes dominate information; so information is presented in ways calculated to influence attitudes. Freedom of speech is very often the freedom to tinker with attitudes for purposes that may or may not serve the interests of those whose attitudes are changed. This is the truth we neglect when the harm caused by free speech is dismissed as a trivial cost.

V. THE BENEFITS AND HARMS OF FREE SPEECH

These remarks have been anecdotal so far. They need more careful formulation. What should our criteria be as we appraise the benefit or harm of free speech?

We know the benefits: namely, the blooming of intellect in individual people, the exchange of information among people coordinating their activities for a shared practical aim, the exchange of ideas (in scientific inquiry or public deliberation, for example) and the defense of societies from rapacious leaders or other citizens. The diversity of these advantages is synergistic: someone who believes that his behavior will not compromise his freedom, take chances out of all proportion to the likely profit to himself. His initiatives are, nevertheless, good for him, and for some of the rest of us, too.

Atomists emphasize such benefits almost as much as they minimize the undesirable effects of free speech. They make several assumptions about us. Why don't names hurt me? Because insults, like promises, require two or more people: one to insult or promise, the other to take the insult or accept the promise. If I ignore the words or hear them as a compliment, there is no insult. Are insults easily ignored? Atomism believes that they may be. For it says of social atoms (in the version of Mill) what I have claimed for systems: that they have an inside and an outside. The inside is the private place of thought, moral reflection, and purpose. This is to be the mediating space between provocation and response, the place where action is inhibited as we appraise information about our circumstances, prospects, and values. Atomism supposes that false and insulting speech will be deflected because reflection counsels that it be ignored. But often it is not, with the result that anger seethes within people and factions where malign speech has a perpetual resonance.

Atomism bets that failures of inhibition will have minor repercussions because effective action, requiring coordination of the actors, is hard to achieve when every atom has its own interpretation of the information supplied, its own projects and values. But isn't this like saying that distributing hand guns is safe, because the guns are hard to assemble and use? Effective associations are frequently achieved, in business, marriage, and government, but also for bank robbing and cross burning. Atomism underestimates the effects of free speech and the reaction to them, because it drastically exaggerates the singularity and irreconcilability of the atoms. Or atomism prays that a huge terrain, or a large and diverse population, will soak up and dissipate the more egregious expressions of speech. Organizations using abusive speech will be too fragile to support their malign causes. Ardor will cool because of difficulty contacting other people, or because most people cannot be diverted from aims of their own. All these defenses are feeble. Distance is no obstacle in an electronic age. Nor is our resistance more than porous when advertisers have learned to promote noxious information in flattering ways.

Is there evidence that viciousness is deterred by the gap between perception and action? Not when desire or fear, not thought, are the typical goads to action. Some of the keenest advocates of unrestrained speech are agencies that are convinced of their power to subvert the integrity of private reflection by sending

Menschenwürde. Das Anliegen der spanischen Kolonialethik des goldenen Zeitalters, or its Spanish translation by F. de Asis Caballero entitled *La Ética colonial española del siglo de oro. Christianismo e dignidad humana,* with an Intro. by A. Truyol Serra; and by K. S. Latourette, *A History of the Expansion of Christianity,* Vol. III: *Three Centuries of Advance A. D. 1500–1800,* pp. 83 ff. See also *infra,* nn. 63–64.

15. IV Esdras 13:40 ff., here cited from the English trans. by G. H. Box in R. H. Charles's ed. of *The Apocrypha and Pseudepigrapha of the Old Testament in English,* II, 619; Gregorio García, *Origen de los Indios de el Nuevo Mundo e Indias Occidentales,* Valencia, 1607.

16. Thomas Thorowgood, *Jewes in America; or Probabilities that the Americans are of that Race,* London, 1650; Menasseh ben Israel, *Miqveh Yisrael Spes Israelis,* Amsterdam, 1650, or the English trans. by Moses Wall entitled *The Hope of Israel,* London, 1650; with the comments thereon and related texts by M. Kayserling in *Christopher Columbus and the Participation of the Jews in the Spanish and Portuguese Discoveries,* esp. pp. 95 ff., 153 ff. App. viii; L. Wolf, *Menasseh ben Israel's Mission to Oliver Cromwell,* pp. xxiv ff., 1 ff., 7 ff.; C. Roth, *The Life of Menasseh ben Israel,* pp. 176 ff., 330 ff., 353; L. E. Huddleston, *Origins of the American Indians: European Concepts, 1492–1729,* pp. 33 ff., 118 ff., 128 ff., 138 ff. See also J. Miranda's succinct observation on "Los Indígenas de América en la época colonial; teorías, legislación, realidades," *Cuadernos americanos,* XXIII, Part 1, pp. 153–61.

The historicity of the "myth" of ancient Israelitic connections with the pre-Columbian population of the Americas has for a long time been curtly dismissed by modern critical historians. However, slowly accumulating new archaeological and other evidence—which would take me too far afield to describe even briefly—has raised some serious questions in the minds of reputable scholars concerning the early presence of peoples of Mediterranean, as well as of Negro and Mongolian, stock, perhaps especially connected with the Phoenician circumnavigation of Africa in the days of Pharoh Necho (609–595 B.C.E.) reported by Herodotus. Nor are direct vestiges of ancient Israelitic influences to be ruled out. See now C. H. Gordon, *Before Columbus: Links between the Old World and Ancient America,* which, however, raises more questions than it answers; the general survey by R. Sanders in his "Who *Did* Discover America?" *Midstream,* XVII, No. 7, pp. 9–21; and J. Lear's succinct reservations against the regnant skepticism on this score in his review of S. E. Morison's recent work, *The European Discovery of America: the Northern Voyages, A.D. 500–1600,* in the *Saturday Review* of Sept. 4, 1971, pp. 61–62. Whatever one thinks of the realities of these East-West contacts in ancient times, however, there is no doubt that the debate about the ancient Israelitic origins of the American Indians had an impact on the readmission of the Jews to England, a matter which will be analyzed in a later volume.

Of the fairly extensive literature relating to the allegedly Indian Jewish tribe living in Mexico today, which consists largely of travelogues and popular essays rather than of rigorously documented studies, we need but mention the following: the older romantic notions well summarized by M. Behar in "Les Sefardís du Mexique: les Juifs indiens," *Les Cahiers Sefardis,* September, 1947; the more restrained observations by some modern anthropologists—for instance, R. Patai's report on "Venta Priesta Revisited," *Midstream,* XI, No. 1, pp. 79–92; and, more decisively, S. B. Liebman, "Mexican Mestizo Jews," *AJA*, XIX, 144–74. See also *infra*, nn. 18 and 63.

17. See the *Recopilación de Leyes de los Reynos de las Indias*, I, vi; VI; *supra*, Vol. XI, pp. 198 ff.; J. L. Mecham, *Church and State in Latin America;* and, more generally, L. Lapétegui and F. Zubillaga, *Historia de la Iglesia en la América Española desde el Descubrimiento hasta comienzos del siglo XIX* [Vol. I]: México, América Central, Antillas; A. de Engaña, [Vol II]: *Hemisferio Sur.* Although deficient in many respects, and particularly inadequate bibliographically, these two volumes offer a fair review of the general evolution.

Most remarkably, the Mexican clergy was so impressed by the royal absolutism that, on its own, it tried to stave off the interference of the papal see. This attitude came clearly to the fore in the resolutions adopted by the Third Mexican Council of 1585. Although convoked for the purpose of introducing the canons of the Tridentine Council into Mexican Church doctrine and practice (these canons became known in Mexico too late to be implemented by the Second Council, which had met in 1565), the resolutions often ran counter to both the Tridentine decisions and earlier canonical legislation. Not surprisingly, when they were submitted to the Roman Congregation on the [Tridentine] Council, they underwent a far-reaching revision. Among other matters, the Papacy insisted upon extending greater protection to the natives than was given them in the earlier formulation. In practice, however, the papal wishes were again disregarded. See L. Hanke, "Pope Paul III and the American Indians," *Harvard Theological Review*, XXX, 74–81 (with an extensive bibliography of earlier studies); E. J. Burrus, "The Third Mexican Council (1585) in the Light of the Vatican Archives," *The Americas*, XXIII, 390–407; and, more generally, P. Leturia, *Relaciones entre la Santa Sede e Hispanoamérica*, rev. by A. de Engaña *et al.* Among other aspects, Leturia also tries to answer the intriguing question of "why the nascent Spanish-American Church was not represented in Trent" (I, 495 ff.).

18. See R. E. Greenleaf, "The Inquisition and the Indians of New Spain: a Study in Jurisdictional Confusion," *The Americas*, XXII, 138–66; Velasco's report of February 7, 1554, reproduced in M. Cueva's ed. of *Documentos inéditos para la historia de México*, p. 190; and, more generally, the mutually complementary studies by R. Konetzke, "El Mestizaje y su importancia en el desarrollo de la población hispano-americana durante la época colonial," *Revista de Indias*, VII, 7–44, 215–37; and by M. Mörner, *El Mestizaje en la historia de Iberoamérica*. A fuller study of Jewish-mestizo relations going beyond S. B. Liebman's essay mentioned *supra*, n. 16, and extending to the South-American countries as well, would be of considerable importance.

From different angles a reexamination of Negro-Jewish relations in the colonial period would likewise be meritorious. For the time being, we must be satisfied with such general studies of the psychological attitudes and sociopolitical realities in both Spain and its colonies as are offered by H. M. Jason in "The Negro in Spanish Literature to the End of the Siglo de Oro," *College Language Association Journal*, IX, 121–31; and esp. F. Tannenbaum in *Slave and Citizen: the Negro in the Americas*, and the literature cited there. See also *supra*, n. 14; and *infra*, nn. 63–64.

19. A. Domínguez Ortiz, *La Clase social*, p. 129 (cites the proverb "Ni judío

necio ni liebre perezosa"); S. B. Liebman, *The Jews in New Spain*, p. 301; E. M. Lohmeyer Lobo, *Aspectos de influência dos homens de negócio na política comercial ibero-americana. Século XVII* (Diss. Guanabara); and L. M. Solís's attempt at reinterpretation of "La Influencia del mercantilismo español en la vida económica de América Latina," *Técnicas financieras*, XXXI, 200–209. Of considerable interest also is the pioneering effort by S. F. Cook and W. Borah to ascertain "Quelle fut la stratification sociale au Centre du Mexique durant la première moitié du XVIe siècle?" *Annales ESC*, XVIII, 226–58. See also, more generally, I. Sánchez Bella, *La Organización financiera de las Indias (siglo XVI)*; and the aforementioned voluminous work by H. Chaunu and P. Chaunu, *Séville et l'Atlantique, 1540 à 1650*. See also *infra*, nn. 50–51.

20. See the twin studies by W. Borah and S. F. Cook, *The Population of Central Mexico in 1548: an Analysis of the* Suma de visitas de pueblos *(Ibero-Americana*, XLIII); and by Cook and Borah, *The Indian Population of Central Mexico 1531–1610* (Ibero-Americana, XLIV); S. B. Liebman, *The Jews in New Spain*, p. 145; and *infra*, n. 24. To be sure, some of Borah and Cook's methods have been criticized by other scholars, and the exact figures given by them are indeed questionable. The uncertainties begin with the very estimates of the American population before Columbus. See A. Rosenblatt, *La Población de América en 1492. Viejos y nuevos cálculos*. Yet there is no doubt about the amazing decline of the native population.

It should be noted, however, that this extraordinary excess of mortality over natality was more a result of the natives' inability to adjust to the new conditions (including the protracted, all-year-round labor, contrasted with an annual average 60–70 working days in the cultivation of maize in the precolonial era; the spread of newly imported communicable diseases; and the great plague of the 1590s) than of any deliberate genocidal tendencies on the part of the conquerors. In fact, even the Iberian immigrants had to overcome tremendous difficulties in adapting their methods of industrial production and the use of European media of exchange and commercial instruments to the exigencies of the new environment. See the plausible arguments presented by A. E. Sayous in "L'Adaptation des méthodes commerciales des pays chrétiens de la Méditerranée occidentale en Amérique pendant la première moitié du XVIe siécle," in *Wirtschaft und Kultur. Festschrift . . . Alfons Dopsch*, pp. 611–25. In vain did the Church try to prevail upon the entrepreneurs, as well as upon the government agents, to be less exacting with respect to the aboriginal population than they had been in their treatment of employees in their home country. See, for instance, S. Poole, "The Church and the Repartimientos in the Light of the Third Mexican Council, 1585," *The Americas*, XX, 3–36; and other data assembled by K. S. Latourette in his aforementioned, somewhat overapologetic, analysis of that subject in *A History of the Expansion of Christianity*, III, 83 ff. Not surprisingly, however, Soviet scholars, although generally concerned with more recent, rather than colonial, developments, have had a field day in describing the oppressive nature of Spanish colonialism. See some of their writings listed by L. Okinshevich and R. G. Carlton in their *Latin America in Soviet Writings: a Bibliography*, Vols. I: 1917–1958; II: 1959–1964. On the small share of women in the Old Christian migratory movement from Spain to the New World, see R. Konetzke, "La Emigración de mujeres españoles a América durante la época colonial," *Revista internacional de Sociología*,

III, 123–50. The paucity of European women naturally led to an increase of the mestizo population.

21. The literature on the cultural evolution of Mexico is enormous. See, for example, the publication by Mexico's Archivo General de la Nación of the *Documentos para la historia de la cultura en México; una biblioteca del siglo XVII; catálogo de libros expurgados a los Jesuítas en el siglo XVIII.* There exist a great many specialized bibliographies of the literature relating to various branches of intellectual endeavor. A substantial compilation of such bibliographies was long ago prepared by C. K. Jones under the title *A Bibliography of Latin American Bibliographies.* Even its revised 2d ed. is now some thirty years old, and thus does not cover the period of greatest qualitative and quantitative work in this field. On the general impact of the Jesuit Order on Mexican culture and its attitude toward *limpieza,* see F. J. Alégre, *Historia de la provincia de la Compañia de Jesús de Nueva España.* New ed. by E. J. Burrus and F. Zubillaga; G. Decarme, *La Obra de los Jesuitas mexicanos durante la época colonial, 1572–1767 (compendio histórico);* and *supra,* Vol. XIV, pp. 13 ff., 306 ff. nn. 12–14. However, there seems to be no way of ascertaining how many New Christians were allowed to join the American sections of the Order even in the less restrictive sixteenth century. A casual review of the biographical data furnished by F. Zambrano in the two volumes of his *Diccionario bio-bibliográfico de la Compaña de Jesús en México* has yielded no satisfactory results. This is the less surprising as the Marrano settlers bore, for the most part, widely used Spanish names, and that none of the nearly 180 prominent members of the Order treated by Zambrano bore a name which could be identified as being of distinctly Jewish origin.

Of special interest to New Christians must have been the inquisitorial censorship of books, particularly of vernacular Bibles, which were their main source of information concerning what they considered their Jewish heritage. See, for example, C. Miralles de Imperial y Gómez, "Censura de publicaciones en Nueva España" (*supra,* n. 10), esp. p. 222; J. Friede, "La Censura española del siglo XVI y los libros de historia de América," *Revista de historia de América,* No. 47, pp. 45–94; and, more generally, A. Flores, ed., *The Literature of Spanish America: a Critical Anthology* (Vol. I is devoted to the colonial period). Understandably, the Church still played a great role in the intellectual evolution of the country. However, there also was a slowly growing lay intelligentsia among both the government bureaucrats and the private citizens. Only thus was the government able to control the Mexican Church to the extent it did.

22. See Pedro Moya de Contreras' *Cinco cartas,* ed. with a Biographical Introduction by S. C. Gutiérrez and F. Sosa; H. C. Lea, *The Inquisition in the Spanish Dependencies,* pp. 534 f. App. No. xi (reproducing a Spanish extract from the Edict of Faith extant in a Riva Palacio MS); *supra,* Vols. III, 194 f., 222 n. 28; XIII, pp. 35 ff., 322 f. n. 37. As usual, the Edict also enumerated certain behavioral patterns by which laymen could recognize their judaizing neighbors. During the subsequent investigation, the phyical examination of male defendants often produced the "incontrovertible" proof of their having at some time submitted to Jewish ritualistic circumcision. True, some American Indian tribes had also practiced circumcision. A graphic representation of such a ceremony on a piece of gold jewelry is briefly described by H. Feriz in "Die Darstellung einer Beschneid-

messages that evade or suppress it. How plausible is it that thinkers will inhibit action while appraising the speeches they read or hear? It was plain to Mill that this ideal is achieved only some of the time by educated people in fortunate material circumstances. Even they frequently respond impulsively, or because of passions that blind them to the likely consequences of what they do. What is the chance that people of little education or impulse control, people anxious and angry, will stop to scrutinize propaganda or bigotry presented as information?

Consider that each system is generated and sustained in the broth from which it derives substance and energy. Without these, it degenerates, thereafter supplying material for some other stability. Consider too that each human being is a system, one that sustains itself by extracting information from the world, either directly or from other thinkers. Idealizing the views of Descartes and Mill, with their emphasis upon the difference between consideration and affirmation, we suppose that thinkers are rightly choosy about the information they accept. Yet each of us, like a shark, swims perpetually in a world where information sustains us. Critical or naive, we must eventually accept, and use, some information or other. Sometimes free speech implies our access to good information. Other times, when free speech is the right to fill every ear with misinformation, we are not surprised if some of the people receiving the "news" use it in ways that are pernicious. "How else should we behave," one imagines them saying, "when this is the information available to us?"

Atomist defenses of free speech are naive, because atomists have no adequate understanding of the harms that speech can do. How extensive can that damage be, given an ontology of systems that are sometimes independent, but often reciprocally related, overlapping, or nested? What are the effects of false and malicious speech, given the ramifying character of this world's ontology and the choice of ourselves as primary goods? Here are some considerations to weigh when deliberating about the limits of free speech:

(i) Individuals are affected by the things said of them. This is so because of the structure (the cognitive-affective balance) acquired as we develop and coordinate information, skills, and attitudes in circumstances that articulate our innate talents and inclinations. The result is idiopathic: the combination of information, skills, and attitudes within each person is unique, given our powers at birth, our circumstances, and development. This is the motor that energizes and explains us. Even a sturdy posture is sometimes fragile. For one of the factors that organizes a person's psychic posture is the story he or she tells him or herself about the perception of his or her worth in the eyes of others. This story is partly a surmise founded in the nonverbal behavior of people who respond—approvingly or not—to us. Partly it is constructed from the words that others use when speaking to or about us. They say that we are good or bad, clumsy or graceful, with the result that these views inflect, somewhat, our self-perception. Or they apply one or another of the contraries (each one a compliment or an insult) that are used to describe people who look or believe or support themselves as we do. Sometimes the words make sense in their own right: one is dirty or dumb. Other times, they have no independent sense, though one hears the loathing they voice. How do we factor this information and these feelings into the verbal picture we have of ourselves or of our kind? How should we defend the people abused when their self-valorizing stories are laced with these words, then bound tightly to attitudes of self-approval or rejection. Speech cuts deep.

(ii) Speech that affects an individual affects every system in which this individual fills a role that is performed better or worse because of the way the speech is heard. These effects are facilitated or impeded by the hierarchical relations among systems. Information is spread more quickly because of the nesting which gives authority to a higher-order stability as its views are represented to those of a lower order. Religions, unions, and regimes take advantage of this nesting when presenting their ideas to a captive audience. But equally, nesting impedes the efficacy of speech, when the words addressed to systems of one order are filtered through an embedded or embedding order. This is the effect when family structure distorts or obstructs information intended for children, or when information intended for a company's stockholders is tied up in its finance committee.

Atomism convinces us that the essential separability of persons makes systems unstable, ephemeral even. It should follow that the effects of words on persons cannot be passed along to the systems in which they participate. Equally, systems that never were cannot retain the effects of these words, or interpret their sense to current or future members. But atomism is wrong. Associations are often stable, as we discover when observing that we are a factionalized society, but not an atomistic one. It becomes urgent that we avert the malign speeches which linger in the reactions and rituals of factional memories.

(iii) Speech affects the speaker and the systems in which he or she participates. Some of Joe McCarthy's Republican friends were disabled by the things he said, as Eisenhower shrank—without replying—from the slanderous treatment of

Marshall, his secretary of state. Saying something or nothing, they feared, would damage the party. McCarthy, too, was affected. People treated him differently, so that he drank himself to death.

(iv) Language is fragile, meaning that our confidence in it is enhanced or sabotaged by the uses made of it. Certainly, language has many uses, but one—truth telling—is primary. We rely on the information that language is used to communicate; and because of this reliance, we are mostly flat-footed and credulous in our reception of other people's speech: expecting them to tell the truth, we are prepared to believe them. A language used carefully and responsibly earns credit for its speakers and their language. A language used dishonestly or maliciously comes to be seen and heard as untrustworthy in itself. This is apparent when languages spoken by vicious peoples are shunned for a time, however splendid the previous history of their literature and philosophy.

(v) Every jurisdiction wanting to enforce a policy of free speech has its particular history, with implications for the constraints it imposes on speech. Germany restricts some forms of speech—including publications and the display of flags, even singing and songs—because they are incitements to behaviors like those of Germany's Nazi past. Germans remind us that their democracy is less permissive then ours because their history is different. Should we snigger, saying that our democracy is better than theirs? Or is it more accurate that local history makes them sensitive to the danger that some speech is an incitement to factional violence?

(vi) Speech enhances or hinders the common good. This good is complex. It comprises the tolerance, respect, and dedication that we show one another as we discover our affinities, our mutual dependence, and our fellowship within stable systems. It also includes the instrumental good of the many systems in which we participate and our procedures for self regulation, including our system of public education and deliberation, the neutral judicial procedures that arbitrate our differences, and the legislative ones that establish our priorities and rules. Realizations of this complex good are always imperfect; but this is our aim and the standard for rectifying our failures. Language is the principal instrument for creating this loosely packed one from a fractious many. It codes the information that systems require if they are to coordinate their aims and behaviors. In words or the tone of a speaker's voice, it expresses the attitudes of partners or competitors. Use the words maliciously, and we put dirt in the gears. No other medium has this power. Tyrannies respond with repression. Democracies tell heroic stories of speech's defenders, while giving it special protection.[6]

These six considerations complicate the atomists' hypothesis. They know well enough that speech makes a difference, but not how much difference it makes. Atomists suppose that the effects of speech are benign, either because thought inhibits action, or because the effects dissipate on account of our separability. These assumptions are naive.

VI. MONOPOLISTIC SPEECH

I have been supposing that abuses of free speech are excused by the ontology that promotes it. There is, however, a third abuse, one that makes little sense in atomist terms, though it is explained by the substitute ontology proposed here. This other harm is monopolistic speech. Atomists make little sense of monopolies, because they can only understand them in either or both of two ways: as expressions of power or as the acts of an aggregate. The first is thought to be a function of the second, for the aggregate pools the power of its members to create a force that overwhelms individuals or aggregates that are smaller or less well organized. This is inaccurate, because it fails to acknowledge the character of monopolistic power.

Suppose we live and work in a company town. General Banana owns our houses, pays our wages, and runs our schools. It also publishes and edits our only local newspaper. This is a story of eighty years ago, so there is no radio or television, hence no alternative source of information. We learn, and mostly believe, what the owner-editor prints about the world and ourselves. He is free to print (thus, to say) what he likes. Not liking views different from his own, he doesn't print them.

Atomists will likely describe this situation (after Machiavelli and Hobbes) as the stabilized outcome of power and coercion: the weaker among us submit to the will of the strong. The ontology of systems tells a different story. It says that the mutual dependency of people filling complementary roles is characteristic of utilitarian organizations. These organizations are higher-order systems (relative to their human members) having a character, existence, and interests that are distinct from those of the members. The owner-editor may believe that he is the mere instrument—the voice—of the company, including its several parts. He may actively canvass the company's directors, managers, workers, suppliers, and clients for their ideas, printing articles that express their disparate points of view or their shared dedication to the company. The editor and readers may agree that views not printed express ideas that are distracting or demoralizing. He edits to inform, not to distress or arouse. We object that he frustrates readers who need to form reasoned opinions. He replies that his newspaper promotes opinions appropriate to those who work within this company town: there is no advantage to printing views that would disrupt either their work or their commitment to the company, hence to one another. Authority within the system is distributed for the purpose of efficiency. Workers who read his paper don't need—as they may agree—more information than he supplies.

The systems ontology acknowledges the integrity of the company town and meliorates, somewhat, the apparent abuse of monopolistic speech. But equally, this ontology makes monopolistic speech visible in ways that are denied to atomists: they don't see the corporate power of monopolistic speech, because their oblivion to systems makes them blind to monopolizing systems. Homely anecdotes about Colonel McCormick or Arthur Ochs Sulzberger obscure the reality that corporate speech is no mere variant of the free and reflective speech prescribed by Mill. *Monopoly* in the ears of atomists means that a market is dominated by its one supplier, this editor: his newspaper controls the thinking of its readers on all subjects for which it is their only source of information. Atomists would not agree, because their ontology bars them from conceiving that the newspaper is monopolistic in this other respect: it articulates the interests and objectives of the system in which its readers participate—namely, the company. The paper is the expression of a system reflecting on itself.

The superiority of a systems ontology is all the more apparent if we alter our point of reference: we appraise monopolistic speech by citing an affiliation, rather than an organization. Suppose that the house journal is published by a religious sect. Readers want to see views like their own in print. Finding their beliefs and feelings expressed in this "objective" format confirms them, thereby guaranteeing readers' support for the paper. They buy as many papers as the editor prints; he publishes as soon as copies of the previous issue have been sold. An occasional writer is allowed to dissent from some ritually accepted belief, but only because he or she shares the core views that distinguish members of the sect. This, too, is a monopoly that atomists cannot easily explain. Yes, each of the readers, editors, and writers is an enthusiast, and each expresses this enthusiasm to others of the group. But what creates their affiliation? What distinguishes an aggregate from a community whose members feel and believe the same things? Just the reciprocal, causal relations—here the mirroring—that atomists ignore.

Or atomists misdescribe these relations as expressions of sympathy or loyalty. They don't perceive that such relations convert an aggregate into a system.

Both stories illustrate monopolistic speech. Am I obligated to endorse this sort of speech because it provides evidence for the existence of the systems I am describing? This doesn't follow: we are not required to approve all the effects of entities acknowledged by the ontology we favor, more than we who live as natural creatures favor tooth decay. We appraise monopolistic speech, and every other sort, by considering its consequences. The church newspaper seems unobjectionable if it restricts itself to the affairs of its members, and if the members have other sources of information. Monopolistic speech is more problematic in a company town, because people who work for a company also have other interests and other rules, but *ex hypothesi* no other sources of information. This is dangerous, because their one role—employee—comes to overwhelm every other, including family member and citizen. This is plain when the company paper supports candidates for political office. The company's aims are not always identical with those of its workers, thereby confirming that a system's interest may be opposed to the interests of its members. The company newspaper should not have the power to obscure or hide this difference.

VII. DEFENDING THE VICTIMS OF FREE SPEECH

How should we defend the individuals and systems damaged by free speech? There are two choices as we respond to written or verbal assaults on them.

One is the tolerant, prudent response of liberal sentiment. It affirms that freedom of speech—including speech that exposes privacies, speech that is malicious and false, and monopolistic speech—should be almost unqualified. For we are autonomous agents, protected against interference by inalienable rights that include freedoms from and freedoms to. Freedom to speak and freedom from interference with one's speech are two of these elementary rights. Interference with either one would be an unnatural violation of this ontological state of affairs. Exposure can be ignored by those who don't wish to know; those who do want to know have a right to see everything as it is. False and malicious speech will be discerned. The monopolist cannot be blamed for exercising a right that, in principle, everyone has.

We palliate ourselves with these formulas, ignoring the abuses they disguise, by recounting the many splendid consequences of free speech: individuals will not sharpen their wits if they are not freely criticized; inquiry will be stunted if we cannot share and evaluate one another's views; productive activity will be frustrated if we cannot pursue shared, coordinated aims; government will become tyrannical if it is protected from the criticisms of the governed (think of Richard Nixon cutting out John Dean's tongue); there will be cynicism and despair if people cannot express and share their beliefs about the meaning of life. Suppress free speech, and we lose some or all of these advantages. Almost as bad, we encourage gerrymandered constraints on speech. One speech would be intolerable while another is not, merely because of a word or two, or because of an adventitious difference in the circumstances in which the thing is written or said. Remember too that every constraint on speech is the precedent for a limit more insidious. Isn't the lesson plain? Don't avert severe but local effects by murdering freedom everywhere. Never compromise free speech in any but the most dangerous circumstances—war and crowded theaters, for example.

This cannot be the last word, because free speech is a social policy, not a sacred rite. It is a practice formulated within a society having a particular history and a certain idea of itself. We may not be able to sustain the history or satisfy the idea if we do not limit its real but neglected abuses. I agree that restricting the nearly blanket right of free speech is as dangerous as tinkering with the genetic code. We want to be very careful that we have detailed information about the likely consequences of what we do before doing it. Still, a different policy may work better than the one we have.

VIII. USING ONTOLOGY TO DETERMINE
THE LIMITS OF SPEECH

We are rightly suspicious of the corporate state and of every tribe that makes us parochial. Atomists, suspicious since the Enlightenment of every private society, barely tolerate them.

> The current mess shows the consequences of treating people as members of minorities with special rights rather than as people, all of whom should have the same rights. This habit took hold in Canada in the 1980's when Pierre Trudeau brought home Canada's constitution, the British North America Act, which had lain in London serving its purpose rather well since the country was formed in 1867. At the same time he introduced a charter of rights and freedoms, which brought collective rights all round as well as individual ones. Mr. Trudeau now advocates a No vote on October 26th. If enough people take his advice and Canada breaks up, the rest of the world may not mind, or even notice; but those Canadians who would rather be citizens of a country than members of a cluster of interest groups will feel he has a lot to answer for.[7]

Surely, Canada's problem—and everyone else's too—is that of making a country from a mix of interest groups and from people who distinguish character from role. These stabilities often fight with one another; they challenge their government for authority. But persons and systems, together, have shared interests. They can learn to discuss these interests, while agreeing not to talk about one another in ways that are corrosive.

Dewey described an entity he called "the Great Community."[8] This ideal prefigures a system of stabilities, each one prized by members who value its singular privacy and its reciprocal relations—both practical and political—to the others. Individuals therein would often be self-concerned; systems would sometimes be hermetic and mutually suspicious. Competition and misunderstanding among them would probably be commonplace, but there would be procedures for mediating quarrels. For this is to be a ramified system that regulates itself. The community Dewey favored does not require that we tell people what to say, or that we shut them up before they speak falsely. It does require tolerance or respect, even esteem, for systems different from one's own. "Openness" there would not disguise the fear of difference. "Free speech" would not be a sufficient defense of speech that is monopolistic or malicious and false.

Chapter 7 Conflict

The reciprocities that establish human systems require the coordination of a system's parts. This emphasis on coordination—and cooperation—seems to confirm our idealized belief that harmony is the essential characteristic of all human relations. It should follow that disharmony is evidence of an eliminable distortion. This estimate is hopeful but mistaken. Some human relations express the contrary interests of people or systems that are mutually inimical or irreconcilably different.

This chapter argues that conflict is systemic and ineliminable (not merely the effect of scarcity and crowding), and that its expressions take one or another of the classical dialectical forms. Neither-nor is the style of Parmenides. Neither rest nor motion—neither term in a set of contraries—obtains. Platonic dialectic takes its style from the courts. Contrary truth claims or states of affairs cannot both be true: either-or, it says. Hegelian dialectic is synthetic: both-and supersedes contrariety by synthesizing differences that are otherwise mutually exclusive. Or conflict is resolved by mutual tolerance and conjunction, as Leibniz resolves conflicts of perspective. Notice that dialectic is more than a style of argument, or the trajectory of rational thought. All three forms—neither-nor, either-or, and both-and—are applicable to the ramifying structures and evolution of natural complexes, including human societies.[1]

I. SYSTEMS

Several features of the systems described in Chapter One are significant here. (i) Systems are established and sustained by the causal reciprocity of their parts. The result is stability. (ii) Systems are stabilized—in either of three ways—by a balance of forces. They are static (for example, an informal border is stabilized, because communities of roughly equal size or power live on either side of it, offsetting one another). They have the positive feedback of systems that provoke one another to do as they have done before, until their energy supply is exhausted (stability here is ephemeral, unless the energy supply is vast). Or they exhibit the negative feedback of systems whose constitutive reciprocities are mutually controlling because mutually modulating (that is, A and B respond to one another in ways that stabilize or alter B and A's next response, with the effect that the system evolves or remains as before). These are the styles of dynamic equilibrium. (iii) Every system is a module having an inside and an outside. *Inside* are its reciprocally related parts. Their relations somewhat decouple a system from its environment, so serve as a barrier to influences that would otherwise deflect the activities of the parts. Such barriers do not imply that a system's parts are separated physically from other systems, because of being collected within a protective wall. It is sufficient that the parts relate reciprocally to one another, however distributed they are among other systems: Turkic speakers sustain their mutual relations while scattered among people who speak English only. *Outside* are other systems, some related to this one, some not. A module resists intrusions—this is its integrity—though it often requires a source of energy, material, or information external to itself. Modularity may be described in either of two ways: as autonomy or as resistance to determination by others. (iv) Systems relate to one another in either of four ways: they are mutually independent (as your breathing is independent of mine), reciprocally related (partnerships), overlapping (as the system of parent and child overlaps that of student and teacher), or nested (as the Borough of Hackney, London, England, and Great Britain are a nest of successively higher-order stabilities).

II. CONFLICTS EXPOSED BY THE THREE
STYLES OF DIALECTIC

Consider the three styles of dialectic—neither-nor, either-or, and both-and—as each applies to cases of mutual independence, reciprocity, overlap, and nesting.

Mutual independence is satisfied by mutual oblivion; but it doesn't require mutual indifference or even the absence of causal relations. The condition obtains if systems have no causal relations (gravitation apart) that establish a balance of forces between them. Conflict is notoriously a threat to such systems. Neither-nor is mutually annihilating. Either-or implies a winner and a loser. Both-and implies compromise, resolution, and mutual tolerance. *Reciprocity* is usually a paradigm for the dialectic of both-and: systems that are established and sustained by the reciprocities of their parts may lapse if any part is lost. More complicated systems exploit the alternation of either-or, as when a quartet's two violinists alternate chairs. Neither-nor is inimical to reciprocity: it entails that nothing plays a particular role or that none plays any role within a system, thereby precluding its formation. *Overlap* brings to mind children joined separately to each parent. Neither one nor the other, says a child, renouncing both of them. Or the child is unable to reconcile the parents' competing claims and responds to one by rejecting the other. Or the parents are reconciled by a child who makes him or herself the medium of their accommodation. *Nesting* is the predicament of people who are caught between the competing levels and duties of a hierarchy. Someone who is trapped between the unreconciled demands of state and federal laws emigrates: neither-nor, he says. Or a community makes a forced choice—either-or—as border states chose the Union or the Confederacy. Or members force compromise on the two systems in which they nest, as when taxpayers—saying both-and—negotiate reconciling changes in state and federal laws.

The conflicts generated by neither-nor and either-or are pervasive in nature, not only in human societies. For nature is everywhere stressed by contrary demands. Think of cities astride continental plates moving in opposite directions, or of people alternately fried or frozen because they live in places overlapped by polar and southerly winds. Still, human societies are remarkable among natural phenomena for the use they make of these tensions. Earthquakes and civil conflict destroy cities; but societies sometimes harmonize their tensions. We have Cuban-Chinese restaurants and Bach played on synthesizers.

These solutions are odious to purists, who insist that both-and is a formula for capitulation. They are annoyed by a system that responds syncretically to the tensions of its situation, because, as they see it, every accommodation qualifies the uncompromising identity they prize. Either-or, they say, is the condition for stabilizing something worthwhile. This belligerence is consequential: both-and reduces tensions; either-or is a policy that intensifies them.

III. CONFLICT WITHIN AND AMONG SOCIETIES

Conflict is chronic within and among human societies for one or more of four reasons. (i) Every society sustains itself by appropriating people and things. Each differentiates people and systems in ways that are appropriate to its history, technology and resources. But then, every difference of function or altered direction is an open door to competition for resources, position, or opportunities. These conflicts are endemic within societies. They are schismatic, and all the more unequal in the competition among societies. (ii) Each society applies and updates its rationale as its circumstances change. This happens as societies justify themselves to old members when economic or social conditions change, or when war occurs. It happens, too, as societies explain themselves to new members whether converts, immigrants, or the young, in ways that alter with changes in circumstances and these recruits. Every society raises banners, schools, or merely its corporate voice to suppress the din of other voices in the ears of its members: advertisers compete for market share, political parties for votes. (iii) Each society balances its corporate interest against the interests of its members. This tension is never resolved, as states compete with the federal government for tax revenue.

(iv) Reciprocity, overlap, or nesting are three flash points for conflict, three zones of disruption. Multiculturalism is their incubator. It is problematic in different ways, according as cultures are restricted to separate states or, as peoples of different cultures, share the same city or state. These are problems of purpose, coherence, and reciprocity. Purpose is first, because societies have distinguishing values and aims, hence different bases for affiliation: one favors polygamy, another polyandry. Someone who participates in two or more such systems may be confused to the point of paralysis. This effect is commonplace when disparate cultures share the same civil society. For then, schools, work, and intermarriage promote accommodation without eliminating conflict. These conflicts of value make people and systems defensive, at cost to civil society. Unwilling to form associations that engage people of different factions, such people are irreparably alien to those having viewpoints or practices different from their own. With little or no reciprocity between them, there is no mutual dependence or respect to bind them. Hostility and suspicion, not amity and interdependence, dominate their mutual perceptions. How is a one produced from a many such as this? It is created (or intimated) by forced encounters where both sides learn that their differences are variations of the same generic interests and needs; by the bold (or rejected) few who cross from one side to the other in marriage; by the fragile network of mediators who consider tolerable ways of sharing their common space; or by the rare members of either faction who look beyond parochial interests to imagine viable—even fruitful—relations between them. If one faction is rich and fearful, while the other is poor and morose, there may be little chance of strong bonds between them. Give them similar material conditions and advantages, and they may discover the benefits of mutual care. Or find an art or activity—music, for example—that gives pleasure to members of all factions. The bonds made there may slowly extend to other things.

IV. THE DIALECTIC OF CONFLICT

There is conflict among systems because they compete for energy, for position (hence for support or control), or for parts. We sharpen our perception of these conflicts by applying the three dialectical rubrics.

(i) Neither a society nor its competitor can have all the resources for which they compete. We have a struggle—with either-or as our principle—before settling for a distribution in the style of both-and. Societies may be mutually annihilating, but this is rare. More often, competition is resolved—in war or negotiation—by dividing the matters disputed. This strategy is only partially successful: it settles some disputes but merely suppresses continuing points of discord in others. No wonder that "absolute victory"—either-or—is more attractive than having to negotiate a difference. Negotiation is especially irksome when the difference is ideological. For we may not want to be reminded that there are identity-making rationales different from our own. We may tolerate these differences, as we do the choice of chopsticks or knife and fork: both-and is a viable strategy if there is space for both. But we don't always like myths or interpretations different from our own. We get the friction of either-or when neither side can smother or absorb the other. Though each may tire of their conflict, so that both-and becomes acceptable to them. Both survive to declare their anomalous "truths."

(ii) Either-or is the dialectical strategy of the powerful. A system that is convinced of its virtue and strong enough to pilfer another's resources doesn't share the available goods or suffer the effrontery of values different from its own. Societies, at every order of complexity—from families bickering with neighbors to religions and nation-states—are self-valorizing, so each is convinced of its entitlement. Extermination and forced conversion are common features of our history.

The modularity of societies—each one somewhat decoupled from others because of its reciprocal causal relations—already guarantees competition for people and materials. This conflict is intensified by overlap and multiple nesting, for the cost of change is greater if one cannot step off one foot without breaking the other. A growing company chooses between loyalty to its employees and duty to its creditors. A political party faces schism because its members are aligned with opposing sides of an issue that has no middle ground. Either-or is wrenching and destructive. Human systems are chronically made and remade because of it.

(iii) Both-and is the cure for neither-nor and either-or. This is the way of pacifiers everywhere. Nietzsche despised it. Dewey told us how to achieve it. Start, he said, with vast space and resources. Encourage freedom, but teach mutual respect and the prudence that makes us sensitive to the public good. Anticipate conflict or quickly resolve the conflicts that occur by diverting attention from points of conflict to neglected opportunities for community or compromise: why fight over a parking place if there are others across the street, or if walking would avert the conflict.

Both-and is the dialectic of plenty and the promise of harmony. It is a splendid idea, and a working principle in circumstances where space or other resources are amply supplied. But this is also the dialectic of delusion. Its universal application is founded in Luther and Descartes, each emphasizing the dignity and self-sufficiency of the individual. The utilitarianism of Bentham and Mill is also decisive, because the greatest good for the greatest number implies that equally worthy individuals should share, to more or less equal effect, this world's goods. The diversity of our self-interests should be harmonizable in the aggregate of our enjoyments. Too bad that this splendid aim obscures the structural limits to its application. One limit is the consideration that no stability is sustained without a source of energy. Some elementary systems—protons, for example—store this energy within themselves. Social systems must extract it from their environment. Systems that compete for scarce people and materials cannot both survive. Nor is conflict always resolvable—the second limit—in the case of overlapping or multiply nested stabilities. The man forced to choose between his golf club and his principles may not find a harmonizing resolution. Neither-nor, more likely either-or, spoils the syncretist dream.

V. KANTIAN SOLUTIONS

Conflict is pervasive, and ineliminable, if reality comprises stable systems that compete for parts and energy, vindication, or position and control. There would seem to be no way to eliminate this fact about us, given the reality of conflicts within and among systems (because of overlap and nesting), scarcity, contrary world views, and our aggressive self-valorization. But there are some ways to ameliorate it. (i) We inform ourselves about the basis for conflict and its costs. (ii) We anticipate and avert conflict because of its price. (iii) We try to establish a variety of opportunities and resources big enough that competitors may seek and find alternatives to conflict. (iv) We learn tolerance and respect for aims different from our own, hence a willingness to accept less control and fulfillment for the benefit of a personal or group interest in return for viable working relations among systems. Or (v) we enjoy—even celebrate—the competition of systems, taking care to regularize the terms of conflict within a playing field that we call the "market." Or (vi) the many systems renounce self-help and the market for a Hobbesian authority that suppresses obstreperous systems in the name of an uneasy peace.

America goes through cycles in which it cannot decide between prudence, enhanced opportunities, and tolerance (options i–iv), or Spencerian evolution (the survival of the fittest, option v). This is our version of the perpetual standoff between strategies of effective conflict and those of effective cooperation. Kant had a solution. He believed that conflict is averted if each person's every action satisfies the categorical imperative: confirm that your maxim could be a universal law because it entails no contradiction. Kant assumed that universalizable maxims can never conflict (on the principle that everything distinguishable is separable), so that behaviors sanctioned by one maxim cannot have averse consequences for behaviors sanctioned by a different one. Or he imagined (but never stated) a vastly complicated maxim, one that averts every conflict. The first of these alternatives—maxims and their consequences are separable—is false to the inextricable conflicts generated by cultural overlap and multiple nesting. These are principal sites for beliefs and practices that are congenial to one group but anathema to another, and for the conflicting duties of people who are loyal to both sides. The other alternative—a universalizable maxim that averts or re-solves every anomaly—is all but unthinkable. Saying that God can think it is no solution.

Kant's views are also unsatisfactory on their epistemological side. We have his story—embellished by Fichte—of thinkers who schematize thinkable worlds in pursuit of their aims. "No striving," said Fichte, "no object."[2] This is Kant's persuasion in the *Critique of Judgment*,[3] and also the opinion of the many con-temporary idealists who describe themselves as pragmatists. Rightly supposing that we use plans to direct our behaviors, they infer from a successfully executed plan that nothing in the world opposes us: there is no conflict; everything goes our way. A Kantian pragmatist may want to generalize. Install the kingdom of ends; let everyone pursue the plan of his life, satisfying himself of its truth when his days are prosperous and happy. This is problematic. Is there a kingdom of ends, each one ample in itself and remote from, but respectful of, others? Where is the perspective from which to observe the several world-makers, each one making a world that harmonizes with every other? Do we—did Kant or James—have knowledge of a domain so ample that it sustains all projects?

This was an attractive fantasy when, in Locke's words, "All the world was America." We could imagine other thinkers, each one centered in the world of its making, all of them pursuing their aims at a safe distance from oneself. Con-flict among these transcendental egos is only notional if their worlds and pur-poses are never coupled to our own. But actual people and systems are mutually engaged, affecting, and responsible whenever they are reciprocally related, over-lapping, or nested. Conflict is the inevitable consequence of these relations, with nothing but regulated compromise to allay it. Kant would agree about the need for regulation, but he erred by implying that we eliminate conflict by willing the categorical imperative.

We may hope to vindicate Kant in our time by saying that these claims about conflicted systems are merely the features of a story, one we may reject. This is a strategy applicable to every hegemonic interpretation of the world. We save ourselves from it by discovering its motivating values, then by discounting it and them while inventing a more congenial interpretation and world of our own. World-making—in the hands of either Kant or the pragmatic idealists—is a de-vice for abstracting ourselves from conflicts we have not made to better worlds of our own design. But no one lives for ever within his productive imagination. Is there a common domain in which our various world-making stories have ap-plication? These idealists—for whom reality is never more than the projection of a conceptual system—have no way to describe it. They prefer coherent stories about the world—conflict-resolving stories—to the recognition of real conflict. Marx deplored the aestheticized harmonies of his Hegelian contemporaries. We should deplore them too.

VI. REPAIRING CONFLICT

Dialectic is more than talk. Either-or, especially, is a tide that runs simultaneously in opposite directions. Systems are established or sustained by the coordination of their parts, and sometimes by relations that join them to other systems. Conflict is the countervailing tension. Benign conflict is competition; less viably, conflict subverts the relations and parts of human systems.

Structural conflicts are a principal challenge to regulation. They alone would be enough to justify the creation of a public. For there seems to be no way of regulating conflicts from a position among them. Participants restart to power when dividing the spoils leaves some of them dissatisfied; or the shifting alliances that regulate some systems leave others uncontrolled. The public has leverage of a different sort, because it stands outside these conflicts.

Making the public an effective regulator also requires that we supersede this other instance of either-or. We need to establish an informed, stable, uncorrupted citizenry, while finding a place within our deliberations for the systems whose conflicts provoke regulation. Atomism denies the reality of systems, in order to justify their exclusion from the public. One understands the motive, but regrets the result: real systems, vying for advantage, subvert the public. How can we acknowledge these higher-order systems, ontologically and constitutionally, while recovering the powers of a citizenry organized for self-regulation? It isn't enough to repeat that we are self-valorizing goods-in-themselves, while they, whatever their advantages for us, are instrumental goods. How can higher-order human systems be made part of the regulative process without giving them so much power that they overwhelm the voices of private citizens? We need practical solutions to this conflict, while powerful systems still give lip service to the idea that we, the citizens, are sovereign.

Chapter 8 Ecology

Our notions of man and society too often abstract us from the physical context in which we secure and satisfy ourselves. *Ecology* studies the reciprocal relations of contiguous living systems (whether individuals or species) and the relations of these systems to their circumstances, including temperature, radiation, and rainfall. It locates us within nature, as natural creatures.

Five points dominate our thinking about nature's relation to human societies: nature as *constituent material, context, resource, challenge,* and *limit.* We are composed of natural materials (carbon compounds, for example) and subject to whatever laws regulate them. Nature is our context: we live within it as natural creatures. Nature supplies resources used to secure or satisfy us. Its laws and materials challenge our ingenuity: how can they be used for our benefit? Nature is a limit: it resists us, while giving way to careful manipulation. Molecular biology breaches some of the limits that have evolved. But no one expects that we shall one day change the laws of motion.

Nature as context (not merely as resource) would seem to be the ideal test of my claims that systems are reciprocally related, nested, and overlapping, that health is a normative ideal for human systems, and that self-regulation is a principal condition for both the health of individual systems and the stability of their mutual relations. We have Aldo Leopold's remark that nature as context—the "biotic pyramid"—"is a tangle of chains so complex as to seem disorderly, yet the stability of the system proves it to be a highly organized structure. Its functioning depends on the cooperation and competition of its diverse parts."[1] This characterization of nature is unexceptionable, but less than we require of a statement that does justice to some principal ambiguities in the relations of humans to our natural context. For Leopold's focus is narrow: he is writing of food chains:

> The species of a layer are alike not in where they came from, or in what they look like, but rather in what they eat. Each successive layer depends on those below it for food and often for other services, and each in turn furnishes food and services to those above…. Man shares an intermediate layer with the bears, raccoons, and squirrels which eat both meat and vegetables.[2]

Our relations to nature are not adequately characterized by generalizing from food chains. For nothing in our self-conception prepares us to accept a place alongside bears, raccoons, and squirrels, merely because our energy suppliers are comparable. Resembling other animals in many ways, we differ from them in ways that Leopold ignores, such as language, technology, moral sense, and social organization. Haven't we learned from Plato that animal appetites (including those that express a need for energy) are the least ennobling of human virtues and desires? Could we—should we—inhibit these other talents in order to reclaim a place among our biotic peers? What place would this be? Should we abandon cities to live in caves, though most of our principal achievements are created and sustained in the dense networks—cities—where nature often seems reduced to a patch of sky.[3]

We distinguish, accordingly, between nature as context and nature as resource. The idea of nature as context is irrefutable good sense to everyone who believes that we are natural creatures. Yet, the "man-land community"[4] is not a plausible trajectory for us humans, if it implies that we can, should, or will make ourselves suitable companions for creatures having similar animal appetites, and that we should use no more energy than is required to sustain ourselves and reproduce. Nor does Leopold tell us how to reinsert ourselves into nature while preserving our aptitudes and achievements. He only reminds us that nature is our context as well as our resource, so that we sabotage ourselves by poisoning or exhausting it. I acknowledge nature's role as context, but emphasize its use as resource in the remarks that follow.

It will disturb some readers that the value I ascribe to nature is either parasitic on our self-valorization or an instance of the instrumental value ascribed to things because of their effects on us. (I deny that nature is good in itself, for the reason that nothing is good in itself. We humans value ourselves; but this act of self-election falls short of demonstrating, or even implying, that we are intrinsic goods.) Where only two kinds of value are acknowledged, nature is valuable in either or both ways. We extend our self-valorization to nature, our context, as we also value other systems that engage us; or nature has instrumental value as our resource—it supplies goods that secure and satisfy us, and bads that afflict us.

There are two sorts of ecology to which values are pertinent. *Scientific* ecology has two aims: it describes both the reciprocal relations that bind individual species and circumstances within an ecosystem (what does each do to the others, and how is each affected?) and the architecture and economy of each ensemble of reciprocally related circumstances and systems. *Moral* ecology proposes that we acknowledge other systems respectfully, while occupying our place among them. It reproaches us when ignorance of our place in nature makes us heedless about polluting it. It laments the effects of our carelessness on our heirs: the resources exhausted and the places spoiled will diminish their lives. Or moral ecology explains our obsessive consumption as an anxiety: we appease uncertainty about our worth by sating ourselves. We could behave differently, says this view, if we learned to experience the simpler pleasures of our natural rhythms. These moral prescriptions are not universally approved. Should we rise at sundown and sleep at sunset? Should we suffer tooth decay out of respect for the bacteria that cause it? How far must we go to make ourselves authentic in the eyes of moral ecologists?

There is also a prior question about the relations of scientific and moral ecology: do the descriptions of the one entail the prescriptions of the other? How much of the *is* sponsors an *ought?* Three prescriptions are rightly made and observed, even before we consider the injunctions of the moralists. (i) We shouldn't waste our time trying to do what natural creatures can never do, as we cannot leave our place in nature for an extra-physical heaven. We need this maxim, because some people make a contrary assumption. They sacrifice goats or armies in wars that are calculated to save their souls. Doing this is misguided if there is no salvation apart from the system of reciprocities in which we live.

(ii) The power to change our natural constitution (hence the character of our relations to other things and our niche) is limited, though the form acquired over the course of our evolutionary development will surely be altered by genetic management. Nothing we do will change the laws of motion or the structure of spacetime; they express the defining form of the possible world instantiated here. (iii) We should take a sober look at the myths that have shaped the conception of our place in nature. Are we really the beneficiaries of an Earth created only so that there may be ample resources for us, God's creatures? Doubting that this story is true, we want attitudes more appropriate to natural creatures having a short life span and no exalted place in the cosmos, however much we tinker with our genes.

How do we construe our place in the world when our importance is radically diminished? This was a theoretical and theological question in the nineteenth century. Now, when the issue is practical only, we don't want to poison the well from which our water comes. Controlling our effects upon things about us is the condition for our current and future hopes of securing ourselves. Our responsibilities to other species are more vexing: how respectful of them should we be? Should there be no more medical research using other animals as experimental subjects? Should all of us be vegetarians, because destroying vegetables is better than eating other animals, there being no pain for the vegetables; or is meat eating permitted to us because animals without our moral sense are carnivores?

Is there a principled way of choosing a morally superior style of living within our niche? One proposal affirms that harmony is natural to ecological systems, each species having a place appropriate to itself, one it fills while behaving in a way determined by its nature. This is Aristotelian ecology. It would have us identify the styles of health appropriate to reciprocally related species, we humans included. Behaving as our human style requires, we would occupy and hold our place as, presumably, other species hold theirs. For we are the unpredictable species, given the variability of our passions and our inability to discern and keep the mean.

Ignore Aristotle's essentialism and his neglect of evolution. Is there something to rehabilitate in his idea that there is a standard of health appropriate to our engagement with nature? Can we preserve some part of the idea that nature is our context, not only our resource? Here, as in Chapter Four, ecological health is a norm that directs us. Bodily health is achieved when myriad, mutually conditioning processes (in and among cells, tissues, and organs) are maintained within certain ranges of variation by the reciprocities of cells, tissues, and organs. Their complex product is the homeostasis that sustains internal order so long as there is no breakdown within a system, no assault from outside it, and a regular supply of energy. The analogy to ecosystems requires only that reciprocities of species are substituted for the reciprocities of bodily parts. Here, too, health is a dynamic steady state, given an energy supply and no breakdowns or interference. We add the proviso that no dramatic evolutionary changes alter the behaviors of constituent species: vegetarians don't become carnivores. Health is an immanent norm, because bodily health is real, and because its relation to ecological health is a formal identity, not a metaphor: steady-state reciprocity is common to both. Do we challenge this claim by remarking that species and the relations of species change, while the relations of bodily parts are static by comparison? The answer is that relations among some species are also steady; and that relations or bodily organs are altered when one organ accommodates itself to change in another (heart and lungs, for example). The analogy is intact: there may be functional integrity in humans or ecosystems, whether or not there are evolving, mutually accommodating changes in either.

Functional integrity is a physical, not a moral, norm: we acknowledge its implications, but we may or may not choose to conform to it. The fact of having this choice evokes a comparison. We have no margin of freedom with respect to the laws of motion: we conform, always and necessarily. The health of ecosystems is more permissive: it is variable within a range wherein each complex value expresses the mutual accommodation of several or many systems. Nor are homeostases coercive for the subsystems engaged. They change, because their energy supplies are exhausted, because they have evolved, or because they are willfully short-sighted.

There is a cost for failing to do such things as sustain ecological steady states: they break down, so that systems comprising them have to fend for themselves, if they can. This is not a problem from one point of view, because homeostasis re-forms at another level of complexity, usually, though not always, a lower level. It is a problem for us humans, because the span of our projects and even our lives is short. Lost ecological health precludes success in the projects that secure life or make it satisfactory. Systems that lose their niche more often die than adjust.

We prudently manage our reciprocal relations to the other species of our ecosystem in ways that have these two effects: we sustain (or decline to damage) them, while securing and satisfying ourselves. The first constrains the second: it requires that care for ourselves should come at least cost to the systems reciprocally related to us. Why? Because we prize the ground having consequences we desire: namely, the sustained reciprocity between them and ourselves.

This is the least we do to contribute the health of our natural context. For this is modest good sense. It acknowledges Plato's distinction between the simple and luxurious states, the one healthy, the other suffering "a fevered state" because citizens lack self-control.[5] Still, this ecological health is slippery: we may care for it only when health is gone. Worse, ecological health is too often opposed to the interests of bodily health, as we exterminate the smallpox bacterium rather than defend its niche within us. Moral ecology—in the version that promotes a universal good neighbor policy— is offended. Even descriptive ecology is annoyed. Its modest precepts (listed above) assume that there is a natural give-and-take among the species of an ecosystem: we hold the bacteria at bay for a time, but eventually they get us. Nothing in this balanced story acknowledges that the perceived interests and technology of us humans have superseded this natural state. Indeed, my characterization of ecological health is too romantic: it ignores the competition and evolution of species and niches. Nature is not, everywhere, a harmony. Ecological health is not only the task of learning the proper rhythm, then of altering our behavior until it harmonizes, unobtrusively, with the rhythms of others. The more cogent issue is this: what should we humans do to minimize our impact on species and circumstances whose relations establish a niche for us (let alone on those having little or no effect on us)? There is no satisfactory answer, until we respond to an antecedent question: namely, how shall we secure and satisfy ourselves? We regret that our self-concern is morally shocking *sub specie aeternitatis,* and that it is costly to other species. But self-regard demands that we calculate our relations to other species in order to profit by exploiting them. Nothing in this justifies cruelty or vandalism; it implies no desire to subvert ourselves by poisoning things that support us. That we value our reciprocities to the other species of our ecosystem is prudent good sense. That we shape these reciprocities for purposes of our own expresses our self-regard. We take our scruples from the descriptive ecologists: our vulnerability as a species is reduced by our mutually supporting relations to the other circumstances and species of a stable ecosystem. Still, we have come to realize that we humans are viable within many different ecosystems. These include steady states without goony birds or passenger pigeons.

This is ugly opportunism or realism, depending on one's sympathies. I prefer the realist side, because I doubt that value is projected into the world when we humans esteem ourselves as its principal goods. Moral ecologists answer that we are self-deceived. I agree that we misperceive our value; but what is the choice? Should we cease to value ourselves, because of discovering that we are merely self-elected, not intrinsic, goods? It is better to concede our self-importance, then to add that our role in nature was altered irrevocably at the point when human intelligence began to contrive the means for enhancing our security and satisfaction. There would have been little harm had we merely used sticks to knock fruit off trees. But that was not the extent of our ability, or disruption. Technology vastly enhances the ability to control our circumstances, at cost to the species we affect, all of them. The naive story of the give-and-take— the vibrant harmony and ecological health—in which we humans participate is a romantic gloss of our species' relations to others. It has never been more than a myth since the days of our early, concerted interventions in nature, well before the first human settlements. Every technological development since that time deepens the story's fatuity. For there is no harmony and little charity on our part for species different from our own. We have not cared for their well-being, thanks to the biblical story and our ecological ignorance. We would not have cared very much had we known our effects on them, given our self-love.

This is the reason for saying that the least of our concern for environmental health—the desire to sustain the stable, dynamic balance of our natural context—is also the maximum of our concern: not wanting to live with bears and raccoons, we do whatever we need do to raise ourselves above them. Our primary objective—now that we know the ecological costs to *ourselves*—is prudential. Is the progression from small-scale intrusions to pervasive changes irreparably dangerous for us? The changes already accomplished may be deadly; but change itself is not mortal, or even threatening, so long as one or another tolerable equilibrium is established among the circumstances and species that remain. The possibility for a succession of survivable steady states nourishes our hopes: can we navigate ourselves into a series of them? Passive acquiescence, with no further balance-altering assaults on nature, is not a likely choice, given the advantages of our inventive technology. But such assaults may not be intolerable to nature. For consider: which of our intrusions has it failed to support? Should human population growth have been stopped at five million? Should we let it run to six billion? What are the viable limits when the intrusiveness of our numbers and technology have long ago frayed any hope for our discreet presence in nature?

These are questions for scientific, not moral, ecology. For it is no more than affectation when we pretend to find our way politely into nature, rather as someone makes his way back to a theater seat after the performance has started. We can hardly walk so softly or insert ourselves so carefully as not to disturb our seatmates. We are large-scale spoilers, at our best. What would we have to do, given an ecological notion of health, to change this state of affairs? Collecting soft drink cans and recycling paper are a beginning, but these are gestures. They make a very small difference to the magnitude of our intrusion. Should each of us do better, perhaps extending a bare leg to as many bugs as can bite us without making a difference to our health and mobility? Ecologists on the moral side do not go this far. Nor do they argue successfully that we humans may satisfy ourselves while making only a ripple in the systems related causally to us. We are too many; our organizations require more resources than can ever be supplied without vastly altering the balance of nature in every domain where we intrude. What does *ecology* mean in Manhattan or even in Boise? It is too late for us to pretend that we are bees among the flowers.

Suppose we acknowledge the magnitude of our intrusions. Should we apologize? Ice ages, tornadoes, and meteorites also have environmental effects. Like them, we humans are a large-scale ecological disaster; though we, unlike them, have an excuse: we are self-valorizing, while other things have instrumental value only. Some of them have good effects on or for us, so we use them accordingly. Things that have no utility for us are trampled or annihilated. Moral ecologists who deplore this attitude think that the world would be better off without us: nature would restore itself, allowing for long periods of diversity and complexity in places denuded by our excesses. This is not an outcome that most of us would voluntarily choose. The most we can do to satisfy these ecologists is to prudently manage the ecosystems on which our well-being depends. There are six policies that ecologists encourage: (i) We should limit human reproduction: fewer consumers put less pressure on other species and resources. (ii) We should be more efficient in our use of resources, so that pressure is reduced on other systems, while leaving raw materials for future generations of humans. (iii) We should rethink our notions of satisfaction. We want more for ourselves than we need, partly because we have lost sight of simpler pleasures. (iv) We need to replace what we use, planting trees where we cut them, cleaning air and water we have dirtied. (v) We should eliminate industrial and military practices that damage the environment in ways we cannot fix because of inadequate time, resources, or technology (radioactive waste, for example). (vi) Granting that they have no intrinsic value, we may care for the welfare of other species because of their instrumental value: many support our well-being; all enhance the pleasure we take in their beauty and variety.

These policies imply a warning: that we subvert ourselves by ignoring practices that sabotage the material conditions for human well-being. They also imply grim predictions for many niches and species so long as our technological civilization endures. For there is no doubt: thousands of species will be exterminated as we remake the environment to suit us. We risk obliterating ourselves, either directly or by destroying conditions for the biodiversity that supports human life.

Is the loss of other species offset by the goodness and beauty that we create? There is no common measure for things so anomalous. Having no measure, we choose ourselves. Why not choose ourselves, and the other species, too? Because the size of the Ark is limited by the number and appetite of us humans. How many of them? At what cost to us? Zoos, not wilds; many fewer species: this would be a favorable result. Even this outcome will elude us if we ignore those interspecific reciprocities that limit our freedom but save our lives.[6]

Afterword

Metaphysics is often thought to be an a priori discipline, thereby implying that its relevance to matters of fact is indirect: we suppose that metaphysics applies to them only as it discovers universal truths that warp every particular in any possible world. There are universal principles of this sort. There are also some parochial universals, meaning principles that apply to, and distinguish, our world. Such local principles are not known a priori. We infer fallibly to them after examining the states of affairs that obtain here. This cascade of determinations starts in the principles of noncontradiction, excluded middle, and identity and the truths of arithmetic. They apply in every possible world. A more limited set of determinations is established (for example) by the relation of space and time to motion: motion presupposes space and time, wherever it obtains. One step down are the more specific designs—including particular laws of motion and a geometry of spacetime—that differentiate particular worlds. Every such world gives distinguishing expression to universal truths. We know these worlds only as we observe, and make testable hypotheses about, their laws and constituents.

My claims about stable systems (in Chapter One) apply to our world and to those that may be like it in possibility or (if any there be) in actuality. These claims mix empirically grounded arguments (about the determinability of properties) with empirical examples. The other chapters (Chapters Two through Eight) test my ontological hypothesis in particular dimensions (persons, sociality, and value) and domains (deliberation, free speech, conflict, and ecology). It does seem that nature, including human psychology and sociality, comprises systems that are mutually independent, reciprocally related, overlapping, or nested.

Dewey emphasized associations—systems—while denying that we can explain them:

> There is no mystery about the fact of association, an interconnected action which affects the activity of singular elements. There is no sense in asking how individuals comes to be associated. They exist and operate in association. If there is any mystery about the matter, it is the mystery that the universe is the kind of universe it is. Such a mystery could not be explained without going outside the universe. And if one should go to an outside source to account for it, some logician, without an excessive draft upon his ingenuity, would rise to remark that the outsider would have to be connected with the universe in order to account for anything in it. We should still be just where we started, with the fact of connection as a fact to be accepted.[1]

There is no mystery. Determining relations among eternal possibles are realized in our instantiated world as causal relations. Systems are created and stabilized when reciprocal causal relations join their parts. Negative feedback—mutual control of interacting parts— affords self-control in human systems.

Dewey shunned metaphysical hypotheses. This one would have appeased him.

Notes

INTRODUCTION

1. "There is no *social entity* with a good that undergoes some sacrifice for its own good. There are only individual people, different individual people, with their own individual lives": Robert Nozick, *Anarchy, State, and Utopia* (New York: Basic Books, 1974), p. 33.
2. Elaine Sternberg, *Just Business* (London: Little, Brown, 1994), pp. 30–61.
3. For a survey of atomism, see Talcott Parsons, *The Structure of Social Action* (New York: Free Press, 1964), pp. 51–60.
4. Willard V. O. Quine, "Two Dogmas of Empiricism," in *From a Logical Point of View* (New York: Harper and Row, 1961), pp. 20–46.
5. C. S. Peirce, *Collected Papers of Charles Sanders Peirce,* ed. Charles Hartshorne and Paul Weiss (Cambridge, Mass.: Harvard University Press, 1965), vol. 5, pp. 113–127.
6. David Weissman, *Hypothesis and the Spiral of Reflection* (Albany, N.Y.: State University of New York Press, 1989), pp. 102–130.
7. I join *space* and *time* because space and time are jointly presupposed by motion (e.g., of light), this being the point of their integration within relativity theory. We may distinguish them when emphasizing their distinctive roles within art and music, or (*pace* Kant and Bergson) within "lived experience," but there is no compelling evidence that space and time are anywhere separable in our world.

8. Aristotle, *Metaphysics,* in *The Basic Works of Aristotle,* ed. Richard McKeon (New York: Random House, 1941), pp. 783–834.

9. Aristotle, *Physics,* in *Basic Works,* pp. 213–394; *De anima,* in *Basic Works,* pp. 533–603; *Nicomachean Ethics,* in *Basic Works,* pp. 927–1126.

10. Thomas Hobbes, *Leviathan,* ed. Michael Oakeshott (Oxford: Basil Blackwell, 1947).

11. Aristotle, *Metaphysics,* pp. 784–786.

12. Thomas Aquinas, *Selected Writings of St. Thomas Aquinas,* trans. Robert P. Goodwin (Indianapolis: Bobbs-Merrill, 1965), pp. 38–39, 44–45.

13. Plato, *Republic,* in *Collected Dialogues,* ed. Edith Hamilton and Huntington Cairns (New York: Pantheon, 1961), pp. 668–687.

14. Augustine, *The City of God,* trans. Gerald G. Walsh et al. (New York: Doubleday, 1962), pp. 323–425.

15. G. W. F. Hegel, *The Phenomenology of Mind,* trans. J. B. Baillie (New York: Harper and Row, 1967), pp. 293–327.

16. "Sinners are attractive because they are loved; they are not loved because they are attractive": Martin Luther, *Basic Theological Writings* (Minneapolis: Fortress, 1989), p. 48.

17. René Descartes, *Discourse on Method and Mediations on First Philosophy,* ed. David Weissman (New Haven: Yale University Press, 1996), pp. 63–70.

18. Immanuel Kant, *Critique of Practical Reason and Other Works,* trans. Thomas Kingsmill Abbott (London: Longmans, 1963), p. 51.

19. John Stuart Mill, *On Liberty* (New York: Macmillan, 1987).

20. Talcott Parsons, *Structure and Process in Modern Societies* (New York: Free Press, 1960), pp. 110–113.

21. Descartes affirmed thought's freedom when he argued that each of us may assert his own existence as a thinker, though everything else is dubitable: Descartes, *Discourse on Method and Meditations on First Philosophy,* p. 64. Mill makes a similar point by claiming freedom of thought regarding matters of every sort (*On Liberty,* p. 16).

22. Ernest Nagel, "Wholes, Sums, and Organic Unities," in *Parts and Wholes,* ed. Daniel Lerner (New York: Free Press, 1963), pp. 135–155.

23. John Rawls, *A Theory of Justice* (Cambridge, Mass.: Harvard University Press, 1971), pp. 3–192.

24. John Stuart Mill, *Utilitarianism* (Indianapolis: Hackett, 1979), p. 14.

25. Lesley A. Jacobs, *An Introduction to Modern Philosophy* (Upper Saddle River, N.J.: Prentice-Hall, 1997), pp. 103–104. Jacobs is paraphrasing Derek Phillips, *Looking Backward: A Critical Appraisal of Communitarian Thought* (Princeton, N.J.: Princeton University Press, 1993), pp. 14–18.

26. I disagree that nature has no decided structure—no categorial form—of its own, merely because the relative autonomy and incommensurability of our theories are obstacles to discerning it. This holistic construal of meaning, hence of texts, precludes the translation (or reduction) of any theory of nature into any other. Where the incommensurability of texts is evidence for the autonomy of their authors, we reject the idea of a unitary nature and affirm the integrity of the many thinkers, each pursuing his value-driven interpretation of things. Notice the affinity of this view to hermeneutical claims about the autonomy of individual texts (e.g., novels, poems, and plays): each text—and perhaps each in-

terpretation of it—is a domain of meanings, each meaning a function of the others, none separable from the others without distortion of them and itself. This deconstructionist aim is also apparent: we expose and repudiate the realist dream that there may be a good representation of nature itself. For the view at issue, see Paul Feyerabend, *Against Method* (London: NLB, 1975); and John Dupré, *The Disorder of Things* (Cambridge, Mass.: Harvard University Press, 1995), esp. pp. 244–264. Dupré remarks: "There can be nothing unique about science, because there is nothing common to the various domains of science" (p. 263). This implies, contrary to abundant evidence, that astronomy, chemistry, biology, cooking, engineering, and medicine have nothing in common with physics. I suppose that physics describes properties, laws, and processes that are common to all their subject matters, though each domain introduces systems and properties which vary for reasons discussed in Chapter One.

27. David Weissman, *Eternal Possibilities* (Carbondale, Ill.: Southern Illinois University Press, 1977); *Intuition and Ideality* Albany, N.Y.: State University of New York Press, 1987); *Hypothesis and the Spiral of Reflection;* and *Truth's Debt to Value* (New Haven: Yale University Press, 1993).

28. Some contemporary thinkers believe that reality is created when conceptual systems are used to differentiate and organize sensory data, words, or sentences. These idealists have a phrase for us realists: we are "rock-kickers." But my realism is not Johnsonian. I agree that sensory data do not prove the existence of extra-mental causes having properties that are identical with the features of every datum perceived (e.g., as color in us is misconstrued if we regard it as evidence of color in the things perceived). Instead, we infer from sensory data to the conditions for its occurrence within us. Sometimes we infer that these conditions are things perceived and that such things have properties (e.g., geometrical properties) like the properties of our visual data. Other times (e.g., as in the case of giddiness, pain, color, and smell), we explain the inception of the data in other ways. This use of testable hypotheses has a metaphysical complement. Having argued that properties exist in the first instance as eternal possibilities, I suppose that some possibles are instantiated (i.e., as particulars in spacetime). It is these particulars that are the referents of our thoughts and words and the causes of our percepts.

Idealists may want to reconsider the charge that realism is Johnsonian rock kicking. They may also want to examine their commitment to a psycho-centric ontology (i.e., the assumption, usually unargued, that only mind and its contents or constructs are real) and their silence about considerations (including error, death, and the feet bruised by kicking rocks) for which they have no explanation. Skeptical arguments, however clever, are no substitute for testable hypotheses that locate us plausibly within a world that thinking and perceiving do not make.

29. Justus Buchler, *Metaphysics of Natural Complexes,* ed. Kathleen Wallace and Armen Marsoobian, with Robert S. Corrington (Albany, N.Y.: State University of New York Press, 1990).

30. Mario Bunge, *Treatise on Basic Philosophy,* Vol. 4: *Ontology II: A World of Systems* (Dordrecht: D. Reidel, 1979).

31. For example, Brian Goodwin, *How the Leopard Changed Its Spots* (New York: Simon and Schuster, 1994); Stuart A. Kauffman, *The Origins of Order* (New York: Oxford University

Press, 1993); *idem, At Home in the Universe* (New York: Oxford University Press, 1955). I discovered these remarks by Walter Fontana and Leo W. Buss when the manuscript was all but finished. They describe my agenda:

> Self-maintaining natural systems include the global climate system, all living organisms, many cognitive processes, and a diversity of human social intuitions. The capacity to construct artificial systems that are self-maintaining would be highly desirable. Yet, curiously, there exists no readily identifiable scientific tradition that seeks to understand what classes of such systems are possible or to discover conditions necessary to achieve them. Given the ubiquity of such systems naturally and the desirability of self-maintenance as a feature of design, any credible approach to establishing such a tradition merits serious attention. We have recently developed and implemented a framework for approaching the problem. . . . It is based on the premise that *the constituent entities of a self-maintaining system characteristically engage in interactions whose direct outcome is the construction of other entities in the same class. Self-maintenance, then, is the consequence of a constructive feed-back loop: it occurs when the construction processes induced by the entities of a system permit the continuous regeneration of these same entities.* . . . We define an *organization* to be the specific functional relationships between entities that collectively ensure their continuous regeneration. A theory of organization, so defined, is a theory of self-maintaining systems. A prototypical instance of entities are molecules. And organisms are a particularly interesting class of self-maintaining systems generated by their constructive interactions. The atmosphere is another example. And so, perhaps, is the sun at the nuclear level. Walter Fontana and Leo W. Buss, "The Barrier of Objects: From Dynamical Systems to Bounded Organizations," in *Boundaries and Barriers,* ed. John L. Casti and Anders Karlquist [Reading, Mass.: Addison Wesley, 1996], p. 55; emphasis original).

CHAPTER ONE: SYSTEMS

1. Benedict de Spinoza, *On the Improvement of the Understanding, Ethics, Correspondence* (New York: Dover, 1955), p. 68.
2. The determinability of properties and the fixing of determinate (i.e., definite) values by determining conditions are useful for expressing some arcane ideas in quantum theory. It may be equiprobable, for example, that the determinable (i.e., variable), color, shall have red, yellow, or blue as its more determinate expression. The wave function (i.e., a superposition of probabilities that a determinable property shall have one another determinate value) collapses when a determining condition fixes one of these specific values for the determinable. Notice that the wave function continues to obtain when a determinable achieves a definite value: it may, for example, be equiprobable that the determinable, color, shall be red, yellow, or blue in the next instant—we assume that it is currently one of these shades—because a new determining condition succeeds or overrides the previous one. Notice, too, that no determinate value is fixed for a determinable in circumstances where nothing is definite. To the contrary, the array of probabilities is grounded in the fact that some determinate property currently obtains. The probability that the color will be red, yellow, or blue

at any next moment is grounded in the fact that it is currently one shade or the other, or in the fact that some other variable has a definite value. See David Z. Albert, *Quantum Mechanics and Experience* (Cambridge, Mass.: Harvard University Press, 1992), p. 41: "[A]ny quantum state whatever of a given physical system will invariably be associated with some definite value of some measurable property of that system." This is the situation anticipated by the claim that the determination of a determinable requires a laterally related, determining condition and by the claim that determinables and determining conditions are present in actual worlds by way of their lowest-order, manifest expressions (i.e., no determinable achieves a more determinate value—and ultimately a definite value—in the absence of a determining condition (or conditions) whose lowest-order, manifest property is, itself, definite).

3. Artifacts are a limiting case (because they are not self-created), not a counterexample. Their efficient causes (e.g., watchmakers) are external to them, though artifacts are self-sustaining (meaning only that they have the stability of things in which forces are balanced).

4. Weissman, *Eternal Possibilities,* pp. 141–188. Also see Alex Oliver, "The Metaphysics of Properties," *Mind* 105, no. 417 (January 1996): 1–80.

5. Aristotle, *Metaphysics,* pp. 800–802.

6. Ibid., pp. 785, 816–818.

7. Aquinas, *Selected Writings,* pp. 8, 13–14.

8. Weissman, *Eternal Possibilities,* pp. 57–107; *idem, Truth's Debt to Value,* pp. 263–272.

9. Weissman, *Eternal Possibilities,* pp. 110–126.

10. Ibid., pp. 9, 93–95.

11. One version of the one and the many—the one possible and its many, one, or no instantiations—has its basis here.

12. I infer from one of Ernest Nagel's footnotes that a theory of properties at least generically similar to the one proposed here and previously in my *Eternal Possibilities* was formulated by Kurt Grelling and Paul Oppenheim: "For this analysis, and further details involved in its elaboration, see the papers by Kurt Grelling, 'A Logical Theory of Dependence,' and by Kurt Grelling and Paul Oppenheim, 'Logical Analysis of "Gestalt" and "Functional Whole,"' reprinted for members of the Fifth International Congress for the Unity of Science, held in Cambridge, Mass., in 1939, from the *Journal of Unified Science,* Vol. 9. This volume of the *Journal* was a casualty of World War II and never appeared" (Nagel, "Wholes, Sums, and Organic Unities," pp. 154–155, n. 13).

13. See Norbert Wiener, *Cybernetics: Or Control and Communication in the Animal and the Machine,* 2d ed. (Cambridge, Mass.: MIT Press, 1961).

14. Weissman, *Hypothesis and the Spiral of Reflection,* pp. 102–130.

15. We may describe elementary particles as the precipitates of a self-diversifying One. The One was, presumably, the near-homogeneity turned explosive and self-diversifying by some accumulation of destabilizing processes (e.g., what are now elementary particles may be the consequence of self-differentiation in a near-stable system turned unstable, then self-stabilized). It is not unique that a system far from equilibrium should realize unpredicted organizational forms within itself, though the conditions for this happening are not fully understood. Such effects may not be random. There may be an intrinsic form

that constrains a system verging on chaos, diverting it toward an energy-efficient organization. The intrinsic topology and geometry that constrain motion in spacetime may be part or all of this stabilizing form (e.g., random organizations are, perhaps, consolidated and sustained because they satisfy and fill an attractor in spacetime).

16. Alfred North Whitehead, *Process and Reality,* ed. David Ray Griffin and Donald W. Sherburne (New York: Free Press, 1978), p. 23.

17. David Weissmann, *Dispositional Properties* (Carbondale, Ill.: Southern Illinois University Press, 1965), pp. 119–158; *idem, Eternal Possibilities,* p. 250. See John Searle, "Minds, Brains, and Programs," *Behavioral and Brain Sciences* 3 (1980): 417–457.

18. Graham Nerlich, *The Shape of Space* (Cambridge: Cambridge University Press, 1994), pp. 69–93.

19. This is the implication of several claims that David Hume makes in *A Treatise of Human Nature,* ed. L. A. Selby-Bigge and P. H. Nidditch (Oxford: Clarendon Press, 1978): including, space and time are relations among sensory data (pp. 33–34); it is no contradiction to suppose that any two or more things may be related in space and time ("All objects, which are not contrary, are susceptible of a constant conjunction": p. 247); existence is only the force and vivacity of our percepts, so that anything imagined can exist as it is imagined (p. 67). It follows that anything may be contiguous in space and time to anything else.

Wittgenstein argues similarly: Ludwig Wittgenstein, *Tractatus Logico-Philosophicus,* trans. D. F. Pears and B. F. McGuinness (New York: Humanities Press, 1963). The configurations (i.e., states of affairs) into which objects can enter are limited by the objects' own internal properties (par. 2.01231, p. 9). However, the claim that "States of affairs are independent of one another" (par. 2.061, p. 13) entails that neither a state of affairs nor its embedding space or time is a constraint on the character of any other state of affairs. Here too it follows that any two configurations can be joined in space or time.

20. Perhaps there is another explanation, too: properties that are conditioning or mutually conditioning may also be mutually implicative (e.g., as perceived color implicates extension and shape, and spin implies momentum). Causal reciprocities in them may be overlaid on geometrical complementarities (see sec. 4) in spacetime.

21. Kant's Third Analogy is devoted to reciprocity as a factor within experience: *Critique of Pure Reason,* trans. Norman Kemp Smith (New York: St. Martin's Press, 1965), pp. 233–238. Kant emphasizes reciprocity. Yet he can make very little of the reciprocity of efficient causes, because his notion of cause is Hume's idea of constant conjunction guaranteed by transcendental rules (i.e., every event has, necessarily, an antecedent and a successor), and because his "objects" are congeries of sense-data schematized by mind's rules. He would probably have agreed that there are reciprocities—complementarities—in the formal relations of geometrical figures. See his views about the transcendental schematization of space: ibid., pp. 67–74.

22. See also Weissman, *Intuition and Ideality,* pp. 214–219.

23. See the notion of feedback in George Herbert Mead's theory of social meaning: "A gesture is not significant when the response of another organism to it does not indicate to the organism making it what the other organism is responding to": George Herbert Mead, *The Social Psychology of George Herbert Mead,* ed. Anselm Strauss (Chicago: University of

Chicago Press, 1956), p. 183. The meaning of my initial act is not established, this implies, until I construe (by my subsequent conduct) your response to it.

24. D'Arcy Wentworth Thompson, *On Growth and Form,* ed. John Tyler Bonner (Cambridge: Cambridge University Press, 1995), pp. 15–48.

25. For an account of privacy's internal depth and density, see Paul Weiss, *Privacy* (Carbondale, Ill.: Southern Illinois University Press, 1983).

26. Whitehead, *Process and Reality,* p. 23.

27. See Niles Eldridge, *Time Frames* (Princeton, N.J.: Princeton University Press, 1985), and Stephen Jay Gould, *Ontogeny and Phylogeny* (Cambridge, Mass.: Harvard University Press, 1977) for their criticisms of the view that populations are nothing more than gene carriers. For the alternative they contest, see Richard Dawkins, *The Selfish Gene* (Oxford: Oxford University Press, 1976).

28. For a defense of the idea that species are individuals, see Michael T. Ghiselin, *Metaphysics and the Origin of Species* (Albany, N.Y.: State University of New York Press, 1997), p. 15:

> "Species are groups of actually or potentially inter-breeding natural populations, which are reproductively isolated from other such groups." A species is thus a particular, or an "individual"—not a biological individual, but a social one. It is not a strictly nominal class—that is, it is not an abstraction or mere group of similar things—because the biological individuals stand in relation to the species as parts to a whole. To attain this divergence in attitude required more than simple affirmation. It was necessary to conceive of biological groupings in terms of social interaction and not merely in terms of taxonomic characters. The new manner of thinking about groups of organisms entailed the concept of a population as an integrated system, existing at a level above that of the biological individual.

29. Causal lineages—one learning from another what the other learned from a third—are different from the noncausal paths that associate ideas. The latter are created as we assemble ideas in order to exhibit their variations and "development." Thinkers may be affected by their predecessors, though ideas, construed as differences and relations thought—as possibilities—are not affected by other ideas: the idea of square doesn't affect the idea of circle. We sometimes err by inferring from ideas associated by a path to causal relations among their authors. There may be no such relations between or among them, as the lineage of calculus, from Leibniz to Newton, was not causally mediated. See my "Introduction" to Descartes, *Discourse on the Method and Meditations on First Philosophy,* pp. 111–120.

30. Herbert A. Simon, "The Architecture of Complexity," in *The Sciences of the Artificial* (Cambridge, Mass.; MIT Press, 1969), pp. 84–118.

31. The example is Sarah Glenn's. This notion of final cause is Larry Wright's, in "Functions," *Philosophical Review* 82 (April 1973): 139–168.

32. Geometrical examples support this surmise, as when generic angularity, not only an angle of some magnitude, emerges when line segments are joined to create closed figures (i.e., joining lines creates angles of a particular size or sizes; but angularity remains when the triangle's shape is changed from scalene to obtuse). Equally, theorems such as that of Pythagoras cite the emergence of determinables: the relation of the squares on the

sides to that on the hypotenuse is determinable with respect to the magnitude of the squares.

33. John Locke, *An Essay Concerning Human Understanding,* ed. Alexander Campbell Fraser (New York: Dover, 1959), vol. I, pp. 207–210; George Berkeley, *Three Dialogues between Hylas and Philonous* (Indianapolis: Hackett, 1979), pp. 28–35.

34. Hume, *A Treatise of Human Nature,* pp. 17–25.

35. Descartes, *Discourse on Method and Meditations on First Philosophy,* p. 90.

36. Richard P. Feynmann, *QED* (Princeton, N. J.: Princeton University Press, 1985), pp. 141n. and 147n.

37. Ghiselin, *Metaphysics and the Origin of Species,* pp. 226–227.

38. Crossing a finish line before other runners is a physical event. What is there in winning that is ideal and irreducible to a physical state if winning = crossing-the-line-first? Think of a competition for pianists: the winner achieves imagined ideals of musicality and technique. Pursuit of these ideals is a trajectory. A competitor wins by extending this path, perhaps teaching some of the judges that his trajectory is larger than theirs. The trajectory, and every stage along it, is physical. Still, this musician's posture, discipline, and behavior signify an overreaching objective: meaning a possibility that may elude instantiation. Ideals (i.e., these possibles) add an extra-physical constraint to our rules, with nothing magical implied. For we bring the ideal into actuality, in the first instance, by way of the signs, habits, and behaviors that signify it. Runners and pianists do more: they practice to win. Some do, because desire, training, and the rules of the competition shape the striving that achieves—rather than signifies—the ideal.

39. Weissman, *Eternal Possibilities,* pp. 237–290.

40. This concern for possibles is also apparent in thought experiments, where, for example, gravitation is presumed to obey an inverse cube law. Imagination satisfies whatever laws constrain motion in our world, including the inverse square law. The object represented in the experiment observes, in possibility, this other law.

41. John L. Casti, *Complexification* (New York: HarperCollins, 1995), pp. 28–42.

42. The error is magnified, not cured, when ontological reduction deprives a system's parts of the dispositions that qualify them to participate in systems, as Hume, Molière, and the positivists stripped opium of its dormative powers. See Weissman, *Dispositional Properties,* and "Dispositions as Geometrical-Structural Properties," *Review of Metaphysics* 32, no. 2 (December 1978): 276–297.

43. Ernest Nagel, *The Structure of Science* (New York: Harcourt, Brace and World, 1961), pp. 97–105; and Marshall Spector, *Concepts of Reduction in Physical Science* (Philadelphia: Temple University Press, 1978), pp. 29–33.

44. Nagel, "Wholes, Sums, and Organic Unities," p. 140.

45. Ibid., p. 143

46. Ibid., p. 144.

47. Ibid., pp. 149–150.

48. Ibid., p. 152.

49. Nerlich, *Shape of Space.*

50. Aristotle, *Metaphysics,* pp. 784–786.

51. Ibid., pp. 803–804.

52. Ibid., pp. 757–758.

53. Ibid., pp. 752–754, 791–797.

54. Also see Plato's claims about the organization of state and soul: *Republic,* 614–710.

55. Plato, *Parmenides,* in *Collected Dialogues,* pp. 921–929. Aristotle would have had no patience with my claim that properties exist, in the first instance, as eternal possibilities.

56. G. S. Kirk, J. E. Raven, and M. Schofield, *The Presocratic Philosophers* (Cambridge: Cambridge University Press, 1993), pp. 402–404, 405–406.

57. Wittgenstein, *Tractatus,* par. 2.01, p. 7.

58. Whitehead, *Process and Reality,* pp. 18, 22.

59. For a more favorable reading of Whitehead's social theory see Robert Neville, *The Cosmology of Freedom* (New Haven: Yale University Press, 1974).

60. Whitehead, *Process and Reality,* p. 19.

61. Ibid., p. 18.

62. Weissman, *Intuition and Ideality,* pp. 157–171; *idem,* "Metaphysics," in Descartes, *Discourse on Method and Meditations on First Philosophy,* pp. 177–195.

63. Plato, *Sophist,* in *Collected Dialogues,* pp. 1005–1006.

64. "The contemporary world as perceived by the senses is the datum for contemporary actuality, and is therefore continuous—divisible but not divided. The contemporary world is in fact divided and atomic, being a multiplicity of definite actual entities": Whitehead, *Process and Reality,* p. 62.

65. "The consequent nature of God is the fluent world become 'everlasting' by its objective immortality in God": ibid., p. 347.

66. Kant, *Critique of Pure Reason,* pp. 135–161.

67. Ibid., p. 231.

68. G. W. V. Leibniz, *Monadology and Other Philosophical* Essays, trans. Paul Schrecker and Anne Martin Schrecker (Indianapolis: Hackett, 1965), pp. 155–157.

CHAPTER TWO: PERSONS

1. Sigmund Freud, *The Standard Edition of the Complete Psychological Works of Sigmund Freud,* ed. James Strachey (London: Hogarth Press, 1966–74), vol. 1, pp. 283–397.

2. Weissman, *Intuition and Ideality,* pp. 171–194.

3. Weissman, *Hypothesis and the Spiral of Reflection,* pp. 109–117.

4. Friedrich Nietzsche, *The Will to Power,* trans. Walter Kaufmann and R. J. Hollingdale (New York: Random House, 1968), p. 298.

5. Kant, *Critique of Pure Reason,* p. 465.

6. Nietzsche, *The Gay Science,* trans. Walter Kaufmann (New York: Random House, 1974), p. 290.

7. Gibert Ryle, *The Concept of Mind* (New York: Barnes and Noble, 1949), pp. 25–61.

8. J. L. Austin, "Ifs and Cans," in *Philosophical Papers,* ed. J. O. Urmson and Geoffrey Warnock (London: Oxford University Press, 1970), p. 153–180; Weissman, *Dispositional Properties,* pp. 9–10.

9. John Rawls writes:

> The parties [in the original position] regard moral personality and not the capacity for pleasure and pain as the fundamental aspect of the self. They do not know what final aims persons have, and all dominant-end conceptions are rejected. Thus is would not occur to them to acknowledge the principle of utility in its hedonistic form. . . . The essential unity of the self is already provided by the conception of right. (Rawls, *A Theory of Justice*, p. 563).

10. Michael Sandel has said this plainly:

> [We] cannot regard ourselves as independent . . . without great costs to those loyalties and convictions whose moral force consists partly in the fact that living by them is inseparable from understanding ourselves as the particular persons we are—as members of this family or community or nation or people, as bearers of this history, as sons and daughters of that revolution, as citizens of this republic. Allegiances such as these . . . define the person I am. To imagine a person incapable of constitutive attachments such as these is not to conceive an ideally free and rational agent, but to imagine a person wholly without character, without moral depth. . . . A person with character thus knows that he is implicated in various ways even as he reflects, and feels the moral weight of what he knows. (Michael Sandel, *Liberalism and the Limits of Justice* [Cambridge: Cambridge University Press, 1982], p. 179)

11. Martin Heidegger, *Being and Time,* trans. John Macquarrie and Edward Robinson (New York: Harper and Row, 1962), p. 174.

12. Murray Bowen, *Family Therapy in Clinical Practice* (New York: J. Aronson, 1985).

13. Alasdair MacIntyre, *After Virtue* (Notre Dame, Ind.: University of Notre Dame Press, 1981), pp. 204–205.

14. Jean-Paul Sartre, *Being and Nothingness,* trans. Hazel E. Barnes (New York: Washington Square Press, 1969), pp. 712–734.

15. Mill, *On Liberty,* p. 12.

16. John Dewey, *The Public and Its Problems* (Chicago: Swallow Press, 1954), pp. 110–142; Jürgen Habermas, *The Structural Transfiguration of the Public Sphere,* trans. Thomas Burgher and Frederick Lawrence (Cambridge, Mass.: MIT Press, 1991), pp. 89–140.

17. Dewey, *Public and Its Problems,* pp. 110–142.

18. Friedrich Nietzsche, *The Birth of Tragedy and The Genealogy of Morals,* trans. Francis Golffing (New York: Doubleday, 1956), pp. 173–176.

19. Descartes, *Discourse on Method and Meditations on First Philosophy,* pp. 64–66.

20. Mill implies that freedom of thought and conscience are prior to, and independent of, freedom of association, hence that thought may have ample content prior to, and perhaps in the absence of, our relations to other people: Mill, *On Liberty,* p. 16.

21. Albert Camus, *The Stranger,* trans. Joseph Laredo (New York: Random House, 1956).

CHAPTER THREE: SOCIALITY

1. J. L. Austin, *How to Do Things with Words* (Cambridge, Mass.: Harvard University Press, 1975).

2. Aristotle described this work when he considered the "household virtues": *Politics,* in *Basic Works,* pp. 1130–1146.

3. John Lachs, *Intermediate Man* (Indianapolis: Hackett, 1981), pp. 127–145.

4. John Dewey, *The Child and the Curriculum* and *The School and Society* (Chicago: University of Chicago Press, 1956).

5. Ludwig Wittgenstein, *Philosophical Investigations,* trans. G. E. M. Anscombe (Oxford: Basil Blackwell, 1953), par. 208, pp. 82–83.

6. A recent news reports on hermits described them and the priests assigned to care for them. One hermit prepares television programs; all those discussed attend mass every day.

7. The model for controlling a system's members is Plato's, with its emphasis on skills, tempered appetites, and the rational appraisal of one's roles and obligations. Members are educated for their roles: they are skilled for particular tasks, and trained to do them with people in complementary roles. Specialization, cooperation, and self-control are their cardinal virtues. Plato, *Republic,* pp. 615–705.

8. Dewey, *Public and Its Problems,* pp. 12–17.

9. John Locke, *The Second Treatise on Civil Government* (Amherst, N.Y.: Prometheus Books, 1986), pp. 48–50; Jean Jacques Rousseau, *The Social Contract,* trans. Maurice Cranston (London: Penguin Books, 1968), pp. 59–62; Hume, *Treatise of Human Nature,* pp. 534–539; Immanuel Kant, "Perpetual Peace," in *On History,* ed. and trans. Lewis White Beck (Indianapolis: Library of Liberal Arts, 1957), pp. 85–135; Mill, *On Liberty,* pp. 3–19.

10. John Rawls, *Political Liberalism* (New York: Columbia University Press, 1993), p. 18.

11. Plato, *Republic,* pp. 606–607; Rousseau, *Social Contract,* pp. 64–65; Rawls, *Theory of Justice,* p. 529; Sandel, *Liberalism and the Limits of Justice,* pp. 77–82.

12. Charles Taylor, "Alternative Futures: Legitimacy, Identity and Alienation in Late-Twentieth Century Canada," in *Constitutionalism, Citizenship, and Society in Canada,* ed. Alain Cairns and Cynthia Williams (Toronto: University of Toronto Press, 1986), p. 211.

13. Iris Marion Young, "The Ideal of Community and the Politics of Difference," in *Feminism/Postmodernism,* ed. Linda Nicholson (New York: Routledge, 1990), p. 318.

14. Habermas quotes François Guizot:

> It is, moreover, the character of that system, which nowhere admits the legitimacy of absolute power, to compel the whole body of citizens incessantly, and on every occasion, to seek after reason, justice, and truth, which should ever regulate actual power. The representative system does this (1) by discussion, which compels existing powers to seek after truth in common; (2) by publicity, which places these powers when occupied in this search, under the eyes of the citizens; and (3) by the liberty of the press, which stimulates the citizens themselves to seek after truth, and to tell it to power. (Habermas, *Structural Transformation of the Public Sphere,* p. 101)

15. See Jürgen Habermas, "Reconciliation through the Public Use of Reason: Remarks on John Rawls's Political Liberalism," and John Rawls "Reply to Habermas," *Journal of Philosophy* 92, no. 3 (March 1995).

16. Plato, *Republic,* p. 843.

17. Friedrich Hayek, *The Road to Serfdom* (Chicago: University of Chicago Press, 1944).

18. Ibid., pp. 48–49.

19. Ibid., pp. 38–39.

20. Kant, *Critique of Practical Reason and Other Works*, p. 77.

21. Should we infer from this tolerance that each of these persuasions is as (much or little) plausible as the others, so that affirming one is no better than professing another? This implication is detested by people who fear that tolerance in education is a smoke screen for skepticism about the truths of every religion.

22. Kant, *Critique of Pure Reason*, p. 137.

23. Karl Marx, *Early Writings*, trans. Rodney Livingstone and Gregor Benton (Harmondsworth: Penguin, 1992), pp. 123–164.

24. Plato, *Republic*, pp. 772–816.

25. Wittgenstein, *Tractatus*, pars. 2.0251 and 2.0272, p. 13. (Par. 2.0251 mentions "being colored" as a form of objects. But color is later implied to be a relational property [par. 4.123, p. 53], one that is consequent on the configuration—presumably spatial—of objects.)

26. Ibid., par. 5.136, p. 79.

27. Ibid., par. 2.0121, p. 9.

28. Aristotle, *Metaphysics*, pp. 786-788.

29. Hobbes, *Leviathan*, p. 130.

30. Dewey, *Public and Its Problems*, pp. 23–27.

31. I am reading Aristotle's politics in the terms of his ontology, thereby slighting his emphasis on the complementary roles that are constitutive of states. This other emphasis would justify saying that Aristotle's politics—at odds with his ontology—postulates a form for the state that is comparable to forms that fix the character of primary substances. That form is a state's constitution, meaning the prescribed order of relatedness among its citizens: "It is evident that the sameness of the state consists chiefly in the sameness of the constitution, and it may be called or not called by the same name, whether the inhabitants are the same or entirely different" (Aristotle, *Politics*, p. 1179). Aristotle, after Plato, does regard states as systems, if one reads him with this emphasis.

32. Mill, *On Liberty*, p. 16.

33. William Greider, *Who Will Tell the People* (New York: Simon and Schuster, 1993), pp. 141–158.

CHAPTER FOUR: VALUE

1. Nietzsche, *Will to Power*, pp. 275–276, 326, 361.

2. Ibid., pp. 363–364. Also see Rawls, *Theory of Justice*, p. 440.

3. Plato, *Republic*, p. 843.

4. Ibid., p. 607.

5. Ibid., 737–744.

6. Augustine, *City of God*, pp. 443–466.

7. Aristotle, *Physics*, pp. 247–248.

8. John Rawls is an explicit consequentialist: "[I]n justice as fairness the concept of right is prior to that of the good. In contrast with teleological theories, something is good only if it fits into ways of life consistent with the principles of right already on hand." (Rawls, *The-*

ory of Justice, p. 396). For objections to consequentialism see Samuel Scheffler, *Consequentialism and Its Critics* (Oxford: Oxford University Press, 1988); and Shelly Kagan, *The Limits of Morality* (Oxford: Clarendon Press, 1989).

9. Kant, *Critique of Practical Reason and Other Works*, pp. 30–38.

10. Ibid., p. 39.

11. "The natural end which all men have is their own happiness": ibid., p. 48.

12. Ibid., p. 47.

13. Kant, *Critique of Pure Reason*, pp. 180–187.

14. "Looking back now on all previous attempts to discover the principle of morality, we need not wonder why they all failed": Kant, *Critique of Practical Reason and Other Works*, pp. 50–51.

15. Aristotle, *Nichomachean Ethics*, pp. 952–956; Bernard Williams, *Ethics and the Limits of Philosophy* (Cambridge, Mass.: Harvard University Press, 1985), p. 201.

16. Weissman, *Truth's Debt to Value*, pp. 66–100.

17. Weissman, "Metaphysics," in Descartes, *Discourse on Method and Meditations on First Philosophy*, pp. 195–209.

18. Plato, *Republic*, pp. 673–677, 683–688.

19. Hume, *Treatise of Human Nature*, p. 469.

20. "Only by restoring the broken connections can we be healed. Connection *is* health": Wendell Berry, *The Unsettling of America* (San Francisco: Sierra Club Books, 1977), p. 138.

21. Adding the conditions for psychological health would require that we specify the reciprocities that bind a person (i.e., a human body with cognitive-affective posture) to his or her family, friends, work mates, or fellow citizens. This is appropriate, but incidental here, where it is the existence of an immanent ideal, not its full character, that concerns us.

22. We sometimes speak of healthy activities when we mean moral actions (e.g., corrupt governments are unhealthy). This sometimes implies consequences for the stability of systems; but I ignore this use of *health*.

23. Hume, *Treatise of Human Nature*, pp. 69–71.

24. A different problem also has a solution, though again at a limit where analogy looks suspiciously like metaphor. This time we remark that the test of health requires the longevity of systems, for otherwise there is no evidence that the parts and relations are sustained by their reciprocities. Health, as functional integrity over time, would seem to be denied to those subatomic particles that blaze across cathode-ray tubes in a fraction of a second. There are two problems here, one more intractable than the other. Easier, and less important, is our human measure of stability: nothing we experience as having an insignificant duration seems stable to us. We discount this bias in favor of the harder problem: functional integrity requires that a system sustain the ensemble of its internal relations (or those relations systematically evolved). But what is the measure of *sustained* reciprocity? It is satisfied by any balance of forces, no matter how ephemeral, however easily disrupted. We stipulate that two cycles of reciprocity are required to establish negative feedback systems. But this is not a necessary condition for systems that are gravitational, hence dynamic, but immobile—arches, for example. Such systems are stabilized from the moment that each part is joined reciprocally to the others.

25. Weissman, *Truth's Debt to Value,* pp. 315–329.
26. Nietzsche, *Will to Power.*
27. Weissman, *Truth's Debt to Value,* pp. 312–315.
28. Kymlicka remarks that *"no end or goal is exempt from possible re-examination":* Will Kymlicka, *Liberalism, Community, and Culture* (Oxford: Clarendon Press, 1989), p. 52. This claim is all but notional, given the recalcitrance of many attitudes. Their rigidity severely limits the voluntarist belief that selfhood is the power of unencumbered choice.
29. Hume, *Treatise of Human Nature,* p. 500.
30. Aristotle, *Nichomachean Ethics,* pp. 956-957.
31. Though see John Kekes, *Against Liberalism* (Ithaca, N.Y.: Cornell University Press, 1997), pp. 69–87.
32. Descartes, *Discourse on Method and Meditations on First Philosophy,* p. 86.
33. Dewey, *Public and Its Problems,* pp. 176–179.
34. Laws required to preserve the state (e.g. those required to raise an army) are a third category.
35. Plato, *Republic,* p. 744.

CHAPTER FIVE: DELIBERATION

1. There are people who go through a painful deliberation, resolve to act, then fail to do so. Such people may say that, yes, I did decide, but I often fail to act on my decisions; don't count on me now. This is a failure to link thought and action, not a failure of self-perception.
2. Kant, *Critique of Pure Reason,* pp. 105–106.
3. Ibid., pp. 180–187.
4. Ibid., p. 193.
5. Ulrich Neisser, *Cognitive Psychology* (New York: Appleton-Century-Crofts, 1967), p. 66.
6. René Descartes, *The Philosophical Writings of Descartes,* vol. 1, trans. John Cottingham, Robert Stoothoff, and Dugald Murdoch (Cambridge: Cambridge University Press, 1993), pp. 37–38.
7. Deliberation as it applies to individuals reflecting on themselves and their circumstances is a useful paradigm for managers. There are exact applications for the headings of perception, conception, and attitude. Corresponding to an individual's perceptions are questions about the facts of the matter. Corresponding to conception are questions about plans: What do we think we are doing? What do interested others (e.g., suppliers and regulators) think we are doing? Corresponding to attitudes are questions about value: Why do we do it? How well do we do it (from the standpoint of workers, suppliers of goods or capital, and customers)? All the principal questions relevant to individual decision making have currency here: what to do, how to do it, how to appraise what is done. The difference is in the scale of their application, the complexity of deliberation, and the magnitude of its effects.

CHAPTER SIX: FREE SPEECH

1. Anthony Lewis, *Make No Law* (New York: Vintage, 1991), p. 186.
2. Wittgenstein, *Philosophical Investigations,* pp. 119–129.

3. George Herbert Mead, *The Philosophy of the Act,* ed. Charles W. Morris et al. (Chicago: University of Chicago Press, 1938), p. 193.

4. Mill, *On Liberty,* p. 11.

5. Hegel, *Phenomenology of Mind,* pp. 529–530.

6. Frederick Schauer believes that we could defend speech effectively, while reducing its abuses, if its protection were left to the arguments and rules that defend various behaviors, including speech, in specific domains. The free speech encouraged in business would have, perhaps, a defense that is different from the literary uses of speech. The libelous recounting of a business competitor's behavior would be accountable to the standards of speech in business, not the looser ones of literature. We could dispense with the universal permission to say what we like, up to the point of seditious speech or speech that endangers others.

   This strategy is awkward in two respects. First, it does not tell us how to limit the consequences or implications of individual behaviors to single domains (e.g., the domains of their inception or domains where their principal effects are felt). Wouldn't clever lawyers find pretexts for bringing contested actions under the permissions or restrictions of one domain, although they go "more naturally" under the rules of a different one? Schauer's proposal is sabotaged if there are many cases that can be tried under the rules of two or more domains having different—even contrary—restrictions or permissions. Second, Schauer's proposal would eliminate the special protection given generically to free speech. This is a dangerous strategy, because it would deprive speech of its recognition as the principal medium of human affiliation (i.e., it facilitates relations among people and systems, thereby enabling systems to coordinate their parts). This recognition is appropriate to the unique value of speech as we use it to establish self-regulating communities. An alternative strategy is more responsive to this use: namely, encourage speech, but restrict it in circumstances where its effects are inimical to other decisive values (e.g., private behaviors that violate no laws). See Frederick Schauer, "The Second-Best First Amendment," *William and Mary Law Review* 31 (Fall 1989): 11–23.

7. "No, Canada," *Economist,* 17–23 October 1992, p. 19.

8. Dewey, *Public and Its Problems,* pp. 143–184.

CHAPTER SEVEN: CONFLICT

1. The importance of these dialectical styles for human conflict much surpasses the applications considered here. I say nothing, for example, about class conflicts (i.e., conflicts within or among people whose membership in classes is based on a similarity of person or function, not on their reciprocal causal relations), or about the intrapsychic conflicts of people having to choose between contrary aims, though these dialectical styles apply to cases of both sorts.

2. Johann G. Fichte, *The Science of Knowledge,* trans. Peter Heath and John Lachs (Cambridge: Cambridge University Press, 1982), p. 231.

3. Immanuel Kant, *Critique of Judgment,* trans. Werner S. Pluhar (Indianapolis: Hackett, 1987, p. 16; and Weissman, *Truth's Debt to Value,* pp. 2–6.

CHAPTER EIGHT: ECOLOGY

1. Aldo Leopold, *A Sand County Almanac* (New York: Oxford University Press, 1987), p. 215.
2. Ibid.
3. The domains for which Aristotle wrote his *Politics* are cities, thereby implying that the self-regulation of human societies presupposes their relative separation from nature (allowing that Greek cities included surrounding farms, woods, and mines). This may explain his neglect of ecology. Aristotle, *Politics,* p. 1176. (I assume that the translator's use of *city* somewhat corresponds to our use of *state.*)
4. Leopold, *Sand County Almanac,* p. 15.
5. Plato, *Republic,* p. 619.
6. Leopold warns us against too narrow a view of our self-interest:

> [A] system of conservation based solely on economic self-interest is hopelessly lopsided. It tends to ignore, and thus eventually to eliminate, many elements in the land community that lack commercial value, but that are (as far as we know) essential to its healthy functioning. It assumes, falsely, I think, that the economic parts of the biotic clock will function without the uneconomic parts. (Leopold, *Sand County Almanac,* p. 214)

AFTERWORD

1. Dewey, *Public and Its Problems,* p. 23.

Index